Inside TCP/IP,
Second Edition

Matthew Flint Arnett
Mike Coulombe
Emmett Dulaney
Rick Fairweather
Eric Harper
David L. Hill
Jim Krochmal
Peter Kuo
Brent Lebo
Jim LeValley
John McGarvey
Art Mellor
Marcus Miller
Scott Orr
Lee Ray
Steve Rimbey
Choa-Chun Wang

New Riders

New Riders Publishing, Indianapolis, IN

Inside TCP/IP, Second Edition

By Matthew Flint Arnett, Mike Coulombe, Emmett Dulaney, Rick Fairweather, Eric Harper, David L. Hill, Jim Krochmal, Peter Kuo, Brent Lebo, Jim LeValley, John McGarvey, Art Mellor, Marcus Miller, Scott Orr, Lee Ray, Steve Rimbey, and Choa-Chun Wang

Published by:
New Riders Publishing
201 West 103rd Street
Indianapolis, IN 46290 USA

Printed in the United States of America 1 2 3 4 5 6 7 8 9 0

        CIP data available upon request

Warning and Disclaimer

This book is designed to provide information about the NetWare computer program. Every effort has been made to make this book as complete and as accurate as possible, but no warranty or fitness is implied.

The information is provided on an "as is" basis. The authors and New Riders Publishing shall have neither liability nor responsibility to any person or entity with respect to any loss or damages arising from the information contained in this book or from the use of the disks or programs that may accompany it.

Publisher	Don Fowley
Associate Publisher	Tim Huddleston
Marketing Manager	Ray Robinson
Acquisitions Manager	Jim LeValley
Managing Editor	Tad Ringo

About the Authors

Matthew Flint Arnett is a Products Reviews Editor for *LAN Times* magazine. He works in the LAN Times Testing Center in Provo, Utah, where his beats include Internet/online services, optical storage, printing, RAID, security, storage/management/tape backup, UPSs, Unix, and virus protection. Matt's background includes analog and digital hardware development and industry listing testing. He also has extensive experience designing Secure Compartmental Information Facilities (SCIFs), intruder detection systems for multiple government locations. Immediately prior to working with *LAN Times*, Matt owned and operated his own network consulting company in southern California, where he stressed disaster prevention and data recovery.

Mike Coulombe is a computer consultant for Whittman-Hart, a Chicago-based national consulting firm. Mike works out of Whittman-Hart's Indianapolis office, specializing in Internet connectivity and Unix solutions. Mike also worked for Macmillan Computer Publishing as System Administrator for Macmillan's World Wide Web server and Internet connection. He also has been a Network Engineer for INDnet, a state-wide educational Internet service provider for Indiana. He also has taught C and C++ courses for Indiana University's department of Continuing Studies. Mike received his bachelor's degree in Computer Science from Purdue University in 1994.

Emmett Dulaney is Publishing Manager for Networking at New Riders Publishing. The author and coauthor of several computer books, including *Inside UNIX* (NRP) and *Voodoo NetWare* (Ventana Press), he also is a frequent contributor to several magazines. An associate professor at Indiana University-Purdue University of Fort Wayne, Indiana, he has taught continuing education classes in Unix and writing, among other things, for the past five years.

Rick Fairweather is a Senior Systems Engineer for a Fortune 500 internetworking company located in San Jose, California. He is involved in the technical design and sales of routing and switching solutions for high performance local area networks, large multiprotocol routed networks, the integration of IBM mainframe environments with multiprotocol networks, and wide area networking. Rick has extensive experience with network protocols including TCP/IP, Novell IPX, AppleTalk, DecNet, OSI, Netbios, and SNA. He has also designed and implemented many high performance networks using technologies such as Ethernet, Token Ring, FDDI, Frame Relay, X.25, SMDS, point-to-point leased like services, ISDN, and Asynchronous Transfer Mode.

Eric Harper is a Reviews Editor for *LAN Times* magazine. He works in the LAN Times Testing Center in Provo, Utah, evaluating and writing about Windows, Windows NT, DOS, Unix, and network management products. Before starting at *LAN Times*, Eric worked for Novell Technical Support and has done private consulting. He received a B.A. from Brigham Young University. His other writing experience includes projects for New Riders Publishing, Brady Books, and Que Corporation.

David L. Hill holds a B.S. in business from Miami University of Ohio. He has more than 11 years of experience in data processing that includes project management, business analysis, and systems design. David is currently employed by a large telecommunications company and is involved in the development and deployment of client/server-based information systems.

Jim Krochmal has more than 17 years of information systems experience as a systems architect, project manager, and consultant. He currently specializes in distributed systems design, distributed database design, relational technology, and data communications. Jim has also contributed to *Enterprise Computing: LAN Connectivity* (NRP, 1992), and is the lead author of *Enterprise Computing: Client/Server Databases* (NRP, 1993).

Peter Kuo, Ph.D., is the first Canadian Enterprise Certified NetWare Engineer and a Certified NetWare Instructor. His areas of expertise include advanced NetWare topics such as network management, IBM, and Unix connectivity issues. Peter is a sysop on NetWire (CompuServe), supporting many advanced sections for Novell, such as connectivity, network management, NetWare 4.*x*, client software, and OS/2 Requester. He also is a member of Novell's Professional Developer's Program.

Jim LeValley, before joining New Riders Publishing, was employed by GTE Telephone Operation and Contel Telephone, where he developed an appreciation for wide area networking technology.

John McGarvey has worked as a software developer for IBM for the past 11 years, developing programs for the DOS, OS/2, and VM mainframe environments. He is currently a senior programmer at the IBM Networking Systems Division, Research Triangle Park, North Carolina and is the lead developer on the TCP/IP for OS/2 project. In this role, he has been involved in adding Internet access function to OS/2 Warp. John is married and lives in Apex, North Carolina. He is the proud father of a two-and-a-half-year-old boy, and he would far prefer to spend time flyfishing a northwest Montana river than surfing the Internet.

Art Mellor earned a bachelor of science in electrical engineering from MIT. He has spent 12 years working in the computer industry, including five and a half in the networking world developing gateways, training employees and customers, and flying around the country troubleshooting network problems. In the past two years, he has helped found Midnight Networks, Inc., and is Midnight's Vice President of Engineering. Midnight Networks develops and sells software to automate the testing of network protocols. Their customers include most of the major network vendors such as Cisco, Wellfleet, SynOptics, Cabletron, 3Com, Xylogics, AT&T, and many more. Art can be reached on the Internet at art@midnight.com.

Marcus Miller, Ph.D., is a staff member with the TCP/IP Design and Development group at the IBM Networking Systems Division, Research Triangle Park, North Carolina. His research interests include massively parallel architectures, hybrid von Neumann/dataflow architectures, simulation modeling of hybrid architectures, compilation techniques, code generation for functional languages, and packet-switched network architectures. Marcus received the Ph.D. in computer science from the University of Kentucky in 1988, and a B.S. in physics from Western Kentucky University in 1980.

Scott Orr has been involved with the networking efforts of the Purdue School of Engineering and Technology at Indiana University-Purdue University at Indianapolis from the very beginning. Starting out as a 20-node Novell network, today over 400 MS-DOS- and Unix-based workstations are interconnected to each other, as well as to the Internet. Much of the TCP/IP access for these networks was provided prior to any such support from Novell; Scott copresented a case study of this Novell-TCP/IP integration at the 1991 Sun Expo held in San Jose, California. In addition, Scott serves as a part-time instructor on networking and data communication for the Computer Technology Department at IUPUI.

Lee Ray, Ph.D., has been training users in the longs and shorts of Unix for 10 years. He writes computer-based interactive training programs and articles about Unix topics. Lee administers systems used in support of research in digital audio and also operates a technical communications service in San Diego, California. He has a Ph.D. in computer music from the University of California and is a composer and performer.

Steve Rimbey entered the U.S. Navy immediately after high school. He has spent the last 10 years learning about, maintaining, and repairing mainframes, minicomputers, desktop computers, and networks. For the past three years, Steve has been the Systems Manager for a Novell network and a Unix system with connection to the Internet. He is currently pursuing a baccalaureate degree in computer science/electronics engineering and certification from Novell as a CNE. Although still in the Navy, Steve has recently started his own business as a computer consultant specializing in network design, analysis, and installation.

Chao-Chun Wang, Ph.D., works for IBM in Research Triangle Park, North Carolina. He has a B.S. in physics and received his M.A.M.S. in computer science from the University of Georgia in 1988. He earned his Ph.D. in electrical engineering from Purdue University, West Lafayette, Indiana in 1993. His research interests include parallel and distributing processing algorithms, high-performance, multiprocessor systems, parallel processing tools, and high-speed computer networking. His current project involves Point-to-Point protocol, ATM, and the TCP/IP stack.

Trademark Acknowledgments

All terms mentioned in this book that are known to be trademarks or service marks have been appropriately capitalized. New Riders Publishing cannot attest to the accuracy of this information. Use of a term in this book should not be regarded as affecting the validity of any trademark or service mark. NetWare is a registered trademark of Novell, Inc.

Product Development Specialist
EMMETT DULANEY

Acquisitions Editor
ALICIA BUCKLEY

Production Editor
AMY BEZEK

Copy Editors
CLIFF SHUBS
PHIL WORTHINGTON

Technical Editor
RUSS CLARK

Assistant Marketing Manager
TAMARA APPLE

Acquisitions Coordinator
TRACY TURGESON

Publisher's Assistant
KAREN OPAL

Cover Designer
SANDRA SCHROEDER

Cover Illustrator
BORIS LYUBNER

Book Designer
SANDRA SCHROEDER

Manufacturing Coordinator
PAUL GILCHRIST

Production Manager
KELLY DOBBS

Production Team Supervisor
LAURIE CASEY

Graphics Image Specialists
BECKY BEHELER, BRAD DIXON,
JASON HAND, CLINT LAHNEN,
CHERI LAUGHNER, MICHAEL
RENOLDS, DENNIS SHEEHAN,
JEFF YESH

Production Analysts
ANGELA D. BANNAN
BOBBI SATTERFIELD

Production Team
KIM COFER, KEVIN FOLTZ,
MIKE DIETSCH, MIKE HENRY,
ALEATA HOWARD, ERIKA MILLEN
ERICH J. RICHTER, SUSAN
SPRINGER, CHRISTINE TYNER

Indexer
CHRISTOPHER CLEVELAND

Contents at a Glance

Table of Contents

INTRODUCTION

Introduction

I nside *TCP/IP, Second Edition* is designed for system administrators who plan to work with the TCP/IP protocol suite. *Inside TCP/IP, Second Edition* is not vendor specific, which means it strives to address as many different versions and flavors of TCP/IP as possible and to hit all the major operating systems. Numerous books are available that discuss TCP/IP from a philosophical point of view. This book does that also, but it does something they do not do—it shows you how to implement the protocol and to have it up and running on any number of different operating systems.

Who Should Read This Book?

Inside TCP/IP, Second Edition is designed for advanced users and system administrators of the TCP/IP networking protocol. The following chapters contain information and procedures for the average TCP/IP environment and are the product of many hours spent troubleshooting and administering this environment.

How *Inside TCP/IP, Second Edition* Helps You

The information presented in Part One provides an overview of the TCP/IP networking protocol and discusses the various features available regardless of the operating system you are using.

Part Two addresses installation on the different platforms and shows how the protocol is actually implemented on each of these operating systems. Whether you need to install and utilize TCP/IP on its native Unix, or on NetWare, OS/2, or any of a handful of other systems, these topics are addressed in Part Two. Part Two also shows you how to connect to the outside world and obtain the most from the Internet, as well as troubleshoot an established system.

Part Three addresses current vendors, RFCs, ways of officially registering your site, and other miscellaneous useful information.

Conventions Used in This Book

Throughout this book, certain conventions are used to help you distinguish the various elements of Windows, DOS, their system files, and sample data. Before you look ahead, you should spend a moment examining these conventions:

✔ Shortcut keys are normally found in the text where appropriate. In most applications, for example, Shift+Ins is the shortcut key for the **P**aste command.

✔ Key combinations appear in the following formats:

Key1+Key2. When you see a plus sign (+) between key names, you should hold down the first key while you press the second key. Then release both keys. If you see "Press Ctrl+F2," for example, hold down the Ctrl key, press the F2 function key once, then release both keys.

Key1,Key2. When a comma (,) appears between key names, you should press and release the first key, then press and release the second key. "Alt,S" means press the Alt key once and then press S once.

Hot Keys. On the screen, Windows underlines the letters on some menu names, file names, and option names. For example, the File menu is displayed on-screen as **<u>F</u>**ile. This underlined letter is the letter you can type to choose that command or option when it appears on the screen. (In this book, however, such letters are displayed in bold, underlined type: **<u>F</u>**ile.)

✔ Information you type is in **boldface**. This applies to individual letters and numbers as well as to text strings. This convention, however, does not apply to special keys, such as Enter, Tab, Esc, or Ctrl.

✔ New terms appear in *italics*.

✔ Text that is displayed on-screen, but which is not part of Windows or a Windows application—such as DOS prompts and messages—appears in a `special typeface`.

Special Text Used in This Book

Throughout this book, you find examples of special text. These passages have been given special treatment so that you can instantly recognize their significance and so that you can easily find them for future reference.

Notes, Tips, and Warnings

Inside TCP/IP, Second Edition features many special sidebars, which are set apart from the normal text by icons. This book includes three distinct types of sidebars: "Notes," "Tips," and "Warnings."

A note includes "extra" information that you should find useful, but which complements the discussion at hand instead of being a direct part of it. A note might describe special situations that can arise when you use Windows under certain circumstances, and might tell you what steps to take when such situations arise.

A tip provides quick instructions for getting the most from your Windows system as you follow the steps outlined in the general discussion. A tip might show you how to conserve memory, how to speed up a procedure, or how to perform one of many timesaving and system-enhancing techniques. Tips also might tell you how to avoid problems with your software and hardware.

A warning tells you when a procedure might be dangerous—that is, when you run the risk of losing data, locking your system, or even damaging your hardware. Warnings generally tell you how to avoid such losses or describe the steps you can take to remedy them.

New Riders Publishing

The staff of New Riders Publishing is committed to bringing you the very best in computer reference material. Each New Riders book is the result of months of work by authors and staff who research and refine the information contained within its covers.

As part of this commitment to you, the NRP reader, New Riders invites your input. Please let us know if you enjoy this book, if you have trouble with the information and examples presented, or if you have a suggestion for the next edition.

Please note, however, that the New Riders staff cannot serve as a technical resource for TCP/IP or TCP/IP application-related questions, including hardware- and software-related problems. Refer to the documentation that accompanies your TCP/IP network operating system or TCP/IP application package for help with specific problems.

If you have a question or comment about any New Riders book, there are several ways to contact New Riders Publishing. We respond to as many readers as we can. Your name, address, or phone number never becomes part of a mailing list or is used for any purpose other than to help us continue to bring you the best books possible. You can write us at the following address:

New Riders Publishing
Attn: Associate Publisher
201 W. 103rd Street
Indianapolis, IN 46290

If you prefer, you can fax New Riders Publishing at (317) 581-4670.

You can send e-mail to New Riders at the following Internet address:

edulaney@newriders.mcp.com

NRP is an imprint of Macmillan Computer Publishing. To obtain a catalog or information, or to purchase any Macmillan Computer Publishing book, call (800) 428-5331.

Thank you for selecting *Inside TCP/IP, Second Edition*!

Part I

Overview

Chapter Snapshot

Without addressing TCP/IP per se, this chapter provides an overview of all forms of data communication and distributed environments by discussing the factors of each. Protocols and models are discussed as they relate to networking, and the client/server environment. Topics include:

Introduction to Data Communications

"The difference between intelligence and education is this: Intelligence will make you a good living."

—*Charles Kettering*

A distributed environment is comprised of various system resources (data, computing power, programs, and so on) that are spread across multiple locations. These resources utilize a communication system to interact with one another. In this scenario, the communication system is the apparatus that provides the distribution mechanism to exchange control information and data. The communication systems that are essential for information distribution can be made totally transparent to end users, or they may be visible enough for the end users to be aware of the network that provides actual resource interconnection. In either case, communication between nodes is indispensable, requiring a physical network to connect all interacting nodes.

Communication and Distribution

Client/server architecture is a subset of cooperative processing, which in turn is a subset of distributed processing. The distributed processing environment is not designed for just the client/server computing model. The factors that are currently contributing to interest in distributed systems are as follows:

✔ Technological advances in microelectronics are changing the price-performance ratio in favor of multiple low-cost, high-performance systems.

✔ Interconnections and communication costs are falling dramatically.

✔ Users are demanding more economical, rapid, sophisticated, and reliable facilities.

An objective and benefit of distribution is resource sharing. A number of resources (such as computers, peripherals, special-purpose processors, programs, data, and so on), are interconnected by the communications system to allow the sharing of these resources. The interconnected systems form a network that can switch messages, or information *packets,* between different sites, systems, terminals, and programs.

The following definitions are useful to know when you discuss networks and communications:

✔ A *communication system* is the collection of hardware and software that supports intersystem and interprocess communication between software components in distributed nodes. The nodes are interconnected by a network that provides a physical path between nodes. The direct connection between two or more systems is sometimes referred to as a *link.*

✔ A system that performs main application functions and controls the communication system is sometimes called a *host* (or *server*).

✔ In a distributed system, the *name* of an object indicates a system, a process, or a node. An *address* indicates where the named object is, and a *route* tells how to get there.

Data is the most common shared resource in a distributed system. Most applications require that data be shared among diverse users with different computing facilities. By distributing data through replication, reliability may be improved. Local copies of replicated and partitioned data can reduce access time. The communication system is used to transmit both data and data requests between different sites, systems, and programs. Although interconnected systems may or may not form a distributed processing system, the data communication system used for message and data interchange can be considered as a distributed system.

Communication System Functions

The following functions are some of the most important functions of a communication system:

- ✔ Naming and addressing
- ✔ Segmenting
- ✔ Flow Control
- ✔ Synchronization
- ✔ Priority
- ✔ Error Control

Naming and Addressing

A communication system manipulates names for objects. These objects can be such items as processes, ports, mailboxes, systems, and sessions between users. Users typically supply names in symbolic form (such as Filename@DepartmentName@CompanyName) and then the communication system restates this form into a network address. The communication system must maintain translation tables (enterprise directories) to convert logical names into physical names.

Segmenting

If a user message or file to be transmitted is larger than a network packet, the communication system must fragment a single message into multiple segments and reassemble it before delivery to the end user.

Specific reasons for message segmentation include the following:

- ✔ Long messages extend access delays for other users because long messages could hold exclusive control over shared network resources for longer periods of time.

- ✔ Shorter messages improve efficiency and reduce transmission error rates.

- ✔ Internal buffers used by the communication system can optimize the transmitted message size.

- ✔ The networks that comprise a particular transmission route can have different packet sizes.

- ✔ Parallel data links and transmissions are possible in some networks. Breaking long messages into small segments may allow their use, thus reducing overall delays.

Flow Control

Many networks are designed to share limited resources among users on the assumption that not all users demand those services simultaneously. When the resulting traffic exceeds the network throughput capacity, network flow control is designed to optimize network performance by regulating the flow of information between a pair of communicating entities.

Synchronization

Before entities can communicate, their interactions must be synchronized. If the receiver is faster than the transmitter, it may possibly acquire and subsequently misinterpret extra information. Conversely, if it is slower than the transmitter it may lose information.

Because the client/server architecture typically subdivides major processes into component subprocesses, each of which executes on a different host, a mechanism must be in place to ensure that the various subprocesses remain syncronized. Similarly, when data resources are shared or distributed, it is necessary to coordinate all of the distributed resources to ensure that they remain synchronized. IBM *Advanced Program to Program Communication* (APPC) protocol is an example of such a multilevel synchronization protocol.

Priority

A communication system can apply priority to messages to allow preferential handling when competing for resources. High-priority messages (alarms, alerts, interrupts) have shorter delays. The communications system can apply priority statically or dynamically (such as according to message content or based on a message source or destination).

Error Control

Reliable, error-free communication is one of the prime objectives of communication system functionality. Error control functions include error detection, correction, and recovery. Error detection can be performed in three ways:

✔ By including redundant information. Redundant data can be compared to determine a possible error in the case of mismatch.

✔ By using control information that allows determination of information corruption. Control information can use various algorithms to calculate a check digit or a check sum of all information bits. By comparing calculated results with the ones received, errors can be detected.

✔ By assigning sequence numbers to messages and detecting sequence errors. Sequencing is used to determine lost, duplicated, or out-of-sequence messages.

Error correction and recovery are generally implemented by automatic retransmission or error-correction code.

Layers, Protocols, and Interfaces

The communication system is responsible for providing communication between nodes in a distributed system. This system allows any network node to transmit information to any other node connected to the communication network. Computer network architectures facilitate interconnectivity among homogeneous and (especially in an open systems arena) heterogeneous systems.

Because communication systems are complex, it is common to divide them into layers. Some layer structures represent formal models.

A Layered Model of Communication

To illustrate the concepts of layered communication models, it is possible to develop a three-layered model that generally describes communication. Consider the following three layers in terms of standard, person-to-person communication:

✔ The Cognitive layer includes concepts, such as understanding, knowledge, and existence of shared, mutually agreed upon symbols. This is the level at which the information becomes available for human use. Computer user interfaces work at this level.

✔ The Language layer is used to put concepts and ideas into words. Examples for humans are words or mathematics. Computers might use ASCII or EBCDIC characters.

✔ The Physical transmission layer provides the medium for the actual communication. This layer may be exemplified in several forms, such as sound vibrations in the air, written words on paper, or visual signs. Data communication may use electrical, radio, or light signals on a variety of media.

This example illustrates the nature of layered models. The three layers are independent of each other. The "upper" layers require the support of the "lower" ones. To communicate ideas, the language and conveyance are required, but the opposite may not be true.

The goals of a layered architecture mirror the goals of structured programming: to define functional modules with clearly defined interfaces. Modules are conceptually simplified and easier to maintain. Provided that the interfaces for a module remain stable, the internals of the module may be freely modified.

A Layered Model of Client/Server Computing

All major network architectures share the same high-level objectives:

✔ Connectivity permits various hardware and software to be interconnected into a uniform, single system image, networking system.

✔ Modularity allows building of diverse networking systems from a relatively small number of general-purpose components.

✔ Reliability supports error-free communications via error detection and correction availability.

✔ Ease of implementation, use, and modification provides generalized, widely acceptable solutions for network installation, modification and management, and by supplying end users with network-transparent communication facilities.

To achieve these high-level objectives, network architectures support modular design. Each module's functions are organized into functional, hierarchical, architected layers.

A layered approach is especially useful when analyzing client/server computing. Communication between distributed processors takes place on numerous levels, from signals on wires to applications that exchange control information or data. At each level, the nature of the communication is somewhat different. Network hardware works in terms of pulses of electrical voltages and currents. Applications communicate through a number of mechanisms with names such as *Named Pipes* or *Advanced Peer-to-Peer Communication*; between are numerous other mechanisms.

Client/server uses features at all of these layers to facilitate a tight integration of processes running on different computers. Some understanding of the layers involved is necessary in order to understand how client/server computing works.

In data communication models, the layers are composed of entities, which can be hardware components and software processes. Entities of the same layer but in different network nodes are called *peer entities*. Layers at the same level in different nodes are *peer layers*.

The typical distributed system architecture consists of the following functional layers:

✔ **Application Layer.** This is the topmost layer of the architecture. Typically, it performs management of application processes, distribution of data, interprocess communication, and decomposition of application functions into distributable processes. Application layer functionality is supported by lower-level layers.

✔ **Distributed Operating System Layer.** This layer provides the system-wide distributed services required by the application layer. It supports global naming, directory, addressing, sharing of local resources, protection and synchronization, intercommunication and recovery. The distributed operating system unifies the distributed functions into a single logical entity and is responsible for creating the *Single System Image* (SSI).

✔ **Local Management and Kernel Layer.** This layer supports the distributed operating system in the individual nodes. It supports local interprocess communications, memory and I/O access, protection, and multitasking. This layer supports the higher-level layers by providing these services and by communicating with its peer layer in other nodes.

✔ **Communication System Layer.** This layer supports communication required by the application, distributed operating system, and local management layers.

The layered architecture provides several important benefits:

✔ **Layer Independence.** Each layer is only aware of the services provided by the layer immediately below it.

✔ **Flexibility.** An implementation change in one layer does not affect the layers above and below it.

✔ **Simplified Implementation and Maintenance.** The support of a modular-layered design and architected decomposition of overall system functionality into simpler, smaller units.

✔ **Standardization.** Encapsulation of layer functionality, services, and interfaces into a carefully architected entities permits standards to be developed more easily.

Communication over different communications links is a complex task. Aside from its use in computer technology, the term *protocol* is possibly most familiar in diplomatic settings, in which a protocol is an agreement between parties that specifies precise rules of behavior.

Society requires adherance to protocols every day in the use of language. The grammar of any language defines a set of rules that governs interpersonal communication. If two people converse in the same language and dialect they will probably exchange information smoothly and without error. If a German and a Japanese diplomat endeavor to engage in an error-free discussion, they employ translators who understand the language-specific protocols and can perform the necessary translations.

Communication between layers is governed by protocols. Protocols include, but are not limited to, formats and order of the information exchange, and any actions to be taken on the information transmission and receipt. The rules and formats for the information exchange across the boundary between two adjacent layers comprise an interface between layers.

Data communications can easily be compared to the United Nations. Translation between communication protocols is a necessary and exacting process. In both cases, many protocols must be comprehended and carefully translated for information to be exchanged readily and without error.

To make the task of conceptualizing and organizing network communication protocols more manageable, the early designers of networking systems standards divided the process into several discrete parts.

The Seven Layers of the OSI Communications Model

The *Open System Interconnection* (OSI) model breaks up the job of moving data from one point to another into seven different tasks. The tasks are arranged hierarchically. Each layer contributes to the assembly/disassembly of a packet.

Data moves through the communications network in discrete bundles of bits known as *packets*. Each packet in turn, is divided into four distinct parts:

✔ The starting characters alert receiving boards that a packet is on the way

✔ A packet header explains where the packet is going where it came from, and what kind of packet it is (either a data or a network controlling packet)

✔ The data the packet is carrying

✔ The final error-checking bits and the end-of-packet characters

The OSI model is concerned primarily with the contents of the header section of the packet, which is the part the packet which tells it where to go. In the header section, the layers built up on outbound packets and conversely stripped off on inbound packets. The layers are arranged in a hierarchical fashion. Each layer sends information only to the layers immediately above and below it. Figure 1.1 shows the building of a packet.

Each layer sends packets to the layers above it and below it, but each layer only understands and works with information that comes from the same layer on another stack. The network layer (layer three), for example, sends an inbound packet to layer four only after it strips off any layer three information. This same layer three sends an outbound packet to layer two only after it adds layer three information to the packet. On inbound packets, it examines the layer three information to see if it needs to take any action. If the layer three information says that this packet is bound for address 04 and the receiving board is address 90, it discards the packet and does not pass it on to layer seven.

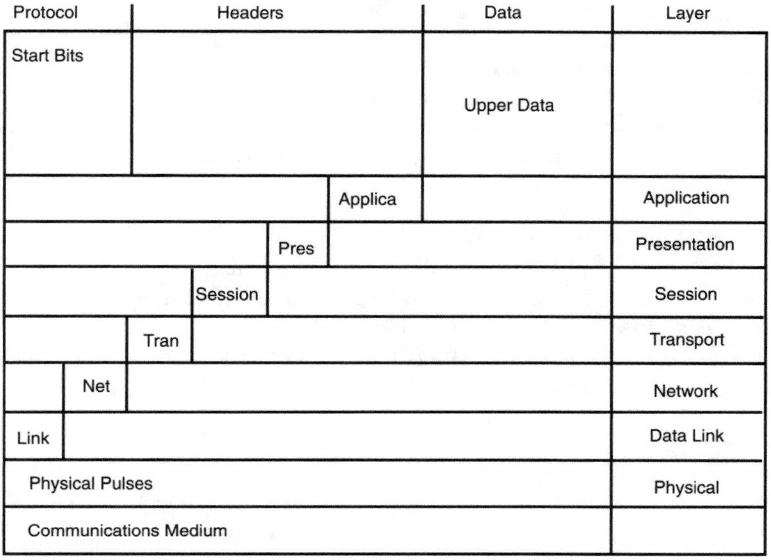

Protocol	Headers		Data	Layer
Start Bits				
			Upper Data	
		Applica		Application
	Pres			Presentation
	Session			Session
Tran				Transport
Net				Network
Link				Data Link
Physical Pulses				Physical
Communications Medium				

Figure 1.1
Building an OSI packet.

Overview

On outbound packets, layer three adds the source and destination addresses to the packet and passes this enlarged packet to layer two for further processing. Layer three on the receiving board responds only to what layer three on the sending board adds to the packet. Each layer on the stack communicates with the same layer on another stack, and is unconcerned with what other layers do.

Physical Layer

The physical layer generates the physical pulses, electrical currents, and optical pulses involved in moving data from the *Network Interface Card* (NIC) to the communications system. RS-232 is an example of physical-layer standard. The units managed at the physical layer are bits.

This layer does not include the communications system, but it does include the connection to it. It handles rise times and pulse durations. The physical layer does not manage the details of connectors and cabling, which are sometimes unofficially nicknamed the "level 0" layer of the model.

Data-Link Layer

The data-link layer is the first level that collects bits and handles data as packets. This level does the final assembly on departing packets and performs first inspection on arriving packets. It adds error correction to leaving packets and performs the checksum on arriving packets. Incomplete and defective packets are discarded. If the link layer can determine where the defective packet came from, it returns an error packet. SDLC and HDLC are examples of protocols operating at this level.

Network Layer

When *local area networks* (LANs) exceed a certain size or geographic area, they must be divided into smaller logical LANs. Devices named routers, bridges, and gateways are used to divide the LAN and create the smaller sub-networks. The network layer routes packets through multiple devices to ensure that a packet arrives at the correct device on the correct sub-LAN.

This level maintains routing tables and determines which route is the fastest available and when alternative routes should be used. This is the first layer at which a device begins filtering out packets that are not going from one network to another so that overall network traffic is reduced. Internet protocol, the IP of TCP/IP, operates at this level, as does NetWare's *Internetwork Packet Exchange* (IPX). This network layer is the level at which "connectionless" or "datagram" services operate. These terms are defined later.

Transport Layer

Transmission Control Protocol (the TCP of TCP/IP) operates at the transport layer. This is a transition level (that is, the last of the levels that manages routing packets and error recovery). It accomodates any deficiencies that cannot be covered at the network level. If packets are received reliably at the network level, this level is a very simple one. If the communications system cannot provide reliable packet transmission, this level compensates by becoming more complex.

Session Layer

In many network settings it is desirable to establish a formal connection between communicating entities. This connection assures that messages are sent and received with a high level of reliability. Such precautions are often necessary when the reliability of a network is in question, as is almost always the case when telecommunications are employed. Therefore, session orientation is the norm in most mainframe communications. LANs are generally regarded as highly reliable, and session control is less common in LAN communication.

The session layer is the level that maintains "connection-oriented" transmissions. The process of making and breaking a connection at this level is one of "binding" and "unbinding" sessions. At this level, packets are presumed to be reliable. Error checking is not part of this level's function. The TCP component of TCP/IP, IBM's NetBIOS and Netware's SPX operate at this level.

Presentation Layer

This level is not yet fully defined or widely used. Processing at this level performs any conversion that may be required to render the data usable by the application layer. Data compression/decompression and data encryption/decryption processes might be implemented at the presentation level. Data encryption and compression, however, can be performed by user applications that run above the OSI application layer.

Translations of data formats also can be performed at this layer. An example is the translation between the ASCII and EBCDIC encoding schemes. This function, however, is most frequently performed by the end-user's application.

The presentation layer is frequently misunderstood as presenting data to the user. The presentation layer is a network communication layer. It does not interface directly with end-user display devices. Production of screen displays is the responsibility of the application program executing on the user's workstation.

Application Layer

The application layer also is in the process of being defined. This layer deals with security issues and the availability of resources. The application layer is likely to deal with file transfer, job transfer, and virtual terminal protocols.

Extra Layers

The OSI model was developed when hierarchy was the norm and before the common LAN protocols (ARCnet, Ethernet, and Token Ring), were widely used. Since its inception, its layer definitions have evolved to make it fit in a world filled with LANs, as well as with minicomputers and mainframes. One of the adaptations is the informal addition of new layers and sublayers to the original seven layers. An example is the informal addition of level 0 to cover hardware details such as cable connectors and fiber optics.

Client/Server Connectivity Components

In a client/server architecture, client and server systems are constructed from a number of interconnected components. Each component provides an interface through which it communicates with other components. Communication between clients and servers can be viewed as the communication between relevant components. The two distinct classes of components are process components and resource components. *Process components* are software components that actively perform some functions. *Resource components* provide the services requested by process components.

From the point of view of client/server interactions, an active resource component acts as a *server*, and the users of the resource component and process components act as *clients*.

Process and resource components, in addition to clients and servers, enter into an association with each other for the purpose of communication. This association is the connection between a sender of information and a receiver of that information. The client/server connections can be static or dynamic. Static connections are set up at compile, load, or at system initialization time and cannot be changed. Dynamic connection can be changed "in-flight" at runtime.

Communication and Synchronization

In a client/server environment, coordination and cooperation between components is provided by the communication system's communication and synchronization actions. Communication functions involve the exchange of information. They are supported by flow control, error control, naming and addressing, and blocking and segmenting. Synchronization functions involve the coordination of actions between two or more components.

Communication and synchronization are closely related. When communication is performed in shared memory, closely-coupled systems, such as Symmetric Multiprocessing systems and software components, such as semaphores or monitors, are used for synchronization. In more traditional loosely coupled systems that are interconnected by communication networks, mechanisms such as message passing must be used for communication and synchronization.

In either case, the communication service provided by a communication system can be connectionless or connection-oriented. Connectionless services are those where each message transaction is independent of previous or subsequent ones. These are low-overhead services that are relatively simple to implement. An example is called *datagram* service, in which the user is not provided with any form of response to a transaction. Typically, datagram services are used for broadcast or multidestination message transmission.

A connection-oriented service provides a relationship between the sequence of units of information transmitted by a particular communication layer. This is similar to the process of establishing a connection between two telephones on the public telephone system. Switches at the telephone central offices establish a route through the telephone system that connects the two telephones. This route will probably be different each time. After the route is established, a *circuit* is established, and the telephones can communicate as if a continuous piece of wire connected them. In the early days of telephone communication, this circuit was literally a continuous set of wires, and it was possible to physically trace the connection between the conversing telephones. Such a connection is a *physical circuit.*

Modern communications systems rarely establish physical circuits. Instead they take advantage of new, high capacity communication channels, such as optical fiber, microwaves, and satelites, that can carry hundreds or thousands of distinct messages. Devices seeking to establish a connection will be routed through an intermediate path. Individual parts of a message may even be disassembled and transmitted through different paths to be reassembled at the receiving end. Such flexible techniques ensure that messages will be handled efficiently, taking maximum advantage of available capacity.

This switching is invisible to the end devices, however, and after a data connection is established between two computer devices, the connection appears to be a continuous wire run between the computers. A connection that appears physical but in fact uses multiple routes is a *virtual circuit*.

The activity to maintain a virtual circuit between two devices is more complex than a connectionless communication service. Most connection-oriented services have three phases of operation:

1. Establishment. An establishment phase can be used to negotiate connection or session options and quality of service.

2. Data.

3. Termination.

A terminal session to a remote computer or X.25 packet-switched network protocols accepted by the CCITT are examples of connection-oriented services.

A connection-oriented system requires a lot of overhead to control session establishment and termination. This effort may be needed to ensure reliable communication over questionable media. However, when the media can be assumed to be reliable, as most LANs are, the virtual connection can be dispensed with. Messages may just be sent with confidence that they will be received by the intended device. The overhead associated with connectionless communication is low, and performance is consequently higher. Therefore, most LANs use connectionless (also called datagram) communication modes.

Connection-oriented communication is often termed *reliable*, not because every message is guaranteed to arrive, but because devices are guaranteed to be informed if a message is not delivered as required.

Connectionless communication is often termed unreliable because the network does not detect the failure to deliver a message. This makes it the responsibility of upper-level software, perhaps the application itself, to determine that an expected reply has not been received in a reasonable time. This approach works well on LANs.

With respect to connections in general, the flow of information can be uni- or bidirectional. The latter involves a return message and synchronization in response to the initial request.

Bidirectional communications are an essential form of communication for the client/server architecture. The client component requests some service from its possibly remote server. It then waits until the results of its request are returned. Bidirectional client/server interactions can be provided by a message-oriented communication implemented in such request-reply protocols as IBM's Logical Unit 6.2 (LU6.2) or by a procedure-oriented communication such as remote procedure calls (RPC).

Procedure-Oriented Communication

Procedure-oriented communication allows applications in a distributed computing environment, such as Open Software Foundation's *Distributed Computing Environment* (DCE), to run over a heterogeneous network. The basic technology that enables this functionality is the *remote procedure call* (RPC).

The RPC model is based on the need to run individual process components of an application on a system elsewhere in a network. RPCs use a traditional programming construct, the procedure call, which is, in this case, extended from a single system to a network of systems. In the context of a communication system role in a client/server environment, an RPC requesting a particular service from a resource server is issued by a process component (client). The location of the resource component is hidden from the client. RPCs are highly suitable for client/server applications. They usually provide developers with a number of powerful tools that are necessary to build such applications. These tools include two major components: a language and a compiler and a run-time facility. A *language and a compiler* simplify the development of distributed client/server applications by producing portable source code. A *run-time facility* enables distributed applications to run over multiple, heterogeneous nodes. They make the system architectures and the underlying network protocols transparent to the application procedures.

The DCE RPC standard appears to be one of the strongest candidates for RPC implementation and deserves close examination.

To develop a distributed, DCE-compliant, client/server application, a developer creates an interface definition using the *Interface Definition Language* (IDL). IDL syntax is similar to ANSI C language with the addition of several language constructs appropriate for a network environment. After the definitions are created, the IDL compiler translates them into stubs that are bound with the client and the server (see fig. 1.2). The stub on a client system acts as a substitute for the required server procedure. Similarly, the server stub substitutes for a client. The stubs are needed to automate otherwise manual operations-copying arguments to and from RPC headers, converting data as necessary, and calling the RPC runtime.

RPC runtimes should have the following features:

✔ Transparency and independence from the underlying networking protocols

✔ Support for reliable transmission, error detection, and recovery from network failures

✔ Support for a common method of network naming, addressing, and directory services, while at the same time being independent of network directory services

✔ Multithreading support for parallel and concurrent processing, and capability to handle multiple requests simultaneously, thus reducing the time required to complete an application

✔ Portability and interoperability with various system environments

✔ Support for resources integrity and application security

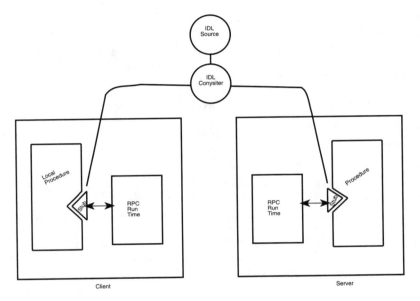

Figure 1.2
An RPC
implementation.

The DCE implementation of the remote procedure calls includes specific semantics for both network transport independence and transparency. DCE RPC includes a pipe facility to eliminate such resource limitations as inadequate main memory. The ISO X.500 standard is used to provide global directory services. DCE RPC utilizes Kerberos authentication and authorization to support security service and asynchronous threads to support concurrent and parallel processing.

Defining Local and Wide Area Networks

Under the client/server model, applications are closely allied with network services. It is, therefore, useful to have a general sense of how local area networks work even if your primary focus will be on programming at the application level.

The proliferation of personal computers throughout organizations has resulted in an increase in the number of PCs used for a wide variety of business functions. It also has resulted in an ever-increasing need for personal computers to communicate. The communication needs include intercommunications among personal computers as well as communication with centralized data processing facilities and the sources of corporate data. Several networking technologies have been developed to support this intercommunication. Among them are wide area networking and local area networking.

Intelligent workstations, such as personal computers or Unix-based technical workstations, can be used as stand-alone systems to support local applications. As workgroup environments become more and more popular, the reasons for interconnecting these intelligent workstations in a network are readily becoming more apparent. Among them are the following:

✔ The need to access data stored in another (not local) system

✔ The need for the members of the workgroup to share devices that are too expensive (such as a duplex PostScript laser printer) to be used only by a single user

✔ The need for the workgroup members to exchange information electronically

The distance between network users is one of the factors that determines the required network type and the underlying technology. One situation includes user requirements for access processing and data storage capabilities typically available from mainframes. Similarly, interconnectivity may be required by geographically widely separated users. In this case, the networking solutions may involve public telecommunication facilities for rapid data interchange. The networks that tie all these users together are called *wide area networks (WANs)*.

It is sometimes useful to distinguish between WANs that can span remote locations at very large distances, measured in hundreds and thousands of miles (for example, users in Atlanta, Chicago, and Tokyo), and networks that link users within a particular metropolitan area. Networks that operate within a city or those that can use physical telecommunications facilities typically associated with the city infrastructure (for example, underground cabling system), are sometimes called *metropolitan area networks* (MANs). A typical MAN provides voice data and video communications at speeds of 45–600 Mbps (million bits per second) at distances ranging from 1 to 50 miles.

Relatively short distance communications between intelligent workstations are supported by a networking technology known as *local area networks* (LANs). The *Institute of Electrical and Electronics Engineers* (IEEE) defines a LAN as a data communication system that allows a number of independent devices to communicate directly with each other, within a moderately sized geographic area over a physical communication channel of moderate data rates.

LANs can be used for shared data, application and device access, electronic mail, process monitoring in a factory environment, and even for alarm and security systems. The most interesting feature of a LAN is its capability to support cooperative applications in which an application runs partly on LAN stations and partly on a LAN server or possibly a mainframe host. The range of LAN applications can be significantly extended by interconnecting several networks. LAN interconnection can be implemented over WANs, thus extending the communication capabilities of LANs far beyond the traditional distance limitations of a typical LAN.

LAN Characteristics and Components

The IEEE definition of a LAN provides characteristics that distinguish local area networks from other networking technologies. This definition is as follows:

✔ By allowing independent devices to communicate directly with each other, the LAN supports peer communication between its nodes. This is in contrast with such centrally controlled hierarchical systems such as IBM's *Systems Network Architecture* (SNA).

✔ By emphasizing a moderately sized geographic area, IEEE separates the LAN from wide area networks. Typically, it does not exceed a distance of about 5 to 7 miles, and often is limited to a single building or a group of buildings placed in close geographic proximity.

✔ By defining a physical communication channel with moderate data rates, IEEE contrasts LANs with wide area networks, which often use public-switched communication facilities.

Moderate data rates are used to imply that LAN data rates are slower than those of the direct mainframe links and channel-to-channel communication, which are measured in several million bits per second. Advances in physical transmission technology, especially fiber-optic communications, allow LANs to support data rates up to 100 Mbps.

A typical LAN that corresponds to the IEEE LAN definition consists of two general types of components: *nodes* and *links* between nodes. In LAN terminology, nodes, which can be any device attached to a network, are generally known as stations. All LAN stations are linked, or interconnected via a cabling system, which includes the physical communication channels and any devices necessary to attach the stations to the network.

To avoid the loss of a signal over the length of the wire, signal regenerators, or repeaters, are sometimes inserted into a LAN. Each station must possess adequate intelligence to handle the communication control functions. With this requirement in mind, peripheral devices, such as printers and hard disk drives, do not qualify as stations themselves, but rather are attached to some of the intelligent stations.

Networks, including local area networks, are characterized by the shape the cabling system takes, that is, the network topology. In addition, different local area networks are characterized by the following:

✔ **The Transmission Medium.** The type of cable that is used in a given LAN.

✔ **The Transmission Technique.** The technique that determines how the transmission medium is used for communication.

✔ **The Access Control Method.** The method by which LAN stations control their access to the transmission medium.

Network Topologies

A communication system has previously been described as the collection of hardware and software that supports intersystem and interprocess communication between software components in distributed nodes.

The actual links between nodes comprise a network. These represent an ordered collection of physical layers between interconnected nodes. This section presents the "basics" of networking-topology and technologies.

Network Switching Techniques

For many network topologies, not all nodes have direct physical links between them. A network must provide a relay function that switches the data between links to provide a point-to-point path between some nodes.

There are two main switching techniques used in modern networks: circuit switching and packet switching.

A *circuit-switching* network operates by forming a dedicated connection between two nodes. While the circuit is in place, the sender is guaranteed that the message will be delivered to the destination. Such a connection is dedicated to the participating nodes until they release it. The dedication of a communication path, however, means that the capacity of the path is reserved whether the communicating nodes are using the full capacity or not.

Packet-switched networks take a different approach. All traffic is divided into small segments (known as packets) that are mapped (or multiplexed) into a high-capacity intersystem connection for transmission from one node to another. The same media path may be shared among a wide variety of communicating nodes, and communication capacity will not be monopolized for any one purpose. To implement packet-switching, packets carry identification that allows *network operating system* (NOS) software to send them to their destinations, where the packets are reassembled by the network software.

The main disadvantage of the packet-switching technique is that as the activity increases, a given pair of communicating partners receives less resource capacity from the network. Opposed to the circuit switching, the available capacity is not guaranteed. New generations of low-cost, high-speed networking hardware are providing for high performance and wide acceptance of the packet-switching networking technique.

Sometimes the *message-switching* technique is described as an alternative to both circuit and packet switching. It involves storing messages (including files) in the switching node's storage. Messages can be stored until the destination node wants to receive the message. This type of packet-switching technique is often implemented in electronic mail applications.

Physical Topologies

A physical topology is the actual way that the wiring is strung between network nodes. Each of these network types is described in greater detail. Of these five types of networks, point-to-point and multi-point networks can be quickly dismissed as special-purpose approaches.

A point-to-point connection is a dedicated connection between two devices. These connections are generally used when performance is the overriding concern. They might be used to implement a high-speed connection between two network servers or multiuser hosts. Point-to-point connections are seldom utilized for normal traffic levels or to service workstations.

Multi-point connections implement a point-to-point connection between each pair of stations that needs to communicate. Cost of such a network escalates astronomically when more than a handful of stations are involved.

The principal idea behind a local or wide area network is that logical point-to-point connections can be established between any two stations on the network while sharing a common, inexpensive medium. A logical connection enables nodes to exchange data as if they were directly connected. These nodes share a common network on which various node-to-node messages are carefully routed and efficiently controlled. By combining a high performance cabling system with efficient protocols, stations can behave as though they are directly connected to each other even though they are "time-sharing" a common network.

The following section discusses the three LAN physical topologies that support efficient use of network resources: the bus, star, and ring topologies. Keep in mind that a network also has a logical topology that defines the way the network functions beneath the surface. A network frequently has a logical topology that is different from its physical topology.

The Bus

A *bus* is the simplest form of multinode network. In a bus topology, all network nodes connect directly to the same piece of cable. Each network node has an address assigned to it, a number that uniquely identifies the node. This address allows nodes to identify messages intended for them and to direct messages to other specific nodes.

A segment of a network that uses a bus topology is a length of wire, generally *coaxial* cable, capped at each end with a *terminator*. It does not wrap back on itself. When a station on the network transmits a message, the electrical signal travels in both directions from the origination point until it reaches the end of the cable, where it is absorbed by the terminators. As the signal propagates down the cable, each station on the cable can examine the data. By adhering to the rules of a network protocol, each station retrieves only those messages that are intended for it.

The primary appeal of the bus topology is its extreme simplicity. Stations in close proximity can be networked simply by stringing a cable from station to station and tapping the station into the cable. A bus is also efficient to install.

The Ethernet networking protocols typically run over a bus topology, but not all buses are required to run Ethernet. Other protocols, such as ARCnet, also can be used for a bus physical topology.

Due to the electrical characteristics of a bus, every component on a bus network is capable of affecting the entire network. If a cable is broken at some point, the problem will be more severe than simply losing contact with stations on opposite sides of the break. The break actually causes each section of the cable to lose its termination, and signals reflect back from the break causing interference on the entire cable. One bad station sending out noise can bring down the entire bus. Under these circumstances it can be difficult to isolate the cause of the problem.

Bus topologies are limited in the number of nodes that can occupy a segment. As each new node is added to the cable, it absorbs a part of the signal on the cable. At a certain level, the signal strength falls to a point so low that it can no longer be relied on without the aid of a repeater. An Ethernet segment can generally only support 30 nodes. Beyond that, repeaters must be added to support additional workstations.

The advantages of a bus topology include that it uses a minimal amount of wire and that it requires inexpensive network hardware.

A single cable break or malfunctioning node, however, can bring down the whole LAN.

Star Topology

In a star cabling topology, a central system, which can be a server or a wiring hub, connects PCs or workstations. Each node is connected to the central system by an individual cable. Because each computer on a network requires its own wire to connect to the network hub, the star topology generally uses much more cable than either bus or ring topologies. The central wiring concentrators also represent a cost that is not required for a bus network. In general, a star network represents the highest-cost physical topology. A simple star network is shown in figure 1.3.

Despite this high cost, the benefits are drawing most network designers toward star topologies. Because each machine in a star network is individually wired, a cable break affects only one workstaion. Concentrators can be excellent places to place network diagnostic devices. Because all signals are routed through the concentrator, they can be monitored from a central location. The higher cost of a star network is generally justified by the greater reliability that it provides.

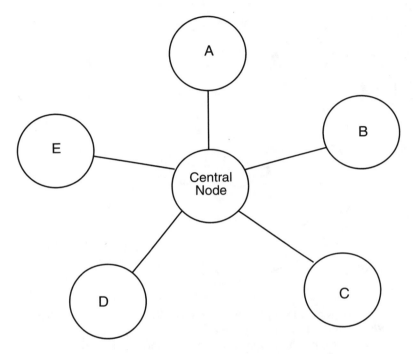

Figure 1.3
A simple star network.

Star topologies are employed for ARCnet, Token Ring, and a version of Ethernet labeled 10BASE-T.

The advantages of a star topology include greater node autonomy—a cable break affects only the machine connected by that cable—and centralized locations for network diagnostic equipment.

The primary disadvantages are that a star topology requires both a large amount of cable and central concentrator components, which adds to network cost.

Ring Topologies

The foundation of a ring network is a loop of cable. Unlike a bus, in which a signal is broadcast throughout the network cable, ring networks operate by passing signals from node-to-node around the ring. Terminal servers, PCs, and workstations connect to the ring, as shown in figure 1.4. Each node receives a message that is passed to it, and, if the message is intended for another node, repeats the signal to the next node. Because this repeating action amplifies and reconditions each message to pass it on, ring networks are less sensitive to signal loss to increasing numbers of nodes on the network.

Figure 1.4
A simple ring
network.

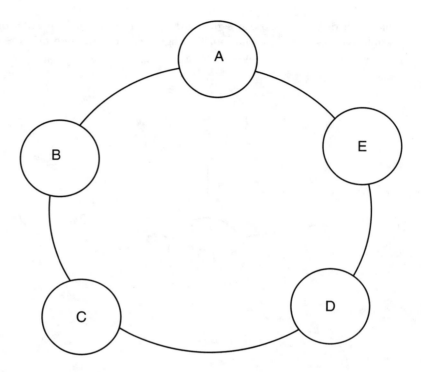

Local area networks are not generally implemented with ring physical topologies. Token Ring, despite the "ring" in its name, is actually wired as a star because the star configuration offers advantages in terms of centralization and troubleshooting. Ring topologies also do not offer a central point for network management.

More frequently, rings are implemented over large geographic areas in which a star would be inefficient. A ring can be run to connect several sites within a city or even several cities across a multistate area. Rings also are implemented for fault-tolerant backbone technologies.

Most ring networks provide fault tolerance by implementing a backup signal path. If a break affects one of the ring segments the signal can often be routed back through the ring's backup unit. When a cable break failure occurs in a ring network, it causes the network to reroute the messages through the backup path, which usually runs in the direction opposite to the mainpath. This doubles the ring distance (and slows the network), but it keeps the network running. Network-management software can monitor the network and notify operators that the backup path has been switched on.

Advantages of a ring topology are that redundant media paths can reroute messages when a cable break occurs; and a ring topology uses cables efficiently when covering a large geographic area.

Disadvantages of a ring topology include no central place to monitor the network and generally lower throughput.

Structured Wiring

Structured wiring is increasingly used as networks become more complicated. Structured wiring systems consist of concentrators that accept plug-in modules. Some of these modules are wiring hubs, which support network connections between stations and the concentrator. Most hub modules support between 8 and 12 connections. Many concentrator types can service several types of logical networks, as well as bridges, routers, repeaters, and terminal servers. Concentrators also may contain component spares or redundant components to make networks fault-resistant or fault-tolerant. Structured wiring is considerably easier to manage than the nonstructured types of daisy-chained or star topologies.

Structured wiring distinguishes between a network's physical and logical topologies. All hubs use physical star topologies, but the logical topology can be ring, bus, or star. Also, several different networks with the same or different logical topologies can exist at once in a single hub. The concentrator conserves cabling by putting the cable backbones in a box.

Some structured cabling systems support stand-alone hubs, which can operate outside of a concentrator. Stand-alone hubs are small units that cannot be expanded. Because each hub is the center of a star topology, the connections from node to hub are star connections. The connections between hubs are a distributed network and can be another hub or a bus, ring, or star. Hub and concentrator architectures are highly modular. Hundreds of nodes can all be connected to one physical star topology.

Hubs can contain bridges, routers, and terminal servers as well as various logical networks. Hubs also may contain network management cards and support *Simple Network-Management Protocol* (SNMP).

Many hubs are sold as segmented products. These can be purchased as a base product with one LAN module that supports 12 nodes on an Ethernet, for example, and with add-in modules to add more nodes, such as a token-ring LAN, router, terminal server, or bridge.

As a general rule, the bigger the network, the lower the hub cost per node. Hubs are more costly than simple networks but offer several savings. The hub's high-performance backplanes allow for better throughput than other networking schemes. Additionally, hubs allow for more flexibility than traditional networks.

Because a hub's logical setup is different from the physical network, changes can be made without changing cables.

Because a hub uses a physical star topology, locating cable faults is easier because only one node is affected by a fault.

Although hubs are extremely flexible and can grow with a network, they generally require a larger initial investment than that needed for more traditional wiring schemes. But the concentration of network components and the separation of physical and logical topologies makes hub-network management simpler and less expensive than other methods.

Advantages of structured wiring systems include the following:

✔ Isolation of cabling for each node, which makes it easy to locate cable faults

✔ Plug-in modules, which make it efficient to move, add nodes, and change the network configuration

✔ Availability of integral network-management support

Disadvantages include the following:

✔ High start-up costs

✔ Higher per-node costs due to the high use of active components

Transmission and Access Control Methods

The physical transmission of information over a local area network can be described by two main categories: the actual medium used for the transmission and the way this medium is used.

Transmission Media

Current LANs are generally implemented with one of three media types: twisted pairs, coaxial cable, and fiber-optic links. Although they will not be discussed further, radio and microwave links also are occasionally employed.

Twisted pairs consist of two individually insulated and braided strands of copper wire. Usually, such pairs form a cable by grouping pairs together and enclosing them in a common protective jacket. The typical intrabuilding telephone wiring is an example of such a cable. Relatively low cost and high availability of such a cabling system have resulted in the popularity of the twisted-pair wire for LAN implementation. Unshielded twisted-pair wire (UTP) can support transmission speeds of up to 10 MB. Figure 1.5 illustrates UTP cable along with the RJ-45 connector usually employed.

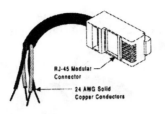

Figure 1.5
Unshielded
twisted-pair (UTP)
cable.

To eliminate possible electrical interference, a twisted pair cable can be enclosed in a special, high-quality protective sheath. Such cable is known as *shielded twisted pair cable* (STP). Although it is slightly more expensive, it can be used where higher reliability and higher transmission rates over longer distances are required. The IBM Cabling System Type 1 and 2 cables are examples of twisted pair cables.

Coaxial cable is familiar to television viewers, especially those with cable TV. Coaxial cable contains a central conducting core (generally copper), that is surrounded by the insulating material, another conductor (braided wire mesh or a solid sleeve), and yet another insulated protective and flexible jacket. Although more expensive, coaxial cable is better isolated from electrical interference than a twisted pair. Coaxial cable can support transmission rates of up to 100 Mbps. DECconnect Communication System's Thin and Standard Ethernet cables are examples of the coaxial cable used in LAN implementations. Figure 1.6 shows an example of coaxial cable along with a typical connector.

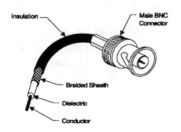

Figure 1.6
Coaxial cable with
a typical
connector.

Fiber-optic links are the newest transmission medium available for commercial LAN implementations. Optical fiber contains a core of an extremely thin glass thread, surrounded by a concentric layer of light insulator, called *cladding.* Optical signals take the form of modified light beams that traverse the length of the fiber-optic link. The cladding is made of a material whose refractive index is lower than that of the core. The light signals traveling along the core are reflected from the cladding back into the core. A number of these optical fibers are bound together into one fiber-optic cable, surrounded by a protective sheath. Fiber-optic cables are characterized by lighter weight than coaxial cables and significantly higher costs. The light signals transmitted over a fiber-optic cable are not subject to electrical interference. Optical transmission medium can support extremely high transmission rates. Rates of up to 565 Mbps can be found in commercially available systems, and experiments have demonstrated data rates of up to 200,000 Mbps.

IBM Cabling System's Type 5 cable is an example of fiber-optic cables used for computer network. Figure 1.7 shows how fiber-optic cable and connectors are constructed.

Figure 1.7
Fiber-optic cable with a typical connector.

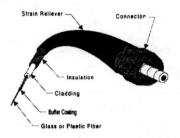

Various implementations of these physical links can be found in a large number of commercially available cabling systems offered by general-purpose communication vendors as well as vendors of various computer networks.

Transmission Techniques

Whichever transmission medium is used in a given LAN environment, the LAN designer must select a technique that the LAN will use to transmit signals over a physical communication link. In general, there are two available transmission techniques for transmission over a physical communication channel: baseband and broadband.

Baseband transmission uses discrete signals (pulses of electricity or light that represent a binary 0 and 1) to carry information over a physical transmission medium. This signaling technique is called *digital signaling.* Baseband transmission uses the entire communication channel capacity to transmit a single data signal. LANs typically employ digital, baseband signalling.

By dividing the available transmission time into time slots, multiple stations attached to a network can share a common communication channel. This technique is known as *time-division multiplexing* (TDM). TDM frequently is used to combine several LAN baseband signals for transmission through a high-speed network such as a fiber-optic backbone, which can be used to interconnect various buildings or departments in large installations.

Broadband transmission typically employs analog (continuously varying) signals. Digital information is encoded into analog waves by using amplitude, frequency, or phase modulation of the base (carrier) signal. This technique is comparable to the practice of combining multiple television signals so that they may be transmitted over a single cable in a CATV system. A tuner can select the frequency for any individual signal and isolate it from the many signals that are being carried on the cable. Because the signals are each identified with a different frequency on the cable, this technique is known as *frequency-division multiplexing* (FDM).

In general, the higher the frequency of the carrier signal, the higher the volume of information that can be carried by this signal. The difference between the highest and lowest frequencies that are carried over the channel reflects that channel's information-carrying capacity and is referred to as the channel bandwidth. The bandwidth is directly related to another measurement of channel capacity the number of bits per second that can be carried over the channel, known as the *data rate.*

Typical baseband LANs operate at data rates of 10–20 Mbps. When networks grow to "campus" size, 10–20 Mbps of performance may be inadequate to connect large numbers of workstations in multiple departments or buildings. A common strategy is to interconnect local baseband networks via broadband networks, (frequently designated as backbones), which simultaneously transport multiple signals.

Transmission Control

Technologies covered in this section are frequently referred to as "media access control" methods in that they are used to ensure that nodes on the network access and share the nework media in an organized fashion. In general, various transmission control methods can be classified as follows:

- ✔ **Centralized control.** One station controls the entire network and gives other stations permissions to transmit.

- ✔ **Random control.** Enables any station to transmit without being given specific permission.

- ✔ **Distributed control.** Gives the right to transmit to only one station at a time. The right to transmit is passed from one station to the all stations cooperate to control access to the network.

Each of these transmission control methods offers its own advantages and disadvantages and has access control methods specifically designed to work best with that particular transmission control.

Centralized Access Control

Centralized transmission control provides for easier network coordination and management and requires simple station-to-network interfaces. At the same time, centralized transmission control, by definition, provides a single point of failure and a potential network bottleneck. Centralized control may employ the following access control methods:

- ✔ **Polling.** A master station sends a notification to all other (secondary) stations indicating that a given station is allowed to transmit. Media access conflicts are eliminated since only the polled station may transmit.

✔ **Circuit Switching.** This can be used successfully in a centralized control LAN implemented by using a star topology. Here, a central station receives requests for a transmission from a secondary station and establishes a connection between the sender and its intended receiver. Circuit switching is widely used in telephony, especially in *private branch exchanges* (PBX).

✔ **Time-Division Multiple Access (TDMA).** This provides a specific time slot for each station on a network. The station is allowed to transmit only during this time slot. The time cycle is started and synchronized by a master station. TDMA can be successfully used on a bus topology.

Random Access Control

One of the best-known access control techniques for random transmission control is *Carrier Sense Multiple Access with Collision Detection* (CSMA/CD). Using this method, stations listen politely to determine whether the network is in use. If not, a station will attempt to transmit. The mechanisms are discussed later in this chapter when Ethernet is described in greater detail.

Carrier Sense Multiple Access with Collision Avoidance (CSMA/CA), used in Apple's LocalTalk networks, is very similar to the CSMA/CD access methods. However, stations utilize a variety of timing strategies to reduce the likelihood that collisions will occur.

The performance of both CSMA schemes is random since it cannot be predicted when stations will attempt to transmit. CSMA is an extremely simple access control mechanism, and there is little work associated with managing network traffic. However, the random element can cause problems when network traffic demands are high, and CSMA network performance can deteriorate rapidly as demand approaches capacity limits.

Distributed Access Control

Token ring passing is the most widely used method of distributed access control and is most frequently used in ring topology networks (for example, IBM's Token Ring). A token is a small message that is constantly circulating around the ring. Token passing can be used in a bus, star or tree topology. Token bus methods are similar to a token ring, emulating the token ring method on a logical topology level. IBM Token Ring is the most commonly cited example of the use of token passing to control media access and is described in detail later.

Token passing is a more complicated mechanism than the CSMA schemes just discussed. It is, therefore, more expensive to implement and the network must have more controls in place to ensure proper operation. When network traffic is high, however, token passing becomes an effective means of ensuring that all network stations are allowed equal network access.

When designing local area networks, many interdependent factors should be taken into consideration: the transmission medium, transmission control and access methods, network topology, bandwidth, and data rates. All these factors affect network performance and cost. Decisions regarding network topology, transmission control, and access control methods should be made based on the processing and cost requirements of a particular LAN.

IEEE Local Area Network Standards

The IEEE undertook Project 802 in February of 1980 to identify and formalize LAN standards for data rates not exceeding 20 Mbps. Standardization efforts resulted in the IEEE 802 LAN standards.

The IEEE standards divide the OSI data-link layer into two sublayers: the *Media Access Control* (MAC) layer and the *Logical Link Control* (LLC) layer. The MAC layer deals with media-access techniques to access shared physical medium. Token ring and Ethernet have different implementations of the MAC layer because their methods of sharing the physical media are different.

All IEEE LANs have the same LLC layer, as defined by standard 802.2. The advantage of a common sublayer, such as the LLC, is that upper layer mechanisms can be the same, regardless of the type of networking hardware.

The 802.3 and 802.5 standards define both the physical and AC components of Ethernet and token ring.

Major network vendors, including IBM, recognize that Ethernet and Token Ring will coexist for the foreseeable future and are rushing tools to market for integrating the standards. Network planners are free to match the cabling system to the application, with the understanding that future network-integration issues can be successfully dealt with.

Ethernet LANs

Ethernet was developed at Xerox Corporation and is the prototype for networks based on CSMA/CD media access control. The system was called Ethernet in honor of that elusive substance called *ether*, through which electromagnetic radiation was once thought to propagate.

Ethernet was proposed as a standard by *Digital Equipment Corporation* (DEC), Intel, and Xerox. The Ethernet proposal became known as the IEEE 802.3.

Before an Ethernet station can transmit, it listens for activity on the transmission channel. Ethernet frequently is described as a "listen before talking" protocol. Activity is defined as any transmission caused by other Ethernet station. The presence of a transmission is called a *carrier*, which can be sensed by the network interface card.

If an Ethernet station detects a busy channel, it refrains from transmitting. After the last bit of the passing frame, the Ethernet data-link layer continues to wait for a minimum of 9.6 microseconds to provide proper interframe spacing. Following that gap, if a data frame is waiting for transmission, the station initiates the transmission. If the station has no data to transmit, it resumes the carrier sense (listening for a carrier) operation. The interframe gap provides recovery time for other Ethernet stations.

If a station tries to transmit when the channel is busy, it results in a garbled transmission, known as a *collision*. If the channel is free (no carrier is detected), the station can transmit. Because multiple stations attached to the Ethernet channel use the carrier-sense mechanism, it is called *carrier sense with multiple access* (CSMA).

Collisions occur during the normal operation of Ethernet LANs because stations transmit based only on one fact: the presence of a carrier on the channel. They do not know whether packets are queued for transmission on other stations. Furthermore, the CSMA operation is complicated by propagation delay in LANs. In Ethernet, for example, signals propagate at 0.77 times the speed of light on standard (thick) cables and at 0.65 tines the speed of light on thin Ethernet cables. A delay occurs before a transmission is heard by all stations, and a station may transmit because it has yet to hear another station's transmission.

Collisions are a fact of life in Ethernet LANs. Ethernet stations minimize the effects of collisions by detecting them as they occur. The stations involved in the collision abort their transmissions. The first station to detect the collision sends out a special jamming pulse alert all stations that a collision has taken place. After a collision is detected, all stations set up a random interval timer. Transmission takes place only after this interval timer expires. Introducing a delay before transmission lessens the probability of collision.

When successive collisions occur, the average random time-out value is doubled. This doubling takes place up to 10 consecutive collisions. Beyond that, doubling the average random time-out value does not significantly improve the performance of the network.

Under the worst-case scenario, a station may wait indefinitely for an opportunity to transmit. Because this scenario is not acceptable for real-time applications, Ethernet is not well suited for real-time applications. Although this potential problem is frequently mentioned when comparing Ethernet to other LAN standards (such as token ring), problems with truely excessive collisions are seldom encountered on real-world Ethernet LANs.

At moderate traffic levels, Ethernet is an extremely efficient protocol. The next section will show that token ring requires a wide variety of control mechanisms that generate network traffic. Apart from collisions, however, most of the network traffic on an Ethernet is related to network transmission. As a result, Ethernet offers very high performance at most data rates. A 10M Ethernet often provides comparable performance to a 16M token ring until high traffic levels are reached.

Token Ring LANs

Ring-based logical networks have existed for many years. Ring LANs are a sequence of point-to-point links. They may be considered to be sequential broadcast LANs, with the point-to-point links forming a circle. Unlike that of Ethernet LANs, in which the carrier-sense mechanism may be analog, the technology of ring LANs is digital. An attractive feature of ring-based LANs is the deterministic response time, even under heavy load conditions.

The token ring LAN encountered most often is the IEEE 802.5. This LAN is often referred to as the IBM Token-Ring because IBM was the prime mover behind the IEEE 802.5 standard.

A special group of bits, called the token, is used to arbitrate access to the ring. The token circulates from station to station around the ring. If a station wants to transmit a frame, it must wait and seize the token. While in possession of the token, it can transmit a frame. At the end of the transmission, it must release the token so that other stations can access the ring.

For proper operation of the ring, the token must circulate continuously, even if there is no activity on the ring. There are 24 bits (three octets) in the token, and the ring must have enough latency or delay to hold 24 bits. If the bit rate on the ring is 4Mbps, the ring must have a latency of 24/4Mbps = six microseconds. While six microseconds may seem like a very short delay, consider a twisted-pair medium in which the propagation velocity is 0.59 times the speed of light. The minimum size then of the ring with these parameters is 1 kilometer. To bring the ring to a realistic physical size, a special station designated as the active monitor adds a 24-bit delay buffer to the ring. This buffer also compensates for any accumulated phase jitter on the ring. The active monitor is important for maintaining normal operation of the ring.

A token ring station operates in one of the following three modes:

✔ Transmit mode

✔ Listen mode

✔ Bypass mode

Protocols

Data communications protocols are used to coordinate the exchange of information between different network devices. They establish the mechanism whereby each device recognizes meaningful information from another device. In the communications world today, there are a number of protocols in use, along with several basic structures that handle different aspects of data communication.

While this book is about the TCP/IP protocol, it is important to understand the alternatives available to it. This section looks at four of non-TCP/IP protocols that are most widely implemented in the context of the OSI Reference Model and the ways that protocols communicate over a network.

Once the domain of the small workgroup or office department, local area networks are becoming the major integration platform for enterprise-wide computing. The simple twenty-user network has now expanded to the three or five thousand-user enterprise internetwork, spanning time zones almost as easily as it used to span office cubicles. To match these new demands, LAN protocols have become increasingly powerful and flexible. The following four major LAN protocols support the workgroup and the enterprise model to varying degrees:

✔ Xerox Network Systems (XNS)

✔ Novell IPX/SPX

✔ NetBIOS

✔ AppleTalk

IPX/SPX

The Novell NetWare protocols are based on the *Xerox Network Systems* (XNS) protocols developed at Xerox Corporation's *Palo Alto Research Center* (PARC). The layer structure, protocol interaction, and network addressing closely correspond to XNS.

Novell's primary protocols are the *Internetwork Packet Exchange* (IPX) and *Sequenced Packet Exchange* (SPX). SPX is a reliable, connection-oriented protocol, while IPX is the unreliable datagram protocol.

NetWare uses a slightly modified version of the *routing information protocol* (RIP) originally developed as part of the TCP/IP Internet protocol suite to query and maintain routing-information tables on workstations and servers.

Network packets must be directed not only to a particular device but to a particular process running on the device. Devices are identified in the form of addresses, which are associated with a particular subnetwork on a LAN. The target process on the device is identified by a socket number. Novell adopted the internetwork-addressing structure of XNS in which a complete address is given by the network number, the host number, and the socket number on the host. The network number is 32 bits long, the host number is 48 bits long, and the socket is 16 bits long.

IPX

The *Internetwork Packet Exchange* (IPX) is Novell's network layer protocol. IPX provides a connectionless, unreliable, datagram service to workstations and servers. IPX makes a best-effort attempt to deliver a packet to the destination but requests no acknowledgment to verify if the packet has indeed reached its destination. IPX relies on high-layer protocols, such as SPX or NCP, to provide a reliable, sequenced datastream service.

An IPX packet consists of a header (30 bytes) and data section. Because IPX does not provide any facilities for packet fragmentation, IPX implementations must ensure that the packets they send are small enough to be transmitted on any physical networks they want to cross. IPX requires that all physical links be able to handle IPX packets that are 576 bytes long. (Therefore, the safest approach is to send no packet larger than 576 bytes.) Many implementations refine this process slightly by detecting when they are sending packets directly to the destination over a single physical link. If this physical link can handle packets larger that 576 bytes, larger packets are used.

SPX

The *Sequenced Packet Exchange* (SPX) is the Novell transport layer protocol. It was derived from the Xerox *Sequenced Packet Protocol* (SPP).

SPX provides a reliable, connection-oriented, virtual circuit service between network stations. SPX makes use of the IPX datagram service to provide a sequenced data stream. This is accomplished by implementing a system that requires each packet sent to be acknowledged. It also provides flow control between the network stations and ensures that no duplicates are delivered to the remote process.

SPX reduces the number of times that an unneeded retransmission occurs to decrease the congestion on the network. Retransmissions normally occur after the sending station has timed-out waiting for an acknowledgment of a packet that is lost or damaged or dropped. SPX uses a heuristically enhanced timing algorithm to estimate accurate retransmission times. It also uses historic information to determine the initial time, and it then increases the time by 50 percent if a time-out occurs. The process continues until a maximum time-out value is reached or until acknowledgments return in time and retransmissions are no longer required. In the second case, the time-out stabilizes at a value that is accurate for the network conditions.

SPX adds 12 bytes to the IPX packet header, mostly to carry connection control information. Added to the 30 bytes of the IPX header, this results in a combined header of 42 bytes. The maximum size of an SPX packet is the same as the maximum for an IPX packet.

NetBIOS

The *Network Basic Input/Output System* (NetBIOS) is a high-level *application program interface* (API) that was designed to enable programmers to build network applications by using a network of IBM type PCs. It was developed by Sytek, and was originally implemented on an IBM PC Network Adapter card. NetBIOS was introduced by IBM in 1984 and adopted by Microsoft for use with its MS-Net network product. Later, IBM provided an emulator which enabled NetBIOS to work with network interface cards used with its Token-Ring networks.

NetBIOS is not really a protocol; it is an interface that provides network applications with a set of commands to establish communications sessions, send and receive data, and name network objects.

Today, all major networking companies, including IBM, Novell, Microsoft, and Banyan, support the NetBIOS interface either directly or through the use of emulators over their respective protocol stacks. Novell implemented NetBIOS support using the IPX protocol stack. Regardless of the implementation, the NetBIOS interface presented to the distributed application on the network remains consistent.

Many network applications are written using the NetBIOS interface. Because of its ubiquitous character, it continues to be a popular vehicle for developing distributed applications.

As seen from the perspective of the OSI Reference Model, NetBIOS provides a session-layer interface. At this level, NetBIOS is capable of providing a reliable, connection-oriented data-transfer stream, along with a naming system for identifying stations on the network. While NetBIOS can provide an unreliable connectionless datagram service, it does not provide a routing service, making the construction of internetworks very difficult.

AppleTalk

Apple Computer began to design a set of communication protocols, called AppleTalk, in late 1983 and early 1984. The goal was to connect Macintosh personal computers, along with printers, print servers, file servers, routers, and gateways, to computer systems built by other manufacturers. The most common first use of AppleTalk was to connect the graphical computer to an Apple LaserWriter laser printer.

Each Macintosh and Apple LaserWriter includes native hardware support for the AppleTalk networking architecture. Additionlly, the system software includes comprehensive network support. This combination of bundled hardware and software helps make AppleTalk one of the most common networking solutions for personal computers in use today.

AppleTalk was designed from the ground up, to be an open, extensible network architecture to support new physical network technologies and new protocol stacks. It provides for the connection of large numbers of computers and peripherals over a potentially large geographic area by linking local networks into internets.

AppleTalk is designed to support peer-to-peer networking (where there is no need for a separate name server to control the assignment and use of network names). The overall (workstation-centric) design philosophy of the Macintosh computer also extended to the network design. The user's model of interaction with the network had to be as transparent as possible so that the standard operations and paradigms are extended in accessing resources across the internetwork. This means that users can mount remote volumes on their desktop and make use of the files and folders by using the standard select and click operations.

The installation of the network nodes was designed to support a "plug-and-play" model, in which the user attaches the physical link. Most of the configuration is then automatically managed by the system software.

AppleTalk Phase 2 was introduced in June 1989 as an upwardly compatible extension to the existing AppleTalk (Phase 1). AppleTalk Phase 2 provides support for larger, enterprise-wide networks by enabling a greater number of nodes (workstations, printers, and servers) on the network. Although AppleTalk Phase 1 supported a maximum of 254 nodes on a single network, Phase 2 enables multiple network numbers to be associated with a single network, while enabling 253 nodes per network number. AppleTalk Phase 2 provides support for LocalTalk, EtherTalk and TokenTalk. LocalTalk is the physical and data-link specification for Apple's familiar shielded twisted-pair cabling scheme. EtherTalk and TokenTalk are Apple's implementation of Ethernet and Token Ring. The AppleTalk Internet Router also was modified to enable the connection of up to eight AppleTalk networks in any mix of LocalTalk, EtherTalk, and TokenTalk. (Each individual network must have only one type of physical link.)

Designers have used AppleTalk to provide a wide assortment of distributed applications, supporting the Apple Macintosh, the IBM PS/2 and PC-compatible computers, workstations and running Unix. These applications include file sharing, print spooling, printer sharing, and electronic messaging. In addition, gateways are available for linking AppleTalk networks with DEC mini- and mainframe computers.

Other LAN Implementations

While dozens of LAN implementations exist, this section covers the non-native TCP/IP choices currently popular for client/server LAN Designers. It is important to note that they are not TCP/IP native, but most now offer additional packages allowing them to connect to TCP/IP.

Novell NetWare

Novell NetWare is one of the most pervasive LAN implementations, with direct support or a comprehensive protocol gateway on every major platform. NetWare can be used with Ethernet, CSMA/CD networks, as well as with token ring architectures. NetWare emulates NETBIOS, supports file and printer sharing, electronic mail, remote access, inter-LAN communication via a NetWare Bridge, and a gateway to IBM's SNA over a *synchronous data link control* (SDLC) line.

NetWare provides a number of utility and monitor programs that allow network administrators to add new users to the network, open/close files, and maintain system resources and security. NetWare provides for security down to a file level.

Both DOS and Unix vendors and developers offer direct support for Novell NetWare. Some Unix hardware vendors have released versions of Portable NetWare. To provide a more seamless link between standard NetWare and Unix hosts, Portable NetWare is implemented as "not native" to its host hardware platform. It runs as a guest under another operating system. As a result, high levels of Unix/NetWare connectivity can be achieved, along with the support of all traditional NetWare clients (DOS, Windows, OS/2, Macintosh) available for the Unix host.

Novell and various third party vendors support NetWare on such client platforms as Apple, DOS (including Windows), OS/2, and Unix. NetWare servers can be hosted under Unix, IBM MVS, IBM VM, OS/400, and DEC VMS. Novell NetWare licensees include Data General, Hewlett-Packard, ICL, Interactive, Intergraph, MIPS, NCR, Prime, Pyramid, Unisys, and Wang.

Banyan VINES

Banyan Systems VINES is one of the most technically advanced distributed *network operating systems* (NOS) on the market today. VINES is designed to seamlessly support large PC networks and internetworks. Compaq, one of the Banyan Systems's largest customers, runs its internal network of approximately 11,000 geographically dispersed PCs using VINES.

VINES distributed architecture integrates directory, security, and network management services on interconnected servers, each of which supports one or more PCs. A VINES server, a version of Unix system V, can run on Intel 386 and 486 based PCs, and over a SCO-Unix-compliant version of Unix system V. Workstation clients include DOS, Windows, Macintosh, and OS/2.

The VINES architecture supports many types of network topologies, including Ethernet and Token Ring. VINES provides support for a variety of communication protocols, including 3270 Emulation, TCP/IP, and X.25 packet switching protocols. In addition, VINES can run over WAN server-to-server interconnections, providing a single, global view of an enterprise network.

VINES provides the user with a single, integrated view of the network VINES uses an authorization mechanism to support network-wide security. Network administrators are provided with easily managed configuration and monitoring tools. VINES offers a set of services that include a file and print services as well as VINES Network Mail.

SNA

The IBM *Systems Network Architecture* (SNA) was first introduced in 1977 and has dramatically changed since that time. It supports a wide diversity of applications over a large user base of approximately 40,000 SNA licenses. With the thousands of networks installed worldwide, SNA is one of the most accepted *de facto* network standards. SNA provides a consistent set of communication protocols, and the communication access method, known as *Virtual Telecommunications Access Method* (VTAM).

SNA is designed to satisfy large network user requirements for efficiency and cost-effectivity:

- ✔ SNA provides resource sharing. It eliminates the need to install separate communication links for different types of workstations applications, because networking enables access to an application of any host processor and from any workstation.

- ✔ SNA enhances network dependability. SNA protocols recognize data loss during the transmission, use data flow control procedures to prevent data overrun, avoid overload and congestion, recognize failures, and correct many errors. Network availability is high due to such SNA features as the extended recovery facility, alternate routing, backup host, and built-in control procedures in workstations, modems, and controllers.

- ✔ SNA helps users with network expansion and maintenance by providing open, documented interfaces, which are implemented in all SNA products. This reduces the amount of programming involved in system integration.

- ✔ SNA facilitates problem determination by providing network management services in each network component plus global management software, such as NetView.

- ✔ SNA maintains an open-ended architecture that helps to accommodate new facilities, such as digital networks, digitized voice, distributed systems, electronic document distribution, fiber optics, graphics, satellites, Token-Ring networks, Videotex, and Viewdata.

- ✔ SNA provides a network interconnection facility that enables the users in one SNA network to access information and programs in other SNA networks by using SNA gateways. These gateways make SNA network boundaries transparent to the network users.

✔ SNA provides network security through logon routines that prevent unauthorized users from accessing the network. SNA also provides encryption facilities.

SNA handles connections between users in a network so that the underlying physical aspects of network routing is transparent to the user. The end-points of a communication link are defined as logical units. The logical unit provides facilities which isolate the user from the physical characteristics of the network devices.

Historically, the application ran on a special network node, the host processor. The user used a terminal connected to the network's peripheral node, thereby supporting a host-to-terminal, master/slave hierarchical relationship.

One of SNA's objectives, especially in the framework of IBM's *Systems Application Architecture* (SAA), is to support distributed processing. SAA distributed processing implies a peer-to-peer relationship between applications, rather than the older master-slave type communication. In SNA, the necessity for peer-to-peer communications originated the creation of a new logical unit type (Logical Unit type 6.2), a new physical unit type (SNA Node type 2.1), and a new set of rules, called the LU6.2 protocol. This new protocol provides peer-to-peer communication capabilities and is marketed as *Advanced Program-to-Program Communication* (APPC).

SNA Components and Links

An SNA network consists of many hardware and software components connected via links. A link consists of a link connection and two or more link stations. A *link connection* is the physical transmission media connecting two or more nodes. Link stations use data link control protocols to transmit data over a link connection. The transmission media can be telephone lines, microwave beams, fiber optics, coaxial cables, etc.

Data link control protocols specify the rules interpreting the control data and providing the transmission across the link. In a LAN environment, SNA data link control protocols support IEEE 802.5-Token Ring.

SNA Compared to OSI

The structures of the OSI model and the SNA model are very similar. Both represent a hierarchical architecture consisting of seven layers. The layers of both models have the same properties. Each layer performs a specific model function (SNA function or OSI function); lower layers provide services for higher layers, and layers of the same level can communicate with each other as peers. Both models are built to formally describe how their respective communication networks should be implemented.

The purpose of the OSI model, however, is different from that of the SNA model. The goal of the OSI model is to bring "law and order" into the diverse world of network communication architectures to provide standard information exchange protocols for communication between autonomous, heterogeneous architectures.

Conversely, SNA is designed for the exchange of information between network nodes on the homogeneous architecture on which IBM builds its enterprise program offerings. This architecture allows IBM to tailor the network hardware and network components to achieve maximum efficiency and performance.

The functions of the SNA and OSI layers (compared in the following), are similar, even though there is no one-to-one correlation between SNA layers and OSI layers.

- ✔ Level 1SNA Physical Control Layer and OSI Physical Layers are functionally equivalent.

- ✔ Level 2SNA Data Link Control Layer can use SDLC and the OSI interface. SDLC is a subset of HDLC, which is used by OSI Date Link Layer.

- ✔ Level 3SNA Path Control Layer provides functions similar those defined for the OSI Transport and Session Layers.

- ✔ Levels 4 and 5SNA Data Flow Control and Transmission Control Layers provide functions similar to those defined for OSI Transport and Session Layers.

- ✔ Levels 6 and 7SNA Presentation Services and Transaction Services Layers provide functions similar to those defined for the OSI Presentation Layer and the Common Application Services in the OSI Application Layer.

- ✔ Level 7OSI Specific Application Services in the OSI Application Layer are considered to be end-user exchanges in SNA.

IBM recognizes the significance of the OSI model as the common standard for heterogeneous system interconnection. Various mixed-vendor networking organizations, such as the Department of Defense, plan to migrate to OSI by the mid-1990s, provided that the model is finalized and OSI-compliant products are available. SNA currently offers more and better functionality for IBM-based networks. As an interim solution, IBM has adopted the concept of the SNA/OSI Gateways and is pursuing the dual strategy of developing gateways from SNA to OSI, in addition to developing products based on the OSI architecture.

Summary

This chapter examined generic networking technology as it relates to protocols, standards, and things that old men discuss in barber shops. This will be the only chapter providing such information and all others will assume a working knowledge of networking concepts and a goal to implement TCP/IP.

Chapter Snapshot

TCP/IP is used as a common language for computers and other devices to exchange information over a network. TCP/IP enables applications to be written so that users can share resources such as printers, disk drives, and information over the network without having to reconnect devices. This chapter examines the following topics:

Introduction to TCP/IP

"A learned fool is one who has read everything and simply remembered it."

—Josh Billings

TCP/IP is a family of protocols used for computer communications. The letters stand for *Transmission Control Protocol/Internet Protocol*, but other than in the press, the full name rarely is used. TCP and IP are both individual protocols that can be discussed separately, but they are not the only two protocols used in the family. Often a TCP/IP user does not use the TCP protocol itself, but some other protocol from the family. To talk about using TCP/IP in this situation is still proper, however, because the name applies generically to the use of any protocol in the TCP/IP family. Because TCP/IP was developed by the Department of Defense, the protocol family is sometimes called *The DoD Suite*, but does not have a classical "marketing" name as does Apple's AppleTalk suite of protocols.

Protocols usually are grouped into "families" (sometimes called *suites* or *stacks*). Which protocols are grouped together is usually determined by the protocols' implementors. Many protocol families are developed by commercial organizations; for example, AppleTalk is a family of protocols developed by Apple Computers. Each protocol in a family supports a particular network capability. No protocol is of much use on its own and requires the use of other protocols in its family. In some ways, protocol families are like a set of golf clubs; each club is used for a particular purpose, and no one club can be used to play an entire game. Usually a golfer purchases all the clubs in a set from the same vendor. Just as each vendor might offer a slightly different set of clubs, network protocol families try to solve the same network problems with a slightly different set of protocols, but many are similar from family to family.

The TCP/IP protocol family includes protocols such as *Internet Protocol* (IP), *Address Resolution Protocol* (ARP), *Internet Control Message Protocol* (ICMP), *User Datagram Protocol* (UDP), *Transport Control Protocol* (TCP), *Routing Information Protocol* (RIP), Telnet, *Simple Mail Transfer Protocol* (SMTP), *Domain Name System* (DNS), and numerous others. Keeping all the acronyms straight can be difficult, especially because some are reused by other protocols (for example, the Novell, or IPX, family has a RIP protocol different from the TCP/IP family RIP protocol). An understanding of all the protocols in a particular family is not a prerequisite to knowing how a network basically works. This chapter concentrates on the IP and ARP protocols (mentioning the RIP and ICMP protocols briefly). This focus, coupled with a minimal discussion of a particular link protocol (Ethernet is used for the examples in this chapter), illustrates how a TCP/IP network causes data to flow smoothly across an internet.

Understanding TCP/IP: Six Questions

In TCP/IP, all protocols are transported across an IP internet, encapsulated in IP packets. IP is a *routable protocol*, which means that two nodes that communicate using IP do not need to be connected to the same physical wire. To have a basic understanding of how information travels across a routed network, it is only necessary to understand the answers to the following six questions:

1. What is the format of an address in this protocol?

2. How do devices get an address?

3. How is the address mapped onto a physical address?

4. How does an end node find a router?

5. How do routers learn the topology of the network?

6. How do users find services on the network?

The rest of this chapter answers these questions and illustrates by example how these answers tie together to explain how information flows across a TCP/IP-based network.

Understanding Basic Network Concepts

Before answering the preceding questions (or possibly even before understanding what they are asking), you must know the meanings of some terms and concepts discussed in this chapter.

Addressing

The central concept of networking is *addressing*. In networking, the *address* of a device is its unique identification. Network addresses are usually numerical and have a standard, well-defined format (each defined in its specification document). All devices on a network need to be given a unique identifier that conforms to a standard format. This identifier is the device's address. In routed networks, the address has at least two pieces: a *network* (or *area*) piece and a *node* (or *host*) piece.

In this chapter, *network* refers to a set of machines connected to the same physical wire (or set of wires connected only by bridges and repeaters). *Internet* means one or more networks connected by routers. The word *internet* (lowercase *i*) is not to be confused with the *Internet* (uppercase *I*). The Internet is a specific internet that connects millions of computers worldwide and is becoming predominant in the press and elsewhere.

If two devices on an internet have addresses with the same network number, they are located on the same network and thus on the same wire. Devices on the same wire can communicate directly with each other by using their data link layer protocol (that is, Ethernet). The examples in this chapter use Ethernet as the medium connecting the devices. Although some particulars might differ, the concepts are the same if the networks are built on Token Ring, *Fiber Distributed Data Interface* (FDDI), or many other common physical media.

Correct addressing of devices on a network requires that every device connected to the same network (wire) be configured with the same network number. Also, every device with the same network number must have a different node (or host) number from every other device with the same network number. Finally, every network in an internet must have a unique network number. To rephrase, every network on an internet must have a unique network number, and every node on a network must have a unique node number within that network. This rule ensures that no two devices on an internet ever have the same network *and* node number and therefore have a unique address within the internet.

In addition to a unique address for every device on an internet, special addresses often are used to address multiple nodes simultaneously. These addresses are called *broadcast* or *multicast* addresses.

The following discussion references two different types of addresses—network layer addresses and *Media Access Control* (MAC) layer addresses. These two address types are completely independent of each other. The network layer addresses are all IP addresses. These addresses are used to communicate between nodes across an IP internetwork. The MAC addresses are used to communicate from node to node on the same wire and often are built right into the communications card (for example, the Ethernet card). MAC addresses are the lowest level addresses and are the means by which all information is ultimately transferred from device to device.

Packets

On most networks, such as TCP/IP networks, the information sent is broken down into pieces called *packets* (or *datagrams*) for two main reasons: resource sharing and error detection and correction. On networks that have more than two computers (for example, Ethernet or Token Ring), the medium connecting the devices is shared. If any two devices are communicating, no other devices can communicate at the same time. A network works like a party line in that respect. If two devices want to share a very large amount of information, it is unfair for them to become the sole users of the network for a long period of time; other devices might have urgent information to transfer to other parties. If the large block of information is broken into many small blocks, each of these can be sent individually, enabling other devices to interweave their own messages between the packets of the extended conversation. As long as each piece is individually addressed to the intended destination and contains enough information for the receiver to piece it back together, the fact that it is broken into pieces does not matter.

The other main use of packets is for error detection and correction. Networks are ultimately made up of wires (or radio waves or light beams) that are prone to interference which can corrupt a signal sent across them. Dealing with corrupted messages is a big part of networking; in fact, most of the complexity in networking involves dealing with the what-if-something-gets-corrupted scenarios. Many error detection and correction tech-niques are based on *checksums*; when a sender transmits information (as bytes of data), a running total adding up all the bytes sent is kept and then transmitted at the end of the data transmission. The receiver computes the total of the data received and compares it to the total transmitted. If a difference exists between the total bytes received and the total bytes computed, then the data or the total is corrupted. The sender is asked to retransmit the data. This version is much simpler than what really happens, but is sufficient to illustrate the concept.

If the medium on which the transmission takes place has an average error rate of one bit in one million (that is, for every one million bits sent, one is corrupted on average), then there is a practical upper limit to the amount of data that can be sent in one transmission. Imagine that ten million bits are sent. Normally a transmission of this size contains ten errors, the checksum is wrong, and the sender is asked to retransmit. The retransmission size is the same as the original transmission, so it contains on average ten errors again. The only way to break out of this loop is to break the data into smaller pieces, each with its own checksum, that can be retransmitted individually.

Protocols

Each of these packets is a stream of bytes. For true communication to occur, these bytes must have meaning associated with them. This meaning is provided by the protocol specification. A *protocol* is a set of rules that defines two things—the format of the packets and the semantics of their use.

Most packets have a format that includes a header and a body. The *header* often includes information such as a source and destination address, the length of the packet, and some type indicator so that the receiver knows how to decode the body. The *body* can be raw data (for example, a piece of a file or an e-mail message), or it can contain another packet that has its own format defined by its own specification. Packet formats usually are depicted in a specification by a rectangular picture that gives the order, size, and names of the pieces of information that make up the packet. Figure 2.1 is an example of an Ethernet frame.

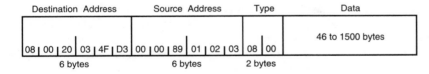

Figure 2.1
An Ethernet frame.

You must know more than the format of a packet to understand the protocol. You also must know when to send which packets and what to do when they are received. Many protocols have very simple formats, but their use is very complicated. Imagine teaching a non-English speaker to behave as an English-speaking receptionist. The "packet formats" might be as follows:

> "Hello, this is company X."
>
> "How may I direct your call?"
>
> "Please hold."
>
> "Good bye."
>
> "That line is busy, may I take a message?"
>
> "That person does not work here."

The "protocol" for answering the phone needs to include when to say each of these phrases, how to look up an extension in the company phone book, what to say if the party being called is not in, how to take a message, what to do with the message after taking it, what to do with a wrong number, and so on.

A protocol specification specifies the format of the information exchanged (the packets) and the correct sequencing of that information as well as the additional actions (logging, mail delivery, table updates, and so on) that might be required. Just as the receptionist described earlier was only trained to direct incoming calls (and not answer tech support questions), each protocol has a specific set of functions with which it is designed to deal.

In the TCP/IP world, most protocol specifications are available online as *Requests For Comment* (RFCs). These specifications tend to be very technical in nature and are directed at engineers who intend to implement these protocols. One site (of many) on the Internet that makes the RFCs available for anonymous ftp is ftp.internic.net. An index is available at that site in the file /rfc/rfc-index.txt.

Routers and End Nodes

Routed networks have two classes of devices: end nodes and routers (see fig. 2.2). *End nodes* are the devices with which users interact—workstations and PCs, printers, file servers, and so on. *Routers* are devices that connect networks. Routers have the responsibility to know how the whole network is connected and how to move information from one part of the network to another. They shield end nodes from needing to know much about the network so that the end nodes can spend their time doing user tasks. Routers are connected to two or more networks. Every device on a particular network must have the same network number as every other device on that network, and every network must have a different network number. Thus routers must have a separate address for every network to which they are connected. Routers are very much the "post offices" of the network. End nodes send information they don't know how to deliver to the local router, and the router takes care of getting it to its final destination. Sometimes a device such as a file server also is a router, for example, when that end node is connected to more than one network and is running software that enables it to route information between those networks. Routing is often a CPU-intensive chore and can significantly impact the performance of a machine doing tasks other than routing. For this reason, most routers are dedicated machines.

Routers are introduced to networks for several reasons. Routers enable more devices to ultimately be interconnected because they extend the address space available by having multiple network numbers. Routers help overcome physical limitations of the medium by connecting multiple cables.

The most common reason for using a router is to maintain political isolation. Routers enable two groups of machines to communicate with each other while remaining physically isolated, which is especially important when the two groups are controlled by different organizations. Many routers have filtering functions that enable the network administrator to strictly control who uses and what is used on the network. Problems that occur on one network do not necessarily disrupt other networks.

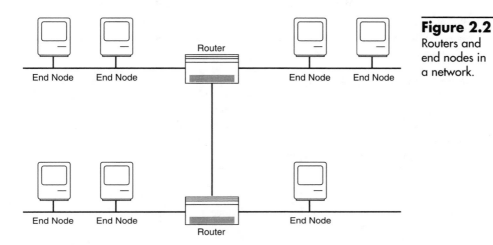

Figure 2.2
Routers and
end nodes in
a network.

End Node Network Send and Receive Behavior

When a node on a TCP/IP network has an IP packet to send to another node, it follows a simple algorithm to decide how to proceed. The sending node compares the network portion of the destination address with the network portion of its own address. If the two networks are the same, it implies that the two nodes are on the same wire—either directly connected to the same cable or on cables separated only by repeaters or bridges (see fig. 2.3). In this case, the two nodes can communicate directly using the data link layer (for example, Ethernet). The sending node uses ARP to discover the destination node's MAC layer address and encapsulate the IP packet in a data link layer frame to be delivered directly to the destination node.

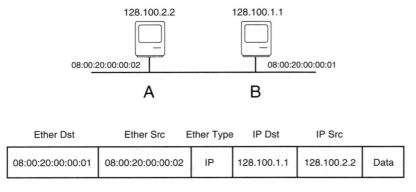

Figure 2.3
Two end nodes
communicating on
the same network.

Ether Dst	Ether Src	Ether Type	IP Dst	IP Src	
08:00:20:00:00:01	08:00:20:00:00:02	IP	128.100.1.1	128.100.2.2	Data

If the network portions are different, the two nodes are separated by at least one router, which implies that the sending node cannot deliver the packet without using a router as an intermediary. The packet is encapsulated in a data link layer frame addressed to the

MAC address of a router on the same wire (if no router is on the wire, then that particular network is isolated and cannot send IP packets to other networks). The router delivers the IP packet to the remote network.

When an end node receives an IP packet, it compares the destination address in the IP packet to its own address and to the IP broadcast address with which it is configured. If the destination address matches either of these addresses, the end node accepts the packet and processes it further. The way it is processed depends on which subprotocol of IP it is. If the destination address does not match, the packet is dropped (ignored), as shown in the following end-node algorithm:

```
Receive

if((dst addr == my addr) or (dst addr == broadcast)){
   process packet
}
else{
    drop (ignore) packet
}

Send
if(dst net = my net){
  deliver (may need to "ARP")
}
else{
    send to router
}
```

Router Send and Receive Behavior

When a node is functioning as a router and it receives an IP packet, it examines the destination IP address in the packet and compares it to its own IP address. If the addresses are the same or the destination IP address is the IP broadcast address, the packet is processed as it would be for an end node. Unlike an end node, a router does not automatically drop packets that are received but not addressed to it. These are packets that end nodes on the network are sending to the router to be forwarded to other networks (see fig. 2.4). All routers maintain routing tables that indicate how to reach other networks. The router compares the network portion of the destination address with each network in its routing table. If the router cannot find the destination network in its routing table, it checks for a default route (typically listed as a route to 0.0.0.0). If it does not find a default route, the packet is dropped (and an ICMP destination unreachable message is sent to the source IP address in the dropped packet).

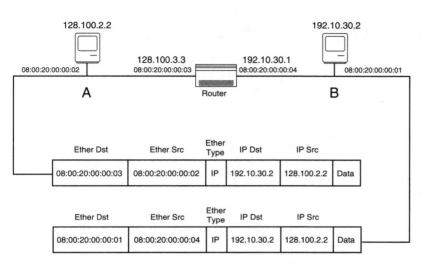

128.100.2.2
08:00:20:00:00:02

A

128.100.3.3
08:00:20:00:00:03

192.10.30.1
08:00:20:00:00:04

Router

192.10.30.2
08:00:20:00:00:01

B

Ether Dst	Ether Src	Ether Type	IP Dst	IP Src	
08:00:20:00:00:03	08:00:20:00:00:02	IP	192.10.30.2	128.100.2.2	Data

Ether Dst	Ether Src	Ether Type	IP Dst	IP Src	
08:00:20:00:00:01	08:00:20:00:00:04	IP	192.10.30.2	128.100.2.2	Data

Figure 2.4
Two end nodes communicating on different networks.

When a matching route to a network is found (or a default route exists), the router checks the distance to the remote network. If the distance is listed as 0, the network is directly connected to the router. In this case, the router sends an ARP request for the destination IP address and encapsulates the IP packet in a data link layer frame addressed to the MAC address of the destination returned in the ARP response. If the distance is greater than 0, the packet must travel through at least one more router. In this case, the router uses the next router field from this route and sends an ARP request for that router, encapsulating the IP packet in a data link layer frame addressed to the MAC address of the next router. This way, an IP packet travels across an internet, maintaining the same source and destination IP addresses the entire time, but having the source and destination MAC addresses change for each hop. The algorithm a router uses when receiving a packet is as follows:

```
Receive
if((dst addr == my addr) or (dst addr == broadcast)){
   process packet
}
else if(dst net is directly connected){
   deliver (may need to "ARP")
}
else if(dst net in table){
   deliver to next router
}
else{
   drop (ignore) packet
}
```

Examining the Format of an IP Address

For any routable protocol to be efficiently routable, the address must have two parts. TCP/IP addresses have two components—a *network component* and a *host* (or *node*) component. Addresses used with TCP/IP are four-byte (32-bit) quantities called simply *IP addresses* (not TCP/IP addresses) (see fig. 2.5). These addresses are written in *standard dot notation*, which means that each byte is written as a decimal number separated by dots (the period character)—for example, 192.37.54.23 (pronounced "192 dot 37 dot 54 dot 23"). Because each piece of the IP address is 1 byte, its value must be between 0 and 255 inclusive—for example, the IP address 125.300.47.89 could not be a legal IP address because 300 is greater than 255 and would not fit in a single byte.

Figure 2.5
Format of an IP address.

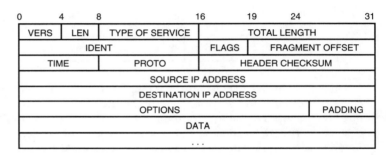

IP addresses are composed of a network portion and a host portion. The split is not as simple as the first two bytes being the network portion and the last two being the host portion. The designers of the TCP/IP protocols were concerned that they not limit the size of potential networks too severely, so they opted for a graduated method of network and host division. If the split was to be two bytes for each, no network could have more than 2^{16} hosts on it. Also, smaller networks would waste much of the address space by using only a fraction of the available nodes on any given network.

To provide for efficient address use, IP addresses are divided into *classes*. The three most important classes of networks are A, B, and C. IP addresses are split into these classes according to the first few bits of the address (or the value of the first byte, if you don't like working in binary), as in figure 2.6.

An IP network is customarily referred to as an IP address whose host portion consists of all zeroes—for example, 10.0.0.0 or 128.37.0.0 or 200.23.45.0. For example, 137.103.210.2 is a class B address that has a network portion of 137.103 and a host portion of 210.2. This network, the 137.103.0.0 network, can have up to two bytes worth (2^{16}) of hosts on it—all of which must share the exact same first two bytes 137.103 and must have unique host portions.

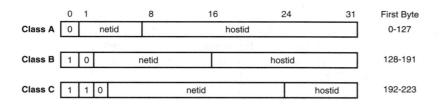

Figure 2.6
The three classes of IP addresses.

Assigning IP Addresses to TCP/IP Devices

IP addresses can be assigned in a number of ways. If an organization wants to build a TCP/IP internetwork that never will be connected to any other TCP/IP network outside the organization, then it is acceptable to pick any class A, B, or C network number that allows an appropriate number of hosts on it. This method is rather short-sighted, as much of the benefit of having a TCP/IP network is the capability to connect to the outside world and share resources beyond those in the organization—for example, connecting to the Internet. A better strategy is to contact the InterNIC's registration services at Network Solutions, Inc. and request an officially assigned network number. The InterNIC ensures that the network number assigned to each applicant is globally unique. All the host ids on that network are free to be assigned as the assignee sees fit.

Sometimes when an organization connects to the Internet through another organization (for example, a commercial service provider or a university), that second organization provides the network number. In addition, many larger organizations have internal network administrators in charge of assigning IP addresses to individual users within the company.

When an IP network number has been acquired from an internal network administrator, service provider, or the InterNIC, it is possible to start assigning specific host IP addresses from that network to individual devices. Usually an organization keeps records of which IP addresses are assigned already and has some method of distributing the unused IP addresses to individuals who need to configure new IP devices. IP addresses must be configured into devices with the same network number as all other devices on the same wire but with a unique host portion. If two or more devices have the same IP address, they will not work reliably and will present a very difficult situation to debug.

Most IP devices require manual configuration. The person installing the device must obtain a unique and correct IP address and type it in to some configuration program or console, usually along with other information such as IP broadcast address, subnet mask, and default gateway address.

Some sites support dynamic configuration of IP devices. Protocols such as *Boot Protocol* (BOOTP) and *Dynamic Host Configuration Protocol* (DHCP) enable the use of centralized servers to hand out unique IP addresses and other configuration information on an as-needed basis. At the time of this writing, this sort of configuration is not a mature enough technology to find widespread use.

Mapping IP Addresses to MAC Addresses

Ultimately, all computer communication takes place by moving data from node to node over some form of link such as Ethernet, Token Ring, FDDI, and the *Point-to-Point Protocol* (PPP). Many links support attaching more than two nodes and therefore require that all data sent over them be addressed to a specific destination to be delivered correctly. These addresses have nothing to do with IP addresses; they are completely separate and in addition to IP addresses. These addresses are MAC addresses—sometimes called *physical*, *hardware*, or *link addresses*. Unlike IP addresses that are assigned, most MAC layer addresses are built into the hardware by the manufacturer of the device or *network interface card* (NIC).

On an Ethernet network, every device on the network has a built-in Ethernet address. This address is a six-byte quantity usually written using hexadecimal numbers with a colon separating the bytes—for example, 08:00:20:0A:8C:6D. Ethernet addresses are assigned by the *Institute of Electrical and Electronics Engineers* (IEEE) and are unique among all Ethernet devices. No two devices should ever have the same Ethernet address (manufacturing errors do occur on occasion). The Ethernet address is divided into two parts; the first three bytes constitute the *vendor code*. Each vendor of Ethernet equipment obtains a unique vendor code from the IEEE. Every piece of equipment supporting Ethernet made by that vendor is programmed with an Ethernet address that begins with that vendor code. In the preceding example, the vendor code 08:00:20 corresponds to Sun Microsystems; every Ethernet device manufactured by Sun begins with those three bytes (see fig. 2.7). The vendor is responsible for making sure that every Ethernet device it manufactures has the same first three bytes (vendor code) and a different remaining three bytes to guarantee that every Ethernet device in the world has a unique address built in.

If every Ethernet device already has a unique address, why are IP addresses necessary? First of all, not every device has Ethernet support; IP addresses enable devices that connect to fiber and Token Ring and serial lines to use IP without having to get an Ethernet address. Secondly, Ethernet addresses are organized by equipment vendor rather than by owner organization. To come up with an efficient routing scheme based on who made the equipment rather than on where it is located would be impossible. IP addresses are assigned based on a network topology, not on who manufactures the device. Finally, and most important, is that devices can be more easily moved or repaired when an extra level of addressing exists. If an Ethernet card breaks, it can be replaced without getting a new IP address. If an IP node is moved from one network to another, it can be given a new IP address without getting a new Ethernet card.

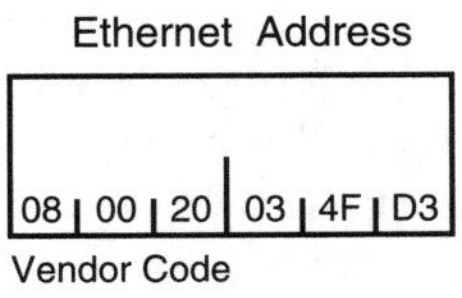

Ethernet Address

| 08 | 00 | 20 | 03 | 4F | D3 |

Vendor Code

Figure 2.7
A typical Ethernet address including a vendor code.

Network hardware communicates only with other network hardware (for example, two Ethernet cards on two network devices). This network hardware often uses an addressing system that is not friendly to humans, but is convenient for the hardware itself. Users and services on networks communicate with other users and services. These services are easier to access if they are addressed in a way that makes sense to people. Addressing that is easy for humans to understand, however, is not always easy for hardware to manage. To solve this problem, a method of mapping user-level addresses to hardware is needed.

Ethernet addresses are long and cryptic and not meant to be regularly dealt with by users. To provide a mechanism for nodes to determine each other's hardware addresses without intervention from the user is possible. For TCP/IP, this mechanism is ARP. When an IP node wants to communicate with another node with the same network number, it assumes that having the same network number implies that the destination is on the same wire. On an Ethernet, for example, the source Ethernet card can directly communicate with the destination Ethernet card if it knows the Ethernet address. To determine the Ethernet address of a node on the same wire, the sending device sends an ARP request to the Ethernet broadcast address (see fig. 2.8). This address is a special address that all Ethernet cards are configured to listen to (it consists of six bytes of all ones, written in hex as FF:FF:FF:FF:FF:FF). Setting the destination Ethernet address to this value and sending an Ethernet packet causes every device on the Ethernet to accept the packet as if it were addressed specifically to it. It is the Ethernet equivalent of the U.S. postal address "Occupant."

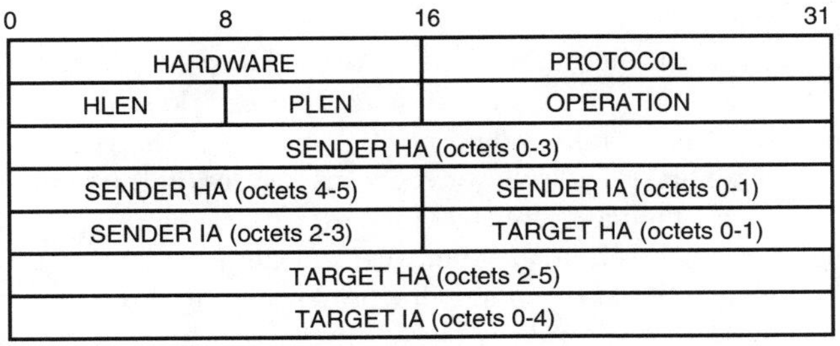

0	8	16	31
HARDWARE		PROTOCOL	
HLEN	PLEN	OPERATION	
SENDER HA (octets 0-3)			
SENDER HA (octets 4-5)		SENDER IA (octets 0-1)	
SENDER IA (octets 2-3)		TARGET HA (octets 0-1)	
TARGET HA (octets 2-5)			
TARGET IA (octets 0-4)			

Figure 2.8
The format of an ARP packet.

An ARP request asks every node on the wire what is the Ethernet address for a particular IP address. The ARP request contains (among other things) the sender's source IP address and Ethernet address as well as the IP address with which the sender wants to communicate. Every Ethernet device on the network accepts this packet and, if the receiving device supports IP, recognizes that it is an ARP request. The receiving device then compares its configured IP address to the IP address being looked for. If an exact match occurs, the receiving device sends an ARP response back to the sender (through the Ethernet address in the ARP request, not as a broadcast) containing its Ethernet address. The sender can then encapsulate the IP packet it wants to send in an Ethernet packet with a destination Ethernet address as specified in the ARP response.

Why doesn't the sending node simply broadcast every packet it sends? On a large or busy network, this would require every node to be interrupted to process every packet on the network to determine whether the packet was destined for it. This interruption would be very inefficient and would slow the network down considerably. To make sure that broadcasts are minimized, nodes on broadcast networks requiring the use of ARP maintain a list of IP addresses and the Ethernet addresses that correspond to them (determined by previous ARP requests). This list is called the *ARP cache* and is updated whenever an ARP response is received. A node needing to send many IP packets to the same destination sends an ARP request the first time it tries to contact the node and records the Ethernet address it receives in the ARP response. Subsequent IP packets use the Ethernet address in the cache instead of sending another ARP request. Each entry in the cache is kept for some amount of time decided by the implementor of the TCP/IP software in use. This timeout might be as little as 30 seconds or as much as several hours or even be configurable. The shorter the time, the more broadcast ARP requests there are. But if the time is too long, then a node that changes its Ethernet address (because the Ethernet card was replaced, for example) cannot be contacted until the entry is updated.

Examining How End Nodes Find a Router

To send a packet to a node on another network, an end node requires the aid of a router. If two nodes on the same network want to communicate, they can do so directly by encapsulating their IP datagrams in link level frames (for example, Ethernet frames) and sending them to each other. This procedure works because nodes on the same network are attached to the same wire (separated only by cable, repeaters, and bridges). When a destination is on another network, it is on another wire and can't be reached directly. The end node encapsulates the IP datagram in a link level frame destined for a router. The router then determines where to send the packet next. Because a router is needed to contact a node on another network, it is necessary for the router to be on the same network as the source node (otherwise the source node would need a router to reach the router!). Routers behave much like a post office for U.S. mail. If you want to deliver a message to someone very close (for example, next door), you would most likely deliver the message yourself. But if the destination is unfamiliar or is far away, you would deliver the message to the nearest post office. The post office would deliver the message for you if the message is for a local address serviced by that post office; otherwise it looks up which post office should deal with it next. The letter might pass through a number of post offices before being delivered.

To deliver a packet to a node on a different network, a source node sends the unmodified IP packet to the local router by encapsulating it in a link level packet addressed to the router's MAC address. If the link level is Ethernet, the source node needs to know the Ethernet address of the local router. For reasons given previously, nodes should not deal with Ethernet addresses directly; therefore, TCP/IP end nodes need to know how to obtain the Ethernet address of a router. By using the ARP protocol, an end node that knows the IP address of a router can obtain the Ethernet address. TCP/IP end nodes need to be manually configured with the address of at least one router (usually called a *default gateway*). Some TCP/IP implementations enable the router's address to be obtained dynamically by "eavesdropping" on the routers' conversations. In this case, the node is configured to "listen" to a particular routing protocol such as RIP.

How Routers Learn the Network Topology

For routers to fulfill their role as "post office" of the network, they need to know which networks are reachable and how to get to them. To accomplish this, routers store information about the topology of the network. This topology is usually stored as a *routing table* that lists each known network, tells how "far" away the network is, and indicates which router is the next one to send a packet to to reach a network not directly connected (see table 2.1 and fig. 2.9).

Table 2.1
A Routing Table for a Three-Router Network

Network	Distance	Next Router
Router 1		
1	0	—
2	0	—
3	1	222.222.222.2

continues

Table 2.1, Continued
A Routing Table for a Three-Router Network

Network	Distance	Next Router
Router 1		
4	1	222.222.222.2
5	2	222.222.222.2
6	0	—
Router 2		
1	1	222.222.222.1
2	1	222.222.222.1
3	0	—
4	0	—
5	1	200.15.22.3
6	0	—
Router 3		
1	2	200.15.22.1
2	2	200.15.22.1
3	1	200.15.22.1
4	0	—
5	0	—
6	1	200.15.22.1

The *cost* of a network can be declared in many ways (depending on whose network you look at), but is most often simply a count of how many routers a packet must go through to reach a network. The cost to a network is often called the *distance* or *number of hops* to a network.

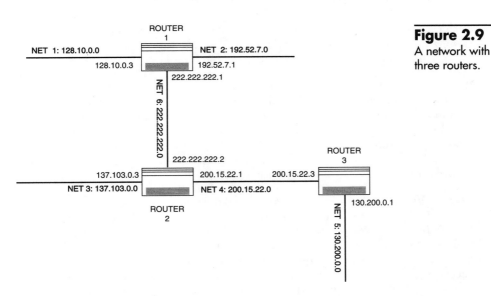

Figure 2.9
A network with
three routers.

A cost of zero means that the specified network is directly connected to the router. Packets destined for such a network can be delivered from the router to the final destination by encapsulating the datagram in a data link layer frame (for example, Ethernet) by sending an ARP request for the node. For this reason, the next router field for directly connected networks is meaningless.

When the cost is non-zero, the network in question is not directly connected and requires routing through at least one more router. In this case, the routing table indicates which router is the next one to send to. The router sends an ARP request for this "next hop" router and encapsulates the datagram in a data link layer packet addressed to the MAC address of the next router. When this router receives the packet, it checks its routing table and determines if the packet can be delivered locally or needs to be routed to yet another router.

If the destination network (or default network) does not appear in the routing table, then the packet cannot be delivered and is dropped (ignored). This could happen for a variety of reasons, including the following:

✔ The sending node was mistaken or misconfigured

✔ The router was misconfigured and does not know about the network

✔ All routes to that network are no longer operating (a router farther along the path to the network went down)

Usually when a packet is dropped due to the lack of a route, the router sends an ICMP Destination Unreachable message to the source, which should cause the node to log a message informing the user that data is not getting through.

Routing tables are set up in routers by two means: manual configuration and dynamic acquisition. (Sometimes a combination of both methods is used.) Manual configuration is the most straightforward method, but the least robust in the face of a changing network, and also can be impossible to maintain in a very large network. When *manual configuration* is used, the person installing the router is responsible for typing in the various fields for the routing table—telling the router which networks are reachable, how far away they are, and which routers should be used to reach them.

Dynamic acquisition of routing tables is achieved by means of one or more routing protocols. In TCP/IP, the most commonly used routing protocol is RIP (not to be confused for the IPX routing protocol of the same name). *RIP* is a simple protocol that enables routers to tell each other what networks they know about and how far away they are. With this information, each router can assemble a table of every network on an internet, enabling packets to be sent from any network to any other network, which could mean excessively large routing tables if the network were attached to a worldwide network such as the Internet. Therefore, provisions are made to "clump" many networks together in a default route represented by the IP address 0.0.0.0. Routers advertising connectivity to network 0.0.0.0 are saying, "If you don't see the network number anywhere else, send the packet to me."

RIP updates are broadcast by every router on every network every 30 seconds. Because these updates can impact network performance considerably on very large or slow networks, more efficient (in bandwidth, at least) protocols are being developed. *Open Shortest Path First* (OSPF) is a routing protocol becoming popular. OSPF provides a number of benefits to large networks, such as less traffic and faster "flooding" of information regarding changes to the network, but at the expense of a more complex algorithm (implying the need for more memory) to implement. Other protocols are used by routers to learn dynamically the topology of the network and advertise changes in that topology. The mechanics of each one is different, but the general purpose of binding the network together is the same.

Finding and Using Services

In the end, the purpose of all this encapsulating and routing is to provide users access to services. Users are interested in terminal emulation, printing, file sharing, and e-mail; they're not concerned with how these services are created.

Services require support to make them easy to find and use. Most people are not very good at dealing with numbers even if they have sensible structures like IP addresses (never mind Ethernet addresses), for example. People like to deal with names that are like words (if not words themselves). The command Telnet server is far easier to remember than telnet 192.34.50.3, for example.

Most services in the TCP/IP world are found through well-known names. Such services are found published in books, in company documents, or by word-of-mouth from the system administrator to users. You can access services if you know the name of the device that provides the service and what program to use to access it. FTP the file printers.txt from server.company.com might be the directions to access the file that describes the names of all the printers you can use. A user would type **ftp server.company.com**; log in; and type **get printers.txt** to access the file.

IP packets cannot be addressed to a name; they require a four-byte IP address. Much like ARP is used to map an IP address to a hardware address, a service name can be mapped to an IP address in a number of ways. The simplest way is to maintain files that contain the name and IP addresses of devices of interest. This file is often called the *hosts file* because in Unix it is found in the file /etc/hosts, and many IP implementations for other platforms have maintained the convention of calling the file hosts. This solution is simple, but not efficient on large networks. To maintain an up-to-date file on every single IP device can be difficult.

Usually a network administrator configures one or more servers to maintain a network-accessible database of name-to-IP mappings. Two commonly used methods are the *Domain Name System* (DNS) and Sun's *Network Information System* (NIS). Maintaining such a database requires that one or more machines be designated as "keepers of the database," and all other machines send requests to these servers to have a name converted into an IP address or vice versa. A network-accessible database of name-to-IP mappings is easy to maintain on a large network and requires little per-device configuration (only needing to know which machine to go to for lookups).

Given the amount of information currently available on the Internet and the rate at which that amount is increasing, obviously, to have just the files and lists of where to find information is entirely inadequate. To ease the burden of locating services and information on a network of the scale of the Internet, many different applications are being built. Applications such as Mosaic, gopher, archie, and *World Wide Web* (WWW) are being worked on by many people, companies, and universities. These applications try to make wading through the vast amount of information available a little easier (or at least more fun). These applications usually have a graphical user interface or a simple text-based interface that makes sorting through some subset of everything out there much easier.

TCP and UDP

Transmission Control Protocol (TCP) and *User Datagram Protocol* (UDP) travel encapsulated in IP packets to provide access to particular programs (services) running on remote network devices.

Throughout this chapter the discussion of TCP/IP has revolved entirely around IP. IP addresses enable data to be addressed to a particular node on an internet. After the data arrives, some mechanism is needed to enable the proper service within the device to receive the data. The data might be e-mail or a file or part of a print job. To direct the data to the appropriate program, another level of addressing is needed. Each service available on a node is accessed through a unique address called a *port* (sometimes also referred to as a *socket*). Ports are identified by a simple decimal number. For example, port 25 is the SMTP address. These numbers are contained in the TCP and UDP headers of TCP and UDP packets, which are encapsulated within IP packets (see figs. 2.10 and 2.11).

Figure 2.10
Format of a UDP packet.

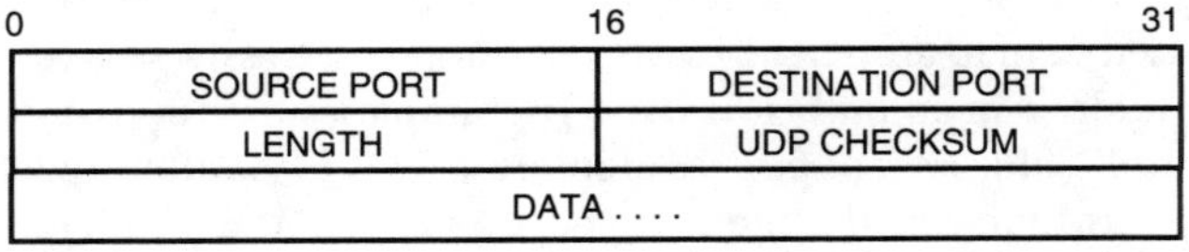

0	16	31
SOURCE PORT	DESTINATION PORT	
LENGTH	UDP CHECKSUM	
DATA		

Figure 2.11
Format of a TCP packet.

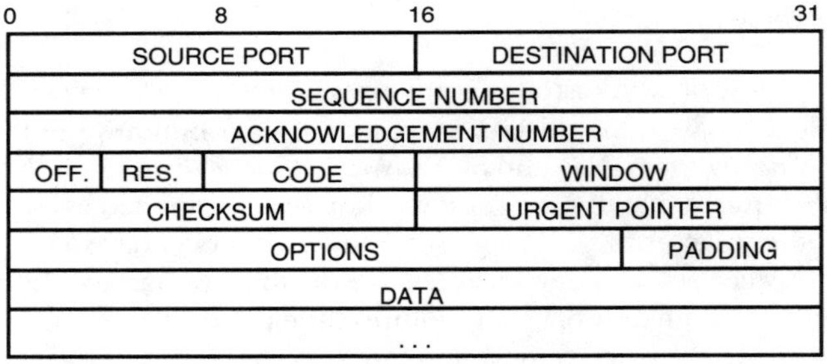

0	8	16	31
SOURCE PORT		DESTINATION PORT	
SEQUENCE NUMBER			
ACKNOWLEDGEMENT NUMBER			
OFF.	RES.	CODE	WINDOW
CHECKSUM		URGENT POINTER	
OPTIONS			PADDING
DATA			
. . .			

To understand the difference between UDP and TCP, you must know what is meant by datagram versus stream-oriented protocols, and what is meant by reliable versus unreliable protocols.

A *datagram-based protocol* is one that imposes a maximum size on the amount of data that can be sent in a single transmission. Ethernet, IP, and UDP are all datagram-based protocols. An upper limit to how much data can be sent in a single transmission exists. This type of protocol is analogous to sending a normal letter through the U.S. Postal Service. A single stamp limits the amount of "data" you can send at one time.

TCP is a *stream-oriented protocol.* A user of a TCP-based protocol does not need to worry about the maximum size of a transmission. TCP breaks the transmission into smaller sizes, retransmitting lost pieces, reordering data delivered out of order, and filtering out any extras that might occur due to faulty retransmissions. This type of transmission is analogous to a commercial freight carrier that can deliver as much "data" as the customer wants. The overhead necessary to support TCP is proportionally higher than that of UDP. An application that uses TCP requires more memory and more bandwidth to ensure that the transmission is completed properly.

The other factor that differentiates UDP from TCP is reliability. UDP is an *unreliable* or *best-effort* protocol. This definition does not mean that reliable data transfer cannot happen if based on UDP, but that the UDP protocol itself does not handle reliable data transfer. An application using UDP is responsible for implementing retransmissions, duplicate filtering, and so on, itself. If a UDP packet is lost or corrupted in transmission, it must be noticed by the application sending the data, which is again analogous to the U.S. Postal Service for normal mail. If the post office loses a letter, the letter is gone. They do not store a copy of it and "retransmit" it. Ethernet and IP also are best-effort protocols.

By pushing the overhead needed for reliability into an application, it is possible to make a reliable protocol or application that uses UDP. Sun Microsystems has implemented an entire file system—NFS—on top of UDP. NFS uses a less efficient set of algorithms than TCP to implement reliability, but the overhead is far less. UDP is appropriate for networks in which an application like NFS is used because the level of loss and corruption on a LAN is usually very low.

TCP is a *reliable protocol.* This definition does not mean that TCP guarantees delivery of the data it sends, but that TCP delivers the data if at all possible and reports back to the application if the data cannot be delivered (for example, if the destination node crashed). This reliability requires a great deal of overhead compared to UDP. Overhead is incurred to provide this service efficiently. TCP fragments and reassembles the data stream (so that the data can fit in datagram-based IP packets), retransmits lost packets, filters out duplicates caused by hasty retransmissions, handles flow control between computers of different speeds, and maintains *windows* (packets sent ahead that don't wait for an acknowledgment). If the network connectivity is preserved during the transmission, the data arrives in order and uncorrupted. If the connectivity is lost (the receiving program or machine crashed or an intermediate router went down), that fact is reported to the application using TCP.

Applications that invoke *sessions* usually use TCP to transfer data. These applications usually require the user to log in or connect before data can be moved. Applications that claim to be *stateless* are usually built on UDP, such as NFS.

Applications and protocols that use UDP include the following:

- ✔ NFS

- ✔ RIP

- ✔ *Trivial File Transfer Protocol* (TFTP)

- ✔ *Simple Network Management Protocol* (SNMP)

Applications and protocols that use TCP are as follows:

- ✔ FTP
- ✔ Telnet
- ✔ SMTP

Summary

This chapter covered the basic concepts of TCP/IP and how members of the TCP/IP protocol family interplay to enable users to access services across an internet. Basic network concepts applicable to any protocol family—such as packets, protocols, addressing, routers, and end nodes—were covered. These general concepts were then applied to the specifics of the TCP/IP protocols. The formats of IP, UDP, and TCP packets were explained, as well as how ARP is used to enable IP addresses to be mapped to MAC addresses. Lastly, UDP and TCP were shown to be the means of addressing individual services within a network device whereas IP is the means of addressing specific devices on an internet.

Chapter Snapshot

In this chapter you will learn the basics of TCP/IP and its addressing. Even if you are currently using the Internet or another form of the Internet Protocol, odds are that you will benefit from learning why TCP/IP addressing has been established the way that it has. In this chapter we will review:

Although TCP/IP in general is foreign to even the most experienced system administrator at first, addressing is frequently perceived as nothing short of magic until a few basics are understood. This chapter should help the Internet novice and TCP/IP expert alike obtain a better grasp on how TCP/IP functions by breaking the whole down into manageable sections.

Host Names and
Internet Addressing

"To my extreme mortification, I grow wiser every day."

—*Lord Byron*

Before you begin your TCP/IP installation, you must first understand the concept of the Internet and how it applies to your network. Without going into all the details of how the Internet began and how it got to where it is today, realize that its main purpose is to bring a multitude of computers together in as efficient a manner as possible to share data.

Describing the TCP/IP Foundation

Quite certainly a vast majority of the readers of this book has at one time or another needed some information or an updated file without delay. Suppose that you are trying to install a SCSI host adapter into a computer when you realize that it is not recognized by your version of DOS. And the computer is that of your boss, and he needs it immediately after he returns from lunch. What do you do?

Before the advent of *bulletin board systems* (BBSs), you might have found yourself hurriedly updating your resume, but not any more. Now most commercial hardware manufacturers maintain a BBS for just such instances. In this case, instead of searching for a new employer you would simply go to a computer, dial the SCSI adapter manufacturer's BBS, and download the latest driver that works with your version of DOS. But then you realize that another portion of your boss's computer system needs to be updated to function with the new SCSI adapter. No problem, call another BBS and download their latest drivers.

No matter the size of the network, every system administrator has a telephone book full of BBS numbers for just such emergencies. But having to dial in and out of multiple BBSs located around the globe can become quite timely and costly (while logged on to the different BBSs, you will probably want to enter into discussions about their products or other related items). The Internet's popularity is due at least in part to its alleviation of this problem.

What the Internet offers to other users (or hosts) connected to its services is a seamless connection to literally thousands of other host computers (or BBSs). You can connect to the Internet either through a local telephone number or some point-to-point high-speed connection, but the constant is that you have one entry point for all the Internet assets.

With access to all these other BBSs, you also can contact the users thereof. And thus begins the reason for the standardization of an addressing scheme that can identify each and every host using the Internet.

Bearing this in mind, you can see that the apparently simple task of how one computer can either get data from or give data to another computer can get quite complex. If you only had to connect two computers, one bit would suffice (one computer would be addressed as 0, and the other as 1). Double the number of computers to four, and you require two bits of addressing (00, 01, 10, and 11). Double it again, and you need three bits. Keep in mind that every doubling of the number of computers (or hosts) involved in your network requires the addition of another bit. A hypothetical ceiling of four sets of eight bits or 4,294,967,296 (2^{32} or 256^4) addresses was established with some restrictions, which are discussed later. (The ceiling is only hypothetical because certain addresses are used for other than addressing. The four-octet addressing scheme was created with TCP/IP during the late 1960s when Stanford, California State Berkeley, UCLA, and Utah University were all linked together by this brand-new concept). Specifically, class A has 2^{24} addresses (16,777,216); class B has 2^{16} addresses (65,536); and class C has 2^8 addresses (256).

To draw an analogy, look at the U.S. Postal Service—how it transfers mail and how this process affects you. First, your main goal is to get a letter to another person intact and in an expedient manner. You really don't care how many stops are between you and the receiving party, just that your letter gets there. Second, you don't care that other carriers such as Federal Express or UPS are on the same road with your carrier (unless they have a collision that delays your mail).

For this to happen, you must conform to certain requirements made by the mail system. You have to put the recipient's name, address, and ZIP code on the mail for it to get there as efficiently as possible. You should write clearly for the postal workers to avoid slowing down the process.

Simplistically, the U.S. Postal Service is no different from the Internet and the associated addressing scheme. The air services and roadways are the medium upon which your mail travels, not unlike the cable that carries your computer-generated messages. The other mail carriers that use the same road are like other protocols that share your cable (for example, Ethernet 802.3, Ethernet 802.2, and Ethernet II). They all can coexist on the same roadways with a minimum number of collisions.

The addressing is very similar in both cases. For you to send mail to your cousin four states away, you tell the post office how to locate the other party. The post office has in place a most efficient route for your mail to get to your cousin, but should that route have a problem (for whatever reason), alternate post offices can get your mail to its proper destination. If you send mail to your cousin's home, you give the final destination to the post office so that it can get the mail into your cousin's hands. If you want to send mail to your cousin's office in a large corporation, you will likely include a mail address specific to the corporation. The post office, therefore, only needs to deliver the mail to the corporation's facility. From that point the corporation itself will act as a subnet and distribute the mail to the individual employees.

Whether the U.S. Postal Service delivers to every individual in a residential area or drops it off at the front desk of a corporation may not mean much to you now, but the differences parallel those of Internet addressing. The following list shows the three primary types of Internet addressing used:

✔ Type A has few large corporations and many houses (or few networks and many hosts per network)

✔ Type B has more corporations and fewer houses than type A (or more networks and fewer hosts per network)

✔ Type C has many corporations and few houses (or many networks and few hosts per network)

As you can see in the Type C example in the previous list, you can replace corporations with networks and houses with hosts. If a city has only corporations that use mail stops to deliver the mail to the final destination (or basically sub ZIP codes), then the mail service delivers large quantities of mail to few locations. But if a city is predominately residential with many disassociated houses, then the postal service delivers small amounts of mail to multiple locations.

Two additional classes are reserved for multicast addressing and future Internet needs. They begin at 224.0.0.0 and continue to (but exclude full system broadcast) 255.255.255.255.

When deciding what pattern your host naming conventions should follow, you should take your time and think about causes and effects. Look at the whole of your network entity. If it is a corporation, is the company logically broken geographically or departmentally? Are there already sub-groups defined or will you, as the network administrator, need to find some commonalties?

Once you have determined your pattern, you should implement a logical naming convention that people can remember. Naming a host after the user (e.g. my TCP/IP hosts on two different internets are marnett and arnettm), a region (e.g. ut001), or a sub-unit (e.g. ltlabut0) is much easier than having to remember some convoluted machine name.

Determining an Addressing Scheme

Whether you plan on attaching to the official Internet, or if your corporation will be creating its own internet outside of the Internet, you will need to determine an addressing scheme for your network.

Every node on any TCP/IP network must have a unique address. In order to obtain an Internet address you need to apply to the Network Information Center (NIC). Should you already have access to the Internet, you can request a copy from:

Network Solutions
InterNIC Registration Services
505 Huntmar Park Drive
Herndon, VA 22070

(703) 742-0400

If you are a network administrator wishing to obtain a network address or domain name, you will need to request either a Network Number Assignment or Internet Domain Name Registration form. Once completed, you will need to return the completed forms to either the same Herndon address or if you have access to the Internet, you can e-mail it to hostmaster@nic.ddn.mil.

Depending on the number of hosts which will be included in your local network (or internet), you will either be assigned a class A, class B, or class C network address. As is discussed later in this chapter, the class of network determines what section of your overall Internet address is to be used for your network, how much (if any) will be used for a subnet mask, and the remainder for your separate hosts. A class A network has a hypothetical maximum of 16,777,216 hosts; class B can have 65,536 hosts, and class C can have 256 hosts.

Since this network/host addressing is at the Internet level, should you be a class B network (which can have 65,536 hosts), you will probably want to break your hosts into logical groupings, or subnets. Depending on the number of sub-groups you desire, you will take the first x number of bits of your host address block and designate them as your subnet address. If you only wish to have two subnets you would use the first one bit of the host address, four subnet groups would require the first two bits, eight would use the first three, and so on. This is simply a manner with which you can more logically group your users within your own internetwork.

If you are even remotely considering entering the Internet at some point, do it now. Not setting your host(s) up as a registered Internet address undoubtedly means headaches later when you do (because you will need to change your addressing scheme). And the more hosts you have, the more complex the change is. In addition to just changing your /etc/hosts file, you need to reconfigure your address and subnet mask using netconfig, alter /etc/hosts.equiv, or /etc/hosts.lpd, and make changes on any other attached NOSes. If you plan to never enter the Internet, or simply thrive on complications, you can address your network however you desire.

If you want to join the extensive Internet, you must apply for and register an IP address with the Registration Service (the address of which was listed a few paragraphs earlier). They will then issue you a network address depending on your needs. You (or your network administrator) can then allocate the host portion of the IP address as you see fit.

Each Internet address consists of four eight-bit numbers separated by periods. These four eight-bit numbers, or *octets*, represent your ZIP code and address in the preceding example. They typically are displayed in decimal form; an example of a class B address is 134.135.100.13.

If you want to access the Internet by yourself (disassociate from any group of users), you more than likely will be assigned a class C address. Your address must be unique so that no other person (or host) also receives your mail. Simply stated, a class C host address allows three octets of Net addressing with one octet for the host address. This means that class A addresses technically range from 0.0.0.0 to 127.255.255.255; class B addresses range from 128.0.0.0 to 191.255.255.255; and class C addresses range from 192.0.0.0 to 223.255.255.255.

This addressing scheme has a few exceptions. The first one to remember is that address 127 is reserved for loopback testing and for occasions when a host needs to communicate with itself. 127 is by default known as the *localhost*, which is an alias for your own host. This address will be invaluable after you install TCP/IP (which is discussed later). Other exceptions are class D and class E, which are reserved for special broadcasts and future development.

With some technical exceptions that are not worth mentioning here, there are 127 network addresses available for class A (0–127), 1600 for class B ((192–128)*(255)), and 2,080,800 for class C ((224–192)*(255²)).

Broadcasting Messages

At some point, you will want to send a message to all hosts on your network. To perform this, TCP/IP uses a special host address to send data to a group of hosts rather than a single host. This is done by keeping the network portion of the address the same and changing the host portion to all 0s or all 1s (depending on the Unix system you are using). To broadcast to all hosts in all address classes, you send 255.255.255.255 (or 1111111.1111111.1111111.1111111 in binary and 0xFF.0xFF.0xFF.0xFF in hexadecimal). Consequently, if you are a member of class B network 134.135 and you want to broadcast to all hosts in your network, you address your message to 134.135.255.255.

Defining SubNet Masking

Subnet netmasking is used to route data to the different subnets within the entity, thus freeing the Internet from having to route all the information. Unless subnetting is implemented, the Internet literally has to perform all the routing within every company's domain (or network).

Understanding Internet Domain Naming Conventions

Domain names are another means by which your network can be accessed. If you are familiar with the Internet, you are more than likely also familiar with names such as NETCOM.COM, SPRY.COM, or LANTIMES.COM. These are all domains and are registered in a like fashion to address registration.

Various top-level domain extensions exist, but the most popular are GOV (any government body), EDU (an educational institution), ARPA (ARPANET), COM (commercial enterprises), MIL (military organizations), and ORG (any other organization not covered in the preceding descriptors).

Understanding Internet Newsgroup Naming Conventions

If you intend to connect to the Internet to access the vast amounts of information available for the asking, you undoubtedly want to investigate every tool it has to offer. If you are in search of some bit of information and do not know where to begin, a good place to start your search is with a newsgroup. *Newsgroups* are groups of people with common interests who like to gather and share related information. Information about newsgroups and their interest focus is published in a variety of publications, but if you do not have access to such literature, you must perform a little "net stalking" (once you are in any newsgroup whatsoever you can query other users as to how you can find other nonrelated groups).

Now that you at least know that such a beast as a newsgroup exists and you are looking around to get a grasp on how newsgroups are structured, you will find that they all have different prefixes to their names, such as alt, comp, sci, misc, rec, soc, and talk. These prefixes, like Internet addressing, are followed by a period. After this period, subdivisions of the same group can be observed (for example, alt.fan.jimmy_buffett or alt.fan.dead). Although the prefixes, like most other items involved with Unix, are cryptic at best, there is a method to the madness. Each prefix has some related definition and narrows your focus to a more limited group. Definitions of the eight main class prefixes that you see while surfing the net are as follows:

- ✔ **alt.** An "alternative" discussion on a wide variety of topics (for example, alt.fan.jimmy_buffett)

- ✔ **comp.** Computer-related information and discussions (for example, comp.bugs.sys5)

- ✔ **sci.** Science news and information (for example, sci.space.news)

- ✔ **misc.** "All other" category (for example, misc.health.diabetes)

- ✔ **news.** Issues concerning USENET itself

- ✔ **rec.** Recreational activities such as fishing (for example, rec.fishing)

- ✔ **soc.** Topics of interest for students of sociology and psychology (for example, soc.college)

- ✔ **talk.** USENET's version of talk radio

Additional groups have smaller followings than those mentioned in the preceding list, but should you be interested they are as follows:

- ✔ **bionet.** Newsgroup related to biologists and their interests (originating from net.bio.net)

✔ **bit.** Discussions redistributed from BITNET mailing lists

✔ **biz.** Newsgroup for those mainly concerned with computer business products and services

✔ **clarinet.** Material distributed from commercial news sources

✔ **gnu.** Information on the GNU Project of the Free Software Foundation

✔ **hepnet.** High Energy Physics and Nuclear Physics related discussions

✔ **ieee.** Area in which Institute of Electrical and Electronics Engineers (IEEE) matters are discussed

✔ **Inet/DDN.** Internet mailing list discussions

✔ **Info.** The "bit bucket" of mailing lists; a concatenation of social and cultural discussions connected to the news discussions at the University of Illinois

More newsgroups are spawning all the time; therefore this list is up-to-date as of its writing. Again, ask around or get into the different newsgroup list newsgroups to find out what is most currently available for access.

Describing the OSI Stack

Now that addressing and naming conventions have been discussed, it is time to describe the manner in which the data gets from one host to another. On any large network it is enough for most users to simply understand that when they need data their application will get it for them. As a network administrator, however, you need to understand where the bits are stored and how they are accessed.

In the instance of TCP/IP, you—the user—make your request upon another host in the form of an application. You ping, telnet, or mail another host and await a response. But how does your query get from your keyboard to the other host and back (frequently in the form of a display on your console)?

This is where the protocol stack comes into play. As an example, you ping another host to see if it responds. When you type **ping** and an address you access a utility that is associated with the application layer. From there your request (in the form of data) passes to the next layer, which either interprets and translates the data or appends information to it before passing it to the next layer. This continues until the packet is literally sent along the wire to another host where the process is reversed (please see the following OSI stack process).

The typical *Open Systems Interconnection* (OSI) model consists of seven layers (see fig. 3.1). When you initiate a transaction to perform some task at another host, your initial action begins at the top of one stack on your host and ends at the top of an OSI stack at the destination host. Each layer in the stack interacts only with its neighboring two layers, but it passes information to its counterpart layer at the destination host.

DoD	OSI	TCP/IP
Process	Application	Application
Process	Presentation	Application
Process	Session	
Host-to-Host	Transport	Transport
Host-to-Host	Transport	Internet
Internet	Network	Internet
Network Access	Data Link	Network Interface
Network Access	Physical	Physical

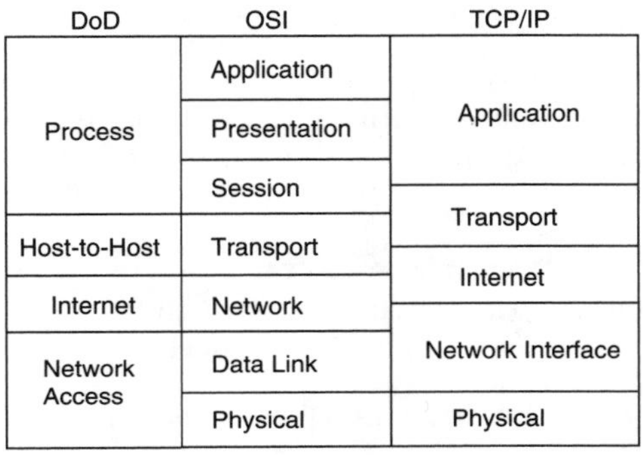

Figure 3.1
A representation of the OSI seven-layer and DoD four-layer stacks.

The typical seven-layer OSI model looks like figure 3.1 and consists of the following layers:

✔ **Layer 7—The Application Layer.** This layer, which most commonly is in the form of a program or application, is the interface point between the OSI stack and the user.

✔ **Layer 6—The Presentation Layer.** Application programs and terminal handler programs are translated in this layer. Typically, this is done through formatting and data translation.

✔ **Layer 5—The Session Layer.** This is where communication between cooperating applications is controlled.

✔ **Layer 4—The Transport Layer.** End-point data transferral, end-to-end data recovery, and flow control occur here.

✔ **Layer 3—The Network Layer.** Connections are established, maintained, and terminated at this layer. This layer enables the upper layers to be independent from the data transmission and switching technologies.

✔ **Layer 2—The Data Link Layer.** Synchronization, error control, and flow control are maintained here to ensure that data crosses the physical layer and is reliable.

✔ **Layer 1—The Physical Layer.** This layer, which can be Ethernet or another medium, is the physical link between the hosts.

TCP/IP frequently has a slight derivation from this seven-layer OSI model in that it commonly has five layers. These five layers are subtle combinations and slight derivatives of the seven-layer model as is depicted in figure 3.1. The layers are as follows:

✔ **Layer 5—The Application Layer.** Applications such as ftp, telnet, SMTP, and NFS relate to this layer.

✔ **Layer 4—The Transport Layer.** In this layer, TCP and UDP add transport data to the packet and pass it to layer 3.

✔ **Layer 3—The Internet Layer.** When you initiate an action on your local host (or initiating host) that is to be performed or responded to on a remote host (or receiving host), this layer takes the package from layer 4 and adds IP information before passing it to layer 2.

✔ **Layer 2—The Network Interface Layer.** This is the network device as the host, or local computer, sees it (for example, /dev/tty1a, /dev/ttys0, or /dev/wdn0). It is through this medium that the data is passed to layer 1.

✔ **Layer 1—The Physical Layer.** This is literally the Ethernet or *Serial Line Interface Protocol* (SLIP) itself.

At the receiving host, the layers are stripped one at a time, and their information is passed to the next highest level until it again reaches the application level.

If a gateway exists between the initiating and receiving hosts, the gateway takes the packet from the physical layer, passes it through a data link to the IP layer where it is analyzed, and then resends through the data link to the physical layer to continue (see fig. 3.2).

Figure 3.2
The seven-layer OSI model with gateways.

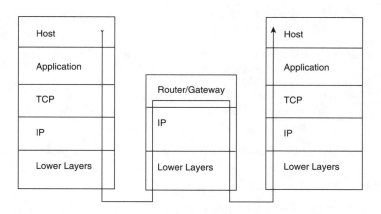

As a message is sent from the first host to the second, gateways pass the packet along by stripping off lower layers, readdressing the lower layers, and then passing the packet toward its final destination.

Preinstalling TCP/IP

Prior to TCP/IP installation, you must determine what equipment you already have in place and what you require to attach to the net. Assuming that you are using an Ethernet adapter to connect TCP/IP hosts, before you install the card you must consider many factors. Will you have interrupt, I/O base address, or RAM base address conflicts? You also need to know the name of your *network interface card* (NIC), your Internet address, your netmask, and your broadcast address.

The best way to begin the hardware portion of your preinstallation is to run hwconfig to determine what your system already has in it. The system returns screen output similar to the following:

```
name=fpu vec=13 dma=- type=80387
name=serial base=0x3F8 offset=0x7 vec=4 dma=- unit=0 type=Standard nports=1
name=floppy base=0x3F2 offset=0x5 vec=6 dma=2 unit=0 type=135ds18
name=console vec=- dma=- unit=vga type=0 12 screens=68k
name=parallel base=0x378 offset=0x2 vec=7 dma=- unit=0
name=e3B base=0x300 offset=0xF vec=3 dma=- type=3c503 addr=02:60:8c:1a:85:7b
name=disk base=0x1F0 offset=0x7 vec=14 dma=- type=W0 unit=0 cyls=919 hds=16 secs=17
```

This screen tells you what hardware you have, the associated vector (or interrupt), the I/O base address, the dynamic memory addressing, and some other various hardware-specific information.

With this information in hand, you can then cross-reference the hardware options that your Ethernet adapter supports and determine what addressing to select. In our instance, prior to installing our 3Com 3C503 Ethernet adapter, we determined that we had no communication port 2 or 4, or any other adapter using vector 3. Because our board supports vector 3 (which most do) and we believe that we will not install any vector 3 devices in the near future, we decided to use this interrupt for our Ethernet NIC.

In the case of our example shown in the preceding hwconfig output, you can determine that neither communication port 2 nor 4 are being used (nor any device which uses vector 3). This is done by reviewing the output and looking for any device which is listed as using vector 3 on its line. If it is not in the list, you can use it.

If you are planning on adding another communication port but not another parallel port, you could have elected to use vector 5 instead of vector 3.

To continue, note that the adapter supports various I/O base addresses, including 0x300 (which was not previously being used). Again this is a standard port to use for NICs, so this is a good choice. Notice that the name "e3B" is associated with this adapter. This NIC is supported directly by SCO, in order to keep you from prematurely losing your sanity you should use an interface adapter that is similarly supported. Your installation process will be much simplified if you do.

In lieu of using hwconfig to determine what equipment your system currently holds, you can use /etc/conf/bin/idcheck or /etc/conf/cf.d/vectorsinuse. Idcheck has quite a few flags which enables you to display specific details about specific attributes, whereas vectorsinuse simply displays which interrupts are presently in use (and will suffice in most instances).

Take into consideration which other hosts you want to allow access to your system and to what degree. The more time you take to perform your installation, the higher the probability that something will crash, and you will have to start the whole process all over again. Have your ducks in a row from the beginning, and your installation will be much smoother.

Installing TCP/IP

Now you are ready for the fun part—the actual installation. The first task you need to perform is the software installation. This can be performed either through the system administrator shell (sysadmsh) or the custom command. If you are not familiar with SCO Unix (or any other Unix for that matter), suffice it to say that most tasks that you can perform through the *system administrator shell* (SAS) also can be performed through the command line. If you did not know this, I suggest that you stick to sysadmsh; it takes care of flags with which you might not be familiar and is a menu utility to boot.

Assuming that you are going to use the SAS, you want to choose SYSTEM from the main menu, SOFTWARE from the system submenu, and INSTALL from the software submenu. Again, in most instances you want to use the default selections. Here you choose to install a new product, the entire product, and then the floppy from which you want the installation to be performed.

After the software installation is complete, you need to address the issue of the NIC installation. As previously covered, you need to know what parameters you are using. Use the /etc/netconfig command to perform the NIC installation. The netconfig utility not only enables you to set hardware parameters, but to logically link your NIC to the TCP/IP stack as well. The first screen output that you see should look like the following code less the third item (which is what you want after you are finished). This output might look a little daunting at first, but if you break it down, it really is quite logical. What you are trying to do is link the different items together.

```
Currently configured chains:
    1. nfs->sco_tcp
              nfs SCO NFS Runtime System for SCO Unix
              sco_tcp SCO TCP/IP for Unix
    2. sco_tcp->lo0
           sco_tcp SCO TCP/IP for Unix
           lo   SCO TCP/IP Loopback driver
    3. sco_tcp->e3B0
           sco_tcp SCO TCP/IP for Unix
           e3B0 3Com 503 ethernet driver, board 0
Select a chain to reconfigure ('q' to quit): 3

These elements support reconfiguring:
    1. sco_tcp SCO TCP/IP for Unix
    2. e3B0 3Com 503 ethernet driver, board 0

Select an element to reconfigure ('q' to quit): 2

Reconfigure e3B0 (y/n): y
Configuring 3Com503 board 0

Reconfiguring the e3B driver
Enter IRQ (2 3 4 5) [3] or 'q' to quit: 3
Enter I/O base address (250 280 2A0 2E0 300 310 330 350) [300] or '1' to quit:
Does this 503 board use thick (AUI ethernet? (y/n) [n] or 'q' to quit: y
```

 Make sure that you do not use values already in use during this process. You are allowed to do so, but the outcome is at best erratic system performance.

This initial screen displays that NFS is chained to SCO_TCP, which is chained to both LO0 and e3B0. This is a "Y" of sorts and basically means that SCO NFS runtime system for SCO Unix is linked to both the TCP/IP loopback driver and the 3Com 503 Ethernet driver through SCO TCP/IP for Unix. If you have more NICs or other logical peripherals, you can link them to some portion of this "Y."

To create the third link on this display, the sco_tcp->e3B0 chain, you need to select the first option from this main menu, "Add a chain." After doing this, you are prompted to select where you want to chain your item (an NIC in this example). Choose to chain it to the SCO TCP/IP for Unix module. If you want to add another 3Com Ethernet board to your system, again select Add a chain from the main menu and repeat the previous steps.

Now your preinstallation information will be of assistance. After choosing to add the 3Com NIC chain to sco_tcp, you are prompted for the IRQ setting for the second board. The next step is to establish the I/O base address and then some hardware-specific selections (for example, whether you will use the thinnet or AUI port for your connection).

Now that the NIC itself is configured, you need to establish who you are to the rest of the world and to whom you will listen. The first question you receive is that of your host Internet address. If you followed the earlier suggestion and already have this written down, enter this information in either hexadecimal or decimal form. If you are not going to use netmasking, then leave the next input as the default (255.0.0.0 for class A, 255.255.0.0 for class B, and 255.255.255.0 for class C).

If you are using SCO Unix, your answer to the next question is irrelevant. You are asked if you want to broadcast all 1s for broadcast messages. Some Unix systems recognize all 0s for a broadcast address, whereas others recognize all 1s. SCO recognizes both, but 1s are pretty standard. If, for example, your network is a class B network with the net address of 134.135, the netconfig utility asks you if you want to use a broadcast address of 134.135.255.255. There are few reasons to deviate from the standard, the best being that you are subnetting and that you would wish to only broadcast messages to your specific subnet.

The data you have entered is displayed, and if it is correct, select yes in response to the prompt Are these values correct? (y/n):. At this point, your NIC configuration is complete. Because the NIC is a new device to the system, you need to create a new kernel. You must do this for your changes to take effect. This step takes several minutes in most instances, so do not worry that your system is experiencing problems.

The next couple of steps will be familiar to those of you who have been dealing with Unix for any period of time. You are prompted whether you want this kernel to boot by default. If you do (which is in most cases), you might as well go ahead and answer yes to the kernel boot question. You can perform this task from the command line, but for simplicity let the system do it for you. After this, you need to rebuild the kernel environment. If you wish for the kernel which you have just built and linked to be the default kernel, then you will answer yes when prompted if this is so. Suffice it to say that there are reasons for you not to wish to do so, but this issue is non-TCP/IP related and more in-depth Unix related.

At this point, changes occur only on your hard disk—your system needs to be rebooted for them to take effect. Congratulations! Your NIC is now installed.

Configuring your TCP/IP Connection

During the preceding netconfig process, an entry was made in the /etc/hosts file that reflects the address of your host. You need to add the Internet addresses, host names, and aliases (including full domain names) of other hosts to which you will allow access to this file. This file looks very similar to the following screen:

```
#     @(#)hosts          1.2 Lachman System V STREAMS TCP source
#     SCCS IDENTIFICATION
237.0.0.1            localhost localhost.jbtestip.lantimes.com
134.135.100.1       jbsco jbsco.lantimes.com
134.135.100.2       test test.jbtestip.lantimes.com
134.135.100.3       jb311a jb311a.lantimes.com
134.135.100.5       jbsco jbsco.lantimes.com
134.135.100.11      jblabvectra1 jblabvectra1.lantimes.com
134.135.100.12      jblabvectra2 jblabvectra2.lantimes.com
134.135.100.13      jblabvectra3 jblabvectra3.lantimes.com
134.135.100.14      jblabvectra4 jblabvectra4.lantimes.com
134.135.100.15      jblabvectra5 jblabvectra5.lantimes.com
134.135.100.16      jblabvectra6 jblabvectra6.lantimes.com
134.135.200.1       talula talula.lantimes.com
134.135.200.2       pugsley pugsley.lantimes.com
0xff.0xff.0xff.0xff            broadcast
~
~
~
~
~
~
~
~
"/etc/hosts" 16 lines, 745 characters
```

When determining which hosts should be allowed access to your host, you will modify the /etc/hosts file. In lieu of setting up multiple host security portfolios, you can grant multiple hosts previously defined levels of access by including them into the /etc/hosts.equiv file.

Testing your TCP/IP Connection

Simple as it might be, you will thank the creators of the *Packet InterNet Groper* utility, otherwise known as *ping*. The ping is used to verify that a TCP/IP connection has been established and that data can be sent and echoed. If you are unsure that your installation and configuration is complete or correct, the first step is to ping localhost or ping 127.0.0.1. If your basics are sound, your terminal displays a series of lines reflecting how many bytes were sent from a host (and address), the sequence, the ttl, and the time in milliseconds required for the round-trip of sending and receiving a 64-byte packet, as in the following example:

```
# ping jb311a
PING jb311a 9134.135.100.3): 56 data bytes
64 bytes from jb311a (134.135.100.3): icmp_seg=0 ttl=255 time=0 ms
64 bytes from jb311a (134.135.100.3): icmp_seg=1 ttl=255 time=0 ms
64 bytes from jb311a (134.135.100.3): icmp_seg=2 ttl=255 time=0 ms
64 bytes from jb311a (134.135.100.3): icmp_seg=3 ttl=255 time=0 ms
64 bytes from jb311a (134.135.100.3): icmp_seg=4 ttl=255 time=0 ms
64 bytes from jb311a (134.135.100.3): icmp_seg=5 ttl=255 time=0 ms
64 bytes from jb311a (134.135.100.3): icmp_seg=6 ttl=255 time=0 ms
64 bytes from jb311a (134.135.100.3): icmp_seg=7 ttl=255 time=0 ms
64 bytes from jb311a (134.135.100.3): icmp_seg=8 ttl=255 time=0 ms
--- jb311a ping statistics ---
9 packets transmitted, 9 packets received, 0% packet loss
round-trip min/avg/max = 0/0/0 ms
#
```

If your netmask was set incorrectly, every other line states that the network is unreachable via your sendto. (This is verbatim from what is displayed on your screen. The sendto is the host with which you are attempting to communicate.) Check the information that you set in netconfig by running it once again and choosing the modify chain selection.

If you see one line that appears normal and then your screen stops, either the host at the other end is not online or you have not properly configured your NIC. A common mistake is to fail to set your interrupt or I/O base address to the same setting on your NIC. The easiest way to determine if your Unix host has recognized your NIC at the address that you have set is to run the hwconfig and see if your card is listed in the devices. If it is not, either change your NIC hardware to reflect your software settings or change your software settings to reflect your NIC hardware.

If your NIC is listed in the hwconfig response, verify that you are physically connected to the AUI port, that you have configured the card to use the AUI port, and that you have told Unix that you will be using the AUI port as well (via netconfig). If it is not, modify it, rebuild the kernel, and reboot the system. I know that this might sound a little ridiculous, but if none of these are the case, make sure that you have only one of your NIC connections connected. You should be able to select whether to use the AUI or the Thinnet connection via software or hardware. You also might want to connect the two for testing purposes, but don't. Don't count on the hardware manufacturers to produce a product that functions as they claim; doing so will cause you more hassles than it is worth.

If you are not familiar, most 10BASE-T (twisted-pair) and 10BASE2 (thinnet) NICs also have what is called a AUI (thicknet) port. This is most commonly in the form of a female DB15 connector located next to the RJ-45 or BNC connector on the back of your card.

Summary

Although companies such as Microsoft and Novell have created transport protocols which rival TCP/IP, they have also created modules which make their products compatible with TCP/IP. Windows NT, for instance, includes TCP/IP support out of the box. This chapter has reviewed the foundation upon which TCP/IP was built, as well as how to implement TCP/IP on a Unix platform. If you have the opportunity, play connect-the-dots and follow our examples step-by-step. When you feel comfortable doing so, deviate, see what happens, and analyze where the changes occurred. It may seem trivial right now, but the better you understand the protocol stack, addressing, and subnetting, the more easily you will fully comprehend TCP/IP.

Chapter Snapshot

The two primary functions of a network are remotely connecting to another host and transferring files back and forth between that host. This chapter examines those two topics by looking at the utilities that make such possible. These include the following:

4

CHAPTER

Remote Access and Network File Transfer

"There's too many kids in this tub.
There's too many elbows to scrub.
I just washed a behind
That I'm sure wasn't mine,
There's too many kids in this tub."

— *"Crowded Tub," Shel Silverstein, from* A Light in the Attic

T his chapter is a medley, if you will—a collection of information that you need to know that may not fit elsewhere.

When you think about it, the reason that you install and maintain a network is to provide access to remote sights and to transfer files back and forth. With that said, this should be the only chapter in the book because that is what you want to know. Ah, but if it were only that easy.

The remainder of this book tells you how to install and maintain the network—the things that an administrator must do. This chapter tells you how to use that network after it is installed—things an administrator wants to do, but also things that a normal user must do.

Several utilities must be discussed that enable you to perform these functions, and they fall into two categories: those that are Unix-specific and those that are not. TCP/IP came to life on the Unix operating system, and several Unix utilities were created to marry the two together. Since that time, TCP/IP has been ported to virtually every major operating system still in use, and other utilities have come about to handle the issues of interaction. These utilities (such as telnet and ftp) are available on Unix now, as well as the other operating systems.

Examining Unix-Specific Utilities

The Unix-specific utilities are common on almost all vendors' versions of Unix. They may or may not be available with other operating systems, depending upon the vendor, and all share a common denominator of starting with an "r." As a rule of thumb, utilities beginning with that letter work only when two or more Unix stations are involved and not with connected processors running another operating system.

rwho

The rwho utility, much like the who utility but on a larger scale, shows who is logged into each host machine attached to the network. This can be crucial in verifying that users on other hosts can access a machine. The following listing shows the output from a typical running of the utility:

```
# rwho
chris     TEXAS:ttyv00b Nov 01 20:24 :48
jenna     MAINE:ttyv00a Nov 01 21:12
root      NYORK:ttya    Nov 01 17:49 :36
sunadmin  TEXAS:ttyv008 Nov 01 13:17 :39
sunadmin  TEXAS:ttyv009 Nov 01 13:53
#
```

 For those not overly familiar with the Unix operating system, it is case-sensitive, and commands are lowercase.

By default, the only users shown are those who have not been idle for an hour or longer. Idle time is depicted in minutes at the right-most column of the display. Constant activity is depicted without a time in this column, as with the second listing—user jenna.

Users who have been idle an hour or more are not shown. Using the -a option, however, causes all users to be shown, regardless of idle time, as shown in the following listing. The entries that have been highlighted are the ones that did not appear in the regular rwho listing.

```
# rwho -a
chris     TEXAS:ttyv00b Nov 01 20:24 :48
cameron   TEXAS:ttyb    Nov 01 01:52  8:01
cameron   MONTA:ttyb    Nov 01 07:25  2:27
cameron   MAINE:ttyb    Nov 01 01:52  8:00
cameron   FLORI:ttyb    Nov 01 01:54  7:57
cameron   INDIA:ttyb    Nov 01 07:25  2:27
cameron   NYORK:ttyb    Nov 01 01:14  8:35
jenna     MAINE:ttyv00a Nov 01 09:30    :21
root      NYORK:ttya    Nov 01 17:49 :36
sunadmin  TEXAS:ttyv008 Nov 01 01:32    :12
sunadmin  TEXAS:ttyv009 Nov 01 09:07
#
```

ruptime

As rwho is a who process for the entire network, ruptime is an uptime process for each machine on the network, letting you know if a host machine is up and able to be reached. The following is a sample listing from this command:

```
# ruptime
TEXAS      up  2+09:49,    4 users,  load 1.07, 1.13, 1.15
MONTA      up 10+13:43,    1 user,   load 0.18, 0.18, 0.15
MAINE      up 20+11:29,    2 users,  load 1.00, 1.09, 1.14
FLORI      up 20+11:28,    2 users,  load 0.03, 0.13, 0.14
INDIA      up 10+13:43,    3 users,  load 0.03, 0.12, 0.14
NYORK      up 20+11:28,    1 user,   load 1.00, 1.00, 1.00
#
```

Each machine's host name is given, as well as the amount of time the host has been on the network in terms of days and hours. MAINE, for example, has been on the network 20 days, 11 hours, and 29 minutes. Following that is the number of users and the load. Loads are averages in three columns—the last one minute, last five minutes, and last fifteen minutes.

You should know one very critical piece of information: both ruptime and rwho obtain their information from the rwhod daemon process running on every host machine:

```
# ps -ef ¦ grep rwho
    root   264    1  0  Nov 9  ?        21:57 /usr/etc/rwhod
#
```

This daemon maintains files traditionally kept in the /usr/spool/rwho subdirectory, and it updates the information every three minutes. Thus, it is possible for a user to be logged in for two minutes and not show up in a rwho listing if the files have not updated yet.

It is the responsibility of the rwhod daemon process to produce a list of who is on the current machine, broadcast that to all other machines, and listen for other rwhod daemons' broadcasts of their status to this host. This information is kept in data files within the subdirectory—one for each host. Listing these files, you can check the last update time, and using the od—*octal dump*—utility, the contents can be viewed.

rlogin

After a host machine is up and talking to the network (as verified with ruptime), the next step is to test access to the machine. To log in on a remote machine as the same user you are on the current machine, use the rlogin utility with a parameter of the remote host name. This establishes a connection as if your terminal were directly connected to the remote host. The rlogin process first attempts to log you in without a password by checking for entries in the /etc/hosts.equiv file. If it cannot find the file, or an entry for you in it, next it checks the /etc/passwd file to find your $HOME directory. It looks in there for a .rhosts file that enables you to log in without verification. If it cannot find that, it then prompts you for a password.

Giving the password correctly allows you access into the system. If given incorrectly, you must give the login and password combination all over again, but the connection stays live. After you are connected and successfully logged in, you can perform any Unix command as if you were sitting at a terminal connected to that host. When you are finished with the session, typing **exit** closes the connection and returns you to your own machine.

To connect to the remote machine as another user (suppose that you are user hanna_d on this machine, but have an account as hanna on the other machine), follow the normal command with -l and the name of the user you will be on the other machine. For example:

```
$ rlogin MAINE -l hanna
```

When a remote login has been established, this will appear in the process table as the rlogind daemon:

```
# ps -ef | grep rlogind
root  5924   259  0 19:39:28 ttyv00a  0:00 rlogind 197.9.200.12
#
```

The user name is not given, although it appears in who listings; instead, the address of the remote host is shown—in this case 197.9.200.12.

Toggling Back and Forth

When remotely logged into a host, you can jump back and forth between it and the one at which you are truly sitting. To come back to your host, enter a tilde (~) and <z>. To return to the remote host, type **exit** on your machine. A representation of this is shown in the following example:

```
# uname -n
NYORK
# rlogin MAINE -l hanna
You have mail.

$ uname -n
MAINE
$

$~z
# uname -n
NYORK
#
# exit
$ uname -n
MAINE
$
```

The tilde is interpreted as the default escape character. If this is inconvenient, for whatever reason, you can redefine the escape character by using the -e option. For example, to change it to the dollar sign, the syntax is as follows:

```
rlogin MAINE -e$ -l hanna
```

remsh

One of the most useful methods of testing the status of a host in relation to the network is to remotely run a job on that machine. This can be done without the necessity of logging in there to perform the action. TCP/IP has a utility for doing so. The name of the utility is dependent upon the vendor who supplied the version, but it will usually be "rsh" or "remsh"—both indicating that you are remotely running a shell process. Here, remsh is used to mean either/or.

For remsh to be successful, the local and remote host must have proper permissions into each other. /etc/hosts.equiv and/or .rhosts files must allow one machine to access another without password verification. The following list demonstrates using the df utility to test this:

```
NYORK> df -t
/          (/dev/dsk/38s1   ):    246688 blocks     30275 i-nodes
total: 571496 physical (71437 4096-byte logical) blocks 35712
NYORK>
NYORK> remsh MAINE df -t
/          (/dev/dsk/38s1   ):    162968 blocks     30855 i-nodes
total: 571496 physical (71437 4096-byte logical) blocks 35712
NYORK>
```

If one user does not have permission to remotely run the desired process, the -l option can be used, as with rlogin to specify another user. If no command is given following the host name:

```
remsh MAINE
```

then an rlogin session is initiated. Quotation marks become all important with remsh commands:

```
remsh MAINE cat this >> that
```

appends the contents of MAINE:this file to the NYORK:that file. The following command:

```
remsh MAINE "cat this >> that"
```

appends the contents of MAINE:this file to the MAINE:that file. You will always get what you ask for, so be careful to specify exactly what you want.

Non-Unix-Specific Utilities

The non-Unix-specific utilities can be found on virtually every Unix vendor's product. Their strength, however, comes from the fact that they are also available with every other TCP/IP product available for different operating systems and are not OS-dependent.

telnet

telnet is both a program and a protocol. telnet (the program) uses telnet (the protocol) to provide an interface to remote logins to other machines on the network. A telnet session provides a *virtual* character-based terminal, in which the user can type commands and other text and also see the output from processes on the remote machine. telnet sends all the characters from your side of the connection to the machine on the other side.

Using telnet, you can log into other machines on the network on which you have an account. For instance, you might have many files on another machine. Rather than copying all of them over to the machine to which you are currently attached, it might be simpler to switch to the other machine and work on them there. Or take another example: To win a bet, you need to know the billion-and-first digit after the decimal point in the value of pi. But you were planning a night-long session of playing hack on your machine. You know your algorithm for calculating the value of pi will slow your local machine to a crawl. Problem? Not with telnet! Just telnet over to another machine, start your calculations, and exit.

The basic virtual terminal has a minimal set of features and can conveniently be thought of as a dumb terminal. It reads input from the user's keyboard and displays output on the user's screen. Usually the display shows or "echoes" what is being typed. It can show the 7-bit *ASCII* (American Standard Code for Information Interchange) character set, which includes the English alphabet, punctuation marks, and some control characters. Everything you type is stored locally in a buffer, and then after you enter the * (and then press Enter), everything is sent to the remote machine. Some control codes may not be supported on your local machine, even though they are in the 7-bit ASCII character set. Table 4.1 shows some control codes that may produce no effect on your local terminal.

Table 4.1
Some Optionally Supported ASCII Control Codes in telnet

Name	Number	Description
BELL (BEL)	7	Produces an audible or visible signal without showing on-screen.
Back Space (BS)	8	Moves the screen cursor one character position toward the left margin.
Horizontal Tab (HT)	9	Moves the screen cursor to the next horizontal tab stop.

The protocol allows many extensions and options to this basic terminal. For example, you can try to use the 8-bit ASCII character set, which includes many characters used in European languages. Of course, the remote machine to which you connect must be able to interpret characters from that set. You can also specify how the telnet session interprets such keyboard characters as those that you use to backspace over a character, kill a whole line, or send a break to kill the process you started with a command line.

In the simplest case, you use telnet to connect to another machine. To initiate a telnet session with an imaginary machine named ohio.aco.com, type the following:

```
% telnet ohio.aco.com
```

Next, you should see the following list:

```
Trying...
Connected to ohio.aco.com.
Escape character is '^]'.

SunOS Unix (ohio)
login:
```

Enter your login name and password—that's all there is to it. You are connected and can begin typing commands as if you were on a terminal physically connected to the remote machine.

You also can use an equivalent sequence of commands. Type the following:

```
% telnet
```

You see the telnet prompt:

```
telnet>
```

You can type the telnet program command **open** followed by the name of the remote machine. For example, type the following:

```
telnet> open ohio.aco.com
```

The connection is made, and you see the login prompt from the remote machine.

```
Trying...
Connected to ohio.aco.com.
Escape character is '^]'.

SunOS Unix (ohio)
login:
```

Getting Help within telnet

If you prefer to use telnet from its prompt, it is easy to get a quick reminder of various commands. Type either:

```
telnet> help
```

or

```
telnet> ?
```

You see the following:

```
Commands may be abbreviated. Commands are:
close       close current connection
display     display operating parameters
mode        try to enter line-by-line or character-at-a-time mode
open        connect to a site
quit        exit telnet
send        transmit special characters ('send ?' for more)
set         set operating parameters ('set ?' for more)
status      print status information
toggle      toggle operating parameters ('toggle ?' for more)
z           suspend telnet
!           shell escape
?           print help information
```

I

Overview

Many of these commands are adequately explained in the table, but a few call for some additional comment. The send command can be used to send special characters or character sequences through to the remote machine. The toggle command turns various attributes on or off. Together, these attributes determine how telnet responds to certain events or character sequences, such as those representing flush, interrupt, quit, erase, and kill.

telnet Variables

After you telnet over to a remote machine, you may need to temporarily interrupt the transmission of characters. But how? Remember, everything you type is being sent by telnet to the other machine. Even pressing Ctrl+Z, the signal that would stop a process on your local machine, is simply relayed over. To get the attention of telnet, type the escape character; by default, this is specified to be Ctrl+]. You can specify any key combination you want as the escape character for telnet. From the telnet prompt, set the value of the telnet variable *escape* by typing the following:

```
telnet> set escape ^[
```

By pressing Ctrl+], you force telnet to stop sending characters to the remote machine, Instead, it must attempt to process them. In general, you can set the values of telnet variables with a command using the following form:

```
telnet> set variable value
```

Several telnet variables are described in table 4.2.

Table 4.2
telnet Variables

Name	Use
echo	Specifies whether what you type appears on-screen. (This is set to a value of "off" when the remote system prompts you for your password.)
escape	Specifies the escape character that halts the flow of characters to the remote machine and forces them to be interpreted by the telnet process running on your local machine.
interrupt	Specifies the Interrupt Process character that interrupts the user process currently running on the remote machine.
quit	Specifies the character used to indicate that the Break or Attention key on the user's keyboard has been entered.

continues

Table 4.2, Continued
telnet Variables

Name	Use
flushoutput	Specifies the character to be used to signify an abort output function on the remote machine.
eof	Specifies the character to be used to send an eof to the remote machine.

You can see the value of telnet variables in your current session by typing the following:

```
telnet> display
```

The preceding command produces something like the following:

```
will flush output when sending interrupt characters
won't send interrupt characters in urgent mode
won't map carriage return on output
won't recognize certain control characters
won't turn on socket level debugging
won't print hexadecimal representation of network traffic
won't show option processing
```

The following list contains characters that can be entered to obtain special results.

Key Combinaton	Result
Ctrl+E	echo
Ctrl+]	escape
Ctrl+?	erase
Ctrl+O	flushoutput
Ctrl+C	interrupt
Ctrl+U	kill
Ctrl+\	quit
Ctrl+D	eof

Sending Special Character Sequences to the Remote Machine through telnet

You can use the send command from within telnet to send certain character sequences to the machine on the other end of your connection. Use the following syntax to do this:

```
telnet> send sequence
```

The variable *sequence* is one or more of the options listed in table 4.3.

Table 4.3
Character Sequences That Can Be Sent with the send Command

Name	Use
?	Displays help about the send command.
escape	Sends the escape character (without forcing telnet to stop sending characters).
ip	Sends the telnet protocol IP sequence. (The remote system should abort the process it is currently running for you. Remember that you can specify what is sent by using the set variable command.)
ec	Sends the telnet protocol EC sequence. (The remote system should erase the last character you typed.)
el	Sends the telnet protocol EL sequence. (The remote system should erase the line you are currently typing.)
ao	Sends the telnet protocol AO sequence. (The remote system should flush all output to your terminal.)
brk	Sends the telnet protocol BRK sequence. (The remote system must provide the response.)
ayt	Sends the telnet protocol *AYT* (Are You There) sequence. (The remote system must provide the response.)

Possible telnet Errors

After you have telnet set up so that it sends the right characters according to your keyboard preferences, the only likely error will be if telnet cannot connect to the machine you name. You will see an error message like the following:

```
Host unknown
```

The problem here is not with telnet, but with the name you used. Use ping with the machine name to which you are trying to connect. If it is not accessible to ping, then you must have the name and associated address added to your machine's table of hosts.

You do not need to be physically near a system to have a terminal-type connection to it. All you need are a valid IP address and telnet. By providing virtual terminals that can open onto any machine on which you have a login, you can work with data or computational resources anywhere on the Internet.

ftp

ftp is both a program and a protocol. ftp (the program) uses ftp (the protocol) to provide file copying to and from other machines on the network. Note that these other machines are not limited to workstations running Unix; they can be anything from mainframes to small personal computers, running operating systems from VMS to Macintosh and DOS. One of the virtues of ftp is that it provides a common interface to many different file storage methods and directory structures. ftp (as with all the Internet protocols) can run over many different kinds of connections. It works over serial (dial-in) lines, Ethernet, Token Ring, and other connections. However, it is worth noting that ftp does not itself perform any data compression. (Of course, it can copy compressed files.) It also has no "smart restart" features that allow it to pick up where it left off in the event of an interruption to its flow of data.

ftp's many capabilities can be grouped into the following five areas:

✔ **Operation.** How to begin and end ftp sessions, see status, see online help, and create macros. Any ftp commands can be entered either at the command interpreter prompt (ftp>) or from a command line. This flexibility makes it easy for machine processes, as well as human users, to use ftp.

✔ **Remote accounts.** Accessing your remote accounts. You can use ftp with any account for which you have a password. This does not mean that you must have your own individual account on every machine to which you connect through ftp. "anonymous ftp" is available on many file archives on the Net. By using the user name "anonymous" and a password (usually your user ID in the form user@machine_name.domain), you can ftp the files placed in the public access directories. For example, the machine nic.merit.edu has a set of public access directories in /document that holds IPs, Requests for Comment, Standards, For Your Information documents, and more.

✔ **Types.** File types. ftp can copy both ASCII (or plain text) files and binary files, that is, any files that have some internal structure of their own such as a spreadsheet, formatted document, or executable program. Binary files are transferred as *images*—a stream of bytes without any modification or interpretation of any kind.

✔ **Names.** File names. You can use regular file names when performing operations on files. ftp also supports *globbing*, Unixese for the use of wildcard characters, single characters that can be used as abbreviations in file names. For example, file?.txt can stand for filea.txt, filer.txt, filez.txt, or file6.txt. Globbing in ftp can be turned on or off.

✔ **Files.** File and directory navigation and management. Once ftp connects to a remote machine and account, you can navigate in the directory structure, make directories, list files, put (send) and get (receive) files, and delete and rename files. Versions of commands such as mget and mput also work on multiple files.

Using ftp

Imagine that you receive e-mail from a colleague from whom you have not heard in weeks. She tells you what a great time she had on a faraway island from which she has just returned. But in case you want to know more, she informs you that there is a document called a *FAQ*, a list of answers to frequently asked questions. The FAQ is available through anonymous ftp; she gives you the name of the machine and the directory and file name. Perversely, you decide you want to know more about this island paradise, knowing full well that it would be years before you could get any more vacation time or could possibly save enough money to go. To log in to the remote machine and get the FAQ file, type the following:

```
% ftp vacations.bigbux.com
```

If the name vacation.bigbux.com is in your machine's database of known names, you are connected, and you see the following information:

```
% ftp vacations.bigbux.com
Connected to vacations.bigbux.com.
220 vacations.bigbux.com FTP server (Version 4.81 Mon Feb 18
14:33:38 PDT 1994) ready.
Name (vacations.bigbux.com:your_userID): anonymous
331 Guest login ok, send your email address as password.
```

A few comments are in order here. ftp always attempts to log in under a name unless you start it up with the -n option. In this example, it will send the name your_userID by default unless you enter something different at the Name prompt. Enter **anonymous**. In response, you see that the remote ftp server will accept that name if you send your user ID and machine name as the password. This should be entered in the form userID@machine.domain, as depicted in the following example:

```
Password:
230- Guest login ok, access restrictions apply.
230- Local time is: Mon Mar 17 17:26:14 1993
230
ftp>
```

Now you can enter the command to list the files in the current working directory, the one you logged into. Type the following:

ftp> ls -F

Use the -F option to ls so that directories will be listed with a / after them. You see a list of files between some other information:

```
ftp> ls -F
200 PORT command successful.
150 Opening ASCII mode data connection for file list.
golf/
islands/
jungles/
tennis/
226 Transfer complete.
57 bytes received in 0.01 seconds (5.6 Kbytes/s)
ftp>
```

The lines about PORT, Opening ASCII, and so on are information from ftp. If you don't want to see them and their ilk, enter the following command:

ftp> verbose

You change directories to islands with the next command:

ftp> cd islands

If you are curious about what directory you are in, you can type the following:

ftp> pwd
257 "/v/public/travel/islands" is current directory.
ftp>

Once again, you list the files in the current directory by typing the following:

ftp> ls -F
200 PORT command successful.
150 Opening ASCII mode data connection for file list.
beautiful
dismal
impressions/

```
ok
226 Transfer complete.
32 bytes received in 0.01 seconds (5.6 Kbytes/s)
ftp>
```

The file beautiful is presumably the one for which you are looking. To get your own copy of this file, type the following:

ftp> get beautiful

If you use wildcard file name expansion, you can just type the following abbreviated version:

ftp> beau*

Or type enough of the file name to distinguish it from any others in the same directory.

Another directory is listed in our example, impressions. Curious, you change directories to it and, after typing an ls command, find files with names like the following:

```
10on11.28.89

5on3.12.88

7on4.3.90
```

With a little ingenuity, you surmise that perhaps these are files containing impressions that various people have had of the islands listed in the parent directory, with a rating from 1 to 10, followed by the date of their vacation. You decide to add a file of your own impressions. You press Ctrl+Z to temporarily disconnect your terminal from ftp. Opening up a new file with your word processor, you jot down your impressions of expensive island vacations. After saving the file under the name forever, you type **fg** or the job number to reattach your terminal.

Then, to upload your file, you type the following:

ftp> put forever

You see the following feedback from ftp:

```
ftp> put forever
200 PORT command successful.
150 Opening ASCII mode data connection for forever.
226 Transfer complete.
local: forever remote: forever
30 bytes sent in 0.01 seconds (2.9 Kbytes/s)
ftp>
```

You disconnect from the remote machine by typing the following:

```
ftp> quit
```

ftp responds with the following output:

```
221 Goodbye
```

You see your command shell prompt.

Using ftp—Operations

ftp can connect to any host on the Net for which you have a name or IP address. You can get online help at the ftp command prompt ftp>. You can also set *toggles*, variables that are either on or off, to specify what information about its operations ftp displays on your screen (see table 4.4).

Table 4.4
ftp Operations/Connections

Name	Use
open name	Opens a connection using the ftp protocol to the machine specified by name. (ftp defaults to starting the login process on the remote machine. If you do not want this behavior, use the -n option on the command line.)
close	Closes the current connection, but keeps ftp operating.
bye	Closes the current connection and terminates ftp.

The machine name for the open command must be of the form machine.domain. Use close when you want to end the connection to a particular machine and start another one with all your macros still in effect. Table 4.5 shows the ftp operations and the type of help given:

Table 4.5
ftp Operations/Getting Help

Name	Use
help, ?	Shows a list of all commands for which online information is available.
help command	Shows a short line of information about the named command.

help shows terse descriptions. For example, the following:

```
ftp> help
```

yields this:

```
ftp> help help
help    print local help information
```

The remote help command shows you what the remote machine's idea of help is. Table 4.6 shows ftp operations and the returned on-screen information:

Table 4.6
ftp Operations/On-Screen Information

Name	Use
status	Shows current settings.
prompt	Switches on or off prompting during operations on more than one file. (Multiple files are specified by using the following wildcard globbing characters: ? for any single character, * for any string of characters. This can be annoying when copying files with mput or mget, but reassuring when deleting files with mdelete.)
verbose	Switches on or off verbose mode. (Use this toggle to see file transfer efficiency statistics and also the replies from the remote ftp process. Replies usually show a completion or error code and a text string.)

A sample response to the status command might look like this:

```
ftp> status
Connected to vacations.bigbux.com.
No proxy connection.
Mode: stream; Type: ascii; Form: non-print; Structure: file
Verbose: on; Bell: off; Prompting: on; Globbing: on
Store unique: off; Receive unique: off
Case: off; CR stripping: on
Ntrans: off
Nmap: off
Hash mark printing: off; Use of PORT cmds: on
ftp>
```

To abort a file copy in mid-stream, press Ctrl+C. This makes your ftp send the ABOR command, which is defined in the ftp protocol. The file copy interruption might take a while to happen, depending on how attentive the remote machine is to your instructions. If the remote ftp *hangs*—that is, does nothing in response to your commands, however patiently you wait—then just kill the local ftp process.

Using ftp—Remote Accounts

After ftp establishes a connection, you need a valid account name and password to begin file transfers. Table 4.7 shows the ftp Remote Accounts.

Table 4.7
ftp Remote Accounts

Name	Use
user name	Provides a user name to ftp on the remote machine. (You are prompted for this name after connecting to the remote machine unless you start your local ftp with the -n option. After you send the name, you are prompted for a password, which does not echo on your screen as you type it.)

Anonymous ftp

Use the user name anonymous when prompted for a user name. You might see instructions about what to type for your password. If not, try your e-mail address in the form userID@machine.domain.

Using ftp—File Types

ftp can copy ASCII text files and binary files. Binary files are copied literally, without ftp adding or subtracting anything from the stream of bits between local and remote machines. To see the different ftp file types, refer to table 4.8.

Table 4.8
ftp File Types

Name	Use
ASCII	Transmits files as 7-bit ASCII. (Lines end with a combination of two characters: Line feed and Carriage Return.)
cr	Switches on or off the removal of the Carriage Return character. (Unix uses Line feed to delimit lines.)
binary	Transmits files as literal images without altering their internal format (if they have one).
type	Shows the current file type.
type name	Sets the type for file transmission to a name that can be either ASCII or binary.

When copying text files that will ultimately end up on a DOS system, you should switch Carriage Return removal off—use cr because DOS uses both Carriage Return and Line feed to delimit a line, whereas Unix uses only a Line feed.

The binary or image type should be used for everything else. This ensures that however the bytes are lined up in the original, they will stay that way in your copy.

Using ftp—File Names

ftp refers to files by name. For convenience, ftp allows the use of wildcard characters to substitute for parts of file names that you do not need to write out in full. Refer to table 4.9 for a listing of ftp file names.

Table 4.9
ftp File Names

Name	Use
glob	Switches on or off file name expansion.
case	Switches on or off the translation of file names that are all upper-case to all lowercase when using the mget command.
runique	Switches on or off the adding of digits to the end of file names for files being received to ensure that they are unique. (Starts with .1 and goes up to .99.)
sunique	Switches on or off the adding of digits to the end of file names for files being sent to ensure that they are unique. (Starts with .1 and goes up to .99.)

Use runique and sunique to ensure that you do not overwrite a file on either the local or remote machine that already has a name identical to one you propose to use.

Using ftp—File and Directory Navigation and Management

Using ftp, you can move within a directory structure, display the names of files within directories on the remote machine, add and delete files, rename them, and, of course, copy files back and forth. Table 4.10 shows the methods of navigating in ftp files and directories.

Table 4.10
ftp Files and Directories: Navigation

Name	Use
cd name	Changes the current working directory on the remote machine to name. (On some implementations of ftp, you can add arguments to cd such as ~ for the login directory and .. for the parent directory.)
cdup	Changes the current working directory on the remote machine to the parent directory.
pwd	Prints the working directory of the remote machine.
lcd name	Changes the current working directory on the local machine to name.
ls	Lists files in the current working directory on the remote machine. (Some implementations may accept ls options such as -l and -F.)
dir	Lists files in the current working directory on the remote machine.
dir name	Lists files in the directory name on the remote machine.
rename	Renames the file on the remote machine named "from" to "name to."

You do not know whether the remote machine's implementation of ftp allows options such as ls -F or cd ~ until you try them. No harm is done if the remote machine does not respond to unknown options; it simply ignores them. The management of ftp files and directories is expounded upon in table 4.11.

Table 4.11
ftp Files and Directories: Management

Name	Use
put local-file remote-file	Copies local-file to the remote machine and gives it the name remote-file. (If you don't specify remote-file, it just uses the name local-file.)
mput name	Copies all files specified by name, which may include wildcard characters, to the remote machine under the same names.

Name	Use
`get remote-file local-file`	Copies remote-file from the remote machine and gives it the name local-file. (If you don't specify local-file, it just uses the name remote-file.)
`mget name`	Copies all files specified by name, which may include wildcard characters, on the remote machine to the local machine under the same names.
`delete remote-file`	Deletes the file named remote-file on the remote machine.
`mdelete name`	Deletes all files specified by name, which may include wildcard characters, on the remote machine.
`append local-file remote-file`	Adds the contents of local-file on the local machine to the end of remote-file on the remote machine.
`mkdir dir-name`	Makes a directory named dir-name on the remote machine.
`rmdir dir-name`	Removes the directory named dir-name on the remote machine.

ftp copies files back and forth to and from machines anywhere on the Internet and beyond. ftp programs run on machines using many different architectures and operating systems. The fact that ftp works more or less the same for all machines makes it a very useful tool.

Understanding NFS

Network File System (NFS) is a separate component often used in conjunction with TCP/IP. Developed by Sun Microsystems, NFS enables you to mount a remote machine's hard disk and view it on your host as if it were local.

Summary

This chapter discussed the utilities relevant to remote system access and file transfers. The utilities can essentially be broken into two categories: those native to Unix and run only on that platform, and those that run across multiple platforms.

Chapter Snapshot

When working with Unix, you inevitably encounter TCP/IP networks. A major headache consultants and administrators face is TCP/IP routing. In this chapter, you look at the various devices used in internetworking as well as some of the protocols used in routing TCP/IP.

These topics, and others, are discussed in the following sections, starting with a brief review of the *Open Systems Interconnection* (OSI) and *Department of Defense* (DoD) models:

5

CHAPTER

TCP/IP Routing

"I don't think we're in Kansas anymore, Toto."

—*Dorothy,* The Wizard of Oz

J ust as stand-alone computers have readily become relics of the past, so too now are stand-alone networks. What was once simply a LAN must now become part of a WAN or MAN. Faced with the requirements to connect to wider geographical locations and more users, administrators have quickly had to embrace bridges, routers, and gateways.

This chapter examines routing on the TCP/IP protocol, how it is implemented, why it is implemented, and what you need to know to implement it.

Examining the OSI Model

Every technology has its own jargon; computer networks are no exception. No matter what the protocol is—TCP/IP or NetWare—the basic underlying concepts are the same. Today they all start with the *Open Systems Interconnection model*, more commonly referred to as the *OSI model*. Chapter 2, "Introduction to TCP/IP," discusses the OSI model in detail, so it is only briefly touched upon here as it relates to this chapter's topic.

Because of the existence of numerous types of computer operating systems, the OSI model was developed in 1977 by the *International Standards Organization* (ISO) to promote multivendor interoperability.

The OSI model itself does not specify any communication protocols. Instead it provides guidelines for communication tasks. It divides the complex communication process into smaller, more simple, subtasks. This way, the issues become more manageable, and each subtask can be optimized individually. The model is divided into seven layers as shown in figure 5.1. Note that the layers are numbered from the bottom up.

Figure 5.1
The OSI model.

Layer	
7	Application
6	Presentation
5	Session
4	Transport
3	Network
2	Data Link
1	Physical

Each layer is assigned a specific task. Also, each layer provides services to the layer above it and uses the services of the layer directly beneath it. For example, the network layer uses services from the data link layer and provides services to the transport layer.

In the context of this chapter, it is important to explain the services provided by the first three layers of the OSI model:

✔ The *physical* layer (layer 1) provides the physical connection between a computer system and the network wiring. It specifies cable pin assignments, voltage on the wire, and so on. The data unit at this layer is called a *bit*.

✔ The *data link* layer (layer 2) provides the packaging and unpackaging of data for transmission. The data unit at this layer is called a *frame*. A frame represents the data structure (much like a database record template).

✔ The *network* layer (layer 3) provides routing of data through the network. The data unit as this layer is called a *datagram*.

The TCP/IP protocol suite was developed before the OSI model was defined and is based mostly on the U. S. Department of Defense's own networking model, known as the *DoD model.* The DoD Model also is known as the *Internet model.* The DoD is discussed in the next section.

Examining the DoD Model

In the mid-60s, the U.S. Department of Defense defined its own networking model. The DoD model, which defines only four layers, is much simpler than the OSI model. Figure 5.2 compares the DoD model to the newer OSI model.

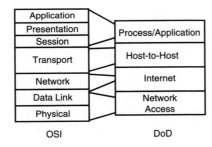

Figure 5.2
A comparison of the OSI and DoD models.

Although the DoD model predates the OSI model by some ten years, a comparison between the two can still be made:

✔ The *process/application* layer in the DoD model maps to the top three layers of the OSI model.

✔ The *host-to-host* layer in the DoD model maps to OSI's transport layer.

✔ The DoD *internet* layer corresponds to the network layer in OSI.

✔ The *network access* layer in the DoD model maps to the bottom two layers in the OSI model.

Associated with each layer is one or more protocols that specify how certain networking functions behave. The Internet/Network layer protocols for TCP/IP are discussed in a later section. The next section examines the internetworking devices associated with the first three layers of the OSI model (the first two layers in the DoD model)—physical, data link, and network.

Internetworking Devices

The basis for all TCP/IP routing decisions is a table of routing information maintained by the stack and routing protocols. The routing table is one of the most frequently accessed structures in the TCP/IP stack; on a busy host this can be hundreds of accesses in a second. The TCP/IP netstat command can be used to view the contents of the routing table. The following table illustrates the output from the netstat -r command used to display information stored in the routing table.

destination	router	refcnt	use	flags	snmp metric	intrf
132.1.16.0	132.1.16.3	1	63	U	-1	lan0
132.1.16.5	132.1.16.4	0	22	U	-1	ppp0
127.0.0.1	127.0.0.1	1	0	UH	-1	lo0
default	132.1.16.1	2	1351	UG	1	lan0

Each entry in the table contains a destination and router (sometimes referred to as an IP gateway) address pair. For a given destination address, the router address indicates the host to which an IP datagram should be forwarded to reach that destination. The following minitable should help alleviate confusion about what a router does.

The flags in the table can have the following values:

Flag	Description
D	The route was created via a redirect message.
G	The route is to a gateway/router.
H	The route is to a host. If this flag is not set, the route is to a network or subnetwork.
M	The route has been changed by a redirect message.
U	The route is currently up.
<null>	If this flag is not set, then the destination can be reached directly.

A few comments are in order regarding the routing flags. If the G flag is not set, then the destination can be reached directly, i.e. the host has both the IP address and the physical or link layer address of the final destination workstation. The net result is that the IP datagram can be sent simply by encapsulating it in the physical network frame.

For indirect routes (G flag set), the IP address corresponds to that of the final destination workstation and the link layer address is the physical address of the gateway. The *Address Resolution Protocol* (ARP), an integral part of the TCP/IP stack, maintains a cache of local IP address and link layer address pairs to facilitate the translation of IP addresses to link layer addresses.

The *Simple Network Management Protocol* (SNMP) metric indicates the desirability of a given route; a positive metric indicates a more preferred route. The intrf field indicates the interface (transport type and unit number) that the route is associated with. Possible interfaces include lan<n> (Token Ring; IEEE 802.5), le<n> (Ethernet; IEEE 802.3), sl<n> (*Serial Line Internet Protocol* or SLIP), ppp<n> (*Point-to-Point Protocol* or PPP), and lo<n> (the Loopback interface). The terminal string <n> represents the interface unit number. Note that the actual name assigned to an interface is vendor specific and varies from system to system.

This section defines the terms *repeater, bridge, router, gateway,* and *brouter* and their functions. It is important to understand how each of these devices functions so that you can make an informed decision when it comes to time for you to either connect your network with another, or segment your existing network into smaller networks to improve performance.

Repeaters

When electrical signals traverse a medium, they attenuate (or fade) as a function of distance traveled. The longer the distance a signal travels, the lower the signal comes out at the other end. This shortcoming can be overcome with the use of a repeater. A *repeater* simply reconditions the incoming signal and retransmits it—in other words, it can be used to extend distance. Therefore, it works at the physical layer of the OSI model.

Because a repeater simply "passes on" the signals it receives, it performs no error checking. Therefore, any errors (such as CRC in Ethernet) are passed from one segment to another.

Repeaters cannot be used to connect segments of different topologies, such as Ethernet and Token Ring. However, repeaters can be used to connect segments of the same topology with different media, such as Ethernet fiber to coax Ethernet.

A repeater, such as an Ethernet multiport repeater, also can act as a signal splitter.

A repeater does not slow down your network because it performs no filtering. A repeater is transparent to protocols; however, because a device is involved, you can expect minute delays (one to two seconds).

Bridges

A *bridge* is usually used to separate traffic on a busy network. A bridge keeps track of the hardware addresses of devices for each network to which it is directly connected. The bridge examines the hardware destination address of the frame and, based on its tables, decides if the frame should be forwarded or not. If the frame needs to be forwarded, a new frame is generated.

A bridge is a *store-and-forward* device; it does not pass the original signal to the destination segment.

Consider figure 5.3. When Earth sends a frame to Jupiter, the bridge knows that (based on its internal tables) Jupiter is on the same segment (Segment A) as Earth; no frame is forwarded to the segment on the right (Segment B). However, if Earth sends a frame to Saturn, the bridge, knowing Saturn is not on the same segment as Earth, forwards the frame.

Figure 5.3
A bridged
network.

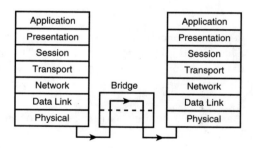

Because the bridge has access to information at the frame level, it "operates" at the data link layer of the OSI model (see fig. 5.4).

Figure 5.4
A bridge in
reference to the
OSI model.

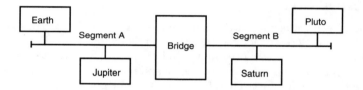

Like repeaters, bridges are transparent to protocols. Because the bridge "operates" at the data link layer, it also can perform physical layer functions. Therefore, you can use a bridge to extend the distance of a segment.

Unlike repeaters, bridges do not propagate errors from one segment to another.

The four types of bridges available today are as follows:

✔ **Transparent bridge.** The *transparent bridge* is the most common type of bridge. It does not care about the protocols on the wire. A transparent bridge also is known as the *learning bridge* because it "learns" about the hardware addresses of the devices to which it is directly attached. It also is referred to as *spanning tree bridge* because of the spanning tree algorithm (IEEE 802.1D) it uses to manage paths between segments with redundant bridges.

✔ **Source routing (SR).** The *source routing bridge* (SR) is popular in IBM Token-Ring environments. IBM uses source routing to determine whether a frame needs to cross a bridge based on ring number information within the frame.

✔ **Source route transparent (SRT).** The *source route transparent bridge* (SRT) is a combination of a transparent and a source routing bridge. It "source routes" if the data frame has the SR information, or "bridges transparently" it if does not.

✔ **Translational bridge.** Some manufacturers produce *translational bridges* that connect Ethernet to Token Ring. An example is IBM's 8209 bridge.

In general, a bridge connects segments of similar topology such as Token Ring to Token Ring. They also can connect segments of the same topology with different media (much like a repeater).

If bridges are connected through a WAN link, they are known as *remote bridges*.

Some bridges have security features that you can define—by hardware address or protocol type—as to whether frames are passed to a certain destination address. This feature enables you to filter traffic that might be destined for a specific server.

A workstation accessing resources across a bridge has slightly slower performance than a workstation accessing resources across a repeater because a bridge performs more functions than a repeater.

Routers

A *router* can determine the best route between two or more networks. A router has access to the network (software) address information, which means it operates at the network layer of the OSI model (see fig. 5.5). Because it needs to access the network address information, it is very protocol-specific. When a router encounters a datagram with a protocol it does not support, the datagram is dropped.

Figure 5.5
A router in reference to the OSI model.

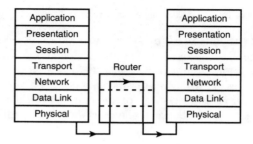

For example, if one of your networks has TCP/IP and NetWare traffic, and your router only supports TCP/IP (or only TCP/IP routing is switched on), no NetWare traffic will ever leave that segment. Therefore traffic is confined to a local segment.

A router is a much more intelligent device than a bridge; it can make decisions on selecting the best route for a datagram to reach its destination. This path can change depending on a number of factors, such as availability of link, traffic level, and others. A bridge, on the other hand, simply decides whether a frame needs to be passed on.

Routers do not pass errors from one network to another.

Because a router works at the network layer, it has no information about the topology (the frame information is stripped off by the data link layer). As a result, you can use a router to connect segments of different topologies.

Routers usually have some built-in filtering capability. The filtering is based on upper-layer protocols. For example, you can set up the filter table such that users cannot see certain servers across a given router. This type of filtering is much more powerful than filtering done with bridges.

A workstation accessing resources across a router has a slower performance than a workstation accessing resources across a bridge, which in turn is slower than when a repeater is involved. A router performs more complex functions than a bridge or repeater, resulting in slower workstation performance.

Traditionally in the IP world, routers were called *gateways* because they were the "gateway" to the outside world. However, with the accepted definition of the OSI model and standardization of internetworking terms within the industry, gateways are now called routers. Be careful, however, when reading some of the RFCs because the term "gateway" is still used liberally. Do not confuse that with the "OSI definition" of gateway as discussed in a following section.

A router connected to two or more physical networks has two or more IP addresses. In rare instances a TCP/IP host has two or more physical connections. Such a host is called a *multi-homed host*. If a multi-homed hosts's routing table is configured properly, it can function as a router.

Brouters

A *brouter* (bridging router) is a device that first routes the protocols it understands. Tailing that, it attempts to bridge the traffic.

Certain protocols (such as NetBIOS) cannot be routed because they have no network information. If you need to pass these protocols together with, for example, TCP/IP traffic, you need to use a brouter for your network.

In most cases, hardware-based routers, such as 3COM, Cisco, and Wellfleet are capable of being a brouter. Software-based ones, such as Novell's Multiprotocol Router, cannot (even though Novell's MPR 2.11+ supports Token Ring SR bridging).

Check your router documentation; not all hardware routers can function as brouters.

Gateways

A *gateway* is a device that translates between two different protocols and sometimes topologies. For example, a gateway is needed to translate between TCP/IP over Ethernet to SNA over Token Ring.

Gateways tend to be upper-layer-protocol specific, as is the e-mail protocol, for example. Therefore, if you need to exchange both e-mail and printing traffic between two hosts, two separate gateways may be needed.

Because a gateway translates most, if not all, protocol layers, it covers the entire seven layers of the OSI model.

Deciding Which Device To Use

Oftentimes, you need to do modify your current network—expand, improve performance, or add new services, for example. How can the different internetworking devices discussed in the preceding sections help? What should you use when? Look at the following two simple case studies and apply what you learned in the preceding sections.

Case Study 1

You are given a task to extend the distance of your current Ethernet coax (10BASE2) network to include another floor of the building. What device should you use?

Before you answer, ask yourself the following questions:

✔ How long is the existing network?

✔ Is traffic an issue right now? Will it be an issue with the additional distance?

✔ Is there more than one protocol on the wire? Do you need to separate them?

If the current network is within the distance specification of 10BASE2 Ethernet, and the addition of the new segment does not exceed that, you can use a repeater to extend the distance. This is the lowest cost solution.

If the addition of the new segment exceeds the 10BASE2 distance limitation, you need at least a bridge to extend the distance because the bridge has (at least) two network cards, and the other side of a bridge is considered a new network (as far as cabling goes, not protocol). Of course, you can use a router here, but it is more expensive.

A router needs to look at the software address "buried" deep within a frame; therefore, it has to do more work to get at the information. A bridge only needs to look at the hardware address, which is near the beginning of the frame, requiring less work. Therefore, as a rule of thumb, a bridge can forward data much faster than a router. A repeater does not look at any "data"; therefore, it is faster than a bridge.

In reference to the second question, if traffic is a consideration, then a bridge should be used even if distance is not an issue. A bridge keeps traffic local and only passes frames to the other side when required.

If (data link layer) broadcast traffic (frames addressed to all devices on a network) is an issue, a bridge is not a good internetworking device to use. By definition, a broadcast address is not "local"; therefore, broadcast traffic always propagates across a bridge. In such case, use a router.

Use a router if multiple protocols are on the wire. A router helps you isolate the protocols, if desired. It also helps you reduce the amount of broadcast traffic as well as manage multiple paths.

Case Study 2

Today some sites do not want multiple protocols on the wire for various reasons. In such an instance a gateway serves as an ideal solution. Consider the sample network in figure 5.6.

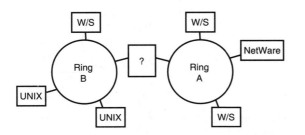

Figure 5.6
A sample network for Case Study 2.

This network contains two (Token) rings. The users on Ring A are Novell NetWare users with a NetWare server on the local ring. The Unix servers are located on Ring B; some Unix users also are on Ring B. Users on Ring A need to access a custom application on the Unix servers on Ring B, but the network management folks don't want NetWare traffic on Ring B or TCP/IP traffic on Ring A. What is the best solution?

If both TCP/IP and NetWare traffic is allowed on the rings, the solution is quite straightforward: load dual protocol stacks on the workstations on Ring A and put in either a bridge or a router to connect the two rings. Multiple protocols, however, are not permitted on the ring, which leaves only one solution: an IPX-TCP/IP gateway.

The workstations on Ring A will speak IPX (NetWare) to the gateway; the gateway will convert from IPX to TCP/IP and put them out on Ring B. Two examples of such a gateway are NOV*IX for NetWare (NLM-based) from Firefox, Inc. (408-321-8344; 800-230-6090) and Catapult (OS/2-based) from Ipswitch (617-246-1150).

Now that you know the difference between repeaters, bridges, routers, and gateways, take a look at the various routing protocols associated with TCP/IP.

IP Routing Protocols

Initially, a router only knows about the networks or subnets to which it is directly connected. It learns about other networks by two means: static routes and routing protocols.

A *static route* is a path in a router's routing table that is manually configured by a network administrator. For each network or host destination, the network administrator configures the next hop router and the cost associated with the route. This information is never changed, even if a portion of the path becomes unavailable. For example, in figure 5.7, a static route is configured for Router 1 so that to reach Network C, it must use Router 2.

Figure 5.7
A static route
example.

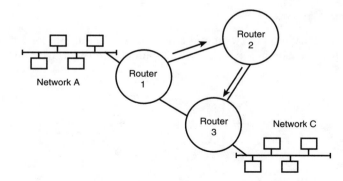

Should the path between Routers 1 and 2 or between Routers 2 and 3 go down, Router 1 cannot reach Router 3 through an alternate path until it is manually reconfigured.

This is not a problem if the connectivity between Network A and Network C is not critical, because it will take some time before Router 1 can be reconfigured. However, this option is not viable if the link is important or automated path reconfiguration is desired. In such a case, a *routing protocol* is required so that routers can exchange path information automatically and update any route changes dynamically.

A number of different routing protocols are used in the TCP/IP world. They are not compatible with each other, though. Therefore, to resolve IP routing problems it is essential that you understand them.

The four routing protocols discussed in some detail in later sections are as follows:

✔ *Routing Information Protocol* (RIP)

✔ *Open Shortest Path First* (OSPF)

✔ *Interior Gateway Routing Protocol* (IGRP)

✔ *Internet Control Message Protocol* (ICMP)

This chapter does not explain all the details of each of these protocols because you can easily refer to the *Request For Comments* (RFCs)—documents that detail the protocol—for such information. The information presented here, however, gives you a working understanding of each of the protocols.

Before learning about the individual routing protocols, however, you must understand the classification of routing protocols used today.

Classification of Routing Protocols

When dealing with internet routing, routing protocols are divided into different "classes"—*interior routing protocols* and *exterior routing protocols.*

Interior routing protocols, sometimes known as *interior gateway protocols* (IGPs), are generally used within an autonomous system to dynamically determine the best route to each network or subnet. An *autonomous system* (AS) is a group of routers that share information through the same routing protocol. Each autonomous system is assigned a unique identification number by the Network Information Center. The AS number is used by some routing protocols to control the exchange of routing information.

Exterior routing protocols, sometimes known as *interdomain routing protocols,* are used to exchange routing information between different autonomous systems.

Depending on the algorithm used to determine routes, cost of paths, and so on, routing protocols are further classified as either *distance-vector routing protocols* or *link state routing protocols.*

In *distance-vector routing protocols,* each router keeps a routing table of its perspective of the network. For example, as shown in figure 5.8, Router 1 sees that Networks A and B are one hop away (connected to directly), whereas Network C is two hops away. However, Router 2 sees Networks B and C as one hop away, and Network A as two hops away. The two routers "see" the network differently.

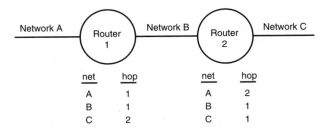

Figure 5.8
A sample network consisting of two routers and three network segments and its corresponding routing tables.

The distance-vector protocol is sometimes known as the *Ford-Fulkerson routing algorithm,* named after the inventors of the algorithm (L.R. Ford, Jr. and D.R. Fulkerson, *Flows in Networks,* Princeton University Press, 1962). The distance-vector protocol also is sometimes referred to as the *Bellman-Ford algorithm* because it was based on the Bellman Equation (R.E. Bellman, *Dynamic Programming,* Princeton University Press, 1957).

Each router takes the routing information passed to it, adds one hop to the route (to account for its own presence), and passes the updated information to the next router in line. In essence, distance-vector routing protocols use "secondhand" information from their neighbors.

Distance-vector routing protocols select the "best route" based on a *metric* ("some" unit of measurement). The metric used is different based on the actual protocol. One drawback of distance-vector routing protocols is that when routers send updates, they send entire routing tables. To keep the information up to date, the updates are *broadcast* at regular, fixed intervals.

The opposite of distance-vector routing protocols are link state routing protocols. With a link state routing protocol, a router calculates a "tree" of the entire network with itself as the root (see fig. 5.9).

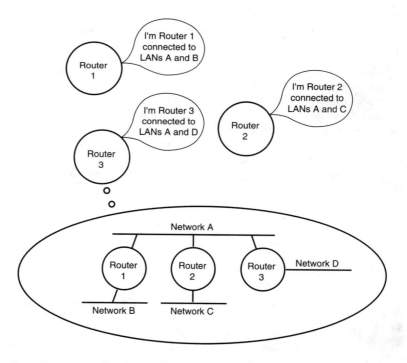

Figure 5.9
Network layout as "seen" by Router 3 using link state protocols.

In this example, Router 3 constructs a network layout based on the route information received *directly* from the other routers. Under link state, each router distributes information about its directly connected networks and their associated metrics only.

The routers only include the best path derived by the metric to other nodes (routers). When a router detects changes in the state of its direct link (for example, a link comes up or goes down), the router distributes (broadcasts) the change to all other routers through a process called *flooding*. Flooding updates every router's database because it only sends state change information (hence the name link state).

In general, these flooding packets are very small and are sent infrequently. They contribute very little to the overall broadcast traffic unless routes change often.

The following sections examine the individual routing protocols.

Routing Information Protocol (RIP)

The *Routing Information Protocol* (RIP; RFC 1508/1388) was first introduced in 1988. RIP is a *distance-vector* routing protocol as discussed earlier.

Because distance-vector routing protocols have regular, fixed update intervals, RIP's update is sent every 30 seconds.

For readers familiar with Novell's protocols, do not confuse this RIP with the RIP used by NetWare. Although they bear the same name and perform a similar function, NetWare RIPs are sent once every 60 seconds.

Therefore, in an environment in which you have both NetWare and TCP/IP, you will have RIP broadcasts from both protocols.

If a route is learned through RIP update messages, and then a subsequent update message does not refresh this route within 180 seconds (six update cycles), the route is assumed to be unreachable and is removed from the routing table.

RIP is probably the most common routing protocol used today because it is easy to implement. RIP has some serious limitations, however. For example, RIP data carry no subnet mask information, which limits RIP to advertise only network information (no subnet information), or requires RIP routers to make assumptions about the subnet mask. The latter makes it very vendor-implementation-specific and often causes interoperability problems.

If you are experiencing routing problems, check the routing tables of the routers involved and see if RIP is enabled. Some network administrators who want to cut down on the amount of broadcast traffic on their network disable RIP on the routers and use static routes instead.

Some routers enable you to adjust the RIP update timer to reduce broadcasts. If you do this, check that all other routers are configured similarly. Otherwise, you might see routes "come and go" on certain routers, resulting in intermittent routing problems.

For RIP, hop count is used as the metric. In figure 5.8 Router 1 "sees" that Network C is farther away than Network A or B because Network C has a metric (hop count) of two, whereas the others have a metric of one. If Router 1 learns (from another router not shown in the figure) of another path to Network B with, say, two hops, it discards that new route because it has a higher metric.

A RIP metric of 16 (hops) means that the destination is not reachable.

Recently some routers started supporting RIP II (RIP version 2; RFC 1388). RIP II is an enhancement over RIP that includes the subnet mask in its routes and variable length subnets, which enables subnet information to be passed on correctly. Also, authentication on routing update messages can be performed.

Not all RIP routers support RIP II. Make sure that your routers use the same protocol.

Some routers, such as Novell's Multiprotocol Router, can support RIP I and RIP II simultaneously.

The biggest disadvantage of distance-vector protocols such as RIP is the time it takes for the information to spread to all routers. This period is known as the *convergence* time. For a large network, the convergence time can indeed be long; and during this time, data frames have a much greater chance of getting misrouted and lost because of the "count-to-infinity" problem illustrated as follows.

Using the distance-vector algorithm, the distances between Network D and the various routers are as follows (see fig. 5.10):

✔ One hop from Router 3 (directly connected)

✔ Two hops from Router 2 (through Router 3)

✔ Three hops from Router 1 (through Routers 2 and 3)

If Router 3 fails or the link between Routers 2 and 3 is down, Router 2 removes Network D's route from its routing table by setting the metric for Network D to 16. However, Router 2 sends a RIP update to Router 3 indicating that it can reach Network D at a lower cost (two hops). Router 3 then adds one hop count to this route and updates its routing table with this new route (reach Network D through Router 2).

Router 2 thinks it can reach Network D through Router 3 (in two hops), and Router 3 thinks it can reach Network D through Router 2 (in three hops). You now have a routing loop! In this case, any data destined for Network D is routed back and forth between Routers 2 and 3 until its time-to-live counter expires.

However, over time as the routers continue to update among themselves, the hop count to Network D continually increases and eventually reaches 16 hops (infinity; unreachable), and the entry is removed from all routers. But as you can see, it can take a while, especially if you have a large network of routers.

RIP uses a technique called *split horizon* to prevent such routing loops—no routing information is passed back in the direction from which it was received. For example, Router 1 informs Router 2 that it is one hop away from Network A. Router 2 takes that information, adds one to the hop count for Network A, and passes that to Router 3 on Network C, but *not* back to Router 1 because that is the router from which it received the information.

Split horizon helps solve the count-to-infinity problem if you have a linear network. Most networks, however, contain redundant routes for fault-tolerant purposes, which reduces the effectiveness of split horizon. Figure 5.11 shows a network with multiple paths.

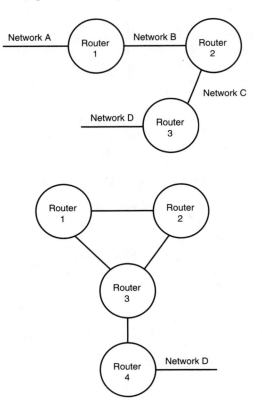

Figure 5.10
A simple count-to-infinity problem.

Figure 5.11
A complex count-to-infinity problem that involves multiple paths.

I

Overview

Router 3 informs Routers 1 and 2 that Network D is two hops away from it; thus the routing tables in Routers 1 and 2 list Network D as three hops away. If Router 4 fails or the link between Routers 3 and 4 goes down, Router 3 will know that Network D is no longer reachable and will inform Routers 1 and 2 of the fact. Through split horizon, Routers 1 and 2 cannot tell Router 3 about their routes to Network D right away. However, between Routers 1 and 2 a "valid" path still exists.

Router 1 learns from Router 2 that it is two hops away from Network D. Router 1 adds one hop to that route and passes the information (3 hops to Network D) to Router 3, but not to Router 2 because of split horizon. Router 1 can pass information about Network D to Router 3 because Router 3 no longer advertises a route to Network D. Router 3 now thinks it is four hops away from Network D through Router 1. Router 3 passes that information to Router 2. Router 2 now thinks it is five hops away from Network D through Router 3. Router 2 propagates this to Router 1. Router 1 turns this into six hops, and passes this information to Router 3. Eventually, a hop count of 16 is reached, and split horizon didn't help much!

What can you do? You can use two more tricks: *poisoned reverse* and *triggered updates*, described in the following paragraphs.

With split horizon, routes are not advertised back onto the interface from which they were learned. With *poisoned reverse* enabled, however, such routes *are* advertised back to the same interface from which they are learned, but with a metric of 16. This immediately breaks the routing loop between any two routers. It helps to speed up the convergence time in the count-to-infinity problem, but does not necessarily eliminate it entirely.

Following are two packet captures taken using Novell's LANalyzer for Windows v2.1. This sample IP network has two routers. Router 1 is connected to IP networks 126.0.0.0 (with address 126.1.1.1) and 125.0.0.0 (with IP address 125.1.1.1). Router 2 is connected to IP networks 126.0.0.0 (IP address 126.2.2.2) and 120.0.0.0 (IP address 120.1.1.1). Router 2 has poisoned reverse enabled. Following is the RIP update from Router 126.1.1.1:

```
    Station:126.1.1.1 ---->255.255.255.255
    Protocol: UDP
        Version: 4
        Header Length (32 bit words): 5
        Precedence: Routine
               Normal Delay, Normal Throughput, Normal Reliability
        Total length:   52
        Identification:        802
        Fragmentation allowed, Last fragment
        Fragment Offset: 0
        Time to Live: 128 seconds
        Checksum: 0xB895(Valid)
udp: ================== User Datagram Protocol ==================
```

```
            Source Port: ROUTER
            Destination Port: ROUTER
            Length = 32
            Checksum: 0x0000(checksum not used)
rip: ============== Routing Information Protocol ===============
            Command: Response
            Version: 1
            Family ID: IP
                  IP Address: 125.0.0.0
                  Distance: 1
```

The RIP update from Router 126.2.2.2 when poisoned reverse is used is as follows:

```
            Station:126.2.2.2 ---->255.255.255.255
            ...
            Precedence: Routine
                      Normal Delay, Normal Throughput, Normal Reliability
            Total length: 92
            ...
 udp: =================== User Datagram Protocol =================
            Source Port: ROUTER
            Destination Port: ROUTER
            Length = 72
            Checksum: 0x0000(checksum not used)
rip: =============== Routing Information Protocol ===============
            Command: Response
            Version: 1
            Family ID: IP
                  IP Address: 120.0.0.0
                  Distance: 1
            Family ID: IP
                  IP Address: 125.0.0.0
                  Distance: Not Reachable
            Family ID: IP
                  IP Address: 126.0.0.0
                  Distance: Not Reachable
```

As you see in the first of the preceding two examples, Router 1 advertises to network 126.0.0.0 a route to network 125.0.0.0 with a hop count (distance) of one as expected. In the second example, Router 2 advertises a route to network 120.0.0.0 with a hop count of one, also as expected. Because it has poisoned reverse enabled, however, Router 2 also advertises network 125.0.0.0 (its local network) and network 126.0.0.0 (learned from Router 1) as not reachable.

A quick comparison between the RIP packets in the preceding examples shows that poisoned reverse generates more update traffic (larger update messages). On a large network, especially on a backbone, this level of traffic can cause traffic problems.

Consider the case of a building backbone connecting a number of different floors. On each floor, a router connects the backbone to a local network. Using split horizon, only the local network information is broadcast onto the backbone. But with poisoned reverse, the router's update message includes all the routes it learned from the backbone (with a metric of 16), as well as its own local network. For a large network, almost all the entries in the routing update message indicate unreachable networks.

In many cases, network administrators choose simply to use split horizon *without* poisoned reverse to conserve bandwidth and accept the slower convergence time.

If your router supports triggered updates coupling it with poisoned reverse can greatly minimize convergence time. *Triggered updates* cause the router to send a RIP update when a route's metric is changed, even if it is not yet time for a regular update message.

Be careful in the use of triggered updates because they can cause much broadcast traffic, similar to a broadcast storm.

The count-to-infinity problem in using RIP can be avoided by designing your network without router loops.

If you must have multiple paths for redundancy, consider using a routing protocol other than RIP, such as OSPF as discussed later. Or simply keep in mind how RIP works, fix your downed link as soon as you can, or reset the routers to force a new routing table to be built.

Configuring Interface Routes

At boot time most hosts run a network configuration file, and each interface is configured. A routing table entry also is created for each interface. The interface is normally configured by the TCP/IP ifconfig command, as shown in the following example:

```
ifconfig lan0 9.67.111.214 netmask 255.255.240.0
```

This command configures the lan0 interface with an IP address of 9.67.111.214 and a netmask of 255.255.240.0. This IP address is on network 9.67.96.0 (obtained by performing a BITWISE AND between 9.67.111.214 and 255.255.240). The following routing table entry is created for the interface:

```
destination        router    flags intrf
    9.67.96.0   9.67.111.214    U     lan0
```

The H flag is not set because this is not a route to a host, and the G flag is not set because this is not a route to a router.

Assigning Static Routes

For simple networks, or networks whose configuration changes relatively infrequently, creating a static routing table using the TCP/IP route command is often efficient. This command provides a mechanism to manipulate the routing table by adding, modifying, and deleting table entries. For example, you can use the following command to create a default route to a network router whose IP address is 9.67.96.1:

```
route add default 9.67.96.1 1
```

The digit 1 following the IP address is referred to as the "hop count" and represents the distance (in number of routers) to the destination host or network.

Interior Gateway Routing Protocol (IGRP)

For a long time on the Internet, routers used the *Interior Gateway Routing Protocol* (IGRP) to exchange routing information. Although IGRP is a distance-vector routing protocol, it uses a number of variables to determine the metric, including the following:

✔ Bandwidth of the link

✔ Delay due to the link

✔ Load on the link

✔ Reliability of the link

By considering these variables, IGRP has a much better, and real-time, handle on the link status between routers. IGRP is much more flexible than RIP, which is based solely on hop count. IGRP can better reflect the type of link and choose a more appropriate path than RIP. In figure 5.11, the links between Router 1 and Router 3 and Router 1 and Router 2 are T1 links, whereas the link between Router 2 and Router 3 is a 56K line. RIP doesn't know the difference in line speed between the paths and sends traffic over the slower 56K line rather than the T1 lines simply because it has a lower hop count. IGRP uses the more efficient T1 lines.

The update interval for IGRP is every 90 seconds, as compared to every 30 seconds for RIP. However, like RIP, when an update is sent, the whole routing table is sent also.

IGRP was developed by Cisco Systems, Inc., which is why for a long time when you acquired a link to the Internet, you were required to use a Cisco router. Now IGRP is supported by many other router vendors.

Open Shortest Path First (OSPF)

Open Shortest Path First (OSPF) is a link state routing protocol first introduced in 1989 (RFC 1131/1247/1583). More and more IP sites are converting to OSPF from RIP because of its much lower traffic overhead and because it completely eliminates the count-to-infinity problem.

Using "cost" as the metric, OSPF can support a much larger internet than RIP. Remember in a RIP-based internet, you cannot have more than 15 routers between any two networks, which sometimes results in having to implement more links for large networks.

Similar to RIP II, OSPF supports variable length subnetting, which enables the network administrator to use a different subnet mask for each segment of the network. Variable length subnetting greatly increases the flexibility and number of subnets and hosts possible for a single network address. OSPF also supports authentication on update messages.

Using cost, an OSPF metric can be as large as 65535.

Other than exchanging routing information within an autonomous system, OSPF also can exchange routing information with other routing protocols, such as RIP and *Exterior Gateway Protocol* (EGP). This exchange can be performed using an *autonomous system border router.*

If you are using multivendor routers in a mixed RIP and OSPF environment, make sure that routes are redistributed between routing protocols in a consistent manner. To create routing loops because a vendor does not increment the hop count when going from RIP to OSPF and back to RIP is possible.

To go into the details of OSPF concepts, OSPF areas, and other OSPF protocols (such as the OSPF Hello Protocol) is beyond the scope of this chapter. Refer to RFC 1583 for the latest definition of OSPF Version 2.

Internet Control Message Protocol (ICMP)

Sometimes even if you have not configured dynamic routing on an IP router, routes can be automatically added to your routing table by the *Internet Control Message Protocol* (ICMP).

ICMP was first introduced in 1980 (RFC 792/1256). Its function is to provide a dynamic means to ensure that your system has an up-to-date routing table. ICMP is part of any TCP/IP implementation and is enabled automatically. No configuration is necessary. ICMP messages provide many functions, including route redirection.

If your workstation forwards a packet to a router, for example, and that router is aware of a shorter path to your destination, the router sends your workstation a "redirection" message informing it of the shorter route.

The newer implementation of ICMP (RFC 1256) contains a *router discovery* feature. Strictly speaking, router discovery is not a routing protocol, but a way of finding neighboring routers. When a router starts up, it sends a router discovery request (multicast address 244.0.0.2; broadcast only if the interface does not support multicast) asking neighboring routers to identify themselves. Only routers directly attached to the network that the new router is on respond.

Router discovery is a rather new implementation for some routers and therefore is not supported by all routers.

Other Routing Protocols

The protocols discussed earlier are all *interior gateway protocols* (IGPs), and they are by far the most often encountered routing protocols in the field. However, at times you might encounter some exterior routing protocols. *Exterior routing protocols* are used to connect two or more autonomous systems (see fig. 5.12). Two exterior routing protocols—*Exterior Gateway Protocol* (EGP; RFC 827/904) and *Border Gateway Protocol* (BGP; RFC 1105/1163/1267)—are briefly discussed in this section so that you can become familiar with them.

Introduced in 1982, EGP is the earliest exterior routing protocol. Routers using EGP are called *exterior routers*. Exterior routers share only reachability information with their neighboring exterior routers. EGP provides no routing information—an EGP router simply advertises *a* route to a network; therefore no load-balancing is possible on an EGP network.

In 1989, BGP was introduced. BGP uses TCP as the transport layer connection to exchange messages. Full path information is exchanged between BGP routers, thus the best route is used between autonomous systems.

Autonomous System 1
RIP
Router 1
Exterior routing protocol used
Autonomous System 2
Router 2
OSPF

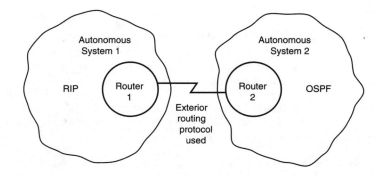

Figure 5.12 Linking two autonomous systems using an exterior routing protocol.

Default Routes

In general, to create a separate routing table entry for every remote network in your internetwork is not necessary. If a *default network* (sometimes called *default router* or simply *default route*) entry exists in your routing table, then packets destined for networks not specifically listed in the routing table are forwarded to that router.

A default router entry is simply an entry in the routing table whose destination is network 0.0.0.0. Figure 5.13 shows an example of such an entry for a NetWare server/router. In this setup, any packets for, say, network 120.1.1.15 are forwarded to router at 126.2.2.2 because the local router doesn't know how to handle it, and 126.2.2.2 is listed as the default router.

TCP/IP Console v1.01 (910801)
NetWare 386 Loadable Module
Host: 126.1.1.1 Uptime: 0 Days 1 Hour 32 Minutes 51 Seconds
Novell NetWare v3.11 (250 user) 2/20/91
ipReceives: 1,285
tcpReceives: 0
udpReceives: 1,246
ipTransmits: 1,524
tcpTransmits: 0
udpTransmits: 1,505
ipForwards: 0
tcpConnects: 0
TCP/IP Tables
Routing Table
Destination Next Hop Intf Cost Type
0.0.0.0 126.2.2.2 1 3 remote
125.0.0.0 125.1.1.1 3 1 direct
126.0.0.0 126.1.1.1 1 1 direct
<End of Table>

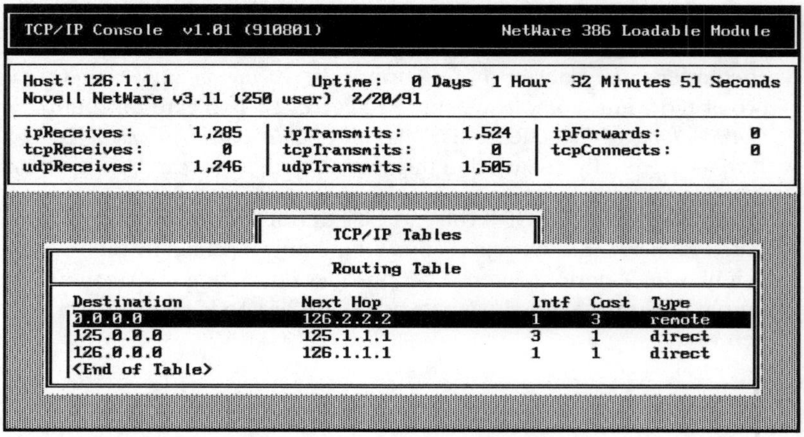

Figure 5.13 A default route entry on a NetWare server/router.

A default route entry is useful when you are not using any routing protocols on your network—for example, if you turned off RIP to save on the bandwidth, but your routers don't support other routing protocols such as OSPF. You do not need to create a static route for each router on your network or subnets on your internet. You can use a default router entry on most routers to "point" to a few central routers that have more complete routing tables.

Some Internet service providers do not use RIP for their connections. Therefore, if you are connected through such a service provider, you might need to use a default router entry to gain access to the Internet.

Path of an IP Packet

Now that you know how routes are determined between your networks and subnet, look at what happens to a frame when it is sent from a workstation to a host as it crosses bridges and routers. The sample network in figure 5.14 consists of two segments bridged together and a router connecting them to a third segment; the default network masks are used—255.0.0.0 for network 126.0.0.0 and 255.255.0.0 for network 133.7.0.0.

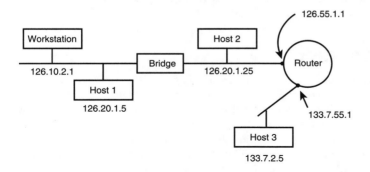

Figure 5.14
A sample network that consists of two bridged segments and one routed segment.

Local Segment

In figure 5.14, the workstation (126.10.2.1) wants to communicate with Host 1 (126.20.1.5). The TCP/IP software in the workstation determines that the destination is on the same network (126.0.0.0); therefore sending data between Workstation 1 and Host 1 does not need to involve a router.

To compose the frame at the data link layer, the TCP/IP software needs the hardware address, also known as the *Data Link Control* (DLC) address or *Media Access Control* (MAC) address, of Host 1. The TCP/IP software finds the hardware address using the *Address Resolution Protocol* (ARP). TCP/IP inserts the DLC address in the destination address field of the frame and its own DLC address (determined from the NIC installed) in the source address field. The frame is then transmitted onto the wire.

Both Host 1 and the bridge "see" this frame. The bridge, however, based on its learned table of addresses, knows Host 1 is on the same side as the workstation; therefore the bridge ignores the frame.

Host 1 sees its own address in the destination field, takes the frame, and processes it. Host 1 uses the DLC address in the source address field as the destination address in its reply messages. In this manner two devices learn about each other's DLC addresses.

Bridged Segment

The communication process in a bridged IP network environment is not much different than the local segment scenario discussed previously. Should the frame need to cross the bridge (to reach Host 2), the workstation uses ARP to obtain the DLC address for Host 2. The workstation then uses the DLC address in the destination field, puts its own address in the source field, and transmits the frame onto the wire.

In this case, the bridge notices that the destination address is listed on its other segment. Therefore, the bridge makes a copy of the frame and puts a copy on the other side—without changing anything, not even the DLC addresses.

Host 2 sees the frame and processes it, not knowing it actually came across a bridge. Remember, bridges are transparent to protocols.

Routed Segment

In a routed environment, the data frame addressing is a little more complicated than in the two cases previously covered. First, the workstation determines that the destination (Host 3) is *not* on its own network; therefore, it needs to use a router. However, which router is used if multiple routers are on the segment? When you install the TCP/IP software on a workstation, you are generally asked to specify a default router. This entry is not used if you are communicating locally. When you need to communicate outside your network, however, all frames are addressed to this default router.

Some workstation software (such as Novell's LAN WorkPlace for DOS v4.1 and higher) enables you to define multiple default routers, which give you some backup paths. Be careful, however, in load-balancing the specification so that no given router is overloaded.

The workstation finds the DLC address of the router by using ARP as in the preceding two cases. The TCP/IP network drive software puts the router's DLC address as the destination, rather than Host 3's address. This key concept is very important—in a bridged environment, the DLC address of the bridge is not involved in data frame addressing. In a routed environment, however, the router's DLC address (and IP address) is involved.

After the router receives the frame, it "unpacks" the frame by stripping off the DLC information. The router looks at the IP information (IP destination address) and checks with its routing table to see where the next stop is. If the destination is on a network directly connected to this router (as in the earlier simple example), the router uses the ARP protocol to determine the DLC address of Host 3 and creates a new *frame* using that information and its own DLC address. Host 3 knows the frame came from a router because the source IP network within the frame is different from its own network. The replies from Host 3 back to the workstation follow the reverse path.

If, however, the first router is not directly connected to the destination network, the router looks in its routing table to find where the next hop is, uses the ARP protocol to determine that router's DLC address, and sends a new frame with the new information. This process continues until the frame reaches a router directly connected to the destination network.

Now you can see why it is important to have the routing tables of *all* your routers up-to-date and consistent with each other. Any old routing information along the path of the frame results in lost data, causing retransmission in the best case and application crashes and incapability to communicate throughout your internet in the worst case.

Summary

This chapter introduced and defined the various devices used in internetworking, such as bridges and routers. Two simple case studies were used to illustrate how to select the appropriate device for a given environment. The various IP routing protocols, such as RIP and OSPF, were discussed in depth, including their strengths and limitations. The chapter discussed the classic count-to-infinity problem and various options, such as poisoned reverse and split horizon, to minimize this effect. Finally, the IP routing process was illustrated.

Chapter Snapshot

This chapter explores the topics of Frame Relay and *Asynchronous Transfer Mode* (ATM). Although popular conversation for many, there are far more people talking about the technologies and possibilities they hold, than there are implementing them. The topics of discussion include the following:

Overview of Frame Relay and ATM

"There is no security on this earth; there is only opportunity."

—*Douglas MacArthur*

Broadband packet networking is an evolving new technology. Although the transport of TCP/IP protocol managed data using this technology is available today, ever-changing requirements and standards require flexible hardware and software implementations. It is important to understand the fundamental building blocks of broadband data transport to get an edge on the technology of the future. Many of these evolving transport schemes are discussed in this chapter.

Frame Relay and Asynchronous Transfer Mode (ATM), two of the most popular broadband packet technologies, provide a great advantage over traditional T-1 for TCP/IP protocol-oriented transmissions. Frame Relay, a packet-based high-speed technology, provides high throughput, low delay, and dynamic bandwidth allocation. Because of Frame Relay's relatively easy upgrade path for X.25 network users, it has gained popularity for use in LAN-WAN-LAN and *Metropolitan Area Networks* (MAN) links.

ATM is a broadband telecommunication network based on the concepts of universal interfaces, bandwidth-on-demand, hardware-based packet interconnects, and multimedia traffic integration. As a result of its versatility, ATM is quickly becoming the standard choice for *Local Exchange Carriers* (LEC) and *Inter-Exchange Carriers* (IXC) that handle public-packet-switched networks. ATM is an excellent service for integrating data, voice, and video.

Some of the terminology used in WAN and internetworking concepts might be foreign to readers unfamiliar with the telecommunications industry. *Public Data Networks* (PDNs) are most commonly maintained by LECs—local telephone service providers — or IXCs — long-distance service providers.

As a result of the AT&T divestiture, *Local Access and Transport Areas* (LATAs) were established to determine if a service was local or long distance. A MAN is a public-switched data network that is operated within LATA boundaries (Intra-LATA) by an LEC or sometimes an IXC across LATA boundaries (Inter-LATA). MAN links are larger in physical size than *local area network* (LAN) links yet typically smaller than *wide area network* (WAN) links. These terms become more important to you when you begin to explore purchasing ATM and Frame Relay services.

Understanding Packet-Switched Networking

The traditional host-to-dumb terminal connections (circuit switching) required continuous links for sending and receiving data. The terminal would signal the host and receive data one screen at a time. As LANs developed into file-based servers and intelligent workstations began appearing on desktops, the type of information requested from hosts changed. File-based networks increased the size of data transmitted but reduced the number of requests for host-to-workstation data transfer. Reductions in the number of requests occurred because workstations could now process the data instead of only receiving results from host data processing.

Transmissions over continuous links began to come in random bursts, and larger files began taking longer and longer to transmit. The bandwidth required for host to terminal connections was much smaller than that needed to transmit the larger files. Smaller LANs that used backbone network connections for server-to-server file transfers began appearing. Economics came into play because more bandwidth required more money, and most networks did not require high bandwidth all the time. Users demanded more bandwidth sometimes and new workstations all the time. This dilemma gave birth to packet-switched networking.

Packetizing Data

Compared to the traditional circuit switching, packet switching excels in its higher reliability and better utilization of bandwidth. Packet switching breaks down the users' data into smaller pieces, and multiple transmissions from several terminals can be mixed into one channel.

Before data can be transported across the network it must be converted into a format that the network transport hardware can manipulate. *Packetizing* data requires the use of a multiplexer to "cut" the signal into frames, a concept that is naturally called *framing*. Two forms of multiplexing are relevant to packetizing data: *Time Division Multiplexing* and *Packet* or *Statistical Multiplexing*.

Time Division Multiplexing and Dedicated T-1

Time Division Multiplexing provides a dedicated and continuous channel for sending data. However, it provides this continuous channel to a greater number of users through multiplexing because the multiplexer enables each user to send a message over a short time slice. The multiplexer cycles through each user's time slice so quickly that each channel signal appears to be continuous.

Fractional T-1 services are provided using Time Division Multiplexing. A bandwidth fractional T-1 line can contain several user channels divided into increments of 64 Kbps. Bandwidth fractional T-1 is fast, cheap, not protocol-oriented, and provides the delay-free transmission required for synchronous protocols, such as X.25 and SNA.

A Time Division Multiplexing frame contains one framing header and one data packet for each of the data channels that make up the T-1's bandwidth.

Figure 6.1 diagrams Time Division Multiplexing data streams in relation to Statistical Multiplexed data streams.

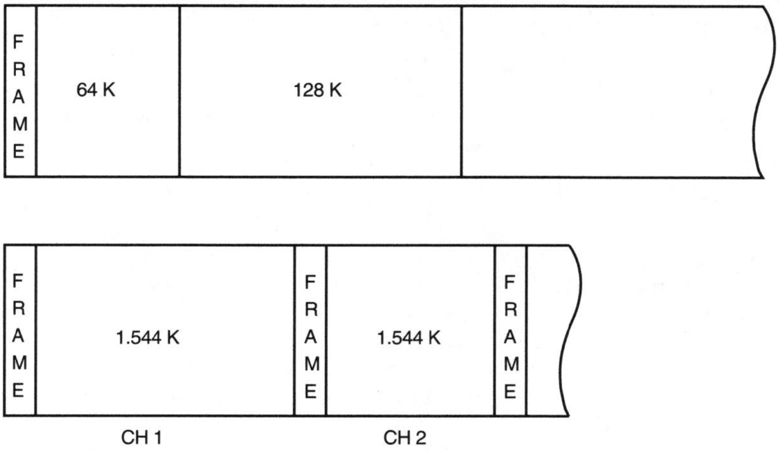

Figure 6.1
Time Division and Statisical Multiplexed Transmissions.

Statistical Multiplexing and Bandwidth on Demand

Statistical or Packet Multiplexing provides for the transmission of data in packets whose sizes are determined by the total available bandwidth. Cutting a data stream into packets enables users to transmit data at greater bandwidths on demand, one user at a time. As previously discussed, bursts of file-sized transmissions require greater bandwidth, but the additional bandwidth is required only occasionally.

Statistical Multiplexing creates a frame that divides each packet up with a framing byte, header, payload, and a trailer. The header contains the channel number or circuit that the data travels on the network. On networks using Frame Relay and ATM, this circuit number changes as the data passes from packet switch to packet switch because of the connection-oriented nature of these technologies. This topic is discussed in more detail later in this chapter.

Frames and Cells

A major difference between broadband packet networks is the structure of the packets—the basic element of transmission. Two types of packets, frames and cells, are constructed by framing to carry data over the network.

A *frame* is a block of variable length identified by a label at layer 2 of the OSI reference model (an HDLC block, for example). Based on a fixed partition, each frame is divided into an overhead and an information payload portion. This payload generally contains an entire native mode message. If the higher-level protocol is TCP/IP, this payload is an IP datagram, which creates a packet of upper-layer TCP data for transporting over the network. This IP datagram, often called a *Packet Data Unit* (PDU), consists of all the upper-layer protocol data and their headers. The entire PDU is encapsulated into the frame payload.

A *cell*, a block of information of short fixed length, contains an overhead section and a payload section. ATM is a data communications network whereby information is organized into cells, fixed in length at a standard size of 53 octets. ATM is regarded as asynchronous because the transmission of cells containing information from an individual user is not necessarily timed periodically.

As a result of the fixed size of the cell, it takes more time to construct a cell than a frame. Whereas frames expand to encapsulate the entire PDU, cells might need to split the PDU into several units of fixed size before they can be sent out. ATM is a multiplexing technique in which transmission capability is organized in undedicated slots or cells that can be filled with data to meet a user's instantaneous need.

The distinction between frames and cells becomes important in relation to different broadband packet technologies. Frame Relay technology uses frames; ATM uses cell payloads. ATM cells are the reason ATM is sometimes called *cell relay*.

Encapsulation

Before data can be transported across the public packet network, it must be loaded into a frame or cell. Frame Relay and ATM do not transport TCP/IP data in native IP datagram format. In fact, neither technology cares what is in its payload; they simply transport frames or cells.

Regardless of ATM and Frame Relay's indifference, the TCP/IP protocol is concerned that the data sent over the packet network is readable. However, the TCP/IP transport layer cannot communicate directly over ATM or Frame Relay circuits. *Encapsulation* is the process by which TCP/IP datagrams are loaded into frames or cells for transport over the network.

Encapsulation really begins with the construction of the PDU. A simple encapsulation sequence looks something like figure 6.2. The process may be initiated at the application layer using a simple FTP request. User data is transferred over the TCP/IP FTP link. FTP sends the data to be transferred to TCP for a protocol-governed transmission over the Frame Relay network. TCP creates what is often called a *TCP segment*, which is created when TCP attaches TCP-relevant information to the FTP data packet. TCP then delivers the TCP segment to IP. IP adds to the TCP segment IP-relevant information and turns the now fully constructed PDU over to the link level control layer for transmission over a Frame Relay network. The Frame Relay frame is completed when the PDU is encapsulated into the payload section of the Frame Relay frame.

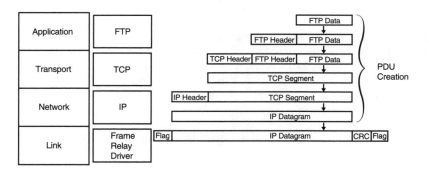

Figure 6.2
Encapsulation of FTP data.

General Broadband Networking Concepts

Even more important to the understanding of TCP/IP protocol transport over WANs is a basic knowledge of the connections that ATM and Frame Relay establish. Complex networks require a complex combination of hardware and software components. Understanding the intercommunications among these components is crucial to establishing host to remote client connections.

B-ISDN

Broadband Packet-Switched Networking or *Broadband Integrated Services Data Network* (B-ISDN) supports switched, semi-permanent and permanent broadband connections for both point-to-point and point-to-multipoint applications. B-ISDN connections support both circuit mode and packet mode services of single media, mixed media, and multi-media. The service can be of either a connectionless or connection-oriented nature. As well, B-ISDN supports bidirectional or unidirectional configurations.

B-ISDN carries two types of traffic: *constant bit rate* (CBR) and *variable bit rate* (VBR). The services that B-ISDN provides are interactive and distribution services. The inter-active services include three classes: conversational services, messaging services, and retrieval services. The distribution services are divided into two classes: one with "user individual presentation control" and one without "user individual presentation control."

Permanent versus Switched Virtual Circuits

Virtual Circuits consist of two components: the *Virtual Path* and the *Virtual Channel.* Each physical link in the network contains several Virtual Paths, each of which contains several Virtual Channels. Between two customer sites there is established a *Virtual Circuit.* The Virtual Path determines the route a particular Virtual Circuit takes between the transmit-ter and receiver. Virtual Paths interconnect user ports. Different portions of a Virtual Path may be carried over different physical links, and the Virtual Paths between source and destination pairs may share the same physical links.

Virtual channels are used to differentiate among several Virtual Circuits that may be established between two users at the same time, all of which share the same Virtual Path. Between two users, several virtual channels can be multiplexed onto the same Virtual Path. Between the same user ports, each Virtual Path may carry several multiplexed virtual channels. The virtual channel number and the Virtual Circuit in the ATM cell header together form the Virtual Path.

A *Permanent Virtual Circuit* (PVC) is a connection established by a broadband packetized network that is never disconnected between two predefined endpoints of the transmis-sion. The predefined endpoints of a PVC are defined for the service provider at the time the connection is established between two user sites—between an office in Portland and an office in Indianapolis, for instance. Hence, a PVC is always established between the two endpoints' hardware links and is never disconnected. Data frames may take many undetermined paths as they travel through the packet-switched network; however, the end points are always predetermined.

Not every packet-switched network uses PVC. X.25 networks use a type of *Switched Virtual Circuit* (SVC). SVCs enable the user to "dial" into the endpoints of the transmission. One thing that distinguishes a SVC from a permanent Virtual Circuit is that SVC establishes a connection between two endpoints only for the period of time needed for transmitting data between the two connections. Both permanent and switched Virtual Circuits appear in B-ISDN. Each endpoint might have one or more permanent Virtual Circuits to each of several other endpoints; these might be used to enable that endpoint to offer connectionless service to its user. Frame Relay is designed to support both PVC and SVC.

Connection Oriented versus Connectionless Communications

Both communications protocols and communications network services take either a connection-oriented or connectionless definition. This distinction is important to understand how the various components of TCP/IP utilize broadband networking technology.

Connection-oriented communications services provide for the establishment of a circuit (continuous open channel) between two sites. Such a connection is often called a permanent Virtual Circuit. PVCs, discussed previously, are a form of Virtual Circuit used in packet-switched networks. In the TCP/IP protocol suite, TCP is a connection-oriented protocol—TCP sets up a connection monitoring session between two hosts for the transport of data and ensures the integrity of the connection throughout the file transport "conversation."

Connectionless communications operate in the absence of a continuous open channel between two communicating host sites. Connectionless communications schemes are used to transport data where speed is more important than the integrity of the data sent, but this doesn't mean that data integrity is not handled at another layer of the communications protocol. Connectionless protocols broadcast packets with addresses on them for eventual delivery at their destination host site. Upper layer protocol functions ensure that the data is correctly rebuilt at the host site or retransmitted if an error is detected.

IP is a connectionless protocol of TCP/IP. However, IP is used on connection-oriented and connectionless communications networks. To clarify this point, it is necessary to understand how TCP/IP transports data over each type of broadband network technology.

Frame Relay and TCP/IP

Frame Relay is a versatile connection-oriented packetized data communications service. It usually provides most users with the most cost-efficient upgrade path for WAN connections previously using X.25 and TCP/IP.

Overview of Frame Relay

Frame Relay is a standard that specifies how the network and DTE interface. Frame Relay is a high-speed multiplexed data networking technology. It carries variable-length data units over an assigned virtual connection. The Frame Relay protocol only supports data transmission over a connection-oriented path. It can be deployed in a private network or obtained from a public network. The Frame Relay services provide shared bandwidth on demand and multiple-user sessions over a single access line that is available in the United States today with a speed up to 1.544 Mbps. If compared with the traditional packet-switched services, the Frame Relay has the benefits of reducing network delays, providing more efficient bandwidth utilization, and increasing communication equipment cost. One of the current major applications of Frame Relay is for LAN interconnection as diagrammed in figure 6.3.

Figure 6.3
A LAN to LAN (WAN) connection using a PDN.

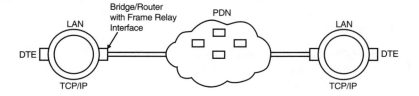

Frame Relay defines a standardized format for data link layer frames transmitted over a network of interconnected LANs or over a public network. User equipment generates a Frame Relay frame that Frame Relay nodal processors or the remote router will process. Frame Relay standards specify the user interface, called *Frame Relay interface* (FRI), between the user and the device or network. An FRI can handle access speeds of 56 Kbps, nx64 Kbps, 1.544 Mbps, and up to 45 Mbps. When using an IXC or VAN service, the user needs a dedicated T1 or 56-Kbps link to the IXC's or VAN's POP. If the LEC serving the user's location provides the service, the dedicated T1 is required only to the serving central office.

Frame Relay, built on the existing X.25 technology, provides a faster, protocol-oriented data transfer. The streamlining of X.25 into Frame Relay data frames is accomplished in several steps. First the X.25 network layer (layer 3) is removed. Then a statistical multi-plexing capability is added through the individually addressed frames to the data link layer. Finally, error correction and retransmission capabilities are removed to reduce the functionality of layer 2. Error detection is retained, but errored frames are discarded by the Frame Relay network. A comparison of X.25 and Frame Relay, and the OSI reference model are shown in figure 6.4.

Frame Relay is designed to support both PVC and SVC services, but currently only PVCs are supported. PVCs form a fixed path through the network so that the receiving end can efficiently reassemble a message or a file. With minimal processing, frames are passed by the network nodes across the network. All of the bandwidth on the physical path of the frame is available for the duration of the frame. The result is a high-speed, low-delay, bandwidth-on-demand network, well-suited for LAN-to-LAN traffic. Frame Relay has the inherent multiplexing capability in which one physical access can support up to 1,024 logical connections.

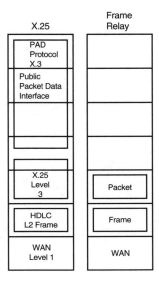

Figure 6.4
A comparison of
Frame Relay and
X.25 OSI.

The main advantages for the Frame Relay user in connecting TCP/IP networks over long distances include the following:

✔ **Protocol-oriented traffic.** Older X.25 networks provided for data integrity checking. This level of error checking is redundant when using TCP/IP, and reducing the overhead required by X.25 to perform it provides for speedier transmissions. This is exactly what Frame Relay does.

✔ **Low noise transmission lines.** Frame Relay is better positioned to take advantage of changes in technology that lead to clearer, thus error-free, transmissions. This occurs because the level of error checking is in your control, because it is at the protocol versus the network level.

✔ **Speed.** Frame Relay is a form of broadband packet switching. Using statistical multiplexing over T-1, T-3, and OC-1, Frame Relay is capable of speeds from 1.56 to 44.6 Mbps.

The Frame Relay Frame

Two basic types of data packets that travel within the Frame Relay network are *routed packets* and *bridged packets*. Because these packets have distinct formats, they contain a fixed number of indicators to assist with transmission. The destination uses this indicator to precisely interpret the contents of the frame. The indicator is embedded within the *Network Layer Protocol ID* (NLPID) and the *Subnetwork Access Protocol* (SNAP) header. For those protocols that do not have an NLPID assigned beforehand, a mechanism is provided to facilitate easy protocol identification. An NLPID value is defined to indicate the presence of a SNAP header. All stations must be able to accept and properly interpret the NLPID encapsulation, as well as the SNAP header encapsulation for a routed packet. This section discusses only the routed packets. Interested readers can refer to RFC 1490 to learn about the bridged packets.

The Q.922 Annex data link layer protocol with two octets address header encapsulate packets of a protocol. Q.922 addresses contain a 10-bit DLCI. In some networks, Q.922 addresses may optionally be increased to three or four octets. Frames contain information necessary to identify the protocol carried within the *Protocol Data Unit* (PDU), thus allowing the receiver to properly process the incoming packet. The format of Frame Relay frames is diagrammed in figure 6.5.

Figure 6.5
Components of the Frame Relay frame.

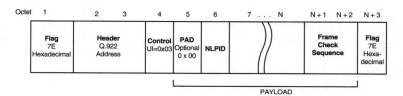

Frame Flag

As shown in figure 6.5, each frame begins and ends with a flag. Frame boundary flags are signaled using the hexadecimal number 7E in Frame Relay and X.25.

Header (Q.922 Address)

Figure 6.6 is the Address field format of the Frame Relay frame defined in figure 6.5. The header provides information necessary for the proper transport of frames to their ultimate destination.

Figure 6.6
Q.922 Address field format.

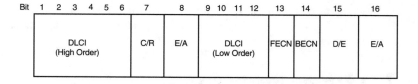

✔ **Data Link Connection Identifier (DLCI).** Identifies the channel or Virtual Circuit the data will take when switched and thus which conversation it belongs to.

✔ **Command/Response (C/R).** Is not used by Frame Relay per se. It is available for use by the protocol initiating the communications.

- ✔ **Extended Address (E/A).** This bit is positioned at the end of each octet within the Frame Relay header. A 0 in this position indicates that the header will continue to include the next octet. A 1 indicates that the header ends with the current octet.

- ✔ **Forward Explicit Congestion Notification (FECN) and Backward Explicit Congestion Notification (BECN).** Both provide network traffic monitoring information important to the handling of frames as they travel through the network. Information contained in these blocks indicates network traffic congestion along a particular link.

- ✔ **Discard Eligibility (D/E).** Alerts the receiving host whether this frame can be discarded and whether another exactly similar frame should appear.

Payload

Each frame also includes a Payload field of undetermined length. The Payload field serves to transport the native mode protocol packet or PDU over the Frame Relay network. When Frame Relay transport services are used to send data between TCP/IP networks, the payload consists of an IP datagram.

A Frame Relay provider specifies a maximum frame size for its network—generally speaking, a value greater than or equal to 1,600 octets. A Frame Relay DTE is configurable to accommodate the maximum acceptable frame size. With a two-octet Q.922 address field, the minimum frame size is five octets between the opening and closing flags. This minimum value increases when the Q.922 address format increases.

Control Field

The control field is the Q.922 control field. The UI (0x03) value is used unless it is negotiated otherwise.

Pad Field

The pad field is used to have the remainder of the frame aligned to a two-octet boundary. There may be a zero- or one-pad octet within the pad field that filled with zero.

Network Level Protocol ID

The NLPID field contains values for many different protocols, including IP, CLNP, and IEEE *Subnetwork Access Protocol* (SNAP). A NLPID value of 0x00 is defined as the Null Network Layer or Inactive Set. A NLPID value of 0x00 has no significance within the context of this encapsulation scheme and cannot be distinguished from a pad field. Thus, it is invalid under the Frame Relay encapsulation.

Organizationally Unique Identifier (OUI)

A distinct protocol is formed by a three-octet *Organizationally Unique Identifier* (OUI), followed by the *Protocol Identifier* (PID). For routed frames, packets that have no pre-assigned NLPID values are routed over Frame Relay networks with the NLPID 0x80 followed by SNAP. If the protocol has an EtherType assigned, the OUI is 0x00-00-00 and the PID is the EtherType of the protocol in use. There is one pad octet to align the protocol data on a two-octet boundary, as shown in figure 6.7.

Figure 6.7
Format of routed frames with EtherTypes.

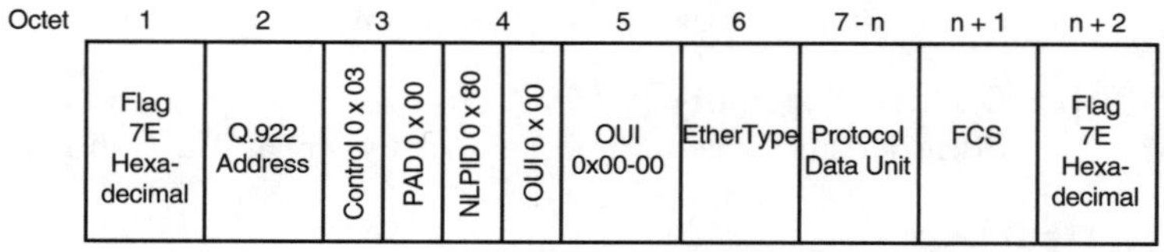

Octet	1	2	3	4	5	6	7 - n	n + 1	n + 2
	Flag 7E Hexadecimal	Q.922 Address	Control 0 x 03	PAD 0 x 00 / NLPID 0 x 80 / OUI 0 x 00	OUI 0x00-00	EtherType	Protocol Data Unit	FCS	Flag 7E Hexadecimal

When a protocol has an assigned NLPID, six bytes can be saved by using the format in figure 6.8.

Figure 6.8
Format of routed NLPID protocol.

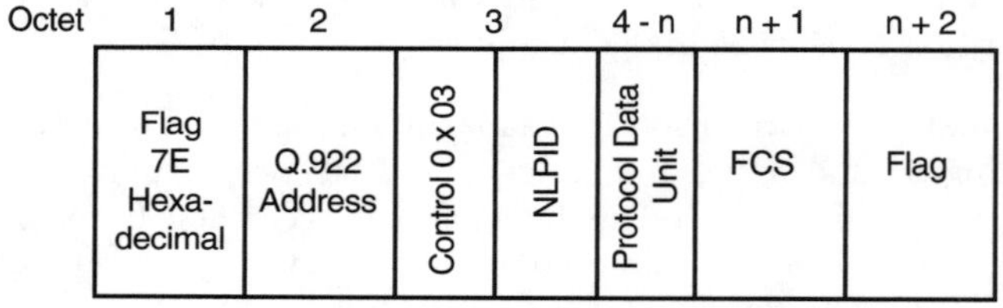

Octet	1	2	3	4 - n	n + 1	n + 2
	Flag 7E Hexadecimal	Q.922 Address	Control 0 x 03 / NLPID	Protocol Data Unit	FCS	Flag

Note that the NLPID encapsulation does not require a pad octet for alignment.

The NLPID is considered the first octet of the protocol data in the ISO protocols. In this case, NLPID need not be repeated. The single octet serves both as the demultiplexing value and as part of the protocol data. IP, on the other hand, has a NLPID defined (0xcc), but it is not part of the protocol itself. The alternative is diagrammed in figure 6.9.

Figure 6.9
The format of a routed IP datagram.

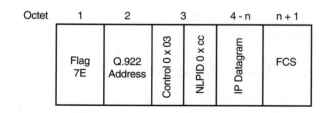

Octet	1	2	3	4 - n	n + 1
	Flag 7E	Q.922 Address	Control 0 x 03 / NLPID 0 x cc	IP Datagram	FCS

Frame Check Sum (FCS)

Although TCP/IP provides for packet transmission integrity checking, Frame Relay provides a check for flaws in the Frame Relay frame as well. The network can detect errors, but the users equipment is responsible for correction and retransmission.

ATM and TCP/IP

LECs and IXCs, as well as some software and switching providers, have moved cautiously toward making a determination as to which broadband technologies they believe will make up the new "information superhighway." Few company executives enjoy explaining to shareholders the extent of their investment in the least favored network technology. Of the many broadband choices, however, many public packet network providers are turning to ATM.

Overview of ATM

ATM-based networks are gaining popularity in both local- and wide-area applications. ATM provides the most chameleon-like services of any of the broadband technologies that integrate data, voice, and video, which demand different services from the network.

Voice data are first converted from analog to digital form before transmission. Analog voice signal is sampled and digitized, and it may be compressed and carried through a network at a typical rate of 64 Kbps. Bandwidth is rarely an issue with digitized voice. The problem is the real-time transport required to keep conversations going without incurring any delay.

Video data are also digitized before transmission. Digitized analog video signal of VHS quality requires a data rate of approximately 100 Mbps without compression, and a data rate of around 1.5 to 6 Mbps with compression. Compressed video presents no serious bandwidth problems like the voice data does. As the case with voice, the biggest concern with video transmitted for playback is that it needs to be done in real time to avoid loss of synchronization.

Data files come in many flavors. A graphics file of a color screen of 1000x1000 pixels with 24-bit color has 2.4 MB (3 MB) of information. A program might have only a few thousand bytes; a transaction that is processing might only require a few hundred bytes to send the query over the network. Various applications require different bandwidths. For example, with the rate of 64 Kbps, it would take more than six minutes to transmit the graphics files mentioned previously, and few milliseconds for the query.

Although ATM can provide voice, video, and data capabilities, it also can emulate X.25 and Frame Relay. Mainly, ATM excels as a technology because of the following:

✔ **Real-time data.** ATM can provide real-time applications with synchronized data; for example, it can synchronize video and sound to arrive at the same time because of the prioritization technology that accompanies an ATM cell.

✔ **Speed.** ATM is faster than Frame Relay because of its cell-based technology. Because of their fixed size, cells are usually much smaller than frames, so they can speed through network switches faster.

The most obvious disadvantages of ATM are as follows:

✔ **Expense.** ATM is expensive to implement because of the lack of an inexpensive upgrade path using existing Frame Relay or X.25 technology. Hardware upgrades are necessary to implement ATM at the PC level.

✔ **Technology.** ATM requires elaborate and expensive technology on the part of the *Packet Data Network* (PDN) provider and with respect to the user's *Customer Premise Equipment* (CPE).

To carry connectionless network traffic over an ATM network, there are LLC Encapsulation and VC-Based Multiplexing. In *LLC Encapsulation*, a single ATM Virtual Circuit supports the multiplexing of multiple protocols. The protocol of a carried PDU is identified by prefacing the PDU with an IEEE 802.2 *Logical Link Control* (LLC) header. *VC-Based Multiplexing*, on the other hand, performs higher-layer protocol multiplexing implicitly by ATM *Virtual Circuits* (VCs).

In the private environment, where large numbers of ATM VCs can be promptly and cheaply created, VC-Based Multiplexing is the better approach. When only *Permanent Virtual Circuits* (PVCs) are supported, LLC Encapsulation might be more desirable. LLC/SNAP encapsulation is the default packet format for IP datagrams.

An ATM cell is a fixed-length, 53-octet cell consisting of a 5-byte header and a 48-byte payload. The fixed-length cell design in an ATM network provides the following benefits: reduced network latency, better statistical multiplexing support than packets of variable length, simplified switching mechanism, and scaleable network performance.

ATM switching is based on statistical multiplexing. ATM cells from different sources are asynchronously multiplexed into fixed-length time slots, with each time slot carrying one ATM cell. Contrary to ATM, the *Synchronous Transfer Mode* (STM) divides the transmission link into fixed-length frames. Cells associated with a given source-destination pair are always transmitted during the same time slot of each frame. These physical framing standards have a number of common transmission rates, with primary rates of 155.52 MBps, 622.08 MBps, and 2.48832 GBps. The multiplexing method is decided either by manual configuration for the permanent virtual channels or by B-ISDN signaling procedures for switched VCs.

ATM Adaptation Layers (AAL)

Before data from upper layer applications can be transported over ATM, it must be encapsulated into ATM cells appropriate for the transmission media being used. The AAL acts as an interface between application data and the transmission media in that it specifies the proper packet components for the type of carrier service in use.

The primary function of the AAL is to segment and reassemble blocks of information of the higher level. In addition, the AAL needs to be able to do the following:

✔ Merge ATM-formatted control signals into the user-generated ATM stream

✔ Detect the appearance of higher-level information blocks arriving at the user interface

✔ Detect the boundaries of reassembled information blocks and have them delivered across the user interface

✔ Detect bit errors and missing cells of arriving signals

For *Constant Bit Rate* (CBR) service, the AAL must compensate for the variable delay of the segments delivered by the ATM network, and for recovering the bit timing clock of the CBR source. The AAL also needs to be able to deliver CBR data continuously across the user interface and synchronize the receiver's bit clock with that of the transmitter.

For ATM to provide the many different networking services it is capable of, the CCITT recommended several service-dependent ATM Adaptation Layers or AALs. Before data from upper layer applications can be transported over ATM, it must be encapsulated into ATM cells appropriate for the transmission media being used. The AAL acts as an interface between application data and the transmission media in that it specifies the proper packet components for the type of carrier service in use. Note that the ATM payload might change with the AAL implementation selected. For example, original AAL4 (described in the following list) makes available only 44 of the 48 octets available for the cell payload. The other four octets are used for additional cell control data. Additional changes of this kind are in order because ATM is a newly evolving technology.

The various AALs and the network technology or services they support are as follows:

✔ **AAL1.** CBR service that is connection-oriented—that is, audio and video over DS-1 and DS-3.

✔ **AAL2.** VBR service that is connection-oriented—that is, certain video/data protocols.

✔ **AAL3/AAL4.** VBR service that is either connection-oriented or connectionless—that is, burst file type data, Frame Relay. Originally, these two layers were defined separately.

✔ **AAL5.** Variable bit rate service that is connection-oriented for broadcast-type transmissions with little or no error checking.

AAL Data Transport

A typical scenario of transferring a block of data from a transmitting customer site with AAL4 is as follows: A block of data originated from a user site that needs to be transferred across the ATM network is presented to the AAL as a User PDU. With the information of the protocol of user PDU, the *Convergence Sublayer* (CS) of ATM will encapsulate PDU with a CS header, trailer, and pad to form the CS-PDU. If necessary, the ATM CS examines the protocol field. The format of the CS-PDU is shown in figure 6.10.

Figure 6.10
The CS-PDU
format.

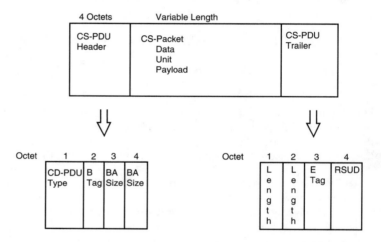

The first field in the CS-PDU header is an 8-bit type field that indicates the type of service being provided to that CS-PDU. For example, all zeroes represent connectionless service. Next is an 8-bit Beginning tag (B tag) field. The content of the B tag must agree with the End tag (E tag) in the CS-PDU trailer. The BA field is a 16-bit Buffer Allocation field. The last 8-bit field in the CS-PDU trailer is reserved for unspecified future use. The CS-PDU Pad field ensures that the overall length of the PDU payload is an integral multiple of four bytes.

The *Segmentation and Reassembly Sublayer* (SAR) of the AAL divides the CS-PDU into 44-octet segments. Each segment is made of the payload of one SAR-PDU. Padding is required if the last segment has a payload less than 44 octets. The SAR-PDU consists of a 2-byte header, a 44-octet payload, and a 2-byte trailer. The format of the SAR-PDU for AAL-4 is shown in figure 6.11.

ST is the segment type field. There are four segment types: *beginning of message* (BOM), *end of message* (EOM), *continuation of message* (COM), and *single segment message* (SSM). MID is the Message ID.

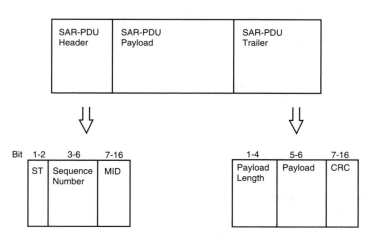

Figure 6.11
The SAR-PDU
format.

Figure 6.12 is an example of the ATM B-ISDN reference model. Note that figure 6.12 also identifies various service control signals for ATM. ATM service control signals provide the AALs with user application data—voice and video data—in a format that the AAL can understand. User services involve Connection-Oriented and Connectionless VBR services, other types of variable bit rate services, and CBR services. The boundary between the user and control interfaces and the AAL is somewhere within layer 2 of the OSI model. The AAL, coupled with the ATM and physical layer, perform services of layer 1 and some of the services of layer 2 of the OSI model. The types of services are as follows:

- ✔ **Class A.** Connection-oriented, CBR class whose interface to the adaptation layer of the ATM B-ISDN Reference Model is AAL1.

- ✔ **Class B.** VBR class interfaced to the adaptation layer by way of AAL2.

- ✔ **Class C.** Connection-oriented, data-only class whose interface to the ATM adaptation layer is AAL3/4 or AAL5.

- ✔ **Class D.** Connectionless, data-only class whose interface to the ATM adaptation layer is AAL3/4 or AAL5.

In the OSI model, the AAL layer is divided into two sublayers: CS and SAR. The former does the encapsulation or deencapsulation for the user and control data, and the latter cuts and reconnects 48-byte segments from each CS-PDU. The ATM layer is responsible for attaching or stripping the 5-byte header from each SAR-PDU, thereby forming the 53-octet ATM cell. The physical layer is responsible for placing these cells onto the transmission link medium.

The transmitting of IP datagrams over ATM networks occurs through adaptation layer 5 (RFC 1577). ALL5 also is called the *simple and efficient adaptation layer* (SEAL).

Figure 6.12
The B-ISDN
Protocol reference
model.

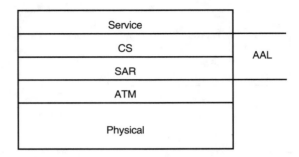

AAL5 Frame Format

This section discusses the AAL5 Frame format for routed packets. Interested readers can refer to RFC 1483 for the bridged packets. Also, this section only describes the frame format for PDU carried directly over the *Common Part Convergence Sublayer* (CPCS) of AAL5. This occurs when the *Service Specific Convergence Sublayer* (SSCS) of AAL5 is empty. If *Frame Relay-Service Specific Convergence Sublayer* (FR-SSCS) is used over the CPCS of AAL5, PDUs are carried using the NLPID multiplexing method. This is discussed in the following section.

PDU is encapsulated within the Payload field of AAL5 CPCS-PDU. The Payload field contains user information up to $2^{16}-1$ octets. The format of the AAL5 CPCS-PDU is shown in figure 6.13.

Figure 6.13
The AAL5 CPCS-
PDU format.

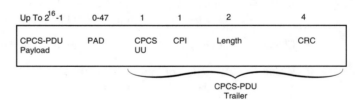

The PAD field ensures that the last 48-octet cell payload fits exactly into the ATM cells. CPCS user-to-user information is embedded in the CPCS-UU (User-to-User indication) field. Currently, this field serves no function and can be set to any value. The *Common Part Indicator* (CPI) field aligns the CPCS-PDU trailer to 64 bits and is coded as 0x00 when only the 64-bit alignment function is used.

The two-bytes-long field represents the length of the Payload field that has a maximum value of 65,535 octets. A payload of zero length is used for the abort function. The CRC field protects the entire CPCS-PDU, except for the CRC field itself.

LLC Encapsulation for Routed Protocols

LLC Encapsulation supports multiple protocols carried over the same VC. An LLC header in the Payload Field, placed in front of the carried PDU, contains necessary information to identify the protocol of the routed PDU. This information enables the receiver to process the incoming AAL5 CPCS-PDU properly.

For the routed PDU with LLC Encapsulation, the PDU is prefixed by an IEEE 802.2 LLC header, which can be followed by an IEEE 802.1a SNAP header. This provides information to the identified protocol.

The LLC header value 0xFE-FE-03 indicates that a routed ISO PDU follows. The Control field for routed protocols has the value 0x03, which specifies Unnumbered Information Command PDU. For routed ISO PDUs, the format of the AAL5 CPCS-PDU Payload field is as shown in figure 6.14.

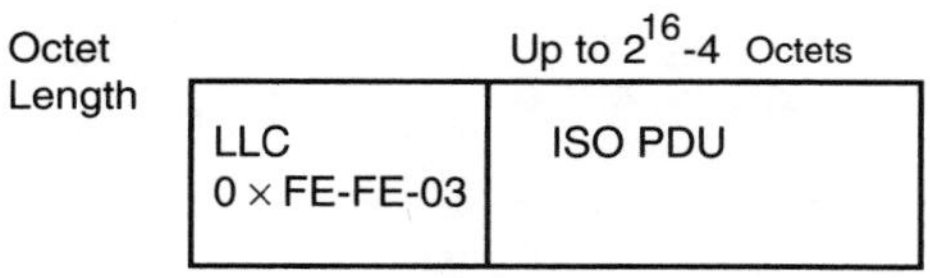

Octet Length	Up to 2^{16}-4 Octets
LLC 0 × FE-FE-03	ISO PDU

Figure 6.14
The routed ISO PDU Payload format.

A one-octet NLPID indicates the routed ISO protocol that is part of Protocol Data. Some of the currently defined NLPID values are listed in the following minitable. An NLPID value of 0x00 is defined as the Null Network Layer or Inactive Set, and is invalid under the ATM encapsulation.

NLPID	DefinitionValue
0x00	Null Network Layer or Inactive Set (not used with ATM)
0x80	SNAP
0x81	ISO CLNP
0x82	ISO ESIS
0x83	ISO ISIS
0xCC	Internet IP

Even though IP is not an ISO protocol, IP has an NLPID value 0xCC. IP is encapsulated like all other routed non-ISO protocols by identifying it in the SNAP header that immediately follows the LLC header. The presence of a SNAP header is indicated by the LLC header value 0xAA-AA-03. A SNAP header has a form, as shown in figure 6.15.

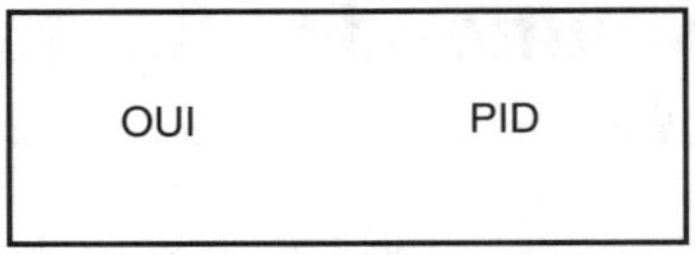

Figure 6.15
A SNAP header.

OUI	PID

The three-octet *Organizationally Unique Identifier* (OUI) identifies an organization that administers the meaning of the two-octet PID. Together they identify a distinct routed or bridged protocol. The OUI value 0x00-00-00 specifies that the following PID is an EtherType.

The format of the AAL5 CPCS-PDU Payload field for routed non-ISO PDUs is demonstrated in figure 6.16.

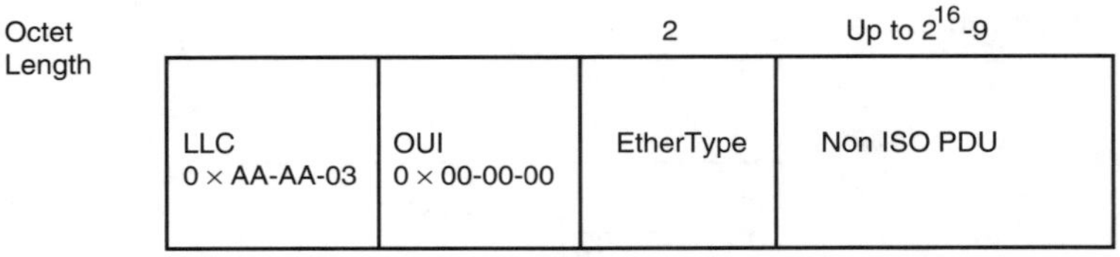

Figure 6.16
The routed non-ISO PDU format.

Octet Length		2	Up to 2^{16}-9
LLC 0 × AA-AA-03	OUI 0 × 00-00-00	EtherType	Non ISO PDU

In the particular case of an Internet IP PDU, the EtherType value is 0x08-00 and has the format shown in figure 6.17.

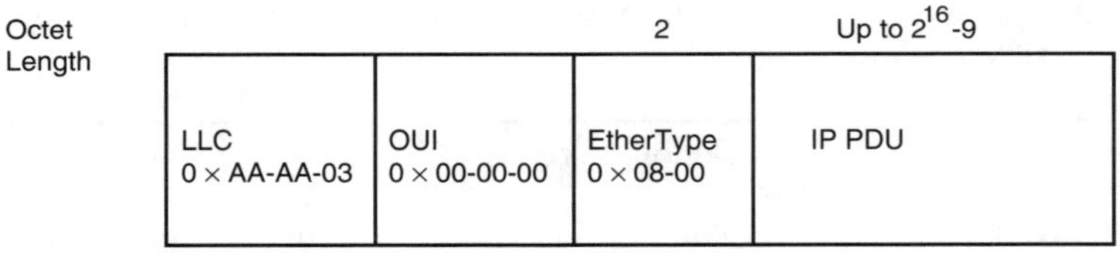

Figure 6.17
The routed IP PDU format.

Octet Length		2	Up to 2^{16}-9
LLC 0 × AA-AA-03	OUI 0 × 00-00-00	EtherType 0 × 08-00	IP PDU

IP Encapsulation over FR-SSCS

Frame Relaying-Specific Convergence Sublayer (FR-SSCS) can be used on the top of the *Common Part Convergence Sublayer* (CPCS) of the AAL type 5 for Frame Relay/ATM internetworking. The service offered by FR-SSCS corresponds to the Core service for Frame Relaying.

An FR-SSCS PDU consists of a Q.922 Address field followed by the payload. Because the corresponding functions are provided by the AAL, the Q.922 flags and the FCS are omitted. Figure 6.18 shows an FR-SSCS PDU embedded in the Payload of an AAL5 CPCS-PDU.

The encapsulation of the Routed PDUs inside the FR-SSCS PDU is defined in RFC 1294 and described in the previous section. The payload starts with a Q.922 Control field followed by an optional pad octet. The protocol of the carried PDU is then identified by prefacing the PDU with an ISO/CCITT NLPID. In the case of an IP PDU, the NLPID is 0xCC and the FR-SSCS PDU has the format shown in figure 6.18.

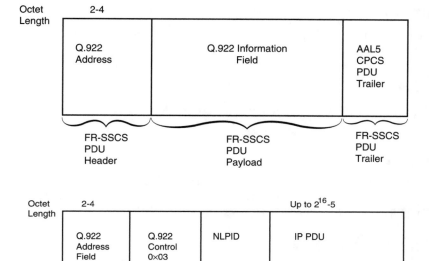

Figure 6.18
A FR-SSCS PDU embedded in the Payload of an AAL5 CPCS-PDU.

Figure 6.19
The FR-SSCS PDU for a routed IP PDU.

The ATM Cell

Figure 6.20 details the composition of an ATM cell. The ATM cell is constructed by the service-independent ATM Layer for transporting over the physical layer.

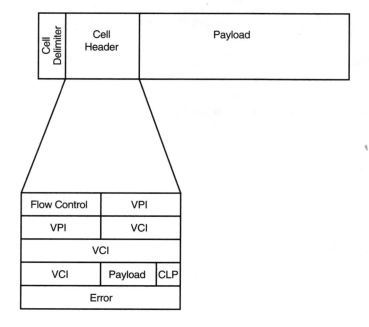

Figure 6.20
ATM cell format.

I

Overview

Cell Delimiter

The cell delimiter designates the beginning of the ATM cell and exists primarily for packet identification purposes.

Cell Header

The header is composed of 40 bits designed to handle network routing of the ATM cell payload.

Flow Control

The four bits that comprise flow control provide a similar service to that of the FECN and BECN bits in Frame Relay. Flow Control bits can also aid in the provision of certain data traffic control characteristics for synchronized voice and video ATM applications.

Virtual Circuit Identifier

Because ATM is connection-oriented, it establishes a Virtual Circuit over which cells can be transported. The VPI serves to identify the Virtual Circuit to which the cell's payload belongs.

Virtual Path Identifier

ATM groups connections that take a common VCI into Virtual Paths. The Virtual Path Identifier is then referenced when communications session management is required instead of each Virtual Circuit. This reduces the total number of session management commands that require issuing, which is an operating advantage of ATM.

Payload Type Indicator (PTI)

The *Payload Type Indicator* (PTI), a three-bit indicator, distinguishes control cells and data cells. Transportation of information important to the handling of each cell can occur in the payload section of a cell. Prioritization data for video and voice synchronization as well as variable versus continuous bit rate switches are examples. The PTI indicates whether one of these items or data is contained in the cell payload.

Cell Loss Priority (CLP)

The *Cell Loss Priority* (CLP) bit indicator performs a similar function to the Discard Eligibility bit in Frame Relay.

Error Control Octet

The *Error Control Octet* provides information to ensure the integrity of the VPI and VCI data. Validation of these identifiers is essential to eliminate misdelivery of ATM cells.

Like Frame Relay, ATM does not concern itself with the validity of the IP datagram encapsulated in the ATM cell. Rather, it relies on higher-level protocols to provide this check.

Cell Payload

The *Cell Payload* is constructed of 48 bytes of data transport space.

Summary

Frame Relay technology provides high throughput, low latency, and bandwidth on demand. The emerging development brings about high-throughput nodal processor, a standard open interface to the bridge and router, and an interface that supports cell relay and switching. It's one of the best choices for the enterprise network.

ATM technology provides high-bandwidth, low delay switching, and multiplexing. Compared with the ATM cell relay, classical packet switching with larger packet size suffers from the problem of response time and throughput. The consensus is that ATM will become the standard of the late 1990s. The ever-changing and progressing technology in high-speed and broadband networking gives the "information superhighway" a brighter future.

Chapter Snapshot

Your job as a network consultant or a network administrator is not finished after you have installed the network and set up user accounts and applications. Your next responsibility is network management, which is a battle that never ends.

Two types of network management issues exist: software-related, such as data security and access permissions; and hardware-related. This chapter focuses on the second of the two issues—management of your network hardware as a whole, using the Simple Network Management Protocol (SNMP) and some ideas on managing the software-related issues. This chapter breaks SNMP down into a number of topics:

Simple Network Management Protocol (SNMP)

"Smile and the world smiles with you.

Frown and they know the network's down."

What is Network Management?

Network management is made up of two similar categories. The first is the management of network applications, management of user accounts (such as file usage), and management of access rights (permissions). These are all software-related network management issues. These are not discussed in this chapter.

The second network management category is comprised of the hardware that constitutes your network. This category includes workstations, servers, network cards, routers, bridges, and hubs. These devices are usually far from your location. For this reason, it would be nice if you could be notified automatically when problems occur. Unlike your users, who will call you on the telephone if there is an application problem, your router will not be able to notify you if it is congested.

To address this issue, vendors have built into some of these devices network management capabilities so that you can query their status remotely as well as allow them to send alerts to you when a certain type of event happens. These devices are usually referred to as "smart" devices. This chapter examines how smart devices function within the scheme of network management.

Network management usually is divided into four categories (see fig. 7.1):

✔ **Managed Nodes (or Devices).** Devices you want to monitor.

✔ **Agents.** Special software or firmware that tracks the status of the managed device.

✔ **Network Management Station.** A centralized device that communicates and displays status of the agents in the various managed nodes.

✔ **Network Management Protocol.** Used by the network management station and the agents to exchange management information.

Figure 7.1
The network management framework.

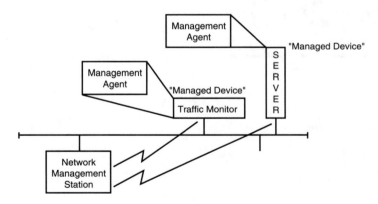

Some vendors use proprietary protocols to communicate with their hardware. For example, IBM's *controlled access units* (CAUs) are manageable devices, but use a proprietary protocol from IBM. That means you need IBM's management console to communicate with their CAUs.

Many vendors, SynOptics, Wellfleet, Cabletron, Cisco, and others, have adopted the *Simple Network Management Protocol* (SNMP) implementation. SNMP is a well-defined, public standard that is widely used by the Internet community (RFC 1157/1098/1067). SNMP is a set of protocols that allows you to remotely query variables from an SNMP device, as well as set new values. An SNMP device can also generate alarms to the management console.

It should be noted that SNMP is *not* protocol-dependent. It can be used over IP, Novell's IPX (RFC 1420/1298), Apple's AppleTalk (RFC 1419), and OSI (RFC 1418/1283/1161). The implementation is most often over IP.

Two Network Management Axioms

When designing and setting up your network management infrastructure you need to keep these network management axioms in mind:

1. The traffic due to management information should not significantly increase network traffic.

2. The protocol agent on the managed device should not significantly increase the processing overhead such that the device's primary function is impaired.

How can SNMP fulfill management needs while obeying the two axioms? This chapter explores the answer.

What is SNMP?

The *Simple Network Management Protocol* (SNMP) was first developed by the *Internet Engineering Task Force* (IETF) study group to address router management issues on the Internet. Many people think that SNMP works over IP because the Internet runs TCP/IP. However, this is not true.

SNMP was designed to be protocol-independent, so it can be used over IP, IPX, AppleTalk, OSI, and other transport protocols as needed.

SNMP is a family of protocol suites and specifications (see table 7.1) that provides a means for collecting network management information from devices on the network. SNMP also provides a way for the devices to report problems and errors to the network management station. The different protocols are discussed in separate sections in this chapter.

Table 7.1
SNMP Family of Protocols

Name	Description
MIB	Management Information Base
SMI	Structure and Identification of Management Information
SNMP	Simple Network Management Protocol

There are two approaches to collecting data from managed devices: a polling-only approach and an interrupt-based approach.

If you use a *polling-only* approach, the network management station is always in control. The drawback to this method is timeliness of information, especially that of errors. How often should you poll and in what device order? If the interval is too small, you generate too much unnecessary traffic. If the interval is too large, and in the wrong order, notification of catastrophic events is too slow. This defeats the purpose of pro-active network management.

The interrupt-based approach provides immediate notification to the network management station should there be an extraordinary event (assuming the device hasn't crashed and there is a valid communication path between the managed device and the management station). However, this approach isn't without its own drawbacks. First of all, resources are required to generate the error or *trap*. If the trap must forward a lot of information, the managed device may have to spend time and resources generating the trap rather than performing its primary functions (and violate Network Management Axiom Number Two).

Furthermore, if several trap events of the same type occur back-to-back, a lot of network bandwidth may be tied up with the same information (violating Network Management Axiom Number One). This would be especially bad if the traps were about network congestion. One way to overcome this is for the managed device to set *thresholds* regarding when to report problems. Unfortunately, this may, again, violate Network Management Axiom Number Two because the device must spend more resources to determine if a trap should be generated.

As a result, the combination of *trap-directed polling* is probably the most effective means of performing network management. In general, the network management station polls the agents in the managed devices to collect data (see fig. 7.2), and displays the data on the console in either numeric or graphical representation. This allows the network manager to diagnose and manage the devices and network traffic.

Figure 7.2
The SNMP management station polls the agent in the managed device for information.

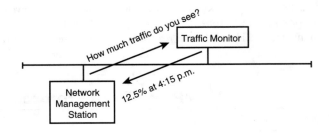

Agents in the managed devices can report error conditions, such as pre-programmed threshold exceeded levels, to the network management station at any time. It does not have to wait for the management station to poll for it (see fig. 7.3). This is known as *SNMP traps*.

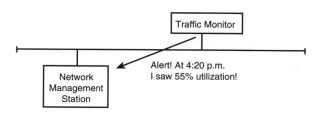

Figure 7.3
The managed device agent reports errors to the SNMP management station, without polling.

Under this combined approach, when a device generates a trap, you can use the network management station to query the device (assuming it is still reachable) for further information.

What is a Managed Device?

You have heard a lot about "SNMP-manageable devices", "SNMP-compliant", or "SNMP-managed" devices. But what exactly are they? How do they differ from a "smart device"?

In simple words, all of the above mean "a network device containing a network management agent implementation." These terms also mean that the agent supports the SNMP protocol for information exchange.

A smart device may not necessarily use or support the SNMP protocol, as previously mentioned. What, then, is an agent? Are there different types of agents? The next few sections address these questions.

Agents

A management *agent* is a specific piece of software (or firmware) that contains information about a specific device and/or its environment. When an agent is installed on a device, the said device is referred to as "managed." In other words, it is a *database*.

When an agent is installed on a device, the device is called a *managed* device. The process of implementing the agent on the device is called *instrumentation*. Thus, sometimes the managed device is also known as an *instrumented device*.

The data contained in the database varies depending on the device on which the agent is installed. For example, on a router, the agent will contain information about its routing table, total number of packets received and transmitted, and so forth. For a bridge, the database may contain information about number of packets forwarded and its filtering tables.

The agent is the software or firmware that communicates with the network management console. The following tasks can be performed over this "link":

✔ The network management station can retrieve information about the device from the agent.

✔ The network management station can update, add, or remove entries, such as routing table entries, in the database maintained by the agent.

✔ The network management station can set thresholds for a particular trap.

✔ The agent can send traps to the network management station.

Remember that the agent in the managed device does not volunteer information, except in the event of a threshold being exceeded. For example, from the network management station you can query your router for the status of the links and their costs (see fig. 7.4).

Figure 7.4
Interaction between the network management station and the agent in the managed device.

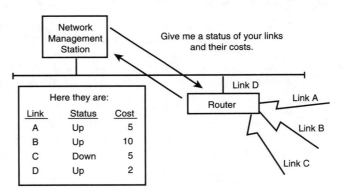

Occasionally, it may not be possible to implement an SNMP agent on a particular device (termed a *foreign* device) because of lack of resources or because the device does not support the transport protocol required by the SNMP agent. Does that mean you cannot monitor such devices? No, all is not lost in such a situation. You can use a *proxy agent*, which acts on behalf of the foreign device.

A proxy agent runs on a different device than the foreign device to be managed. The network management station first contacts the proxy agent, and indicates (somehow) the identity of the foreign device. The proxy agent then translates the protocol commands it received into whatever management protocol is supported by the foreign device. In such an instance, the proxy agent is said to act as an *application gateway*.

If the foreign device does not support any management protocols, then the proxy agent must monitor it using some passive means. For example, a proxy agent for a Token Ring bridge may monitor its performance and generate traps if it detects any congestion errors reported by the bridge.

Fortunately, you can get an SNMP-manageable device for most of the internetworking device types available today, such as hubs, bridges, and routers. Some vendors even offer an SNMP agent on their network cards.

MIBs

It is rare to refer to the database in a managed device as a database. Rather, it is generally referred to as the *management information base* (MIB) in SNMP lingo.

An MIB describes the objects, or entries, that are to be included in the database. Each object, or entry, has four properties:

- ✔ Object Type
- ✔ Syntax
- ✔ Access
- ✔ Status

These properties are defined by the *Structure and Identification of Management Information* (SMI; RFC 1155/1065) specification, one of the SNMP specifications. SMI is to MIB what a schema is to a database. SMI defines what each object "looks like." The properties are described as follows.

Object Type

This property defines the name of the particular object. For example, sysUpTime. It is simply a label.

SMI uses the *Abstract Syntax Notation One* (ASN.1) for data representation. That means it is case sensitive because ASN.1 uses an alphabetic case convention to indicate the kind of objects.

The object also has to be "identified." For the internet network management MIBs, the identifier starts with the following, presented in ASN.1 notation:

```
internet OBJECT IDENTIFIER ::= { iso org(3) dod(6) 1 }
```

or in a concise format:

```
1.3.6.1
```

This is derived from the ASN.1 documents. It defines a tree-like format for the identifiers. The tree consists of a root, connected to a number of labeled nodes. Each node is identified by a non-negative integer value and possibly a brief textual description. Each node may in turn have subordinates, which are also labeled.

When describing an OBJECT IDENTIFIER, there are several formats that one uses. The most concise format is to list the integer values found by transversing the tree, starting at the root and proceeding to the object in question.

From the root level, there are three subordinates (see fig. 7.5):

✔ ccitt(0)

✔ iso(1)

✔ joint-iso-ccitt(2)

Figure 7.5
The ASN.1
OBJECT
IDENTIFIER tree.

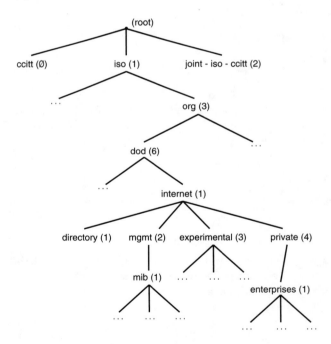

Each of these "branches" is administrated by the respective organizations as shown in the labels.

Using the tree as an aid, you can easily see any MIBs that are represented, using the concise numeric format:

```
1.3.6.1.2.1...
```

or the slightly longer textual format:

```
iso.org.dod.internet.mgmt.mib...
```

Syntax

This property specifies the data types, such as integers, number of octet strings (character strings; ranging from 0 to 255), object identifiers (aliases of predefined data type), or NULLs. NULLs act as place holders reserved for future use.

Access

Access indicates the level of access to this particular object. Legal values are: *read-only, read-write, write-only,* and *not accessible.*

Status

Status defines the implementation requirement for this object: *mandatory* (the managed node must implement this object); *optional* (managed device may implement this object); or *obsolete* (managed device need no longer implement this object).

Consider the fictitious MIB and its SMI components for an address book database as shown in the following example:

Object Type	: name	Object Type	: address1
Syntax	: octet string (20)	Syntax	: octet string (20)
Access	: read-only	Access	: read-write
Status	: mandatory	Status	: mandatory
Object Type	: address2	Object Type	: city
Syntax	: octet string (20)	Syntax	: octet string (20)
Access	: read-write	Access	: read-write
Status	: mandatory	Status	: mandatory
Object Type	: state	Object Type	: country
Syntax	: octet string (20)	Syntax	: octet string (20)
Access	: read-write	Access	: read-write
Status	: mandatory	Status	: mandatory
Object Type	: zip code	Object Type	: telephone
Syntax	: octet string (10)	Syntax	: integer (15)
Access	: read-write	Access	: read-write
Status	: mandatory	Status	: optional

The following example shows the actual database structure (schema):

Name	:	(20 octets: mandatory)
Address1	:	(20 octets: mandatory)
Address2	:	(20 octets: mandatory)
City	:	(20 octets: mandatory)
State	:	(20 octets: mandatory)
Zip Code	:	(10 octets, mandatory)
Telephone	:	(15 digit integer: optional)

The presence of objects, their names, and values are part of the MIB specification. Currently there are three MIB specifications:

✔ Standard

✔ Experimental

✔ Private (Enterprises)

Standard MIB

The *standard MIB* contains a set of objects that are well defined, known, and accepted by the Internet standards group. Two versions of the standard MIB are available today, and are referred to as MIB-I (RFC 1156/1066) and MIB-II (RFC 1213/1158).

MIB-I was first released in 1988 with 114 objects defined within it. These objects were divided into eight groups as shown in table 7.2.

Table 7.2
The Eight Object Groups in MIB-I

Group	No.	Objects for
system	3	the managed node itself
interfaces	22	network attachments
at	3	IP address translation
ip	33	the Internet Protocol
icmp	26	the Internet Control Message Protocol
tcp	17	the Transmission Control Protocol
udp	4	the User Datagram Protocol
egp	6	the Exterior Gateway Protocol

I

Overview

For a managed device to claim to be MIB-I compliant, it must implement all the managed objects in the group whose functions it supports. For example, an MIB-I IP router that supports the EGP routing protocol must implement *all* the above groups. On the other hand, an MIB-I IPX router need only implement the "system" and "at" groups of objects.

In 1990, MIB-I was enhanced and more groups were added. The new information base became known as MIB-II. Two new groups and a much larger set of objects (total of 171 objects) were added; these are listed in table 7.3.

Table 7.3
The Ten Object Groups of MIB-II

Group	No.	Objects for
system	7	the managed node itself
interfaces	23	network attachments
at	3	IP address translation
ip	38	the Internet Protocol
icmp	26	the Internet Control Message Protocol
tcp	19	the Transmission Control Protocol
udp	7	the User Datagram Protocol
egp	18	the Exterior Gateway Protocol
transmission	0	the specific type of interface, such as Ethernet, etc.
snmp	30	the Simple Network Management Protocol

Three differences between MIB-I and MIB-II are worth mentioning:

✔ The *at* (address translation) group will be removed in due time. When it was introduced with MIB-I, it only provided for one-way mapping of protocol addresses to physical addresses. However, certain protocols, such as OSI's *End-System to Intermediate-System* (ES-IS) protocol requires inverse mappings. It is difficult indexing a single table to provide bi-directional mapping. At the same time, the various protocol groups now have one or two tables for mapping in the appropriate direction. This group is expected to be of little use, and will soon be removed from the next revision of the MIB.

✔ The *transmission* group was introduced in MIB-II. It is supposed to contain specific objects for each type of interfaces, such as Ethernet, Token Ring, etc.

At the moment, most of the objects for this group are in the experimental or enterprise "MIB-space" (to be discussed later) and will eventually move to the standard-MIB-space as consensus and experience dictates. This group is mainly used as a temporary place-holder.

✔ The *snmp* group was added in MIB-II. It contains objects about SNMP. This allows network management stations to manipulate the SNMP portion of the agents.

MIB-II is a superset of MIB-I; therefore, the same naming convention is used for the variables. Common objects have identical names in the two MIBs.

Vendors may choose to implement MIB-I or MIB-II for their agents. Likewise, vendors may choose to implement MIB-I or MIB-II for their network management software.

That means if you use an MIB-I network management station to query an MIB-II device, you will not get the full range of possible data. Conversely, if you use an MIB-II network management station to query an MIB-I device, many of the data displays on the console will read blank or zero because of the unavailability of the extra objects.

The following output is taken from the first 100 lines of an MIB-II (RFC 1213):

```
RFC1213-MIB DEFINITIONS ::= BEGIN

-- Extracted from RFC-1213

IMPORTS
        mgmt, NetworkAddress, IpAddress, Counter, Gauge,
                TimeTicks
          FROM RFC1155-SMI
        OBJECT-TYPE
                FROM RFC-1212;

--   This MIB module uses the extended OBJECT-TYPE macro as
--   defined in [14];

--   MIB-II (same prefix as MIB-I)

mib-2      OBJECT IDENTIFIER ::= { mgmt 1 }

-- textual conventions

DisplayString ::=
```

```
        OCTET STRING
-- This data type is used to model textual information taken
-- from the NVT ASCII character set.  By convention, objects
-- with this syntax are declared as having
--
--      SIZE (0..255)


PhysAddress ::=
     OCTET STRING
-- This data type is used to model media addresses.  For many
-- types of media, this will be in a binary representation.
-- For example, an ethernet address would be represented as
-- a string of 6 octets.


-- groups in MIB-II

system      OBJECT IDENTIFIER ::= { mib-2 1 }
interfaces  OBJECT IDENTIFIER ::= { mib-2 2 }
at          OBJECT IDENTIFIER ::= { mib-2 3 }
ip          OBJECT IDENTIFIER ::= { mib-2 4 }
icmp        OBJECT IDENTIFIER ::= { mib-2 5 }
tcp         OBJECT IDENTIFIER ::= { mib-2 6 }
udp         OBJECT IDENTIFIER ::= { mib-2 7 }
egp         OBJECT IDENTIFIER ::= { mib-2 8 }


-- historical (some say hysterical)
-- cmot       OBJECT IDENTIFIER ::= { mib-2 9 }

transmission OBJECT IDENTIFIER ::= { mib-2 10 }
snmp         OBJECT IDENTIFIER ::= { mib-2 11 }


-- the System group

-- Implementation of the System group is mandatory for all
-- systems.  If an agent is not configured to have a value
-- for any of these variables, a string of length 0 is
-- returned.

sysDescr OBJECT-TYPE
     SYNTAX  DisplayString (SIZE (0..255))
     ACCESS  read-only
     STATUS  mandatory
     DESCRIPTION
```

```
                              "A textual description of the entity.  This value
                              should include the full name and version
                              identification of the system's hardware type,
                              software operating-system, and networking
                              software.  It is mandatory that this only contain
                              printable ASCII characters."
                      ::= { system 1 }

             sysObjectID OBJECT-TYPE
                  SYNTAX   OBJECT IDENTIFIER
                  ACCESS   read-only
                  STATUS   mandatory
                  DESCRIPTION
                              "The vendor's authoritative identification of the
                              network management subsystem contained in the
                              entity.  This value is allocated within the SMI
                              enterprises subtree (1.3.6.1.4.1) and provides an
                              easy and unambiguous means for determining 'what
                              kind of box' is being managed.  For example, if
                              vendor 'Flintstones, Inc.' was assigned the
                              subtree 1.3.6.1.4.1.4242, it could assign the
                              identifier 1.3.6.1.4.1.4242.1.1 to its 'Fred
                              Router'."
                      ::= { system 2 }

             sysUpTime OBJECT-TYPE
                  SYNTAX   TimeTicks
                  ACCESS   read-only
                  STATUS   mandatory
                  DESCRIPTION
                              "The time (in hundredths of a second) since the
                              network management portion of the system was last
                              re-initialized."
                      ::= { system 3 }
```

A third MIB exists in the Standard MIB family. It is the *Remote MONitoring* (RMON) MIB. This is a new addition that was only accepted as a Standard MIB in late 1993. It is discussed in a later section.

Experimental MIBs

The experimental MIBs contain MIBs that are not in the standard MIBs and are not part of the private or enterprise MIBs (as discussed in this section). These MIBs may contain specific information about other elements of the network and device management that is deemed important.

When an experimental MIB is proven effective and refined, it is then moved from the experimental "MIB-space" to the standard MIB-space. It is like a staging area, if you will, for standard MIBs. Shown in table 7.4 are some of the registered Experimental MIBs.

Both MIB-II and RMON were Experimental MIBs before they were accepted by the Internet standards body.

Table 7.4
List of Experimental MIBs

Number	Descriptor (label)	Description
0	(none)	(reserved)
1	CLNS	ISO CLNS Objects
2	T1-Carrier	T1 Carrier Objects
3	IEEE802.3	Ethernet-like Objects
4	IEEE802.5	Token Ring-like Objects
5	DECNet-PHIV	DECnet Phase IV Objects
6	Interface	Generic Interface Objects
7	IEEE802.4	Token Bus-like Objects
8	FDDI	FDDI Objects
9	LANMGR-1	LAN Manager v1
10	LANMGR-TRAPS	LAN Manager Traps

Refer to figure 7.5. You can see that the experimental MIB-space is separate from the private/enterprise and standard MIBs. The following is the numeric representation for experimental MIBs:

    1.3.6.1.3...

The numeric representation for the standard MIBs is

    1.3.6.1.2.1...

Private or Enterprises MIBs

Private MIBs, or more commonly called *Enterprises MIBs*, are designed by individual companies for their own networking devices. For your network management software (that is not from the vendor) to read these Enterprises MIBs, you must know the MIB object names (or their numeric representations) to access them.

Often the Enterprises MIBs from a vendor are product-line or model specific. Therefore, make sure you have the correct MIB file if you have difficulties accessing the object values.

In many cases, vendor-specific MIBs are shipped with your SNMP-manageable devices, or you can obtain them from the vendors directly.

Some Enterprises MIBs are available for FTP from the host VENERA.ISI.EDU. Use "anonymous" FTP and look for files in the "mib/" directory.

Some Enterprises MIBs are available on CompuServe. Check the vendor's forum library area.

Listed in table 7.5 are some of the assigned Enterprises MIB numbers.

Table 7.5
Partial List of Assigned Enterprises MIB numbers

Number	Descriptor (label/vendor)
0	(reserved)
1	Proteon
2	IBM
3	CMU
4	Unix
5	ACC
6	TWG
7	CAYMAN
8	PSI
9	cisco
10	NSC

Number	Descriptor (label/vendor)
11	HP
12	Epilogue
13	U of Tennessee
14	BBN
15	Xylogics, Inc.
16	Unisys
17	Canstar
18	Wellfleet
19	TRW
20	MIT

The following is an extract from the Cisco MIB (lines have been removed to conserve space and not the full MIB is shown):

```
-- cisco MIB*

                 -- Wed Jun  3 10:41:46 1992

                 -- cisco Systems, Inc.
                   — 1525 O'Brien
                 -- Menlo Park, CA  94025

                 -- customer-service@cisco.com

-- 1. Introduction

-- This memo describes the variables that are implemented for
-- the cisco Systems, Inc.  set of products including the
-- Gateway Server, Terminal Server, Trouter, and Protocol
-- Translator.  The document relies upon the Structure of
-- Management Information (SMI), RFC1155.  It is presented in
-- a format described in RFC1212, the Concise MIB document.

-- This  document describes the cisco local Management
-- Information Base (MIB) variables for
```

```
-- version 9.0 of the system software.

-- 2. Object Definitions

CISCO-MIB { iso org(3) dod(6) internet(1) private(4)
                        enterprises(1) 9 }
DEFINITIONS ::= BEGIN

IMPORTS
        enterprises, OBJECT-TYPE, NetworkAddress,
/IpAddress,
        Counter, Gauge, TimeTicks
        FROM RFC1155-SMI
        ifIndex, ipAdEntAddr, ipRouteDest,
/tcpConnLocalAddress,
        tcpConnLocalPort, tcpConnRemAddress,
/tcpConnRemPort,
        DisplayString
        FROM RFC1213-MIB;

-- *This file is machine generated. Do not edit.

cisco           OBJECT IDENTIFIER ::= { enterprises 9 }

products        OBJECT IDENTIFIER ::= { cisco 1 }
local           OBJECT IDENTIFIER ::= { cisco 2 }
temporary       OBJECT IDENTIFIER ::= { cisco 3 }

gateway-server  OBJECT IDENTIFIER ::= { products 1 }
...
igs             OBJECT IDENTIFIER ::= { products 5 }

lsystem         OBJECT IDENTIFIER ::= { local 1 }
...
lts             OBJECT IDENTIFIER ::= { local 9 }

decnet          OBJECT IDENTIFIER ::= { temporary 1 }
xns             OBJECT IDENTIFIER ::= { temporary 2 }
appletalk       OBJECT IDENTIFIER ::= { temporary 3 }
novell          OBJECT IDENTIFIER ::= { temporary 4 }
vines           OBJECT IDENTIFIER ::= { temporary 5 }
...
```

```
-- Local System Group
-- This group is present in all products.

    romId OBJECT-TYPE
        SYNTAX  DisplayString
        ACCESS  read-only
        STATUS  mandatory
        DESCRIPTION
                "This variable contains a printable octet
                string which contains the System Bootstrap
                description and version identification."
        ::= { lsystem 1 }

    whyReload OBJECT-TYPE
        SYNTAX  DisplayString
        ACCESS  read-only
        STATUS  mandatory
        DESCRIPTION
                "This variable contains a printable octet
                string which contains the reason why the
                system was last restarted."
        ::= { lsystem 2 }

    hostName OBJECT-TYPE
        SYNTAX  DisplayString
        ACCESS  read-only
        STATUS  mandatory
        DESCRIPTION
                "This variable represents the name of the
                host in printable ascii characters."
        ::= { lsystem 3 }

...
```

RMON

Remote MONitoring (RMON; RFC 1513/1271) MIB is a relatively new standard MIB. Because it serves a different function than MIB-I/II, it is worth discussing separately.

RMON was designed to monitor network media, rather than a particular device. Therefore, it is useful in monitoring your network traffic as a whole. There are nine object groups in RMON (see table 7.6).

Table 7.6
RMON Functional Groups

Group	Function description
statistics	A table that tracks about 20 different network traffic statistics, including total frames and errors.
history	Enables you to specify frequency and intervals for traffic sampling.
alarm	Permits you to establish thresholds and criteria under which the agents will issue alarms.
host	A table containing each LAN node listed by traffic statistics.
hostTopN	Enables you to set up sorted lists and reports based on the highest statistics generated by the host group.
matrix	Two tables of traffic statistics based on pairs of communication nodes. One table is based on sending node addresses, the other is based on receiving node addresses.
filter	Permits you to define, by channel, particular characteristics of frames. For example, a filter may be applied to capture TCP traffic.
packet capture	Works in conjunction with the filter group. Enables you to specify the amount of memory resources to be consumed in storing captured frames that meet the filter criteria.
event	Enables you to specify a set of parameters or conditions to be tracked by the agent. Whenever these conditions or parameters are met, an event log will be recorded.

A number of RMON implementations are available today. Some are software add-ons on existing devices, such as servers and hubs. Novell Inc.'s NetWare LANalyzer Agent, for example, is a set of NLMs (NetWare Loadable Modules) that runs on NetWare 3.*x* or 4.*x* servers. Others are available as specific hardware implementation, such as Novell's (now defunct) LANtern, and the recent announcement by Network Application Technology Inc. (N.A.T.) of their EtherMeterCard/450 RMON probe.

To implement a RMON agent on a device, the network card in the device must be able to operate in the *promiscuous* mode in which it can accept data not specifically addressed to it.

The network management station needs to be RMON-compliant before it can communicate and extract data from RMON devices.

SNMP Traps

SNMP traps are alerts generated by agents on a managed device. These traps can generate five event types:

✔ **coldStart or warmStart.** The agent reinitialized its configuration tables. A cold start may alter the current configuration.

✔ **linkUp or linkDown.** A network interface on the agent either failed or comes back to life. Sometimes these traps are sent when a protocol is bound or unbound from a network interface.

✔ **authenticationFailure.** An unrecognized community name (discussed later in this section) accompanied an SNMP message.

✔ **egpNeighborLoss.** The agent can no longer communicate with its *Exterior Gateway Protocol* (EGP) peer.

✔ **enterpriseSpecific.** Vendor-specific error conditions and error codes. Your network management must have the vendor's Enterprise MIB to decode these messages.

Some sample trap messages are shown in figure 7.6.

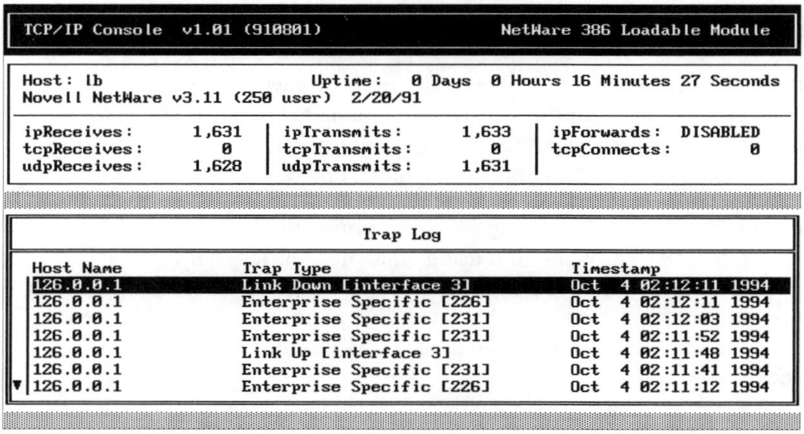

```
TCP/IP Console   v1.01 (910801)              NetWare 386 Loadable Module

Host: lb                        Uptime:   0 Days  0 Hours 16 Minutes 27 Seconds
Novell NetWare v3.11 (250 user)  2/20/91

ipReceives:      1,631    ipTransmits:     1,633   ipForwards:  DISABLED
tcpReceives:         0    tcpTransmits:        0   tcpConnects:        0
udpReceives:     1,628    udpTransmits:    1,631

                                Trap Log

Host Name            Trap Type                      Timestamp
126.0.0.1            Link Down [interface 3]        Oct  4 02:12:11 1994
126.0.0.1            Enterprise Specific [226]      Oct  4 02:12:11 1994
126.0.0.1            Enterprise Specific [231]      Oct  4 02:12:03 1994
126.0.0.1            Enterprise Specific [231]      Oct  4 02:11:52 1994
126.0.0.1            Link Up [interface 3]          Oct  4 02:11:48 1994
126.0.0.1            Enterprise Specific [231]      Oct  4 02:11:41 1994
126.0.0.1            Enterprise Specific [226]      Oct  4 02:11:12 1994
```

Figure 7.6
Sample SNMP trap messages.

SNMP Community Names

Each SNMP request is "signed" with a "password." This password is called an SNMP *community name.* It is a *case-sensitive* text string of up to 32 characters. Each character may take a value from 0 to 255. However, most community names use only printable ASCII characters. Some implementations place a restriction on the characters that can be used. Novell's implementation, for example, allows any characters except for spaces, tabs, open square brackets ([), equal signs, colons, semicolons, or number signs (#).

Three types of communities exist. Each can have a different name (password):

✔ **Monitor Community.** This community name grants read access to SNMP MIBs. Therefore, for each SNMP query, the network management station must include the monitor community name in the message. By default, the monitor community name is set to "public" (all lowercase; without the quotes).

✔ **Control Community.** This name grants read and write access to the MIBs. Recall that certain MIB objects are read-only because of their SMI definition. Therefore, even with the correct control community name, a network management station cannot modify those variables. By default, the control community is disabled so that MIBs are not modified accidentally.

✔ **Trap Community.** This name needs to accompany trap messages. If this name does not match the name setting on the network management station that receives the traps, the trap messages will be rejected (thus lost). By default, the trap community is set to "public," just like the monitor community.

SNMP community names are sent as clear text in the message. Anyone with a protocol analyzer placed on your wire can capture and decode the community names being used (see fig. 7.7). Therefore, do not assume SNMP is secure. This issue is being addressed in SNMP v2 (RFC 1446).

Simple Network Management Protocol

The Simple Network Management Protocol was designed to allow network management station software to communicate with the agents in the managed devices. The communication may involve query messages from the management station, reply messages from the agents, or trap messages from the agents to the management station.

To confirm that traffic due to network management is minimal (the First Network Management axiom), SNMP is implemented using an asynchronous client-server approach. This means an SNMP entity (management station or managed device) need not wait for a response after sending a message; however, a response is generated except for the case of a trap. It can send another message if necessary or continue on with its predefined functions.

```
 ━
 ═  File   Monitor   Alarms   Capture   Decode   Window   Help
 No.  Source            Destination       Layer   Summary
    3 DREAMLAN_312      DREAMLAN_311      snmp    TRAP;126.0.0.2
 ┌─┐
 │←│
         Community: public
         TRAP-PDU: 45 bytes
         Enterprise:
               iso(1).org(3).dod(6).internet(1).private(4).enterprises(1)
               .novell(23).1.6
         Agent Address: 126.0.0.2
         Generic trap: DisplayString(3)
         Time stamp: 6720(00:01:07)
         Variable bindings list: 17 bytes
         Variable binding: 15 bytes
         Name:
               iso(1).org(3).dod(6).internet(1).mgmt(2).mib-2(1)
               .interfaces(2).ifTable(2).ifEntry(1).ifIndex(1).0
         Type: INTEGER
         Value:2
         --A linkUp(3) trap signifies that the sending
         --protocol entity recognizes that one of the
         --communication links represented in the agent's
         --configuration has come up.
    0:  02 60 8C 0B B9 D2 00 AA 00 32 74 62 08 00 45 00   │.`......2tb..E.
   10:  00 58 00 03 00 00 80 11 3E 8F 7E 00 00 02 7E 00   │.X....>.~....~.
   20:  00 01 00 A2 00 A2 00 44 A5 0F 30 3A 02 01 00 04   │.......D..0:....
   30:  06 70 75 62 6C 69 63 A4 2D 06 08 2B 06 01 04 01   │.public.-..+....
   40:  17 01 06 40 04 7E 00 00 02 02 01 03 02 01 00 43   │...@.~.........C
   50:  02 1A 40 30 11 30 0F 06 0A 2B 06 01 02 01 02 02   │..@0.0...+......
   60:  01 01 00 02 01 02                                 │......
                       Packet:  3    Unfiltered:  3
```

Figure 7.7
A LANalyzer for Windows trace of an SNMP trap message.

In SNMP v1 (which is widely used today), there are only four basic operations:

✔ **get.** Used to retrieve a single object in the MIB.

✔ **get-next.** Used to traverse tables within the MIB.

✔ **set.** Used to manipulate (read-write) MIB objects.

✔ **trap.** Used to report alarms.

Rather than use an acknowledge-based protocol, which wastes bandwidth, SNMP uses the response as part of the request acknowledgment.

If you issue a *get* command (the Type and Value fields are set to NULL because the request has no pre-knowledge of what these objects are, as in fig. 7.8) and the named object does not exist, a *get-response* is returned with a *noSuchName* error code. Otherwise, a *get-response* is returned identical to the request, but with the Type and Value portions of the variables filled-in accordingly (see fig. 7.9).

A new *get-bulk* operator has been added to SNMP v2 (RFC 1441-1452). This operation enables the SNMP network management software to retrieve a table with a single request, rather than have to make repetitive calls to *get-next.* This cuts down processing time and network traffic. The main thrust of SNMP v2 is its enhanced security over SNMP v1. As mentioned earlier, community names in SNMP v1 are in clear text and can easily be interepted with a protocol analyzer. SNMP v2 offers a number of secured protocols (RFC 1446) that allow for encryption and authentication. Currently, SNMP v2 is not yet a recommended standard by the *Internet Activities Board* (IAB); it is still an "elective" protocol as per RFC 1600 (dated March 14, 1994), meaning it is not a requirement. SNMP v1 is the current recommended protocol, meaning its implemenntation is strongly suggested. However, SNMP network management software vendors will start implementing SNMP v2 when it becomes more mature. In time, SNMP network management software will all be upgraded to SNMP v2.

Figure 7.8
A SNMP get-request packet.

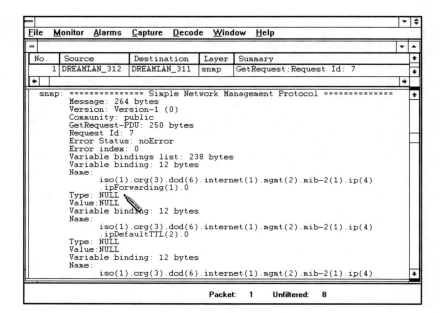

Figure 7.9
A SNMP get-response packet for the request shown in figure 7.8.

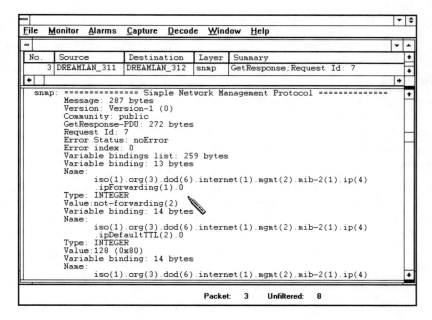

What is a Network Management Station?

A network management station is usually a dedicated workstation (Unix or DOS/ Windows) that runs some kind of network management software. In most cases, this software supports SNMP. Several types of network management software include:

✔ **Novell Inc.'s *NetWare Management System* (NMS).** Runs on DOS/ Windows. Note that NMS is not limited to IPX devices. It also supports the management of IP devices.

✔ **HP's OpenView.** Runs on either DOS, DOS/Windows, or Unix.

✔ **Sun Microsystems's SunNet Manager.** Runs on Unix.

✔ **SynOptics' Optivity.** Runs on DOS/Windows or in conjunction with Novell's NMS or Unix.

✔ **Cabletron's Spectrum.** Runs on DOS/Windows (in conjunction with Novell's NMS) or Unix.

The network management station serves three major functions:

✔ Trap message clearinghouse. It receives trap messages from various managed devices and take any necessary pre-programmed actions (see fig. 7.10). A good implementation also allows you to keep a database of trap messages so that you can have a history of events.

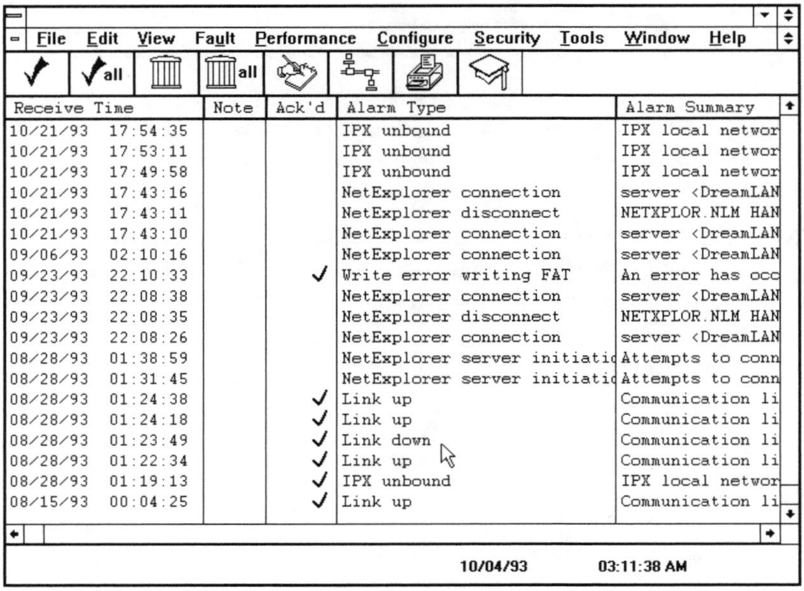

Figure 7.10
The error message report screen of Novell's NetWare Management System (NMS).

✔ Management of SNMP devices by being able to issue SNMP *get, get-next,* and *set* commands (see fig. 7.11). Most management stations provide a nice, user-friendly, interface so that you can avoid using the the complicated ASN.1 representation.

✔ Display of your network layout as well as MIB information in an easy to understand manner. For example, figure 7.12 shows a logical network map based on information collected from various agents. Also shown are alarm symbols alerting network administrators about problematic segments.

Figure 7.11
Sample SNMP query screen from Novell's NMS.

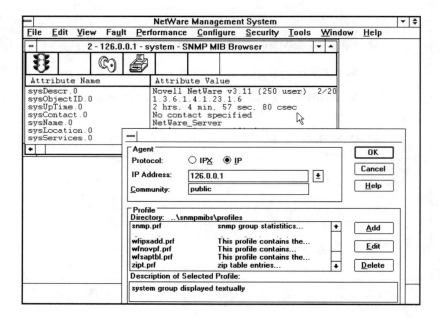

When you invest in a network management station, make sure it has all the functions and features you need to effectively manage your network and devices.

Do not become over-sold on the "gee-whiz" features if they do not provide meaningful information for your particular needs. It will just cost you more money, and not save any time when you are using it.

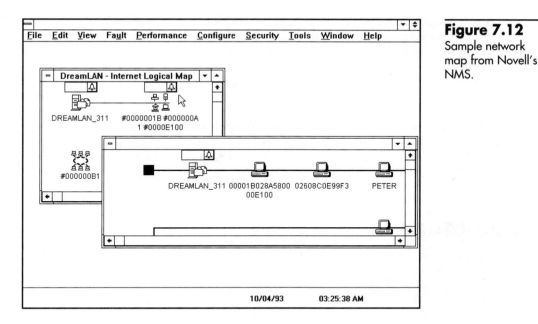

Figure 7.12
Sample network map from Novell's NMS.

Manage Your Network Smartly and Effectively

Two schools of network management are the pro-active approach and the re-active method. Most of the time, we are always reacting to a crisis, which is not effective network management.

To be in the pro-active mode, make full use of your existing resources. Find out if you have smart hubs. Almost all routers support SNMP-management, at least at the MIB-I level. If you are not sure, check with your vendor.

The first thing you need to be aware of when administering a network is to know when the network is getting sick. But, how do you tell? With humans, you look for certain symptoms. You check the temperature and the pulse. Symptoms on your network can also be monitored, such as bandwidth utilization as a function of time, CPU utilization on your servers and routers, and the usual amount of errors on your wire (you will *always* have some errors). Use your network management station to track these statistics for a period of time, say two weeks, and work out some average values for different times of the day. This will be your *baseline*.

A baseline is a set of figures that represent a "healthy" network. With people, a "normal healthy" body temperature is 37C (98.6F). This is your baseline to tell if someone is having a fever. You also need a baseline to determine if anything is wrong with your network. By watching your network's threshold settings in managed devices and looking for symptoms of trouble, you have an early-warning system.

Keep in mind that vendors may have special, proprietary, agents (Enterprises MIBs) for their operating systems, servers, and devices. Make use of them because they provide more information than standard MIBs.

Summary

This chapter presented an overview on Simple Network Management Protocol (SNMP). The most commonly used terms in SNMP, such as *agents* and *MIBs* were defined and discussed. You also learned about the kind of features and information a typical network management station can provide. Finally, some tips on good network management practices were presented.

Chapter Snapshot

In earlier chapters, you learned that 32-bit integers are used for IP addresses to identify machines. Even though such addresses are sometimes easy to remember, most people would rather use names. Names also reduce the chance of "mis-dialing" a host.

This chapter presents one such scheme, called *Domain Name System* (DNS), which is commonly used in mid- to large-size TCP/IP networks and throughout the Internet. This method maps easy-to-use names and symbolic names to IP addresses. This chapter discusses defining what DNS is, its structure, naming conventions, how it works, its implementation, and troubleshooting steps. These topics are presented in the following sections:

Domain Name System

"Don't learn the tricks of the trade; learn the trade."

—*Anonymous*

Defining the Domain Name System

In the early days of computer systems, users had to program a system using toggle switches to set machine addresses and input instructions. As time passed, assembler language was developed so that users could use some simple symbols and instructions to program machines. Today, high-level programming languages accept English-like instructions, which are easier to understand. With newer languages, computer users no longer have to worry about knowing specific memory addresses for variables—they simply refer to them by the variable names.

This analogy is also true in networking. Rather than having to address a specific host by its numeric address, it is much easier to use a symbolic name. This method improves productivity because users make fewer mistakes. It also helps to identify the location of and type of resource a particular machine provides.

Which machine designator is easier to understand: *Customer-Database-Server* or *199.246.41.8*? From the name, you can easily tell that the machine belongs to the Customer Service department, and it is a database server. But looking at the IP number, your guess is as good as any! Another advantage of accessing a resource by name is that your users would not have to know if you moved that service physically from one machine to another.

For example, by using names, your users will connect to *Database-Server* to access the database files. If one day you decide to move the database files from a host with an IP address of 199.246.41.15 to another host with an IP address of 199.246.41.17, you simply have to change the name-to-IP-address mapping. Your users will not even notice. However, if you use IP addresses, you will have to inform all your users of the change—a potential management nightmare.

It is easy to assign a name to any machine at your site. However, how can you guarantee it is unique? In general, if you are not connected to the outside world, such as the Internet, and at a relatively small site, chances are good that you have control over the naming assignments and that every name you use is unique. However, as soon as you join a national, or even a regional network, machines under different administrative control might have name conflicts. Even if you are not joining any outside networks, how can you prevent duplicate names from being used within your organization as your IP network grows?

There are two ways to implement a name-to-IP-address look-up table. You can either have a local table for each workstation or have a centralized table for all your users. The local table solution is ideal for a small number of users or when you want each user to be able to use their own naming convention. Such an implementation is known as a *local hosts table*. However, you have no direct control over the contents of the file because it resides on each machine. When a change is needed, you need to update all machines. The one advantage of this method is that if one user messes up his or her hosts table, it only affects the individual and no one else.

The ideal solution is to use some kind of centralized naming system that translates names to IP addresses. Given the centralized administration of such a database, there is no chance for duplication. The major drawback of this scheme is that if you make a mistake, it affects all users, unlike the local hosts table implementation.

The Internet took just such an approach to managing the large number of names on the Internet. Initially, the Internet's *namespace* was "flat." Each name consisted of a sequence of characters without further structure. Although this kept the naming simple, the Internet quickly found that the flat namespace cannot easily handle a large set of names that exist today. By 1990, there were more than 137,000 host names registered on the Internet.

As the number of registered hosts grew, the workload involved in keeping the database up to date and the amount of traffic going to a single site was just overwhelming. To solve these problems, a *hierarchical* naming scheme, known as the *Domain Name System* (DNS), was developed. To help reduce the traffic bottleneck and add redundancy to the overall system, it was decided that the namespace be partitioned into different domains, with each domain having multiple name-to-IP-address mapping machines.

DNS is mainly used for name-to-address resolution. It should not be confused with *Network Information Services* (NIS; formerly known as Yellow Pages). NIS (the most current implementation is known as NIS+) does more than name-to-address resolution; it also provides user information, such as *user id* (uid) and *group id* (gid).

NIS/NIS+ are most commonly found in NFS environments.

How is DNS Organized?

The current organization of DNS calls for a hierarchical naming structure. On the Internet, a number of top-level domains are defined. Table 8.1 is a sample.

Table 8.1
Top-Level Domain Names

Domain Name	Description
ARPA	Advanced Research Projects Agency network (ARPANET)
COM	Commercial organizations
EDU	Educational institutions
GOV	Government agencies
MIL	Military agencies
NET	Network support centers, such as Internet service providers
INT	International organizations
ORG	Non-profit organizations
country code	Two-letter country codes (as defined by X.500 in ISO-3166)

In most cases, a country may request to use a three-character country code to prevent possible conflict and confusion.

Note that domain names are not case-sensitive at this time. Therefore, *COM* is the same as *com*. As with any hierarchical structure, there is always a *root*. In DNS, the root is simply denoted by a period—no specific name is used.

The proper syntax for a fully qualified domain name should include the trailing period, but most often the "standard" practice is not to include it because it is "understood."

Each top-level domain is divided into a set of second-level domains. The top-level domain reflects the category of domain, such as commercial (*COM*). Second-level domains usually represent a whole organization, such as a company. Third- and lower-level domains are departments and divisions of that organization. Each level of the domain name is separated by a period between the names. The levels move from right (top) to left (bottom). For example, the following name illustrates a three level DNS name:

    Consulting.DreamLAN.COM.

Consulting is the third-level, DreamLAN the second-level, and COM the top-level. This name reflects the Consulting division or department of an organization called DreamLAN within the commercial organizations domain (see fig. 8.1). Each of the names is called a *label* in DNS terms.

Figure 8.1
A sample Internet domain name hierarchy tree.

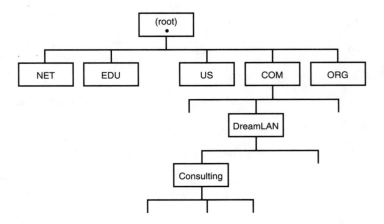

In domain names, the period delimiter is referred to as "dot." Therefore, in the example of *Consulting.DreamLAN.COM*, the correct way of referring to it while speaking is Consulting-dot-DreamLAN-dot-COM. This is the same when you are referring to IP numbers.

The names of the top-level domains are fixed by the *Network Information Center* (NIC). Second-level domain names are unique and must be registered with the NIC before they can be connected to the Internet and be known by the name-to-IP-address mapping servers. Without registering your name, other users on the Internet will not be able to reach you by name; they must explicitly use your IP address.

You can register for a second-level domain name in two ways. First, you can submit your application electronically via email to HOSTMASTER@INTERNIC.NET. A copy of the DOMAIN-TEMPLATE.TXT application form is shown in Appendix C; you can also FTP it from a number of RFC FTP sites, such as NIC.DDN.MIL. If you don't have e-mail access, you can call the numbers listed in the appendix. Note that NIC.DDN.MIL no longer assists non-military users.

When you register a domain name, you are not registering individual host names. This is similar to when you are registering a company for business; you are registering the company, not the individuals who work within the company.

In essence, you are registering the unique "qualifier" for your hosts.

If you simply want to set up a domain for your internal use, you do not need to register with the NIC. However, should you ever have plans to connect with the outside in the future, it is strongly advised that you register for a domain name to avoid future conflicts.

To decentralize the administration workload, each domain is given its own authority to maintain names and to create sub-domains. Sometimes, a domain may subdivide and give some of its authority to the sub-domains. The idea is to keep dividing until each subdivision is small enough to be manageable.

This is very similar to the management of a large organization. It is unreasonable to ask the Board of Directors to be responsible for the hiring and firing of *all* personnel within the organization. Instead, they delegate that authority and responsibility to the various divisions. And each division has different department heads. If the department is large enough, there may be workgroup managers.

The telephone system provides an excellent example of the hierarchical naming system (see fig. 8.2). The telephone number is divided into the following sections (regardless of the number of digits in each "section"):

✔ Country code

✔ Area code

✔ Exchange

✔ Subscriber number

Figure 8.2
A hierarchical tree
for the telephone
number system.

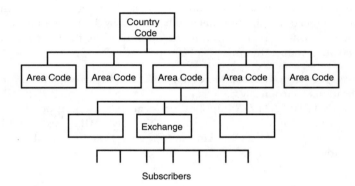

A country is divided into a number of states or provinces. Each state or province is assigned a unique area code to identify it. If the area is large, multiple area codes may be assigned. For each area code, there are different exchanges. Each exchange can handle a preset number of subscribers. If more new subscribers come online, new exchanges are added without needing to modify the area code level. After you are given your own subscriber number, you may choose to have extension numbers (which are independent of the phone company and may be the same as some other company's internal extension numbers).

When ordering telephone service, you generally go to your local phone company office in your area. The people there can assign you a number from that exchange, without having to go back to the head office. If you are a large enough client and want to have a direct-dial number for each person in your company, you may get your own exchange number.

When you register for a domain name, the second-level domain name you choose must be 12 characters or less, as per RFC 1348/1035, the DNS specification.

The fully qualified name, including name, subdomain names, and the top- and second-level domain names, must not exceed 255 characters.

In the DNS world, only the second-level name needs to be unique. Third- and subsequent level domain names are purely administered by the organization. Therefore, the following two names do not constitute a conflict:

```
Consulting.DreamLAN.COM.
```

```
Consulting.Novell.COM.
```

You do not need to register any third- and lower-level names with the NIC; only the second-level name.

> There is no limit on how many sublevels you can have in your domain tree, but it is generally advisable to keep it shallow. You should subdivide it when it makes sense to—for example, to reduce the size of the subdomain so it is manageable.

The division of domains within DNS is purely by organization, rather than by physical location. For example, the COM domain consists of commercial organizations from around the world. A domain (or subdomain) is simply a logical grouping of networks, and may contain, entirely or partially, multiple networks (see fig. 8.3).

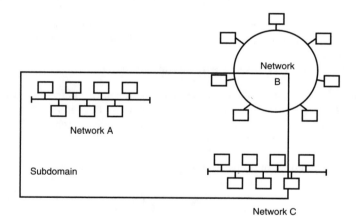

Figure 8.3
A (sub)domain may contain an entire network or only parts of a network.

At the end of each domain tree "branch" (or subdomain) is one or more "leafs" (or objects, as known within the X.500 naming standard). This corresponds to your machine's host name. This name (or label) must be unique within the subdomain. For example,

```
Database-server.Consulting.DreamLAN.COM.
```

and

```
Database-server.Services.DreamLAN.COM.
```

are considered two different and unique machines because they reside in two different subdomains.

When working with domain names, make sure you know the context in which it is referenced. When working with domains, the last item in the list (such as *Consulting.DreamLAN.COM.*) is the subdomain name. When working with a host name (such as *Database-Server.Consulting.DreamLAN.COM.*), the last item in the list is the host name.

In general, you cannot distinguish the names of subdomains from the names of individual objects or the type of an object based solely on the domain name syntax.

Each name stored in the DNS database is assigned an *object type* to identify it. For example, is the name a name for a host, a mailbox, or a user? For example how do you tell if *Consulting* in *Consulting.DreamLAN.COM.* is a host name or a subdomain name? When a client asks the DNS to *resolve* a name (that is, to perform the name-to-address mapping), it must specify the type of answer desired. For example, a remote telnet application should specify that it wants a machine's IP address, not its domain's mail server information. In other words, you must be specific when asking "Consulting, what is your host IP address?"

As part of the DNS specification, the DNS database is distributed among a number of servers. It is unlikely that one single server could hold the database for the entire network. In general, a set of servers located in different locations operate cooperatively to solve the name mapping requests. This is especially true on the Internet.

One of the reasons for a distributed database is efficiency. If you can place the names that are accessed most often on a local machine, you can reduce the DNS lookup traffic on your internet. The other reason is reliability. In a distributed environment, a single machine failure rarely impacts the whole system's operation.

The servers that perform name mapping functions within the context of DNS are called *name servers.* In some cases, they are written as *nameservers* (all one word). A name server performs the function of domain name-to-IP address mapping. If it fails to find the entry in its local database, it may contact another name server for the information. This server software often runs on a dedicated machine.

Name server software is available from a number of sources and can run on a wide variety of platforms. For example, you can get DNS for Unix, DOS, and even NetWare (as a NetWare Loadable Module).

There may be one or more name servers per domain or subdomain.

The client software, called a *name resolver,* uses one or more of the name servers for name lookup. This function is usually built into the client TCP/IP software stack. The next section examines how DNS name servers resolve names requested by clients.

How Does DNS Name Resolution Work?

The easiest way to discuss how the domain name servers are arranged is if they are arranged in a tree format corresponding to the naming hierarchy, as shown in figure 8.4.

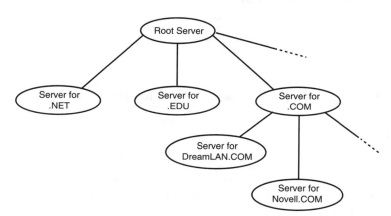

Figure 8.4
Name servers arranged in a tree structure that corresponds to the naming hierarchy.

Each lower-level server knows what the higher-level servers are and where they are located (by IP address). The root server contains information about the root and top-level domains.

When an organization registers for a second-level domain name, it is required to provide and maintain a name server for that subdomain and link it into the tree. This name server is known as the *authority name server* of the subdomain.

If you are using a service provider for your Internet connection, you can use the name servers of your service provider, even if it is in a different subdomain than yours. However, you must obtain that information because it is required for your domain name application.

For example, if a company named ACME Network wants to apply for a domain name on the Internet, it must provide and maintain a name server before a domain name is granted.

To register for a domain name on the Internet, the contact person for the subdomain must have an e-mail address that is reachable via Internet. Although this is not directly related to DNS as discussed here, it is helpful when applying for domain names.

In practice, a single name server usually services numerous subdomains because there is no real need to have a name server for each and every subdomain. In such a case, the set of subdomains forms a *zone of authority*. However, Internet requires that each subdomain provides and maintains two name servers; one acts as the primary and the other secondary should the primary fail.

A name server works in two "modes," depending on the client request. When a name resolver client queries a name server, the message contains the following information:

✔ Name to be resolved

✔ Class of the name (protocol group to be used)

✔ Type of answer desired (that is, IP address associated with this name)

✔ An "action code" that specifies whether the name server should translate the name completely

DNS was designed to be protocol independent. Therefore, the Class field in the query identifies the protocol group of the record of interest. It is possible to have multiple records in the DNS database that has the same data in the "name" field but for different protocols. For TCP/IP users, the class code is *IN* for Internet.

You read previously that DNS can be used to translate a host name to an IP address and also look up a mail server address for a domain. This information is differentiated by the object types. Listed in Table 8.2 are some common object types (better known as *resource record types* in DNS terms) used within DNS.

Table 8.2
Common DNS Resource Record Types.

Type	Meaning
A	Host IP address
CNAME	Canonical domain name for an alias
HINFO	CPU & OS information for a host
MINFO	Mailbox or mail list information
MX	Mail server name for the domain
NS	Name server (that has authority) for the domain
PTR	Pointer to domain name (like a symbolic link in file systems)
SOA	Start of Authority—multiple fields that specify which part of the naming hierarchy a server implements

The majority of the records you find in a DNS database are type *A*, meaning they consist of the name of a host and its IP address. The next common type of records is probably *MX*. It contains host names that act as a mail exchanger (gateway) for a given subdomain. The *MX* records enable you to send e-mail to someone at a given subdomain without having to know the name of the mail gateway. For example, you simply need to address the mail to *Peter@DreamLAN.COM* without having to know that the name of the mail server is *SMTP-GW*. Otherwise, you will have to address your mail to *Peter@SMTP-GW.DreamLAN.COM*.

When a name server receives a query, it checks to see if the name is within the subdomain for which it has authority (that is, is the name in the subdomain in which the name server serves?). If so, it looks up the name in the database and sends back the requested information if present.

If the name server cannot resolve the name completely, it checks to see what "action code" the client specified. There are two possible action codes. If the client requested a *recursive resolution* (complete lookup), the name server will contact another name server to see if it can resolve it; if the contacted name server cannot resolve the name, it will contact the next name server and so forth until it is successful or a time out due to name not found completes (see fig. 8.5).

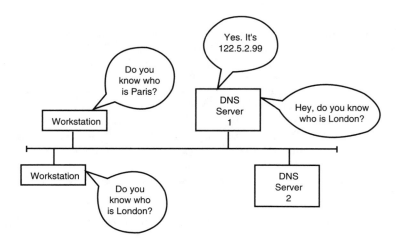

Figure 8.5

In the recursive mode, a name server can ask other name servers for assistance in resolving a name when needed.

If the resolver client asks for *iterative resolution* (non-recursive lookup), the name server will generate an error if it cannot resolve the name. As part of the reply message, the name server will inform the client of a name server that the client should try next (see fig. 8.6).

Figure 8.6
If in the non-recursive mode, a name server that cannot resolve a name will inform the client to try another name server.

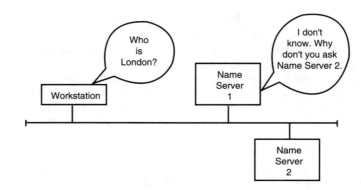

Name resolution is performed from left to right; that is, from the local authority up. This provides the most efficient path for name resolution for a number of reasons. First, a much shorter path for local name resolution is needed. Secondly, if every resolution request starts with the root server, the name server can be easily overloaded with traffic. Lastly, failure of servers at higher levels will prevent name resolution, even if the local authority could resolve the name. Using our telephone system as an example, it is always fastest to contact your local operator to look up a local phone number than to call the overseas operator to look up a local telephone number.

It is very inefficient to contact the root server every time a non-local name needs to be resolved. Internet DNS name servers use *name caching* to reduce such overheads.

Each name server keeps a cache of recently resolved names, as well as a record of where the mapping information for that name came from. When a client queries the name server, the server first checks to see if it can resolve it locally using the standard procedure. If not, the server checks its name cache to see if the name was recently resolved. If found, the server reports the information back to the client, but will indicate that the information might be out of date, and includes as part of the reply the name of the name server and its IP address from which the cached information came. If the name is not found in cache, then the name server will follow the steps described earlier, depending on the "action code" supplied.

It is up to the client software to decide if the returned information is "good enough." If yes, it will go ahead and use that information. Otherwise, it can query the name server that originally supplied the data for verification.

When an authority replies to a query, there is a *Time To Live* (TTL) timer as part of the message that specifies for how long mapping (known as *binding* in DNS terminology) is valid. Thus, the name servers doing the caching will age out the records when the TTL timer expires.

Should a client ask for a name that was once in the cache but has been aged out, the server goes back to the name server with the authority and obtains the binding again.

Now that you have seen how a name server behaves and reacts to client queries, look at how a client makes a request.

How Do You Use DNS?

When a workstation requests a connection to the host, and a name such as the following is used, the TCP/IP software performs a name-to-IP-number look up:

```
telnet database-server
```

Now, depending on the actual software vendor's implementation, the workstation may first look to see if there is a local hosts table (usually a file called *hosts* in a directory called *etc* off the root of the directory path). If the hosts file exists, it checks to see if an entry for *database-server* exists. If so, it uses the IP address corresponding to the entry. A sample hosts file is shown in the following:

```
#
#     Mappings of host names and host aliases to IP address.
#
127.0.0.1        loopback lb localhost    #normal loopback address

#
# examples from Novell network
#
130.57.4.4      ta tahiti ta.novell.com loghost
130.57.6.40                     osd-frog frog
130.57.6.144                      sj-in5 in5
192.67.172.71                     sj-in1 in1

#
# interesting addresses on the Internet
#

192.67.67.20    sri-nic.arpa nic.ddn.mil nic
26.2.0.74     wsmr-simtel20.army.mil simtel20

199.246.41.1                      dreamlan
199.246.40.1                           ast
199.246.41.2                          nw11
```

If a hosts file does not exist and the DNS option is enabled for the workstation software, it will contact the first name server machine listed in the configuration file, known as the *resolve* file; up to three different name servers can be specified in the configuration file. Some software works by looking for DNS first, before checking the local hosts file. A sample DNS resolve file is shown in the following:

```
domain AnyCompany.Com

name server      199.246.41.1
name server      199.246.41.2
```

In the resolve file, typically called *resolv.conf* and often located in the */etc* (or equivalent) directory, the first line indicates the subdomain the workstation is in, or the "default" domain. In the example, the default domain is *Company.COM*. Any host names that are not fully qualified will have *Company.COM* appended to the end. For example, if a user executes the command:

```
telnet database-server
```

DNS will try to resolve *database-sever.Company.COM* for a result.

The remaining lines list the different name servers to contact. Name servers will be queried in the order listed, and up to three name servers can be listed.

You should be aware of the order in which your TCP/IP software searches for DNS name servers and hosts tables. If you do not have DNS name servers, but configured a resolve file, and your software looks for DNS name servers before the hosts file, workstation response time will suffer as a result.

Often, the creation of this resolve configuration file on the workstation is all you need to do for a DNS client to function.

Implementing DNS

Like any public protocols, there are many different DNS name server and resolver implementations. Although the specifics vary from one to another, some general concepts and rules apply. This section discusses general implementation techniques; the next section discusses some troubleshooting tips for DNS. This section uses the *Berkeley Internet Name Domain* server (BIND) as an example for discussion.

As with any client-server type application, there is a server component and a client component. Under *BIND*, the server name daemon is called *named*. The daemon *named* handles the name resolution, queries other name servers when needed, and caches information from previous queries as outlined previously.

Typically, a client's software calls the *gethostent()* and related functions for host information. When *named* is running, such calls are routed to it for resolution. If *named* is not running, calls to the *gethostent()* family of functions are looked up in the /etc/hosts file.

Depending on the implementation, you might need to recompile every program that uses the *gethostent()* family of functions when you switch from /etc/hosts lookup to *named*. The C library should be recompiled for *named* before recompiling the rest of the system. A new kernel would need to be generated.

Some implementations include user-level commands and library functions to query name server databases. *BIND* provides *nslookup* and *resolver*. Shown in figure 8.7 is Novell's implementation of *nslookup* on a NetWare server.

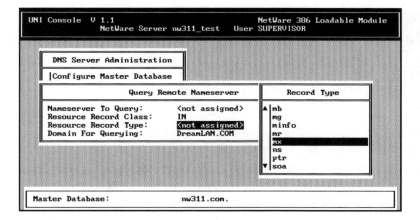

Figure 8.7
Novell's
implementation of
nslookup.

When you set up your copy of *named*, you can configure it to run in one of the following modes:

✔ **Primary master.** All data is stored locally and contains the master copy of the database. All changes and updates should be made to the primary master.

✔ **Secondary master.** Downloads the data from primary master at boot time.

✔ **Caching only.** Contains no local data, queries other servers, and caches the answers.

As mentioned before, to provide fault tolerance, each site needs to have a primary master and at least one secondary master name server.

The *BIND* implementation uses the following three configuration files so that *named* knows about the other name servers:

- ✔ **named.boot**—Name server startup file

- ✔ **named.local**—Client startup file

- ✔ **named.ca**—Initial cache of names and addresses

named.boot

A sample *named.boot* file for the primary master name server is shown in the following:

```
;
; bind boot file - primary server (IP=199.246.41.1)
;
sortlist      199.246.40.0      199.246.41.0
directory     /etc
;
; type         domain              source file or host name
;
cache                                 named.ca
;
primary      AnyCompany.COM        named.hosts
primary      57.130.IN-ADDR.COM    named.novell
primary      0.0.127.IN-ADDR.COM   named.local
```

All lines starting with a semicolon are treated as a comment. The *sortlist* line indicates the order you want addresses to be returned by the name server if there is more than one answer to a given query. For example, this primary name server also acts as an IP router between networks 199.246.40.0 and 199.246.41.0. Thus, the reply to a query of its IP address will cause its address on the 199.246.40.0 network to be returned first.

The *directory* entry states where the data files are located. In this case, their location is in */etc*.

The *cache* line initializes the server name cache from the file *named.ca*. It and other files are to be found under */etc*, as indicated by the *directory* entry.

The first *primary* entry states that the primary source of authoritative data on name-to-IP-address binding for the *AnyCompany.COM* subdomain is the file called *named.hosts*.

You can use an IP address instead of a file name for the location of data sources. If such is the case, the named daemon will attempt to transfer data from that IP host from the named socket (#42).

The second *primary* entry indicates that mapping data for network 130.57.0.0 is in the file *named.novell.* You will only have such an entry if this name server is also the authority for the subdomain on that particular network. Repeat the entry for as many networks/ subdomains for which the name server is the authority. Note that the IP address is *byte-swapped* (reversed). The data listed in the file is also byte-swapped. A sample taken from RFC 1033 is shown in the following:

```
33.12.192.IN-ADDR.ARPA.   IN  SOA KL.SRI.COM  DLE.STRIPE.SRI.COM.  (
                          870404  ;serial
                          1800    ;refresh every 30 minutes
                          600     ;retry every 10 minutes
                          604800  ;expire after a week
                          86400   ;default of a day
                          )


33.12.192.IN-ADDR.ARPA.   NS   KL.SRI.COM.
                          NS   STRIPE.SRI.COM.
                          PTR  GW.CSL.SRI.COM.

; SRI-CSL-NET [192.12.33.0] Address Translations

; SRI.COM Hosts
2.33.12.192.IN-ADDR.ARPA.       PTR     CSL.SRI.COM

; CSL.SRI.COM Hosts
1.33.12.192.IN-ADDR.ARPA.       PTR     GW.CSL.SRI.COM
3.33.12.192.IN-ADDR.ARPA.       PTR     B.CSL.SRI.COM
4.33.12.192.IN-ADDR.ARPA.       PTR     SMELLY.CSL.SRI.COM
5.33.12.192.IN-ADDR.ARPA.       PTR     SQUIRREL.CSL.SRI.COM
7.33.12.192.IN-ADDR.ARPA        PTR     VENUS.CSL.SRI.COM
```

The last *primary* entry is for the localhost information. Some TCP/IP networks do not need this entry, but some do. Note that the localhost address is also reversed.

A sample *named.boot* file for the secondary master name server is shown in the following:

```
;
; bind boot file - secondary server (IP=199.246.41.2)
;
sortlist        199.246.40.0    199.246.41.0
directory       /etc
;
; type          domain          source file or host name
;
cache                           named.ca
```

```
;
secondary       AnyCompany.COM          199.246.41.1    named.hosts
secondary       57.130.IN-ADDR.COM      199.246.41.1    named.novell
secondary       0.0.127.IN-ADDR.COM     named.local
;
forwarders      199.246.41.1
```

You might notice that the format of this file is very similar to that for the primary name server, with a few minor exceptions.

In the *secondary* entries, you specified that the data be read from both the primary master server (by IP address) and from local files.

The primary name server is also a *forwarder*, in that any queries to the secondary server will be sent to the primary for resolution, rather than to a root server. This way, the amount of traffic to the root server is reduced, and the primary server is allowed to build a big cache and is able to resolve most queries locally.

named.local

The *named.local* file is used to specify the local loopback interface for the name server. The file contains only one *Start of Authority* (SOA) record and two resource records. An example is shown in the following:

```
@ IN    SOA     Server.AnyCompany.COM. Admin.Server.AnyCompany.COM. (
                        134.8   ; Serial number
                        3600    ; Refresh time (in seconds)
                        3600000 ; Expiration time (in seconds)
                        3600 )  ; Minimum (in seconds)
    IN    NS     Name server.AnyCompany.COM.
  1 IN    PTR    localhost.
```

The SOA record defines the start of a zone. The @ in the first field on the first line defines the name of the zone. @ denotes the current *origin* or AnyCompany.COM in this example. The fourth field lists the name of the primary master name server for this subdomain. The next field identifies the person in charge of the administration of this subdomain; it must be an e-mail address. The options in parentheses set the parameters for the subdomain.

The SOA record contains a list of five numbers enclosed within parentheses:

✔ **Version or serial number.** The first number in the list should be incremented every time the file is updated. Secondary name servers check and compare the version number of the primary server with their version to determine whether to download the master DNS database.

✔ **Refresh time.** Specifies the time in seconds regarding how often secondary name servers query the primary name server to determine if updated tables are available.

✔ **Retry.** Specifies a time in seconds on how long a secondary name server should wait before a failed refresh should be retried.

✔ **Expiration time.** The upper limit on the time interval, in seconds, that can elapse before a secondary name server should age out its whole database without doing a refresh.

✔ **Minimum.** The default time for the *Time to Live* (TTL) timer on the exported resource records when none is specified.

The NS record states the name server for the current subdomain is called *Server.AnyCompany.COM*. It does not have to be the primary name server. This is how you can distribute workloads onto various secondary name servers.

The last record specifies a reverse pointer to localhost. The 1 in the first column of the last entry is short for 1.0.0.127, which is the byte-swapped version of the localhost address 127.0.0.1.

Note that the fully qualified name is to be used in the DNS server names, including the root—the trailing "dot."

named.ca

The *named.ca* file is used to populate the name cache when the name server boots up. A sample *named.ca* file taken from RFC 1033 is shown in the following:

```
        ;list of possible root servers
        .       1       IN  NS  SRI-NIC.ARPA.
                                NS  C.ISI.EDU.
                                NS  BRL-AOS.ARPA.
                                NS  C.ISI.EDU.
        ;and their addresses
        SRI-NIC.ARPA.           A   10.0.0.51
                                A   26.0.0.73
        C.ISI.EDU.              A   10.0.0.52
        BRL-AOS.ARPA.           A   192.5.25.82
                                A   192.5.22.82
                                A   128.20.1.2
        A.ISI.EDU.              A   26.3.0.103
```

For each entry, the first field indicates the domain or subdomain; the second field is the TTL value; the third field is the class (Internet); the fourth is the record type, such as NS (name server) or A (address); and the last field is either the host name or the IP address.

 A blank entry in a field uses the last entry defined for that field. In the preceding sample, for instance, fields 1 through 3 are blank in record 2—they will take on the value from the previous record: ".," "1," and "IN."

It is important to note the "dot" in the very first entry. It indicates the root domain. Also note the final dot in the host names; all names are specified all the way back to the root domain.

Troubleshooting DNS

Due to the varied implementations of DNS available, not all DNSs will communicate with each other. This section details five common problems and possible fixes regarding this incompatibility. The information presented here is drawn mainly from RFC 1536, "Common DNS Implementation Errors and Suggested Fixes." If the tips presented here do not help with your particular problem, contact your vendor. You might have an implementation-specific problem.

Fast Retransmission Error

Domain name resolution uses the classic client-server technology. It generally works well on local area networks where the geographic extent is small or when traffic is so light that it does not cause bottlenecks. A problem can arise when a client gets no response from its query within a reasonable time and amount of retries. However, how does one classify "reasonable time?"

This is not a straightforward question because there are many variables involved. For example, the platform on which the name server runs, the efficiency of the name server software, traffic on the network, and client TCP/IP software are all variables affecting response time.

Other matters aside, sometimes the main culprit is the client's TCP/IP protocol stack. It may not wait long enough before deciding a time-out situation has occurred and then retransmitting the request. This could result in excessive traffic on the network, and the server will see multiple queries. If the server's software is smart, it would ignore the multiple queries and generate only one reply. Otherwise, even more traffic will be generated as a result.

Some implementations of the client resolver software will back off (increase) the time interval between retries. This, however, is not often the case.

A solution to this type of problem is to tune any time-out parameters that may be available on the client side. Sometimes, the delay on the server side may be due to it waiting for a reply from other name servers when a recursive name resolution is requested by the client. Should this be the case, if the client software can query multiple servers, use the non-recursive query mode rather than the recursive mode. Use the name server list from the server to query other name servers.

Recursion Bug

When a name server receives a query, it first determines its zone data and checks the cache to see if the query can be answered. If the name server cannot satisfy the query, it finds a list of name servers that are more likely to have the desired information. At this point, the name server does one of two things, depending on the client's requested action code.

If the client asks for recursion and the name server allows recursion, the name server queries this list of servers. If the client did not ask for recursion, the name server returns the list of possible name servers to the client. The client will then query the new list of servers. This process repeats until the client is satisfied or gives up.

However, in certain cases, a faulty name server may include itself in the list of name servers as one of the servers to query. The client resolver software may not check and resend the same query to the same name server. This causes a loop.

Another type of loop is possible between name servers. Name server A lists name server B as possible and name server B lists name server A as possible. Such circular reference is difficult to detect, especially if more than two name servers are involved.

Another type of recursion bug is when the client doesn't know what to do with the list of name servers it is given, so it queries the same name server again.

This category of bug is very difficult to track down. In most cases, you will need a protocol analyzer to look at the request and reply packets between the client and name servers. If outside name servers are involved, it makes it even more difficult to identify.

You can, however, help minimize such possibilities by first examining your local configuration and ensuring none of your own name servers are pointing to each other. Sometimes, trying different client resolver software may help to identify the source and cause of the problem.

Zero Answer Bug

Sometimes name servers return no errors and no data to the client. This happens when the queried name is valid, but no records of the desired type are found. For example, you queried for the *MX* record for domain *WhereEver.COM*. The name server may not return an error if the domain name *WhereEver.COM* is valid, but no *MX* record is found (see fig. 8.7).

Depending on the client software, it may treat this "zero answer" reply as invalid, and query the name server again. Because every query results in an "error," you might get into an infinite loop. You can determine if this is indeed the case by using *nslookup* or an equivalent to query for different types of records for the same domain name. If your resolver software permits, limit the number of times the client can query a name server when an "error" condition is detected.

Format Error

Perhaps due to a bug in either the name server or resolver client, the correct format of the request or reply message is not adhered to. This results in the other party not being able to understand the message. The format error might only happen for certain record types.

Similar to the problems discussed here, querying different record types and trying different name servers or resolver clients can help you identify the error resource. Finding the cause is half the battle.

Configuration File Error

As with any software installation, configuration file errors are probably the most common cause of headaches. This is especially true with Domain Name Services. Some common configuration errors include the following:

✔ Syntax error causing part or all the file to be ignored. Sometimes, this is seen when the configuration files were created on a different machine or even different platform (such as MS-DOS), and then transferred to the name server host. Many times the files were not transferred correctly—for example, using binary setting in FTP.

✔ Look at the files on the name server using its native editor to see if you can spot anything. If you are unsure, re-create the files on the name server.

✔ Missing resolver configuration file causing DNS not to function.

✔ Missing the *domain* entry in the resolver configuration file.

✔ Incorrect root name server address.

✔ Forgot to increment the serial number count on the SOA record after updates were made.

✔ Forgot to byte-swap address files.

The configuration file errors are often much easier to troubleshoot and correct than the first four errors described. You will be surprised to find out how much troubleshooting you can do with simple utilities such as *ping, netstat,* and *nslookup.* One of the rules in troubleshooting networks is no matter what software is involved, ensure your connectivity is good. If you have bridges and routers, also check their configurations.

Like any software, should you suspect a software bug, make sure you are running the latest version. Sometimes, it is also important for the client software version to match your server's.

Summary

This chapter presented the Domain Name System (DNS), a popular name-to-IP-address mapping protocol used in many mid- to large-size TCP/IP installations.

In-depth views on the organization of DNS, its naming conventions and its implementations were discussed. In particular, the chapter showed various ways DNS can resolve a name to IP address. This chapter helped you understand DNS functions and troubleshoot some common DNS problems. The Berkeley Internet Name Domain (BIND) implementation was used as an example to illustrate how you configure DNS servers.

Five common DNS implementation errors and possible solutions were presented. By combining the information presented in this last section with your understanding of how DNS should operate, presented earlier in the chapter, you will be well prepared to implement and troubleshoot a DNS server.

Chapter Snapshot

The sendmail program transfers e-mail messages to local and remote users' mailboxes. For local mail delivery, it writes directly to the user's mailbox file. Remote delivery requires the use of whatever networking is available. Where available, sendmail can utilize *Unix to Unix Copy* (UUCP) or TCP/IP networking. The *Simple Mail Transfer Protocol* (SMTP), as specified by RFC 821, is used for TCP/IP networking.

sendmail is not a user interface—in fact, it is not user-friendly in any way. sendmail just delivers preformatted messages. Other programs such as mail, mailx, or elm provide a more user-friendly environment for composing messages. These programs format the entered message accordingly, and then call on sendmail to transfer the data.

In this chapter, you learn about the following topics:

9

CHAPTER

sendmail and SMTP

"Certainties are arrived at only on foot."

—*Antonio Porchia*

Nothing is more capable of bringing a company to its knees than taking away its e-mail system. When looking at the timeline of history, e-mail has been in existence a very short time. Yet, in that time, companies have become so dependent upon it that they barely function when the mail server crashes.

sendmail is the Unix-based daemon (background process) that routes e-mail from user to user and server to server. From an administrative standpoint, no more efficient daemon can be found; from a user's standpoint, no more cursed and confounding beast exists. sendmail is difficult to use and tiresome to learn. Consequently, many third-party applications have been developed to act as interfaces to it. Users can be isolated from the cryptic commands by such e-mail interfaces as ELM, while sendmail continues to function in the background and satisfy all requests.

Understanding the sendmail Command

One of the most confusing components of sendmail is its many options. It is safe to say that the vast majority of these options are not used on a regular basis. The reason for the abundance of options is that sendmail was designed to be customizable to almost any need or requirement; what these options unintentionally did, however, was to make sendmail confusing.

The Options

Several command-line options control the sendmail program. Most are used for testing the configuration file and the alias file. Options such as sendmail -bt and sendmail -bv are used when changing the configuration file to ensure that the new rule sets work properly. Most options are of very little use on a daily basis, though. The most important options to a system administrator are -d# for setting the debug level, -q<time> for setting the frequency to process the queue of messages, -bd for setting the program to background or daemon mode, and -v to set verbose mode for basic testing.

The sendmail program should be started in the background mode by the following entry in one of your startup scripts:

```
/usr/lib/sendmail -bd -q30m
```

This command starts sendmail as a background process and directs it to process queued messages every 30 minutes. The time after the -q option may be specified as any combination of days, hours, minutes, and seconds by following the numbers with d, h, m, or s, respectively. -q2d3h45m10s, for instance, specifies that the queue is to be processed every 2 days, 3 hours, 45 minutes, and 10 seconds.

The sendmail command is usually linked to other command names such as mailq and newaliases. These commands, when invoked, actually run the sendmail command with certain options preset. The mailq command, for instance, is the same as sendmail -bp and displays the contents of the mail queue. newaliases rebuilds the alias database from the alias file, explained later, and is the same as sendmail -bi.

Examining the sendmail Configuration File

The sendmail configuration file is a readable text file that starts with a list of options and macros with which you define your system and preferences. These are followed by very cryptic *rule sets,* which are used by the sendmail program to decipher the addresses in mail messages. This chapter does not attempt to decipher and explain the rule sets; they are beyond the scope of this book and perhaps the English language.

Do not attempt to modify the rule sets unless you are VERY sure of what you are doing. Rule sets are very cryptic and should only be modified by experts. Your system should have a default configuration file with appropriate rule sets. Only the options and macros should be manually manipulated.

Options and Macros

Macros start with D and are followed by a single case-sensitive letter to name the macro and the text for expansion of the macro. Macros are used to define names, such as your host name, domain name, and the name for the From field on error mail messages. Macros can be continued by starting with the letter C, followed by a previously defined macro name and the continuation text. The most important of these is the host name(s) and domain name. The following is a sample sendmail file:

```
############################################################################
###                                                                      ###
###          basic sendmail configuration for generic complex host       ###
###                    with both UUCP and Internet connections            ###
###                                                                      ###
############################################################################

# Our local domain ($D is added to $w [hostname] for official name in
➥rule sets
#
DDbar.com


# All the names we are known by (put all the names & nicknames on the
➥next
# line, separated by spaces. If you need another line, begin it with
➥"Cw")
#
#Dwfoo.bar.com
#Cwns ftp www


# Our UUCP name
DU$w


############################################################################
###    baseline definitions that sendmail needs to operate          ###
############################################################################
```

```
##########################
###    Special macros    ###
##########################

DV25


# my official host name
Dj$w
# my name (the name on mailer bounces)
DnPOSTMASTER
# UNIX header format
DlFrom $g $d
# delimiter (operator) characters
Do.:%@!^/[]
# format of a total name
Dq$?x$x <$g>$¦$g$.
# SMTP login message
De$j Sendmail $v/$V ready at $b


##################
###    Options    ###
##################


# we have full sendmail support here
Oa
# location of alias file
OA/usr/lib/aliases
# default delivery mode (deliver in background)
Odbackground
# (don't) connect to "expensive" mailers
#Oc
# temporary file mode
OF0600
# default GID
Og1
# location of help file
OH/usr/lib/sendmail.hf
# log level
OL9
# Send to me too (even if I'm in an alias expansion)
Om
# default messages to old style
Oo
```

```
# queue directory
OQ/usr/spool/mqueue
# read timeout -- violates protocols (timeout an SMTP idle for 2 hours)
Or2h
# status file
OS/usr/lib/sendmail.st
# queue up everything before starting transmission
Os
# default timeout interval (returns undelivered mail after 3 days)
OT3d
# time zone names (V6 only)
OtPST,PDT
# default UID
Ou1
# encrypted wizard's password (for the undocumented "wiz" SMTP command)
OWjoejoe
# rebuild the aliasfile automagically
#OD
# maximum load average before queueing mail
Ox10
# maximum load average before rejecting connections
OX15


###############################
###    Message precedences   ###
###############################

Pfirst-class=0
Pspecial-delivery=100
Pbulk=-60
Pjunk=-100


#########################
###   Trusted users   ###
#########################

Troot
Tdaemon
Tnews
Tuucp
#############################
###   Format of headers   ###
#############################
```

```
H?P?Return-Path: <$g>
HReceived: $?sfrom $s$. by $j$?r with $r$. ($v/$V-eef)
      id $i; $b
H?D?Date: $a
H?F?From: $q
H?x?Full-Name: $x
H?M?Message-Id: <$t.$i@$j>
HSubject:
H?D?Resent-Date: $a
H?F?Resent-From: $q
H?M?Resent-Message-Id: <$t.$i@$j>


# RULESETS START HERE
#
################################################################################
#                   RULESET ZERO PREAMBLE                                      #
################################################################################
```

The actual macro names in your configuration file may be different from the example here. As long as it is well commented, as they usually are, you should be able to translate well enough.

Make a backup copy of the configuration file before making any changes. The changes do not always work as expected. A backup file saves much time if the file is ruined in the process of modification.

The DD entry defines your domain name and is combined later with the Dw entry to create your official host name. If the server is expected to handle mail for other servers on your network or if your server is known by more than one name, you should include the extra names on the Cw line. Remember, C entries continue a macro. In the case of the host name macro, it is used to list all aliases by which your mail system is known.

The Dn entry is used to define the user name that will be sent in the From field of error messages. Set this macro to send the name POSTMASTER and ensure that an entry for POSTMASTER exists in the alias file. This enables users to "Reply" to error messages without generating yet another error.

Most, if not all, options available on the sendmail command line also can be specified in the configuration file as defaults. Options start with the letter O followed by the option. The option letters that follow the O are the same as those on the command line and have the same effect.

The OL# option defines the log level. This option controls how much information is stored in the log file by sendmail. Larger numbers in place of the # result in more information in your log file. If you are having problems, enter **OL9** for maximum logging. When an error develops, you will have more information for troubleshooting.

The Om option is for alias expansions. If a user sends mail to an alias and his or her name is listed in the alias expansion, the default action is to not send the message to the sender. Om overrides this default and sends mail to the user anyway. Because many users use this feature to verify that their mail was actually sent, it is probably a good idea to make this option a default action by including it in the configuration file.

Or*<time>* and OT*<time>* are timeout options. The OT option causes problem messages to be queued and retried for the amount of time specified before giving up and returning to sender. The Or option specifies a timeout value for read operations. When receiving mail from a remote host and no data is received for the amount of time specified by this option, sendmail gives up and closes the connection. Because this option violates the strict letter of the standard as specified by RFC 821, it should be set to a very high value when used.

The OW option specifies a password for "wizard" functions. Basically, this is a "backdoor" password that enables the user to perform functions not normally required of the sendmail program. It is used by programmers and troubleshooters to find problems with an implementation of the protocol. It is not needed by the average user or administrator.

Change the wizard password. It was set to a well-known default by your installation program. Because this standard is known to those who know how to use it, your system could be vulnerable to malicious misuse. Eliminating the line from the configuration file may automatically enable the default. Ensure that this option is specified and is changed from the default.

When the standards were originally developed for e-mail message transfer, they used spaces to separate multiple names of recipients. The current standard, however, requires the comma as a separator. Many mail programs still use the old style of multiple names separated with spaces. sendmail, therefore, provides an option both on the command line and in the configuration file to ensure that these old mailers will still work. The -o or Oo option tells sendmail that some messages may use spaces to separate recipient names instead of the newer comma format.

OD is another useful option. Whenever you change the alias file, you must run newaliases to rebuild the database that sendmail uses. If OD is set in the configuration file, sendmail automatically rebuilds the database before sending any messages. This may result in extra processing, but will prevent errors caused by forgetting to rebuild the database after changes. It is very useful if you are maintaining mailing lists using the alias file.

"Trusted" users can alter the From name on messages. This is normally only used by special user accounts such as root, daemon, or uucp for sending error messages. Any user listed in the TRUSTED USERS section of the configuration file, however, can use the sendmail -f*<user>* command to alter the From field on outgoing messages.

Examining the alias File

The alias file, usually /usr/lib/aliases, is used for creating mailboxes for which no user account exists. In this file, you define alias names and account names to which the system redirects the incoming mail. You can even redirect the incoming mail to the stdin of a program instead of a user's mailbox with this feature.

The standard alias redirection line is entered as follows:

```
alias: username
```

or

```
alias: username, username, username, ...
```

The first example redirects all mail addressed to the alias to the user name. The second example redirects all mail to each of the user names listed. For long lists of names, you can continue the line by ending with a \ immediately prior to the carriage return. Account names can be simple local accounts such as smith or remote users like green@some.school.edu. Any address that you can specify when sending mail can be specified in the alias list.

For extremely long lists of names, list the names in a separate file and enter a line in the /usr/lib/aliases file, such as the following:

```
authors:":include:/usr/local/lib/authors.list"
```

When sendmail expands the alias, it reads the specified file for a list of account names it needs to send the mail.

Always include an alias for POSTMASTER and, if running a name server daemon, also for HOSTMASTER. These aliases are de facto standards for the administrators of the mail system and domain name system, respectively. When a user on a remote host cannot find a user account name or a host name, a query to one of these aliases results in a helpful answer.

One of the most powerful and therefore most dangerous features of the alias file is the capability to redirect inbound mail to a program based on an alias. When the first character of an account name in an alias expansion is a vertical bar (|), the name will be executed as a program and the inbound mail will be sent to the program as if typed on the keyboard. In an alias file, the vertical bar works the same as in the shell. So,

```
listserv: "¦/usr/local/bin/listserv -l"
```

would send the mail file to the listserv program as if you had entered **cat mailfile¦listserv -l**. In fact, that is how most automated mailing list servers are implemented. The administrator sets up an alias, and the listserv program translates the subject line or body of the message into actions to control the mailing list.

It is a major security risk to include an alias that redirects inbound mail to a uudecode program. Although this was once common and is still useful for transferring files, it is very dangerous. Because no authentication or permission controls are enabled within this system, a Trojan horse or virus could easily be introduced into your system. Do not include any programs in your alias file that would allow transferring executable programs unless you have enabled extra security measures.

An example of an alias file is shown in the following. For those not familiar with the Unix operating system, note that lines beginning with a pound sign (#) are comment lines and ignored by the program.

```
# Alias file for foo.bar.com
# Last update 30 September 1994 SDR
######################################################################
#                                                                    #
#  Don't forget to rebuild the database with 'newaliases' after      #
#  you change this file. -- Not absolutely necessary if OD in cfg    #
#                                                                    #
######################################################################
#Required entries for system administration
POSTMASTER: smith_john
MAILER_DAEMON: smith_john
HOSTMASTER: jones_bill

#Department Heads
CEO: oserr_mary
Accounting: reader_mike@money.bar.com
AIS: smith_john, jones_bill

# Mailing list
listserv:"¦listserv -l"
allusers: ":include:/usr/lib/allusers"
#Printer
hardcopy:"¦lp -s"
```

Understanding SMTP

The sendmail program uses the SMTP to send mail to users on remote hosts. The receiving host must be running sendmail or an equivalent program as a background daemon listening on the well-known port 25. The following steps occur:

1. The sending sendmail establishes a connection on this port to the receiving sendmail.

2. The receiver identifies itself upon recognizing the connection; then the sender identifies itself.

3. After the receiver acknowledges the sender's ID, the sender defines who the mail is from. Again this is acknowledged by the receiver.

4. Next, the sender identifies the intended recipient(s) of the message. The receiver acknowledges or denies the transfer.

5. If denied, the sending sendmail records an error message in the sending user's mailbox.

6. If any of the intended recipients are positively acknowledged, the sender transfers the message, ending it with a period on a line by itself, and the receiver acknowledges and forwards the message to the user's mailbox.

All of this transpires using standard text commands, as in the following example of a typical e-mail message transfer:

```
220 FOO.BAR.COM Simple Mail Transfer Service Ready
HELO SOME.SYSTEM.EDU
250 Welcome to FOO.BAR.COM
MAIL FROM:<Smith@SOME.SYSTEM.EDU>
250 OK
RCPT TO:<Jones@FOO.BAR.COM>
250 OK
RCPT TO:<Green@FOO.BAR.COM>
550 No such user here
RCPT TO:<Brown@FOO.BAR.COM>
250 OK
DATA
354 Start mail input; end with <CRLF>.<CRLF>
From: Smith@some.system.edu
To: Jones@foo.bar.com, Green@foo.bar.com, Brown@foo.bar.com
Subj: Test message
```

```
This is a test. This is only a test. etc. etc.
250 OK

QUIT
221 FOO.BAR.COM Service closing transmission channel
```

The following commands are used:

- ✔ HELO is the command with which the sending sendmail program identifies itself.

- ✔ MAIL FROM is the command to identify the sending user.

- ✔ RCPT TO is the command to identify the intended recipient. (Note that the RCPT TO command may be repeated several times before the actual message is sent. This allows the sendmail programs to send the same message to several users without transferring the data across the network for each user.)

- ✔ DATA signifies that all recipients have been specified, and the sender is ready to transfer the actual message.

- ✔ QUIT is used to tell the receiver that the sender is finished and the connection may be closed.

The responses from the receiving sendmail program always start with a number and are usually followed by text to explain the response to humans. The first digit of the number gives the general category of the message—the one most important to humans reading the messages. $2xx$ is an OK, all conditions normal response. $5xx$ is an uncorrectable error message, such as a syntax error. $4xx$ is also an error message, but implies a temporary condition like "service temporarily unavailable—try again later." These numeric codes are included because the replies are normally read by a sendmail program, and a standard of three-digit numbers is much easier to parse. The text messages are only included for error reports and debugging modes, which must be read by humans.

Summary

The sendmail program is a complex message-transfer utility used to deliver e-mail to both local and remote users. This chapter discussed the sendmail configuration file, which contains many options—most of which are never used by the average network user. The chapter also explains how sendmail uses the Simple Mail Transfer Protocol to send and receive messages. SMTP makes using sendmail easier by specifying the use of a TCP connection and simple commands and responses.

Chapter Snapshot

Security is an item people never tire of discussing. This chapter examines security as it relates to your network and the hosts on that network. Rather than stating the obvious and telling dozens of ways to choose a password, the focus is on more advanced concepts and includes the following topics:

CHAPTER

Network Security

"Through March and early April, the hacker laid low..."

—*Cliff Stoll,* The Cuckoo's Egg

A secure network does not exist; nor does a secure computer. The only secure computer is one that is unplugged, locked in a secure vault that only one person knows the combination to, and that person died last year. When you move beyond that scenario, you must expect lapses in security.

The question is how much "insecurity"—for lack of a better term—are you willing to accept? The next question is to what do you want to apply security? Are you trying to keep people from using your CPU processor? Are you trying to keep them from seeing your data? Are you trying to keep them from ruining your hardware? What, exactly, are you attempting to keep safe?

The Unix operating system inherently contains a few loopholes and inconsistencies that can be exploited by a wily hacker to his or her benefit. Originally, Unix was not written with security in mind, but rather ease of use. In fact, many vendor versions of Unix shipped with known security holes, and it was the responsibility of the system administrator to close those holes. Were it not for events like the Robert Morris Internet Worm of 1988, many of those holes would still exist.

Although Unix sounds less than trustworthy, compare Unix to a DOS-based operating system, which has no security whatsoever. Considered in that light, Unix turns out to be one of the most secure operating systems still considered usable.

What happens when you connect a secure computer to a network, though? Suddenly individuals are allowed to access data and perform operations without the necessity of sitting at the keyboard. A network provides so many advantages over a stand-alone computer, that stand-alones are virtually dinosaurs of the past. At the same time, however, the benefits bring disadvantages. Those disadvantages are risks—you are allowing someone into your system and trusting that they will respect your system and its data.

This chapter looks at ways of reducing the risks to which you expose your system. Understand, however, that no system is entirely foolproof. The first step in risk reduction is to comprehend the different levels of security that can be applied to operating systems.

Understanding Security Levels

The Trusted Computing Standards Evaluation Criteria (also known as the Orange Book), established by the United States Department of Defense, concludes that one cannot simply say that a computer is secure or not secure. Instead, it says that different levels of security can be assigned to an operating system. All these levels are based upon the *trust* you have in the operating system. A highly trusted system prevents intruders from entering the system, whereas a less trusted system has more possibilities of an intruder coming in unnoticed.

Four different levels of security are represented by letters ranging from A to D. Within each level of security, a number can be used to subdivide the level further, as in A1, A2, and so on. DOS is representative of a D1-level operating system. DOS has no security whatsoever; whoever is sitting at the keyboard has complete access to everything on the system. The concept of file ownership and permissions is virtually nonexistent in DOS—all the files are owned by the current user.

At the other end of the spectrum, an A1 level is virtually the machine locked in the vault without power or users. Everything else falls somewhere in-between.

C-level operating systems have more security than D-level ones, and have a means by which a user is identified before he or she is allowed to access and manipulate files. Standard Unix, without any features other than logins, passwords, and file ownership concepts represents C1 security. C2 is a step higher than C1 and includes the capability to keep users from executing commands if they lack certain criteria, as well as the capability to audit every action that takes place. Many Unix systems today, notably SCO Unix, allow for these additional facilities and are C2-certified.

B-level operating systems must offer further security restraints—including an inability for the owner of a file to change the permissions of it. Very few operating systems, and certainly not those readily available in the commercial market, meet any of the B level-requirements.

Deciding How Much Security To Implement

Although some experts issue the blanket statement that you can never have enough security and that the best thing you can do is implement more, more, more security, these generalities could not be further from the truth. Security, inherently, makes it harder to enter a system by providing additional locks that users must pass. Unfortunately, legitimate users must pass those locks as well. Every security measure installed creates more work for someone. In the instance of applying additional passwords, additional work is required by all users to further identify themselves before being allowed to do the transactions they want to do. With auditing, which may be invisible to the end user, the system administrators must assume additional tasks; they must define rights, maintain log files, and audit them on a regular basis.

Figure 10.1 shows a crude representation of the security spectrum. At one end is no security whatsoever; the system is easy to use by virtue of the fact that no constraints are placed on users or administrators.

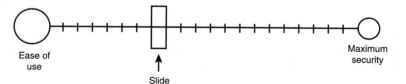

Ease of use

Maximum security

Slide

Figure 10.1
The security spectrum.

At the other end of the spectrum is maximum security—again referring to the unplugged machine locked in a vault. At this end, the system is as secure as it can be, but so difficult to use that no one wants to. The slide in the middle is moveable so that it can be custom-tailored to each site.

Because absolutes rarely exist in life and little can be shown with a straight line, figure 10.2 presents the same information in a more realistic manner. The left side of the graph tracks the number of computer problems relating to security measures (including both user and administrator problems), whereas the bottom represents the amount of security implemented. When no security is implemented, no problems occur. As soon as security is implemented, the number of problems begins to increase. The term "problems" is used to represent legitimate complaints as well as additional workload.

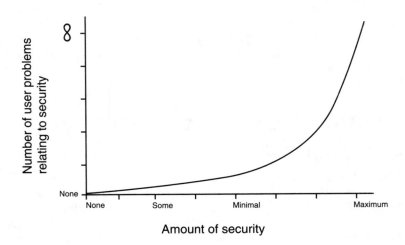

Figure 10.2
Graphing security measures and the number of problems they generate.

Amount of security

In figure 10.2, notice that the line does not grow in a linear fashion; this is known instead as an *indifference curve*. As a small amount of security is implemented, only a few problems occur. It is, in fact, possible to implement more security without affecting the number of problems too significantly. When the security measures begin to tighten significantly, the number of problems begins to increase at a rapid pace.

Just looking at this chart, however, is not enough to formulate an answer as to how much security to implement. For one thing, you need to define what you are trying to secure. This ties in to the earlier question of what are you trying to protect. Is the cost of protecting that entity worth doing so? For example, it can be costly to prevent someone from deleting the operating system from a machine. Is it worth it? Most operating systems can be reinstalled within a short period of time—a day at the very most. After you buy an operating system and install it, no changes are made to it beyond that, so you can always go back and restore it to the way it was when you installed it.

What about your hard drive? Can you protect it from someone driving a tank through the front door and blasting it with artillery shells? The answer is yes, you can, but is it worth the cost of constructing a bunker? Probably not. Most hard drives can be formatted, and reconstructed—again within a day usually.

What you cannot recover, and what your biggest investment is in, is your data. You can run to the computer store and buy an operating system. You can run there and buy a hard drive. But you cannot run to the store and buy a copy of your data that has been in the process of being defined since the day you opened your doors for business. That is what you should devote your time and talents to protecting (and backing up).

With regard to that data, the next item that needs to be investigated is the possibility of a system intrusion that could affect that data. Figure 10.3 shows a simple graph charting the potential/possibility for intrusion against the amount of security implemented. This example is for a small business and not indicative of a giant firm. With no security whatsoever, the potential for intrusion is unlimited. Implementing some security measures reduces this risk significantly, whereas implementing maximum security all but eliminates it.

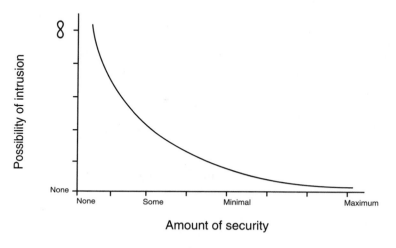

Figure 10.3
Weighing the amount of security against the possibility of intrusion.

The actual representation of the graph shown in figure 10.3 is different for every organization. It depends upon the number of users accessing the system, the value of the data (the more valuable, the more incentive to try and break in), and how access is allowed (must users log in here, or are they granted access to everything on the system by virtue of logging into another host).

Figures 10.2 and 10.3 are different for every organization, and one of the key jobs of management and administration is to define what each graph looks like for their organization. After those two items (potenial for intrusion and number of problems created) have been defined, they can be weighed against each other, as in figure 10.4, to find the equilibrium point at which they meet.

In figure 10.4, an equilibrium point is found by weighing the possibility of intrusion against the number of user problems inherent in implementing security measures. That equilibrium point denotes the point at which the company works the most effectively. The potential for intrusion is curtailed somewhat by the implementation of security measures, yet users are inconvenienced only slightly.

The amount of inconvenience the users tolerate is offset by the gains that come from reducing the possibility for system intrusion. Understanding where the equilibrium lies is essential in planning what measures to take. If the implemented measures fall on either side of the equilibrium, as shown in figure 10.5, then full realization is not obtained.

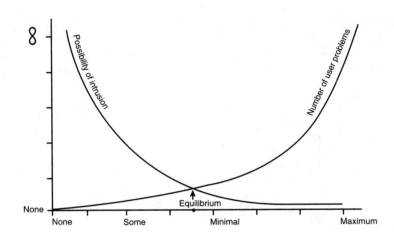

Figure 10.4
Finding the
equilibrium point.

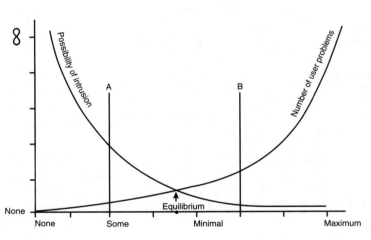

Figure 10.5
Points of non-
equilibrium.

Within figure 10.5, point A represents a conservative attempt at security. The users are not inconvenienced significantly and, at the same time, the potential for system intrusion is still great. Not enough preventive measures have been taken, and intruders can more easily access this system than should be the case. The flip side of this is reflected in point B. Here, security measures have been liberally applied. The possibility of system intrusion is significantly reduced, yet users are required to go through more steps than they should—possibly entering multiple passwords and being forced to log out exactly at 5:00 p.m. The thing to note is that with implementation falling to either side of the equilibrium point, a loss in potential is generated. Falling on the A side, you lose the potential to provide adequate security to protect your system. Falling on the B side, you lose the potential to get more productivity from users by requiring them to deal with more security measures than they should.

One last item of note regarding the amount of security to implement is that after you define your equilibrium point, you should always be cognizant to factors that can cause it to change. Firing a number of programmer/analysts can create an outside body of disgruntled ex-employees who would like to break into your system. Possessing knowledge about the way your system is configured and works, they have enhanced skills that would allow them to break into your system, and the entire possibility of intrusion shifts to the right, as depicted in figure 10.6.

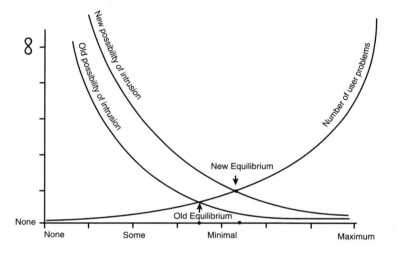

Figure 10.6
A shift in the possibility of intrusion changes the equilibrium point.

The shifting in the indifference curve depicted in figure 10.6 causes the equilibrium point also to shift to the right. More security measures should be implemented to counter the shift. The security measures can be installed locally and across the network—depending upon your actual scenario.

Local Security

Before concerning yourself with the security of a host on a network, it is important to look at how secure the host is as a stand-alone. For much of this discussion, the Unix operating system is used as an example. The reasons for this are that Unix can represent a C2-level operating system, and that the files in question are indicative of those found on other operating systems. Finally, TCP/IP is currently running on more Unix hosts than on any other operating system (not to mention the fact that no local security exists on many other operating systems).

Viruses

Computer viruses are really operating system viruses. They are written to take advantage of the way an operating system works—and here an important distinction must be made: not *any* operating system, but rather *an* operating system. No viruses exist that can work on any computer regardless of the operating system running. The majority of known viruses are written for DOS—an incidental that makes sense given the way the operating system is written: little security, simple file allocation table, and so on. No known viruses exist in Unix, and with the exception of the Internet Worm, most of the problems inherent in Unix fall into the category of loopholes, or poor system administration.

The passwd File

When users log in to a machine, they must supply the following two things:

✔ A user name, or login id

✔ A password

The name appears while it is being typed, for it is assumed to be common knowledge. Whenever another user wants to address this user, such as with the write or mail commands, they must refer to them by their login id. The password, on the other hand, does not appear when it is typed. It is not (supposed to be) common knowledge, and should be changed on a fairly regular basis.

When both these entities are given to the operating system, it compares them with the /etc/passwd file to see if the user has successfully completed the login requirements. If user "hannah" logs in with the password "firewall," the login routine looks through the passwd file to find a matching entry. A sample of this file follows:

```
root:kjsd:0:1::/:/bin/sh
hannah:eadkad:100:9:Hannah Elaine:/usr/acct/hannah:/bin/ksh
karens::101:9:Karen Scott:/usr/acct/karend:/bin/ksh
kristind:djfkjdkfjdk:102:1:Kristin Dulaney:/usr/acct/kristind:/bin/csh
```

This is a colon-delimited file, wherein the first field represents the login id. The second field is the password of the user in an encrypted format—thus "firewall" does indeed match "eadkad" on this system. The encryption is accomplished using hashing routines that add "salt" (extra characters) to an entry before encrypting it. In so doing, it makes it virtually impossible to decipher a password entry from viewing the encrypted listing. The word "firewall" can be encrypted many different ways.

Because one word can be encrypted many ways, the user can use the same password on multiple systems without this fact being readily apparent.

The third field is the *user id number* (uid) that the system uses to actually keep track of the user. The fourth field represents the *group id number* (gid), identifying what other group of users this user is associated with. The fifth field is free text that is useful only to the administrator in trying to identify the listing. The sixth field denotes the home directory of the user, whereas the last field is the shell (command interpreter) they use by default.

It is important to note that not every field need have a value. The fifth field for the root user is blank, meaning that no verbose description of the administrative user exists. More frightening, however, is the blank second field on the karens user. Without an encrypted password here, anyone can log in as karens (login ids are common knowledge), and they will not be prompted for a password. That intruder would appear to the system as karens and be able to change, delete, or modify any files owned by karens, or the group she belongs to (assuming appropriate permissions). There should never be any entry in the passwd file, on a secure system, for which an assigned, encrypted password does not exist.

The /etc/shadow File

On newer Unix systems, the /etc/passwd file contains only an "x" in the second field for every user. If this is so, it indicates that another file is used in conjunction with passwd—the /etc/shadow file. The passwd file, although not writeable, must be readable by every user by the sheer nature of it. This means that every user who can successfully log into the system can view the file. To add an additional level of security, /etc/shadow holds the encrypted passwords, and is readable only by the system administrator.

The /etc/group File

The /etc/group file contains information about members of computing groups. Users can be placed in groups when they need to share information. For example, if a spreadsheet is on the system, the chief accountant may own it, but the entire accounting department may need to view it. By establishing an accounting group, this permission can be applied to all members of that group.

The fourth field of /etc/passwd contains the group number that users belong to. Looking at the earlier example, one security breach is worth noting:

```
root:kjsd:0:1:::/bin/sh
hannah:eadkad:100:9:Hannah Elaine:/usr/acct/hannah:/bin/ksh
karens::101:9:Karen Scott:/usr/acct/karend:/bin/ksh
kristind:djfkjdkfjdk:102:1:Kristin Dulaney:/usr/acct/kristind:/bin/csh
```

The user kristind belongs to group 1. If you look at the first entry, you can see that group 1 is also the group to which root belongs. No user should belong to the same group as the system administrator/root user.

By the same token—and far more critical—it is imperative that no two users have the same user id. Take the following example:

```
root:kjsd:0:1::/:/bin/sh
hannah:eadkad:100:9:Hannah Elaine:/usr/acct/hannah:/bin/ksh
karens::0:9:Karen Scott:/usr/acct/karend:/bin/ksh
kristind:djfkjdkfjdk:102:1:Kristin Dulaney:/usr/acct/kristind:/bin/csh
```

The first thing wrong is that any user can log in as karens without having to supply a password. The second thing is that karens shares the same uid number as the root user. When a user requests an operation—such as creating files, deleting them, and so on—the system checks to see if they have the appropriate permissions to do so. It checks them with their uid number, and the file is read sequentially. Thus, even though karens is not the root user—does not have the same home directory, does not use the same shell, and so on—she essentially has all rights to the system and can do whatever she wants to without restriction. For all practical purposes, she is the root user.

Although root represents a special user, the concept holds true for any duplicated uid. The second user in the list has the permissions of the first user, even though they are not the same person.

Things To Watch For

With regard to local security, the items you should check for mainly include the /etc/ passwd file. Check for the following items:

- ✔ Every user has a password

- ✔ Every user has a unique user id number

- ✔ Users are assigned to the appropriate groups

Other common-sense measures can also be implemented. For example, if the machine hardware you are using allows for a bootup password (contained within the CMOS), then implement that; if you can remove the keyboard from a server that no one uses as a console, then do so; and so on. It is very important to step away from the administrator's role every now and then and view your system as if you were an intruder. Ask yourself how you would get in, what the weak links are, and what you would target. Armed with that train of thought, step back into the administrator's role and look for ways to circumvent those attacks.

TCP/IP Concerns

The TCP/IP protocol represents a security risk simply because it enables remote users to access files and data on machines other than their own. Aside from that, it offers a number of features designed to make using the protocol easier for users. Unfortunately, some of these (such as the .rhost concept) open additional security loopholes. This section looks at those issues and makes recommendations that can save you grief down the road.

Host Equivalency

TCP/IP enables you to create a file on each host system, /etc/hosts.equiv, that defines a list of special hosts. Although intended to be a time-saving device, it creates something of a security risk. The purpose behind it is to enable a user from one system to log into another without requiring them to supply a password. The file says that they are equivalent on this system to the user by the same name on the originating system. A sample file on a host named scott is as follows:

```
lloyd
tim
rob
cheri
drew
matthew
```

The names listed in the file represent the names of host computers other than this one. The hosts.equiv file is telling the operating system that if user karens, who is currently logged in on the lloyd machine attempts to remotely log into this system, then let her in without requiring a password. You are trusting her because she has successfully logged in on host lloyd, and you have an equivalent user on this system.

The security risks here should be readily apparent. If an intruder can successfully break into one system, you are giving them carte blanche to visit your other hosts. The root user cannot be placed into the hosts.equiv file, but that is only of little consolation. Because karens's files are valid on one system, you are trusting that an intruder will not log in as karens on another system.

The /etc/hosts.equiv file is also saying that *every* user on the other host is a trusted user and allowed to log into this host without regard. All that must exist for a user to log in this way is an /etc/passwd entry by the same user name the user is currently using. Imagine the ramifications if this host had a user named Hanna Harrison, and she used the login id of hannah, and the lloyd host had a user named Hannah Alden, who also used a login id of hannah. Even though they are not the same person, and should not be viewing the same files, Hannah Alden has full access to all of Hanna Harrison's files.

To further hammer the point home, suppose that the host computer tim has a user rlawson. No such user exists on our example host, but rlawson, by virtue of the fact that he is coming from an equivalent host, can log in here as any user whose login id he can guess. If he knows that Hannah works on this computer and he always sends mail to her as hannah, then all he need do is issue the following command:

```
rlogin scott -l hannah
```

And once again, because he is coming from a trusted host, he is allowed on this system as hannah without ever needing to supply a password.

It is highly recommended that you not employ /etc/hosts.equiv files if security is of any concern to you.

User Equivalence

Just slightly better than trusting an entire host, is trusting individual users—a process done through .rhosts files. .rhosts files have one good thing going for them right off the bat: by beginning with a period they are "invisible" to all directory listings not using the -a option.

Multiple .rhosts files can exist, and they must reside in the home directory of the user in question. Within the file is a list of the hosts from which the user can log in without needing to supply a password. For example, look at kristind's /etc/passwd entry from earlier:

```
kristind:djfkjdkfjdk:102:1:Kristin Dulaney:/usr/acct/kristind:/bin/csh
```

The sixth field shows her home directory as /usr/acct/kristind. Going to that directory, she can create a .rhosts file with the following information:

```
lloyd
tim
rob
cheri
drew
matthew
```

Now, if she is logged into another system—the matthew host, for example—she can log into this machine without needing to give a password. A quickly visible drawback in the scheme, however, is the rlawson character previously discussed. He can still log in to this system from any of the hosts listed, using the -l option to rlogin to become kristind, and he can get in without needing to know her password.

To circumvent this scenario, a second field can be added to the .rhosts file, denoting how the user must be known on the first machine before they can log in on this system:

```
lloyd kristind
tim kristind
tim emmett
rob kdulaney
cheri kristind
drew kristind
matthew
```

Now, if a user is logging in as kristind on this host, he or she must be known by that name on hosts lloyd, cheri, or drew. If users are coming from the host rob, then they must be known as kdulaney—this is an excellent means of executing remote logins when the user id for the same person is not the same on two different machines. Coming from the host tim, two possibilities present themselves. First, kristind can remotely log in on this system without the need for giving a valid password, and if emmett is trying to come over to this system as her with the following:

```
rlogin scott -l kristind
```

then he is allowed to do so. In other words, he is emmett where he was, he is now kristind here, and will be emmett once more when he exits this host. This procedure provides a means of allowing a support person to access the system when necessary. From the last host listed, matthew, any user can login as kristind without needing to provide a password.

Drawbacks to .rhosts are numerous. The first is if the second field is not used—as with the matthew host in the previous example—and left blank, any user from any host can come over to this system as that user. The second drawback is if multiple users have the same login id on different hosts. The third is that a .rhosts file can exist in the root (/) directory—giving root authority to any user who logs in with the following:

```
rlogin scott -l root
```

Additional Security Steps

You can take a number of security steps above and beyond those required. The more you implement, the more secure you can feel your data is. The more you implement, however—rest assured—the more your users will complain. A painless security does not exist, and all require additional steps that can be viewed as inconveniences by your clientele. You must assess risks and weigh for yourself how much security you consider to be sufficient for your implementation.

Utilize Subnets

Using subnets, you can divide your large network into smaller portions and assign a system administrator to each portion. When viewing the network as a whole (depending upon the size of the system), it can often appear overwhelming; and security is only one aspect for which this holds true. When broken into manageable components, however, each task is smaller and more controllable.

Taken as a whole, the concept of security can never be implemented by one person. Broken into subnets, though, each administrator is responsible for a limited number of local users and hosts, and security stands a better chance of being properly implemented.

Dialup Passwords

If your host is connected to the outside world through modems, consider adding another password before allowing access to the operating system. *Dialup passwords* (implemented with the dpasswd utility) are encrypted the same as other passwords, but reside in a separate file. Additionally, they can be assigned to specific ports, and only used if a user attempts to log in with a given id.

During the login process, the user who is calling in and not connected directly gives his or her login id, followed by a password, and then the dialup password that is the same for everyone on the host. If all three are correct, the user is allowed in. If any of the three are incorrect, the user is asked to log in again; he or she has no indication of which item was incorrect, making it more difficult for intruders to gain access. Because the intruders you are concerned about are not sitting at the terminal most of the time, dialup passwords make great sense.

/etc/dpasswd is the executable file used to manage dialups, and the options that can be used include the following (at least one is required each time you use it):

- ✔ **a {list}.** The list of terminals given is added to /etc/dialups; thus, when a user logs in from one of the terminals and has a shell defined in /etc/d_passwd, the user has to give the dialup password. Entries in the list have to be separated by spaces or commas and enclosed in quotes.

- ✔ **d {list}.** The given list of terminals is removed from /etc/dialups. This eliminates the need for the user to supply a dialup password when logging in.

- ✔ **r {list}.** This option changes the login shell to /bin/sh for every user listed in the list.

- ✔ **s {shell}.** This option updates an entry in the /etc/d_passwd file or adds a new one.

✔ **u {list}.** This option causes a new shell to be created for the names in the list. The list of user names must be separated by spaces and enclosed in quotation marks. Entries are made in the /etc/d_passwd file for the shell, and the password works for all users unless otherwise specified.

✔ **x {shell}.** This option removes the shell and its password from the /etc/d_passwd file.

The file created in all instances (regardless of which option you use) is /etc/dialups. It is nothing more than an ASCII file with each terminal line entry contained on a single line. When a user logs in on one of the listed devices and the user's shell matches an entry in the /etc/d_passwd file, the user is prompted for a dialup password before being allowed to complete the login.

The following example creates a dialup password on device ttya for those using the standard shell:

```
# dpasswd -a ttya
#
# dpasswd -s /bin/sh
New password:     {4Rinfo}
Re-enter new password:    {4Rinfo}
#
```

Now, when a user attempts to login from /dev/ttya, the routine becomes the following:

```
login: jenna
Password:  <------ the password for user jenna must be satisfied
Dialup Password: <----- password for ttya device
```

The dialup password is active only for that device. If the user attempts to log in from a different device, the second password is not asked for. If a user fails the user password, he or she must try again. The dialup password is asked for only after all else has been satisfied.

The two new files created by this utility are in the /etc directory, as shown by the following:

```
# cd /etc
#

# ls -l d_passwd dialups
-r--r--r--   1 root      rootgrp      23 Feb  7  1992 d_passwd
-r--r--r--   1 root      rootgrp      10 Feb  7  1992 dialups
#
```

```
# file d_passwd dialups
d_passwd:       ascii text
dialups:        ascii text
#
# cat dialups
/dev/ttya
#

# cat d_passwd
/bin/sh:sWdYehOXZSGb.:
```

/bin/sh is the name of the shell that must be associated with the user, whereas *sWdYehOXZSGb.* represents the encrypted password.

If your system supports dialup passwords, it is strongly suggested that you use them. This is particularly important on modem connections where hackers can play with less detection. It provides one more firewall toward keeping them out.

Password Aging

Users should not be able to use the same password for their entire life. The more frequently you change passwords, the more frequently you thwart those who may be trying to guess one and become an intruder. Theoretically, you could change passwords every day, but that would start a mutiny among users.

A good recommendation is to change passwords every 30 to 60 days, coupled with the requirement that users use unique passwords for eight times. Be sure you stress to your users the importance of using good passwords, and keeping them to themselves (not scribbling them on post-it notes attached to the monitor).

As an administrator, you should take great pains to disable the accounts of inactive users. These represent open doors for anyone wanting to hack into a system. When a user leaves the organization, remove his or her entry from /etc/passwd, or disable it. The easiest manner in which to disable it is to place a "z" as the only entry in the second field of the listing. Should the user return to the company, you can then remove the "z" and use the passwd command to give them a new password.

Use Firewalls

When apartment complexes are built, brick walls are constructed between townhouses. If a fire occurs at the complex, the walls keep the fire from spreading to adjoining townhouses—hence these walls are called *firewalls*.

When you connect your host to the outside world, you can get much information that you otherwise could not get. Unfortunately, you also leave a means by which the outside world can get into your system and access things they maybe should not. A computer firewall is a router through which your outgoing requests are transmitted, and through which incoming requests are filtered. In other words, you are allowing intruders to break into your router and not into your system—putting a firewall between you and the outside world.

A firewall router is fairly common for many sites connected to the Internet. An existing router can be converted to perform such functions if it can support the more complex filtering configuration. If it cannot, you can choose to build your own from scratch or turn to third-party solutions. One such example is the FireWall-1 product from CheckPoint Software Technologies Ltd.

In September 1994, SunSoft Inc., a division of Sun Microsystems Inc. announced the addition of the FireWall-1 product to their Internet Product Family of products. Coupling FireWall-1 with SunSoft's Internet Gateway software, you can easily turn a Solaris server into a very secure Internet server solution that provides full Internet access for your users, while preventing unauthorized access to and from your networks.

This book does not have the size or scope to detail the method by which you can build your own firewall, but it is highly recommended you read *Internet Firewalls and Computer Security* (New Riders Publishing).

Other Security Options

If you are using a bridge in your network, investigate its filtering capabilities. With some bridges, for example, you can configure a hardware address filter table. Depending on the vendor, the address filter can be applied to either incoming or outgoing addresses. Under this configuration, all frames matching the addresses listed in the filter table are discarded by the bridge. However, this is somewhat labor-intensive to maintain.

For example, if you want to ensure that no one outside of this segment can access one of your servers, put its hardware address in the filtering table. However, if you change the network card in the server, you need to update the filter table.

If you want to limit certain workstations from accessing resources outside their local segments, you can put their hardware addresses in the filter table. Again, if the hardware is changed, remember to update the filter table.

Some more advanced bridges can filter frames by protocols (very much like a router in this sense). All frames carrying that particular protocol are blocked by the bridge. This is one way of localizing certain protocols to a segment, which is a cheaper alternative than using a router.

If you are using routers, you can selectively block protocols or only certain protocols within a protocol suite. For example, if you do not want any RIP traffic on your TCP/IP network, you can block that using the router, and let the rest of the TCP/IP traffic through.

In some cases, for security reasons, you may only allow e-mail to come into your network, but not other TCP/IP services such as FTP (File Transfer Protocol) or Telnet (Terminal Emulation). Using routers, you can selectively filter out those kinds of traffic. You can even set up the filter table such that FTP and Telnet traffic can *go out* of the network, but not come in. You have thus allowed your users to access outside resources, but at the same time shielded yours from others, which effectively turns your router into a firewall (discussed in the preceding section).

Data Encryption

One possibility that should never be overlooked is the encryption and deencryption of data before it is sent over the network. In Sweden, all data communications must be encrypted (per government edict), and a thriving market in encryption modems exists. The United States would do well to consider similar measures.

Numerous utilities are available that enable you to encrypt messages. Within standard Unix, the crypt command enables you to apply to file contents the same hashing routine that you use to encrypt passwords. When received at the other side, they can be unencrypted for viewing.

File encryption and e-mail can be combined into a lethal combination using the following three commands:

- ✔ enroll
- ✔ xsend
- ✔ xget

enroll is used to add a user to the secure mail system. After entering the command, you are required to supply a *key*. The key is a character that is used to determine your encryption/decryption—for example, the letter "a."

You can use xsend in place of regular mail or mailx to send a message, if you want to secure it. This places the utility into input mode, and all other operations are identical to the way they work with the other mail routines. Secured mail can only be sent to one user, however, and you cannot specify more than one name on the command line.

When you login, the message you have mail appears. When you then attempt to view your mail, you are informed that an encrypted message has been sent and the user who sent it (as well as date and time). To read the message, you must use xget.

xget prompts you for the key, and you must enter the same key as was entered during the enroll. If you give the proper key, the message is displayed, and the same options are available as for reading any mail message. If you give the wrong key, the message is still displayed, but it is all control characters and totally unreadable.

NFS (mentioned in Chapter 4) provides a security risk just by the definition of its operation. To compensate for this, you can increase its security slightly by invoking the "secure" option.

Encryption is involved and a public key is assigned to the file system mounted securely. A *public key* is a piece of common knowledge—such as the time—that is encrypted. The client encrypts the public key and sends it to the server with every request. The server decrypts it and compares the value to what it believes it should be. If they match, transactions continue to take place. If they do not match, the client is not allowed access to the host file system.

The root user can create keys to be used in the encryption with the newkey command, or regular users can create keys using the chkey command. When you attempt to remotely log in to the system, the keylogin utility is used to verify the encryption. After you are in, any commands you give are unencrypted by keyserv until you issue a keylogout command.

Log Files

One of the most important things you can do is monitor the transactions that take place in your log files. No one should ever implement auditing on a system just to watch log files grow and their hard drives shrink. Entries are written to log files for a reason, and it is important to monitor them.

The last command shows the contents of /etc/wtmp. This file contains information about who logged in as well as the time, when they logged out, and the total amount of time they were on the system. If you suspect someone is using your system on off-hours, this should be one of the first places to check.

Commands can be placed into queues and executed at later times with the cron and at commands. Each of these commands writes to a cron log file, detailing the name of the person requesting the job, the job, and the time executed. A cursory glance through this file on a regular basis can be of great benefit, as can a glance to see what jobs are currently spooled up to execute at dates in the future. You must have root permissions and a good knowledge of Unix to examine these files. *Inside UNIX* (New Riders Publishing) provides you with the knowledge you need to examine these files.

One file that should NEVER be overlooked is sulog. Any user can become any other user with the su command, providing that they know the password of the user they want to become. The sulog file records each time a user does this. Not only that, but it also reports every unsuccessful attempt. Keep a very close eye on this file because it can provide you with information about users trying to crack passwords far sooner than they are able to do so.

Summary

This chapter examined network security from a variety of angles. Security was examined in terms of what it is, how it is implemented, and how much security should be implemented in relation to what you are trying to protect.

The amount of security you can and should implement depends upon a number of factors. Chief among them is the operating system upon which your network is installed. If you are running DOS-based machines, which have no inherent security, little can be done to thwart a determined intruder. You can put safeguards on the network, but similar measures should also be installed locally.

The Unix operating system represents a C2 security platform at the local level and has enough security to represent a fairly trustworthy operating system. If you monitor login files and log files, you can easily spot intrusion and take significant steps to keep it from happening.

Chapter Snapshot

IP version 6 currently is being defined and developed. This chapter presents IP version 6 as it is currently defined by discussing the following areas of interest:

You can find documentation of a more technical nature in several Internet *Request for Comment* documents (RFCs) and documents of Internet drafts. Look to the end of this chapter for a listing of these documents and sources.

CHAPTER

11

IPng—The Next Generation

"The difference between reality and fiction? Fiction has to make sense."

—Tom Clancy

The *IP layer* is the foundation of the TCP/IP protocol suite. Perhaps the IP layer's most critical function is addressing. The IP address structure was developed with the expectation that it should meet current and future requirements. The current implementation of IP, also known as version 4, which utilizes a 32-bit addressing space, does provide for a large addressing space.

This is illustrated in the following table:

Table 11.1
IP Version 4 Addressing Capabilities

Address Class	First Octet Range	Number of Networks	Number of Nodes per Network
A	1–127	127	16,277,214
B	128–191	16,383	65,534
C	192–223	2,097,151	254

IP version 4's addressing capacity met the internetwork community's requirements when first implemented but has rapidly been exhausted, owing principally to the enormous growth of devices that utilize IP addresses.

The computer environment currently is the largest group of devices that utilize IP addresses and one of the fastest growing areas of technology. Now being purchased in the thousands are personal computers, many of which utilize TCP/IP as a communications protocol and therefore have an IP address. More and more platforms, such as mainframes, utilize TCP/IP and have IP addresses.

The Internet has experienced phenomenal growth over the past several years, and that rate of growth is likely only to increase. As of October 1994, estimations suggested that the Internet consisted of approximately 40,000 networks. Since then, the number of networks in the Internet is rapidly increasing each year. At the same time, the number of users within these networks also is increasing owing to the rapid growth in use of the Internet in both the business and home communities. Another example of the growth in the Internet is quantified by the number of World Wide Web servers. Matthew Gray provides statistics on the number of WWW servers on the Internet, shown in table 11.2.

Table 11.2
WWW Servers in the Internet

June 1993	130 sites
December 1993	623 sites
June 1994	1265 sites
December 1994	11576 sites
Current	More than 15000 sites

*Source: Matthew Gray "Growth of the World Wide Web"
http://www.netgen.com/info/growth.html

Systems and network management also has contributed to exhausting IP addresses. Network and device management is critical for organizations that implement local and wide area networks and for client-server environments that require monitoring, control, and fault detection. Using technologies based on *Simple Network Management Protocol* (SNMP), an IP-based protocol, requires that each device—a network hub, a network interface card in a personal computer, a file server, a router, a LAN switch or other communications equipment—have an IP address.

Although the computer and network market's growth has been explosive, it might not experience the amount of growth now only priming to erupt in the consumer entertainment market. By providing services such as cable television, video on demand, home shopping, and information access, every television could become an Internet device with an IP address. The growth that this market alone can be expected to drive will demand an architecture that provides efficient, easy-to-implement, and easy-to-monitor large scale addressing and routing.

History of IP Next Generation

IP Next Generation, or version 6, actually is the evolution and compilation of a number of proposals and efforts over the last three years within the standards communities. Numerous proposals have addressed some but not all of the IP version 4 issues.

By the end of 1992, the Internet community had developed three primary proposals for consideration: *TCP and UDP with Bigger Addresses* (TUBA), *Common Architecture for the Internet* (CATNIP), and the *Simple Internet Protocol Plus* (SIPP).

TUBA—TCP and UDP with Bigger Addresses

By design, TUBA's primary objective is to address the IP address exhaustion issue; specifically, to provide a significantly larger address space by replacing the current IP layer with CLNP. CLNP uses an address format known as *Network Service Access Point* (NSAP) addresses, which are significantly larger than the IP version 4 32-bit addresses. Furthermore, the hierarchy that can be structured into these address structures would enhance the scalability of the Internet environment and increase the levels of efficiency of routing data through the Internet.

One of TUBA's strongest points is that it doesn't require completely replacing the current transport (TCP and UDP) protocols or application protocols (FTP, TELNET, SMTP, SNMP, HTTP, and so on). TUBA doesn't imply a complete transition to the OSI protocol suite—rather it just replaces the current network layer with CLNP.

Integral to the TUBA proposal is a migration strategy that would allow a gradual transition of Internet devices. The primary devices affected during this migration phase would be host systems that serve as platforms for Internet applications and *Domain Name Server* (DNS) platforms that provide host name to address translation functions. This migration strategy would allow both traditional IP version 4 addresses and NSAP addresses to coexist in the Internet, and this would allow for a smooth transition rather than a large scale conversion effort all at once.

CATNIP—Common Architecture for the Internet

The concept driving CATNIP is to establish a commonality between several of the most prominent protocol environments you see in today's networks: namely, in the Internet, which is predominately TCP/IP based, OSI, and Novell IPX. The objective is to eliminate the architectural and protocol barriers between these environments and to facilitate growth of the Internet. The goal is to extend the life of the Internet and to increase the performance of it.

The CATNIP concept specifies that any of the current transport layer protocols (TCP, UDP, IPX, SPX, TP4 and CLTP) be able to function on any of the prominent layer three protocols (CLNP, IP version 4, IPX, and CATNIP). It also would permit one device that might use IP as a network layer protocol to interoperate with a device that uses IPX as a network layer protocol.

Like TUBA, CATNIP implements OSI Network Service Access Point (NSAP) format addresses.

SIPP—Simple Internet Protocol Plus

Perhaps the primary consideration behind the design of the Simple Internet Protocol is to develop a protocol that would provide an easy transition from IP version 4. It is expected that SIPP would function well in high performance network environments, such as FDDI and ATM, as well as in lower performance networks, such as low bandwidth *wide area networks* (WANs) or wireless networks. The two primary areas addressed are addressing and structure of the IP packet.

The Simple Internet Protocol increases the size of the IP address from 32 to 64 bits, and this larger address space allows for a significantly larger number of addressable devices as well as for a higher degree of hierarchical structure in a network. This would dramatically increase the efficiency of routing data in large networks such as the Internet. Furthermore, the architecture allows the 64-bit address space to be expanded even further in 64-bit increments. Given this, it is projected that SIPP could have a longer viable lifespan than earlier versions of IP.

The structure of the IP packet also has been revised. Functions and fields not functional or deemed unnecessary have been eliminated. Enhancements required have been added to the specifications. A certain capability was added, for example, to enable identifying packets as being part of a "conversation" between two devices that might need special handling as they are transported through an internetwork.

IP Next Generation Overview

Each of the preceding proposals resolved some of the existing issues with IP version 4 and also introduced new functionality necessary for the future requirements of the IP protocol. None of them, however, addressed all of the relevant issues. IP Next Generation, as it is currently defined, is in fact the result of adopting the salient features of these three prominent proposals.

One of the primary objectives of IP version 6 design is to maintain compatibility with higher level protocols that rely on it, such as SMTP, SNMP, FTP, and HTTP. By design, it is meant to be evolutionary, so that it doesn't require completely redesigning the applications that thousands of users currently utilize.

The evolution of IP version 6 can be categorized into several areas:

✔ Expanded addressing and routing capabilities

✔ Header format simplification and improved support for options

✔ Quality of service capabilities

✔ Security and privacy

✔ IP mobility

The following sections discuss how IP version 6 seeks to address the issues and limitations of the current implementation of IP in each of these areas.

IP Next Generation Addressing

One of the most noticeable differences between IP versions 4 and 6 comes in the area of addressing. IP version 4 utilizes a 32-bit address space, whereas IP version 6 increases this address space from 32 bits to 128 bits, which allows a much greater number of addressable devices—a total of 340,282,366,920,938,463,463,374,607,431,768,211,456 addresses. This is 4 billion times 4 billion the number of addresses that are possible with IP version 4.

IP version 6 has three types of addresses, as follow:

✔ **Unicast.** Unicast addresses identify a specific interface on a device. By definition, only one device can be assigned to a specific unicast address.

✔ **Anycast.** Anycast addresses identify a group of interfaces in which a single member of the group receives any packet sent to the multicast address. The device that is "closest"—closest according to the routing metric—receives any packet sent to an anycast address. (The *routing metric* is the unit of measure provided by a routing protocol such as RIP or OSPF, to quantify the end-to-end path between two netword devices.)

Anycast addresses are identical in format to unicast addresses. The only difference is that more than one device can be assigned to a specific anycast address and the device can be specifically configured to know that it has a anycast address.

✔ **Multicast.** Multicast addresses identify a group of interfaces in which all members of the group receive any packet sent to the multicast address.

The type of IPng address is determined by the leading bits in the address. This variable length field is called the Format Prefix (FP).

IP version 4 addresses are distinguished by class, but this is not so with IPng addresses. The IPng concept resembles *Classless Inter Domain Routing* (CIDR), which is discussed in detail in RFC 1338.

This RFC does not explain IPng addressing. It is a source for a similar mechanism, and the reference is provided for someone who might want more technical information.

The leading bits in the address indicate the specific type of IPng address. The variable-length field that comprises these leading bits is called the *Format Prefix* (FP). The initial allocation of these prefixes is as follows:

Table 11.3
Address Distribution for IP Version 6

Allocation	Prefix (binary)	Fraction of Address Space
Reserved	0000 0000	1/256
Unassigned	0000 0001	1/256

Allocation	Prefix (binary)	Fraction of Address Space
Reserved for NSAP Allocation	0000 001	1/128
Reserved for IPX Allocation	0000 010	1/128
Unassigned	0000 011	1/128
Unassigned	0000 1	1/32
Unassigned	0001	1/16
Unassigned	001	1/8
Provider-Based Unicast Address	010	1/8
Unassigned	011	1/8
Reserved for Neutral-Interconnect-Based		
Unicast Addresses	100	1/8
Unassigned	101	1/8
Unassigned	110	1/8
Unassigned	1110	1/16
Unassigned	1111 0	1/32
Unassigned	1111 10	1/64
Unassigned	1111 110	1/128
Unassigned	1111 1110 0	1/512
Link Local Use Addresses	1111 1110 10	1/1024
Site Local Use Addresses	1111 1110 11	1/1024
Multicast Addresses	1111 1111	1/256

*Source: R. Hinden, http://www.playground.sun.com/pub/ipng/html/pingmain.html

I

Overview

Based on this scheme, approximately 15% of the address space has been reserved and 85% is available for future use.

Routing

One of the objectives with IPng was to minimize the effect on other protocols and technologies that rely on the IP protocol. One such example is routing.

Routing in IPng is very similar to routing in IP version 4 environments using CIDR, except for the actual addresses used for routing; that is, IPng addresses being 128 bits long rather than 32 bits.

Therefore, current routing protocols, such as RIP, OSPF, IS-IS, and IDRP can be used to route IPng with modification rather than force the development of entirely new protocols. This too will facilitate the transition to IP version 6.

One of the new capabilities of routing in IP version 6 environments is facilitated by the IPng routing option. An IPng source device uses the routing option to list one or more intermediate nodes it must pass through on its way to a specified destination. This functionality allows the source device to dictate the path that its data takes, enabling such things as provider selection. To illustrate this concept, examine the network depicted in figure 11.1.

Figure 11.1
Source routing in an IP version 6 environment.

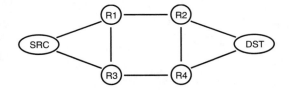

In the network illustrated in figure 11.1, if device SRC (representing a source device) transmits data to device DST (representing a destination device), the routing protocol in use determines its path through the network. A routing protocol may determine the optimal path based on characteristics of the individual connections and devices between the source and destination nodes, such as bandwidth, delay, or hop counts. The path of transmitted data, for example, might be SRC-R1-R2-DST, because the routing metric for this path is the least among the possible paths.

Using the IPng routing option, the device SRC can specify the path of its data through this internetwork. Essentially, this enables the source device, such as a personal computer, to override the router and dictate it's path through the network. If the connection between R1 and R2 is subject to high amounts of delay and the data in question is delay sensitive, for example, SRC might want to specify that the path of its data be SRC-R3-R4-DST.

The IPng routing option also can be used to allow source devices to select which Internet Access Provider (IAP) might handle specific flows of data. If the connection between R1 and R2 is provided by an IAP that might be undesirable for the traffic flow for reasons of cost, bandwidth, delay, or reliability, the source device can direct network traffic onto a favorable path.

IP Next Generation Packet and Header Formats

As mentioned previously, many of the new capabilities of IP version 6 are made possible by a restructuring of the IP header. In this section, you examine the components of the IP version 6 header and explain the capabilities made possible by these components.

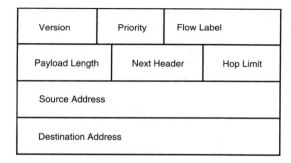

Figure 11.2
The IP version 6 header format.

The sizes of the fields shown in figure 11.2 are illustrative only. The actual size of each field and its function are explained in the following:

✔ **Ver.** 4-bit Internet Protocol version number. The purpose of this field is to identify which version of the IP protocol is being used. For example, the number in this field is 4 in the current implementation of IP. This field will be 6 the headers of IP version 6 packets.

✔ **Prio.** 4-bit Priority value. This allows the source device to mark packets as higher or lower priority relative to other packets from the same source. This will be discussed further later in the section titled "IP Version 6 Priority."

✔ **Flow Label.** 24-bit field. The purpose of this is to allow the source device to identify packets transmitted between a source and destination device that are part of a specific conversation or "flow." An example of this might be a multimedia transmission of time and delay sensitive video and audio material. This will be discussed further later in the section titled "Flow Labels."

✔ **Payload Length.** 16-bit unsigned integer. This file identifies the length of the payload of the packet in octets. The payload is the remainder of the packet following the IPng header.

✔ **Next Hdr.** 8-bit selector. Identifies the type of header immediately following the IPng header. This values for this field are listed in RFC 1700.

✔ **Hop Limit.** 8-bit unsigned integer. The initial value of this field is specified by the source device. It is decreased by 1 by each node that forwards the packet, such as a router. If the value reaches 0, the packet is discarded by the node that is handling it.

✔ **Source Address.** 128 bits. The address of the sender of the packet.

✔ **Destination Address.** 128 bits. The address of the intended target recipient of the packet.

IPng Extensions

In IP version 6, optional IP layer information is placed in separate headers between the IP version 6 header and the transport layer headers of TCP or UDP. A single packet can contain zero, one, or several extension headers. Primarily, only the receiving or destination device uses these headers, and intermediary devices such as routers do not examine them, with the single exception being the Hop-by-Hop Options header (discussed later in this chapter). This serves to improve the performance of routers that process packets that contain IP version 6 options. Unlike IP version 4 headers, IPng extension headers have any length in multiples of 8 octets without IP version 4's 40-byte option limitation.

The header formats shown in figures 11.3 through 11.5 illustrate several possibilities.

Figure 11.3
The IP version 6 header with no options.

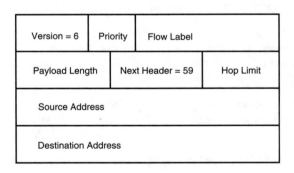

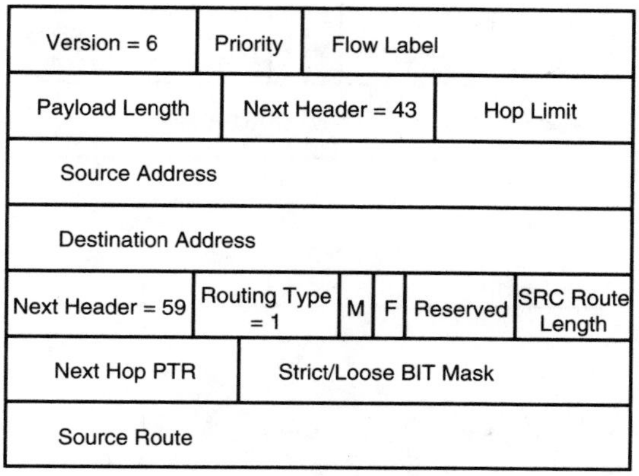

Version = 6	Priority	Flow Label	
Payload Length	Next Header = 43		Hop Limit
Source Address			
Destination Address			
Next Header = 59	Routing Type = 1	M	F	Reserved	SRC Route Length
Next Hop PTR	Strict/Loose BIT Mask		
Source Route			

Figure 11.4
The IP version 6 header with a single option field.

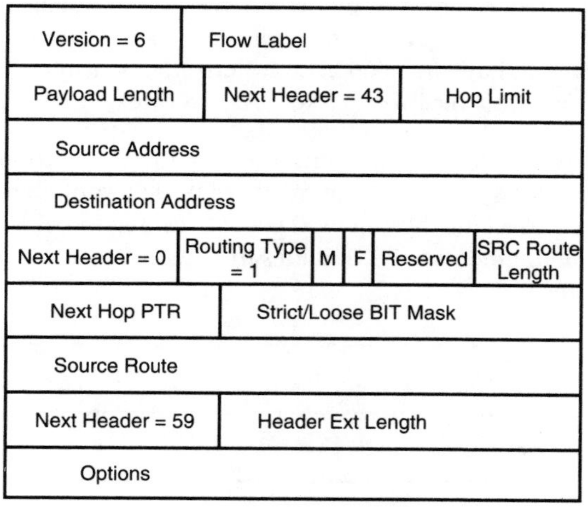

Version = 6	Flow Label	
Payload Length	Next Header = 43	Hop Limit
Source Address		
Destination Address		
Next Header = 0	Routing Type = 1	M	F	Reserved	SRC Route Length
Next Hop PTR	Strict/Loose BIT Mask	
Source Route		
Next Header = 59	Header Ext Length	
Options		

Figure 11.5
The IP version 6 header with multiple option fields.

At this time, the following IPng headers have been defined: Routing, Fragmentation, Authentication, Encapsulation, Hop-by-Hop Options, Destination, and No Next Header. The following sections discuss each of these headers and the function each provides to the IP version 6 protocol.

Routing

The function of the Routing header is to specify one or more intermediate devices to be visited as a packet is forwarded to its destination (see fig. 11.6). This allows a source to specify the "route" to a destination and essentially override the route that might have ordinarily have been determined by the routing protocol.

The Routing header is identified by a Next Header value of 43 in the header that precedes it. This is illustrated more clearly in figure 11.5, in which the entire IP version 6 is illustrated.

Figure 11.6
The format of a
Routing header.

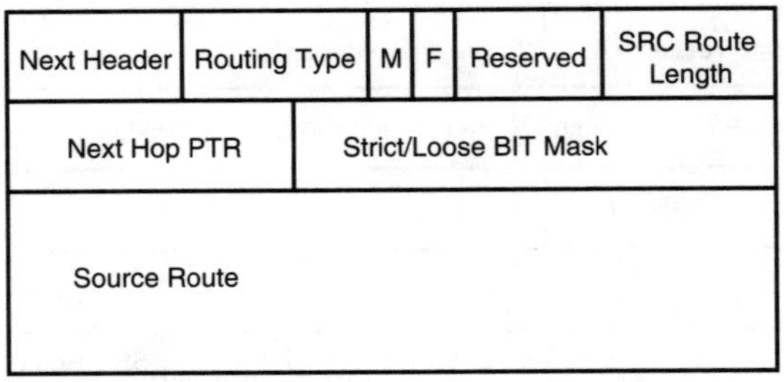

Next Header	Routing Type	M	F	Reserved	SRC Route Length
Next Hop PTR		Strict/Loose BIT Mask			
Source Route					

Fragmentation

In an IP version 6 environment, the source node uses the Fragmentation header to send packets that are too large to fit in the maximum packet size or MTU of the destination. By function, the Fragmentation header addresses the possibility that the network to which the receiving station is attached, or any intermediate networks, cannot accommodate packets as large as the sending station. A device connected to an FDDI network, for example, could send packets as large as 4,000 bytes, whereas a receiving device connected to an Ethernet network could only receive a packet of 1,518 bytes.

In this case, the source node divides, or fragments, the larger packet into smaller packets that can fit the receiving device's MTU. Each fragmented packet would have a Fragmentation header that identifies it as a large fragmented packet (see fig. 11.8). When the receiving node receives the fragments, it recombines the fragments into a single packet and processes it accordingly.

Figure 11.7
The format of a
Fragmentation
header.

Next Header	Reserved	Fragment	Reserved	M
Identification				

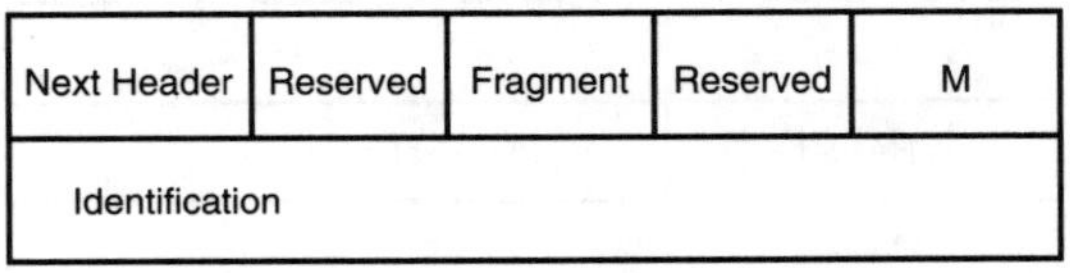

IP version 6 fragmentation works much differently than with IP version 4. Whereas with IP version 4, intermediary devices, such as routers, can handle fragmentation, only the source node performs fragmentation with IP version 6. The Fragmentation header is always identified by a Next Header value of 44 in the preceding header.

Authentication

The Authentication header exists specifically to ensure two significant facts:

    ✔ The destination node receives data that matches the data the source node sends.

    ✔ The sender that the source address identifies truly is the sender of the data.

To accomplish this, the sending station calculates a value based on the headers, payload, and user information within the packet. The receiving node then calculates the value based on the same headers, payload, and user information. If these two values match, the receiver considers the packet authentic as defined; if not, it rejects the packet.

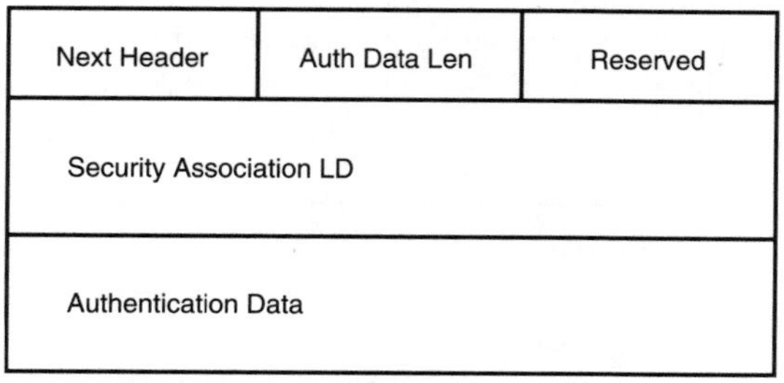

Next Header	Auth Data Len	Reserved
Security Association LD		
Authentication Data		

Figure 11.8
The format of an Authentication header.

The section "Security" discusses authentication in detail later in this chapter.

Encapsulation

The Encapsulation header seeks to provide the same security functions as authentication but also provides confidentiality between the sender and receiver. It achieves confidentiality by taking the IP version 6 datagram and encrypting the data, which is known as the *Encapsulated Security Payload* (ESP). Then a new IP version 6 header is attached to the ESP for transmission through the network. The new header is illustrated in figure 11.9.

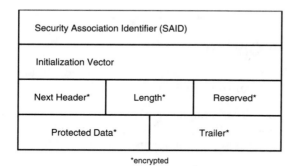

Security Association Identifier (SAID)		
Initialization Vector		
Next Header*	Length*	Reserved*
Protected Data*		Trailer*

*encrypted

Figure 11.9
The format of an Encapsulation header.

After the destination device receives the packet, it removes the new header, decrypts the ESP, and then processes the original IP version 6 datagram.

Obviously, coordination of these encryption formats between the source and destination nodes is critical for the receiver to be able to decrypt the packet. Equally critical is the confidentiality of these encryption keys. The section "Security" later in this chapter discusses the principle of encapsulation in IP version 6 in detail.

Hop-by-Hop Options

The Hop-by-Hop Options header (see fig. 11.10) is the one header option that each node or device examines or reviews along the delivery path to the destination. Its function is to identify specific handling that the intermediary nodes between the source and destination nodes require. It is identified by a Next Header value of 0 in the Next Header field of the IP version 6 header.

Figure 11.10
The format of a
Hop-by-Hop
Options header.

Next Header	Hdr Ext Length
Options	

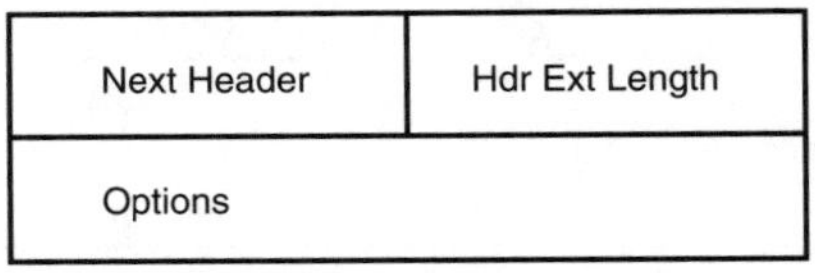

Destination Options

The Destination Options header (see fig. 11.11) accommodates information that only the destination device for the packet or packets will handle. It is identified by a Next Header value of 60 in the preceding header.

Figure 11.11
The format of a
Destination
Options header.

Next Header	Hdr Ext Length
Options	

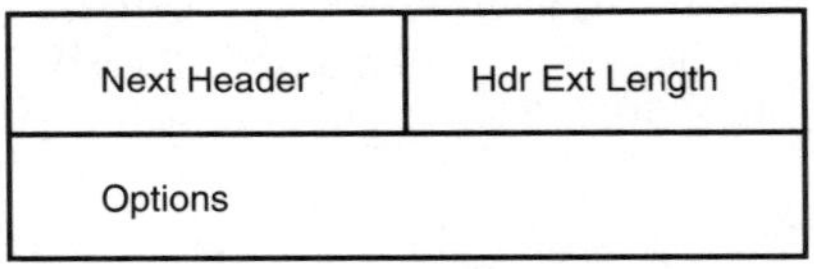

No Next Header Option

The value of 59 in the Next Header value of the IP version 6 header or that of any extension header indicates that no options follow.

As mentioned previously, one of the advantages of IP version 6 is the capability to have larger headers than is possible with IP version 4. This advantage will allow new IP version 6 header options to be defined as new requirements are discovered.

Quality of Service

One of the fastest growing technologies in the internetwork arena is applications that rely on "real-time" data, such as multimedia, multicast, or video applications. These applications have several critical requirements:

✔ A constant level of throughput to ensure adequate bandwidth between the source and destination nodes. If a user tries to view a video presentation using a network, for example, the bandwidth or capacity of the network must be sufficient to deliver the data.

✔ A constant level of delay.

✔ A constant level of jitter, where *jitter* refers to varying amounts of latency in the transmission of packets through a network.

A host can use the flow label and the priority fields in the IPng header to identify packets that might require special handling by IPng routers to ensure throughput, delay, and jitter to meet application requirements.

Flow Labels

A *flow* is defined as a series of packets, sent from a specific source device to a specific destination, that requires special handling by any intermediary IPng routers. RFC 1363 defines a flow as "a data structure used by internetwork hosts to request special services of the internetwork, often guarantees about how the internetwork will handle some of the hosts' traffic." The destination can be a single device (using unicast addresses as a destination) or multiple devices (using multicast addresses as a destination). One example of a flow would be the transmission of a multimedia presentation from a server to a group of client personal computers.

The flow label field of the IP version 6 header is 24 bits long. A flow is identified by having a value other than zero in the flow label field of the IP version 6 header. A packet that isn't part of a flow would contain a flow label value of 0, which a control protocol, such as *Resource Reservation Protocol* (RSVP), would then use. RSVP is an example of a protocol designed to reserve a path through an internetwork that meets the application's requirements for bandwidth, delay, and jitter.

A device that doesn't support use of a flow label must do one of the following:

✔ Set the field to zero if it originates the packet, the function of a destination node that doesn't support flow labels, such as a workstation or server.

✔ Pass the field on unchanged when it forwards the packet, the function of a router that might not yet support flow labels.

✔ Disregard the field if receiving the packet, the function of a destination node that doesn't support flow labels, such as a workstation or server.

Any packets transmitted as part of a flow must contain the same IP version 6 header information, including the source address, destination address, and flow label value, as well as information in any extension headers, such as Routing headers or the Hop-by-Hop Options header.

Flow labels and the protocols that would utilize them still are being designed and can be expected to change, owing to the requirements that present themselves.

IP Version 6 Priority

Often, to meet application requirements in internetworks, you might need to assign certain data higher priority than other traffic from the source. The priority in the IP version 6 header is a 4-bit field, which offers a value range of 0 to 15. The purpose of this field is to allow a source node to identify the priority level for delivering packets. Data that has a priority level of 12, for example, should be delivered before packets that have a priority level of 3.

The traffic to be transmitted is separated into the two following classes:

✔ Traffic in which the source device (a file server, for example) can provide congestion control. Here, in the event of network congestion, the device can "throttle back" until the congestion dissipates entirely. For example, this type of traffic uses TCP as a transport protocol, such as FTP, TELNET, or HTTP. The priority values for this traffic currently range from 0 to 7, with the following categories:

Priority	Description
0	Uncharacterized traffic
1	"Filler" traffic (e.g., netnews)
2	Unattended data transfer (e.g., email)
3	(Reserved)
4	Attended bulk transfer (e.g., FTP, HTTP, NFS)
5	(Reserved)
6	Interactive traffic (e.g., telnet, X)
7	Internet control traffic (e.g., routing protocols, SNMP)

✔ Traffic that cannot be "throttled back" to resolve network congestion: multimedia transmissions that consist of video and audio information, for example. You would use a priority value between 8 and 15 for this type of traffic. A value of 8 identifies real-time traffic that is more acceptable to be discarded in the event of network congestion whereas a value of 15 identifies traffic that is far less acceptable to be discarded.

Security

IP version 6 contains two mechanisms to address security in networks, both of which are optional extensions to the IP version 6 header. The first is the Authentication header, which guarantees delivery of the packet intact and authenticity of the source address. It does not guarantee confidentiality, however; some other device between the sender and the receiving station could potentially also receive the transmission.

The sending value computes a value based on the headers that don't change during delivery to the destination and the payload of the transmission. When the destination node receives the transmission, it also computes a value based on the headers and payload. If these two values match, then the station addresses and the packet's payload are considered authentic and therefore processed. If these two values do not match, the packet is discarded. The algorithm currently used to compute the value for the authentication header is the *MD5 algorithm.*

Using of the Authentication header impacts the processing performance of IP version 6 devices and the communications latency between them, owing to the need to calculate the authentication value in the source and destination devices and to compare the two computed values in the destination node.

Secondly, IP version 6 provides a feature called Encapsulating Security Payload (ESP). As does using the Authentication header, ESP ensures the integrity of the transmitted data and authenticates the sender and receiver. In addition, ESP ensures the privacy of the transmission. Using an encryption algorithm that only the sender and the receiving device maintain prevents other devices from decrypting and processing the transmission unless they too possess the encryption key.

IP Mobility

Assuming that a network user maintains a single unchanging specific location would frequently lead to error nowadays. Many network users are highly mobile, and many work at home or even in different parts of an organization. IP mobility is in fact not unique to IP version 6 and currently is addressed with IP version 4—and can easily be modified to work with IP version 6. The definition of IP version 6 provides a significant opportunity to implement functionality to meet the unique needs of the mobile network user.

In the Internet draft document from the IP version 6 Working Group titled "Mobility Support in IP version 6," by Charles Perkins and David Johnson, it clearly states the primary issue to be dealt with by IP mobility.

> "We believe that the most important function needed to support mobility is the reliable and timely notification of a mobile node's current location to other nodes that need it. The home agent needs this location information in order to forward intercepted packets from the home network to the mobile node, and correspondent nodes need this information in order to send their own packets directly to the mobile node."

IP mobility requires that mobile computers have at least two addresses defined for them—one permanent and any others temporary or care of address. The mobile user would obtain the care of address from a local router or server and then notify the home agent of its temporary location.

You could send information such as e-mail, for example, to a mobile user at the permanent address. If the mobile user is at that location, they receive it. If not, a home agent receives the transmission and redirects the data to the care of the address.

Transitioning to IP Version 6

Clearly, the success of IP Next Generation depends highly on the level of complexity and difficulty in transitioning to this new protocol. A complex, high cost migration plan would dramatically hinder its potential of becoming widely deployed. IPng, however, has number of features that greatly facilitate its implementation.

The most significant feature is the provision for a "phased" implementation. IP version 4 devices, such as client workstations, servers, or routers, can be upgraded gradually with minimal effects on each other. This is due, in part, to the fact that devices upgraded to IP version 6 will essentially run both the IP version 6 and the IP version 4 protocols. This will enable communications with devices that have not yet been upgraded.

The addressing structure of IP version 6 will also ease the burden of transition. Devices that have been upgraded can continue to use their IP version 4 addresses. A server, for example, might be upgraded to support IP version 6 but would still support an IP version 4 address to enable communications to clients that are still using IP version 4. Furthermore, IP version 4 addresses can be "embedded" in the larger address space made possible by IP version 6.

By design, the transition to IP version 6 has been architected to be a smooth, gradual migration. For this reason, it is very likely that the deployment and acceptance of IP version 6 will be swift.

Summary

IP version 6 is designed to be an evolutionary step from IP version 4. It seeks to address known issues with IP version 4 and to introduce functionality to address future requirements of this protocol.

From the start, the issue of migration has been dealt with extensively. As discussed earlier, the addressing techniques designed for IP version 6 allow for the inclusion of IP version 4 addresses to facilitate migration. Hosts that are converted to IP version 6 will be able to maintain their current IP version 4 addresses. By design, IP version 6 hosts will be able to communicate with IP version 4 hosts.

IP version 6 has been designed to work on a variety of networks, ranging from slower technologies such as wireless networks to high speed networks using technologies such as ATM and FDDI.

Perhaps most importantly, IP Next Generation seeks to meet the requirements of the Internet, Next Generation: a large, scaleable, and useable world wide network.

Sources of Information on IP Next Generation

S. Bradner, A. Mankin, RFC 1752, "The Recommendation for the IP Next Generation Protocol," January 1995.

V. Fuller, et al, "Supernetting: an Address Assignment and Aggregation Strategy," RFC 1338, June 1992.

S. Deering, "Simple Internet Protocol Plus (SIPP) Specification (128-bit address version)," Internet Draft, July 1994.

R. Hinden, Editor, "IP Version 6 Addressing Architecture," Internet Draft, April 1995.

R. Gilligan, E. Nordmark, "Transition Mechanisms for IP version 6 Hosts and Routers," Internet Draft, March 1995.

Part II

Enumeration

Chapter Snapshot

In this chapter, you learn how to integrate Unix and NetWare servers. Although these two network operating system platforms are drastically different, this chapter will simplify your task of bringing data and print services from one platform to the other. This chapter covers the following:

Although these two operating systems are about as similar as apples and kiwi fruit, once you understand the areas that the two have in common and the manner in which the two systems communicate, you will realize that melding the two platforms is not as daunting as it initially appears.

Connecting to NetWare

"Every beginning of an idea corresponds to an imperceptible lesion of the mind."
—E.M. Cioran

This chapter covers step-by-step what it takes to interface TCP/IP with a Novell NetWare file server. If at times this very basic interconnection appears a little overwhelming, remember that many great third-party TCP/IP-to-NetWare connectivity packages that simplify many of the complexities are available (for example, Firefox by NOV*IX, Network Chameleon by Netframe, and PC-Interface by Locus to name a few).

And should you want to integrate multiple *network operating systems* (NOSs), you might want to incorporate packages such as LANtastic for TCP/IP with LANtastic version 6, LANtastic CorStream Server, or Central Station II to further broaden and simplify your networking environment. In doing so, you not only can combine a central processor host (Unix) with a distributed processor network with a centralized data repository (NetWare), but also add the ability for people to directly share what is on their hard disks with one another in a peer-to-peer environment (Artisoft).

This chapter focuses on the simple capability to share data between Unix and a NetWare environment. Although Unix-to-NetWare TCP/IP connectivity can be complicated and more than a little convoluted, this chapter presents you with enough data for even the inexperienced network administrator to be able to share data.

Understanding Unix TCP/IP Basics

As previously covered in Chapter 3, "Host Names and Internet Addressing," many considerations must be addressed prior to installing a TCP/IP network. These interconnection decisions are even more important when you decide to link two unlike NOSs. How do two (or more) systems communicate with one another?

Your first consideration must be that of media. Is one of the systems already in place, and if so does its media support the additional operating system workload? If not, what direction should you take to best minimize your cash outlay and prepare yourself for future growth? Ethernet is a popular choice for integrating Unix and NetWare because it is readily supported by both platforms (and is extremely modular).

Third-party packages such as Firefox by NOV*IX provide easy TCP/IP access via DOS workstations. After it's loaded, the Firefox software enables the DOS workstation to select the TCP/IP host to which it wants to attach (see fig. 12.1).

Figure 12.1
Selecting a TCP/IP host from a DOS workstation with Firefox.

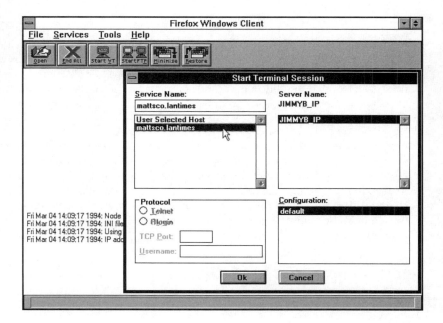

Second, establish your addressing scheme. In the addressing analogy in Chapter 3, you must determine if you ever want to connect to the Internet. If this is even a slightly remote possibility, get your official address and install your hosts accordingly right from the start. If you never plan to enter the Internet officially, you still want to consider establishing a segmentation tree structure for your system design. This structure keeps your addressing scheme much cleaner and simplifies your administrative tasks.

Finally, establish to what areas of which system your users are to have access and to what level. Do you simply want to create one big "bit bucket" in which people can transfer data to and from their respective NOSs? And along these lines, who should have their own login accounts and printing rights? As you can see, the convolutions with which you must work to have a fully functional and secure system are extensive indeed. If your system is in place and requires no breach in security, consider beginning with a system that undoubtedly will have users calling you and asking why they cannot access certain areas until you fix them. If this is not the case, an open system can easily be tightened with a minimal amount of customer disturbance.

TCP/IP routers and gateways are easily identified with the NOV*IX software. In figure 12.2 you can observe the default gateway, its IP address, as well as its physical MAC address.

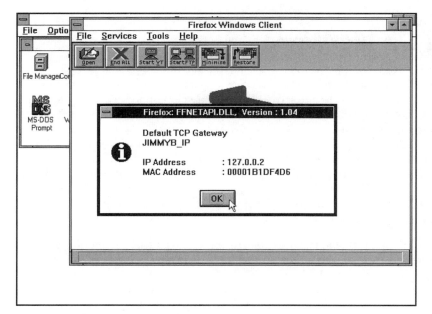

Figure 12.2
Firefox gateway information.

II

Enumeration

Integrating NetWare and Unix

Why would you want to share data between an operating system that allows files to have names up to 255 characters in length and a DOS-based operating system? Many would argue that as the Internet and TCP/IP are becoming more popular, Novell is losing ground in a market it has "owned" for years now. The argument would continue that many corporations have spent vast amounts of money installing and maintaining DOS programs in a NetWare environment, as well as training their staff. Whether this is predominantly true or not, as Unix becomes more graphical and requires less hardware, many companies are merging and frequently end up with these two NOSs under one roof. The question then becomes do the companies fully migrate to one operating system and dump the other, or do they merge the two as best they can?

Until recent years, people knew either NetWare or Unix. Asking a network administrator to include the other NOS in his job description was like asking Jimmy Buffett to sing some Village People songs. Yes, there might be money in the proposition, and he might do it, but he won't like it. But now as the saying goes, "the times they are a changin'." As previously stated, a variety of third-party Unix-to-DOS/Windows/NetWare/everything packages are on the market right now. A couple of these packages are discussed later. The majority of this chapter focuses on a very basic interface between NetWare and Unix that incorporates TCP/IP and a product developed by Sun Microsystems and marketed by Novell called *Network File System* (NFS).

Setting Up NetWare

The setup within NetWare is performed by setting the NetWare environment to cohabitate with Unix and loading a variety of *NetWare Loadable Modules* (NLMs). First you should ensure that your NetWare file server has hardware enough to accommodate your requirements. Start by evaluating your RAM supply and your RAM requirements. Not only will you require more memory to support the NFS name space, but a few of the NFS NLMs that you will load are relatively large in size. Unfortunately, your memory require-ments do not stop there. You also need to accommodate the potential for the larger packets that Unix might send and the additional buffers required for the additional Unix connections. After much NetWare system tuning, a file server can work with 12 MB of RAM, but 16 MB is the realistic minimum for anyone who wants the system to remain online during high use periods.

You next need to confirm that your *network interface card* (NIC) supports Ethernet_II. If it does not, consider adding to your system another card dedicated to the Unix side of the house. If you are not familiar with how you bind multiple protocols to a single Ethernet adapter, you simply load your adapter a second time and bind the Ethernet_II protocol to the second iteration of your NIC. Following are examples of a typical C:\NETWARE\STARTUP.NCF and SYS:\SYSTEM\AUTOEXEC.NCF file for NFS:

```
#SYS:\SYSTEM\STARTUP.NCF

set reserved buffers below 16 meg = 60
set cache buffer size = 4096
autoregister memory above 16 megabytes = off
load nfs
set maximum physical receive packet size = 2048
set minimum packet receive buffers = 100

#SYS:\SYSTEM\AUTOEXEC.NCF

file server name JB311a
ipx internal net CABA
mount all
load ne2000 int=port=300 frame=ethernet_802.3 name=ipxlan
load ne2000 int=3 port=300 frame=ethernet_ii name=tcplan
bind ipx to ipxlan net=a
set maximum directory cache buffers = 1000
set minimum file cache buffers = 200
set minimum directory cach buffers = 200
set minimum file cache report threshold = 10
set reserved buffers below 16 meg = 20
load streams
load clib
load aha1540 port=330
load tcpip
bind ip to tcplan addr=134.135.100.3 mask=0xff.0xff.0x0.0x0
secure console
sys:\system\nfsstart.ncf
```

After you complete these two aspects of the installation, it is time to install the NFS software on the NetWare system. To perform this task, insert the NFS floppy into the appropriate file server drive and load the INSTALL.NLM at the NetWare system console. From the Install Options screen, choose the Product Options option and press Enter. The NetWare optional packages currently installed on your file server appear. Do not worry if nothing is in this panel; this is normal with most basic NetWare installations. At this point, press the Insert key to let the Install program know that you want to install a new package. You are prompted for the drive in which the new product is located; after you furnish this data, your installation proceeds.

You then need to let the installation know the drive and path from which NetWare boots (so it can alter your STARTUP.NCF file). This is usually a DOS drive. The installation program then also copies the NFS name space and the NFS support module V_NFS.NLM for VREPAIR to your NetWare boot directory. The program does this in case your drive becomes corrupt, and you want to attempt to repair it. (You would not be able to reach your VREPAIR.NLM to fix your SYS: volume if it resided in SYS:\SYSTEM.)

Your NFS files then are transferred from the floppy to the appropriate NetWare volume directories (that is, SYSTEM, PUBLIC, and ETC). Now comes the fun part. If you already have set up TCP/IP on your Unix server or read Chapter 3, "Host Names and Internet Addressing," of this book, you should have few problems. If you have not, take some time to understand the addressing conventions of the Internet. Familiarity with addressing is invaluable at this juncture, and the better understanding you have of how it works, the easier your network administration duties will be in the future. Trust me—thousands of network administrators can't all be wrong.

You now are asked to supply your internet address, host name, subnet mask, maximum packet size, and minimum packet receive buffers. If you have more than one NIC, you also have to select which NIC is to be used for NFS. Your Internet Address must be unique to the network upon which your host resides. If you are going to be connected to the Internet in any manner, you need to contact your local Internet committee to have a unique network address issued to you. If you do not know how to contact this committee, call any Internet Service Provider; they are usually kind enough to let you know how you can obtain the information you require (usually only after trying to sell you a connection through their service).

Your host name can be as convoluted or contrived as you like. Assigning a name to your host is simply a way of defining which machine you are on. Again drawing upon information given in Chapter 3, you need to determine what you want your subnet mask to be. If you are a class A network (address 0.0.0.0 to 127.255.255.255), then you typically enter 0xff.0xff.0xff.0x0 (or 255.0.0.0 in decimal). If you are in a class B network (128.0.0.0 to 191.255.255.255), you enter 0xff.0xff.0x0.0x0; and if you are class C (192.0.0.0 to 223.255.255.255), then your subnet mask is 0xff.0x0.0x0.0x0.

Although your subnet mask has a default value of 1514, because Unix packets are frequently as large as 2048, you can avoid future intermittent problems by entering the larger value. The next configuration parameter is that of Minimum Packet Receive Buffers, and the default is 100. Unless you experience problems with these buffers at some point in the future, 100 should be more than enough for you to function efficiently. (NetWare lets you know if your minimum receive buffers drops below 100.) At this point, if you are satisfied with the data you have supplied the NFS installation package, answer Yes when prompted if you want to update the configuration files.

You can update your configuration files using either the EDIT.NLM or a DOS editor. All of the necessary configuration files are located in your SYS:\ETC directory.

The major portion of your NetWare NFS configuration is now complete. You now have the opportunity to choose which NFS modules you will use in an ongoing fashion. I have found that it is best to install all the modules and edit the portions you do not require.

You can perform this by editing the NFSSTART.NCF file located in SYS:\SYSTEM with any editor you want. Your options are to add the following:

✔ Unix to NetWare Print Service

✔ NetWare to Unix Print Service

✔ XConsole

✔ FTP Server

✔ Lock Manager

If you choose to install the Unix to NetWare printing, you are asked if you want this module to be started automatically when you invoke NFSSTART.NCF. Again, answer Yes to at least see how and where the installation process places the module. Editing is much simpler than reinstalling the whole package to change one answer.

The following is a typical SYS:\SYSTEM\NFSSTART.NCF file for initiating NFS, print services, and DOS file locking:

```
#SYS:\SYSTEM\NFSSTART.NCF

load bcastlib
load inetdfix
load nfsserv
#
# Setting up Unix to NetWare Print Service
#
load plpd
#
# Setting up Unix to NetWare Print Service
load lpr_psrv
load lpr_gwy
#
# Setting up the Remote Console for Unix
#
load xconsole
load rspx
#
# Setting up Inet Daemon to start FTP server
#
load inetd
#
# Setting up Lock Manager
#
load lockd
```

If you have not already done so, now is a good time to add name-space support for Unix, which is accomplished once by a couple of NetWare commands. At the system console, first type **LOAD NFS** and then **ADD NAME SPACE NFS TO VOLUME SYS**; your volume is now ready to accept extended name spacing.

Now it is time to configure the NetWare NFS server. To do so, you need to set up five NFS configuration files. The first four (NFSUSERS, NFSGROUP, HOSTS, and EXPORTS) are located in your SYS:\ETC directory. The fifth, LPR$PSRV.NAM, is located in the SYS:\ETC\PLPD subdirectory. These files determine the NetWare user name of a user who logs in to your system with a given NFS *user id* (uid); what NetWare group a user should belong to, given his or her NFS *group id* (gid); which remote hosts should have access to your system; which local NetWare directories you want to make available to NFS users; and NetWare LPR Print Server information.

These files can be edited in a number of ways. The suggested manner is to load the NFSADMIN.NLM and perform your changes there. In doing so, you ensure that the nomenclature is correct, but the file formats are lenient and allow for deviations. Without going into extreme detail of all file concatenations, the first four files warrant further attention.

NFSUSERS takes the NFS user id of a person logging in to the NetWare system and allocates that user a NetWare user name. If the uid does not appear in the NFSUSERS file, the person defaults to the NetWare user NOBODY (created during the NFS installation). You can obtain the NFS uid of your user by using the Unix sysadmsh command on the remote Unix host and selecting ACCOUNTS from the main menu, USER from the ACCOUNTS submenu, EXAMINE from the USER submenu, and IDENTITY after entering the user name. In this information, you see a section that displays the user's related uid. The following is an example of the SYS:\ETC\NFSUSERS file:

```
#"NFS uid", "NetWare Username"
-2 nobody
0 supervisor
200 eharper
201 marnett
237 jbuffett
```

NFSGROUP is the same concept as NFSUSERS in the preceding paragraph. The NetWare NFS server first attempts to match a user's group id to a NetWare group through the SYS:\ETC\NFSGROUP file. If the gid is not listed in the NFSGROUP file, then the user is assigned to NetWare group NOGROUP. As with NFSUSERS, if you want to maintain a wide-open system and have no worries about security, you can assign user NOBODY and group NOGROUP the NetWare security equivalencies of SUPERVISOR. For obvious reasons, this would not be very wise and is strongly NOT RECOMMENDED (except for possible debugging purposes).

SYS:\ETC\HOSTS is identical to its Unix counterpart. This file tells the system what other host systems are allowed access to this NetWare NFS server. The Internet address is required in the HOSTS file. Typically included in this file is not only the four-octet "dot-delineated" Internet address, but also the host name and any associated aliases.

The SYS:\ETC\HOSTS file includes remote host Internet addresses and names, as shown in the following example:

```
# "IP Address", "Hostname"
127.0.0.1 localhost
134.135.100.1 jbsco jbsco.lantimes.com
134.135.100.3 jb311a
134.135.100.11 jblabvectra1 jblabvectra1.lantimes.com
134.135.100.12 jblabvectra2 jblabvectra2.lantimes.com
134.135.100.13 jblabvectra3 jblabvectra3.lantimes.com
134.135.100.14 jblabvectra4 jblabvectra4.lantimes.com
134.135.100.15 jblabvectra5 jblabvectra5.lantimes.com
134.135.100.16 jblabvectra6 jblabvectra6.lantimes.com
134.135.200.1 talula talula.lantimes.com
134.135.200.2 pugsley pugsley.lantimes.com
0xff.0xff.0xff.0xff broadcast
```

EXPORTS is critical to enabling portions of your NetWare volumes to be accessed by NFS users. Be very specific about which directories you allow access to. The whole issue of linking two operating systems that do not have common security and password conventions is potential enough for prying fingers. Do not make their attempts any easier, though, by literally giving them access to your valuable data by offering critical areas for export by including them in the Exports file.

The following example of the SYS:\ETC\EXPORTS file allows access to the SYS:\MARNETT\Unix and SYS:\USER\NOBODY subdirectories:

```
# "Exported Path", "Options"
/sys/marnett/unix
/sys/user/nobody
```

Be wary of who has Read (and most definitely Write) access to the SYS:\ETC directory. If NetWare users are allowed to view the contents of these files, they know who has access to different areas in NetWare (especially by combining the EXPORT and NFSUSERS files). Even worse is if users have the ability to either modify or delete and copy or create attributes to the SYS:\ETC directory. If they do, they can modify which NetWare directories can be accessed by anyone—even NetWare NOBODY! Seriously, consider having a dedicated volume for NFS transactions and not adding NFS name space to any of the others.

Setting Up Unix

As stated in preceding chapters of this book (again including Chapter 3, "Host Names and Internet Addressing"), if you want to allow remote users access to data on your NetWare file server, you need to make certain file modifications. But in the instance of your NetWare server acting as the NFS server (the data repository), setup on the Unix side is minimal. Your Unix host first and foremost needs to have a physical device that can communicate in a manner NetWare can understand. This communication typically is performed through an Ethernet adapter that communicates using the Unix equivalent of NetWare's Ethernet_II.

NOV*IX includes in their Firefox Elite package ftp that provides a more basic application layer ftp interface than the often cryptic command-line alternative (see fig. 12.3).

Figure 12.3
The ftp help available in most software packages.

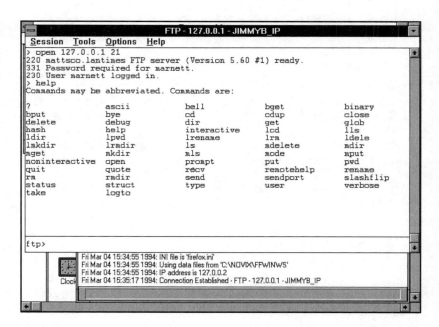

Without repeating what was covered in Chapter 3, make sure that you do not set up your network interface hardware with interrupts already being used by another device. If you do and are lucky, you will only experience minor difficulties and will be able to rectify the problems. If you are not lucky, you will use a vector or I/O base address being used by an integral part of your Unix system and will have to reinstall the whole software package before you can proceed with your installation (or before you can function at all, for that matter).

NIC setup can be accomplished by thoroughly investigating what addresses your current hardware is using. By far the easiest way to do this is to run the hwconfig and study the data it relays. Included in this data are vectors in use and base I/O addresses. The time that you take to review this data is time well-spent.

Run the hwconfig utility to link your NIC to TCP/IP and NFS. Before you begin this process, you should know what your host Internet address is to be, what your network broadcast address will be, and what your subnet mask address should be set to (if you are going to use one at all). After you input this data, you need to rebuild the kernel and then relink it to Unix. You then are prompted to perform these tasks, and unless you have done something incorrectly, you need to complete these actions before your NIC will function. When completed, reboot your Unix system for the changes to take effect. sync your data to the hard disk and perform some form of graceful system shut-down (for example init 0, init 6, or shutdown). When the system reboots, a NIC is available to your network.

Exchanging Data

If you performed the preceding tasks without error, you are now ready to begin sharing and transferring data from one system to another. Realize that as with the Unix doscp command, any Unix files out of the DOS eight-dot-three convention are truncated into the standard. Other restrictions apply, but they are not necessary for this section or chapter. Simply know that restrictions exist (and you will know when you have encountered them).

Exchanging data can be performed between Unix and NetWare in a variety of manners. With NFS, two basic tools are used to perform these tasks—the Unix ftp and mount commands. *ftp*, as mentioned throughout this book, is a basic file transfer protocol that enables Unix users to exchange data with numerous, typically unlike operating systems. ftp is limited, but effective at performing the tasks for which it is designed.

The main configuration that you need to perform for remote hosts to have access to your system is to modify your SYS:\ETC\HOSTS file to include the remote host names. Use any DOS editor to add users to this host access list. Included in the SYS:\ETC\HOSTS file are the Internet addresses, names, and optionally any aliases of the different remote hosts. You also need to create a user for each individual who is going to need access to your local Unix host. The rights you grant your user (for example, the associated groups and user equivalencies) determine to what areas the user has access when communicating with your local host using ftp.

You now have all the necessary tools in place to have remote hosts use ftp to access your local NetWare NFS server. The nuances of how you specifically perform the ftp tasks are best left to the Unix manufacturers' different manuals.

The other more direct (and simple) manner in which you can access data that resides on a NetWare NFS server is to use the Unix mount command. Depending on the type of Unix you are using, the NetWare NFS Supervisor's Guide might or might not be correct in regard to the use of the mount command. If you want to mount the \marnett\unix subdirectory on volume SYS, which is on a server called JB311A, onto your local Unix host at point /buffett (and you are on a Sun Sparcstation), then the book is correct. You enter the command **mount -o soft jb311a:/sys/marnett/unix /buffett**. If you are using SCO Unix, then the command is **mount -f NFS jb311a:/sys/marnett/unix /buffett**. The differences are subtle, but if you do not get them exact (including the letter cases and slash directions), the mount will not work. Remember, for the weak of heart, you always can use the sysadmsh to perform these functions.

If you do not have NetWare NFS server JB311A in your Unix system's /etc/ hosts file, the preceding mount example will not work.

After you mount the NetWare subdirectory, you can access it as if it were part of your local Unix drive. If you successfully perform the preceding mount operation and then enter **cp /.profile /buffett/rootlogn**, you are effectively taking Unix user root's login script from the Unix host and copying it as file name rootlogn in the NetWare SYS:\BUFFETT directory. In like fashion, you can type **mkdir /buffett/songs** to create a subdirectory named songs under the NetWare directory SYS:\BUFFETT.

Understanding NetWare to Unix Printing

NetWare to Unix printing is as simple as printing to any other NetWare queue and printer on a normal Novell file system. The printer installation is the only area on the Unix side that might require some understanding to accomplish; but read on, and you should have no problems.

With an effort to avoid stating the obvious, if you have a printer attached to a parallel port on your Unix host, you must first make your parallel port available for printing. You either can use your sysadmsh utility to create this portion of your system hardware (that is a hint for your menu selections), or you can use the command line. In this instance, the command line is no more difficult than the system administrator shell menu, but those DOS users who are reading about Unix for the first time are probably scratching their heads and asking "make a parallel port, why?" Suffice it to say that vector 7 is not parallel port 1 until you tell it that it is. If you want to use the first parallel port for your printer, then create it using vector 7 and I/O base 0x378.

Now that you have "created" your DOS LPT1: equivalent (which is /dev/lp0 in Unix), attach your printer to the port and proceed to the physical printer configuration. (Here those who are not familiar with Unix should again enter the sysadmsh.) Select PRINTERS from the main menu, and then CONFIGURE and ADD. You then need the following three basic bits of information for your printer to be fully configured:

✔ **A printer name.** Users use this name to direct their print jobs, so a logical and short name is best. In this example, use "test" as your printer name.

✔ **A type of interface.** When you get to this prompt press F3, and a list of available printer types is displayed. If your printer is not listed or you are not sure which type it is, scroll down until you highlight Standard and press Enter. Choosing Standard does not work in all instances, but it is a safe bet for most printers.

✔ **The device name of your interface.** Remember that even devices are files in Unix, and because you just finished creating /dev/lp0, use this port.

Do not worry about the warning that displays when you finish your printer configuration. If you do not want certain individuals to access this printer, refer to your System Administrator's Guide and look up lpadmin.

You now have a printer available for print jobs—almost. The next two tasks are most easily performed through the command line, so either select another virtual terminal screen or exit your system administrator's shell menu all the way to the command line. Type **enable test** and press Enter. Then type **accept test** and press Enter. Indeed you now have a printer available for printing from your Unix host. To test it, enter the lpstat command with the -a and -s flags. You should receive a display stating that your printer is accepting requests. The lpstat command in conjunction with the -s and -a flags as follows gives you a quick but thorough glance at the state of your printers and their associated queues:

```
# lpstat -a -s
jbunixprt0 accepting requests since Sat Sep 17 21:29:50 1994
test not accepting requests since Mon Sep 19 01:53:43 1994 - new
  destination
system default destination: jbunixprt0
device for jbunixprt0: /devlp0
device for test: /dev/lp0
#
```

Typically you want to give access to your printer to those on the NetWare NFS server. On the Unix side, you only need to perform two simple tasks to accomplish this. First, if you have not already done so, enter the Internet address and host name of the NetWare NFS server into your /etc/hosts file. Second, edit the /etc/hosts.equiv file to also include the host name of the NetWare NFS server. As far as the Unix side is concerned, you are done.

From the NetWare side of the world, you need to configure a few items to gain access to the Unix printer. The first few configurations can be made through the PLPDCFG.NLM utility. After this NLM is loaded on the system console, you should select the print queues for use by LPD. If this is a fresh installation, you need to create a queue that uses the Unix printer. Press the Insert key and create a queue name to associate to the Unix printer. If you only want to use one queue, transfer the print queue name from an Available Print Queues window to the Print Queues Selected window. The next step is to select a print filter for the print queue. Typically you select either the Line Printer or PostScript options for the printer. Simply highlight your choice and press Enter. The next step is to select which printer type is associated with your queue. This is straightforward, so simply choose the printer type you have attached to your Unix host. When this is complete, press Esc twice to return to the Main Menu. Select Yes to save the changes and press Esc once again to exit from the program.

The PLPDCFG.NLM utility circumvents the need for you to create queues or printers through the NetWare PCONSOLE utility. You are now ready to print to the Unix host through the LPD_GWY.NLM and the LPD_PSRV.NLM. If they are already running on the NetWare NLM server, you need to unload and then load them. At this point, you should be online with the Unix line printer daemon. You can toggle to the Product Kernel Message Screen on the NetWare NLM server to ensure that you are not receiving any error messages. If you are, the solution usually can be obtained by interpreting the message on the NetWare system console and cross-referencing either the Unix System Administrator's Guide or the NetWare NFS Supervisor's Guide. If everything looks satisfactory on the Product Kernel Message Screen, verify that the LPD Printer Server screen reflects that the Unix printer is online and functional. If it does not appear to be so, reconfigure your remote printers through either the PLPDCFG.NLM or the NetWare PCONSOLE utility.

Now that your Unix printer is configured for use with NetWare and your NFS print daemon is running on your file server, you can use the conventional NetWare CAPTURE command to redirect your workstation print jobs to the NetWare (Unix) printer. If you desire to have everything that would normally go to your local LPT1: port on your DOS workstation, enter the following NetWare command after logging in to your NetWare server:

CAPTURE L=1 S=JB311A Q=TEST NT NB NFF TI=15

Your jobs now are redirected from your local printer port through your NetWare NFS server to the Unix box and out its /dev/lp0 device.

CAPTURE, PSC, and PCONSOLE are all still intact. You can change your local redirection, perform Print Service Commands, and monitor the status of your print job at the NetWare server. After the job leaves NetWare and enters the Unix queue, you need to view the status of the jobs using the netstat -s -a (or similar) commands.

Exploring Unix to NetWare Printing

Printing from Unix to NetWare is much simpler than printing from NetWare to Unix. After you have a valid TCP/IP connection between a local and remote host and you have loaded SYS:\SYSTEM\PLPD.NLM, your connections are made, and only basic configurations need to be made. You first must specify which authorized remote computers have access to the NetWare NFS print server. As with many of the earlier tunable parameters, this is done by manipulating a table through the SYS:\SYSTEM\PLPDCFG.NLM.

When the PLPDCFG.NLM utility is loaded, you see a menu that has the following four options:

- ✔ Select Print Queues for use by LPD
- ✔ Select Trusted Hosts
- ✔ Select Username Mapping Mode
- ✔ Exit

Choose the Select Trusted Hosts option, and you are presented with a Trusted Hosts list. Assuming that this is the first time you have invoked this portion of the PLPDCFG utility, you need to press Ins to select which remote hosts are to have access to your print server.

If you properly configured your SYS:\ETC\HOSTS file, you then observe the list of hosts held within that file. You can select multiple Available Hosts to be added to your Trusted Hosts list by highlighting the desired remote hosts and pressing F5. When you have highlighted all the hosts you want to add, press Enter to transfer the names. Press Esc when you are satisfied with your decisions and exit this portion of the PLPDCFG utility by again pressing Esc.

Because NetWare enables only users designated by the System Administrator to access the various print queues, you now have to select how to associate remote host users with NetWare users (or equivalents). You have three tools with which to accomplish this task. The first option is to select Single Account Mode. In Single Account Mode, every print job that is sent to a queue is associated with a specific NetWare user. In this instance, every job received for a specific queue is associated with one user. Single Account Mode is by far the simplest NetWare printer management selection.

Your second choice is a table-based reference method. This choice is just what it sounds like—a table contains a list of remote user names and their NetWare equivalents. The names do not need to be the same on both sides of the table, so in reality you can create a mini-security grid in which all the names of Unix users in the accounting department equate to one NetWare user named UnixACCT. You can then manage how a whole department prints by changing one user's rights and privileges.

The last mode is Client Username Mode. If—and only if—users have the same names on both your Unix and NetWare systems you can take advantage of this printing scheme. If your remote system has users named eharper, bshimmin, and selder, then your system enables them to access as users EHARPER, BSHIMMIN, and SELDER would have. If there is no direct match between the two systems, then the NetWare NFS print server uses the Single Account Mode Table for specific authorization.

On the remote side of the coin, you need to be concerned with a few configuration settings. The first critical consideration is if your Unix system supports the lpr protocol. If your system does not support the lpr protocol, you will not be able to directly share print devices, and need to purchase either a printer-sharing device for your two systems or a printer for your Unix side. If it does support the lpr protocol, all you need to do is edit the /etc/printcap file to specify the print queue. The following is an example of what you need to add:

```
jbunixprt0:\
            :lp=/dev/lp:sd=/usr/spool/lpd/jbunixprt0:
```

In this example, `jbunixprt0` is the name of the printer; `lp` is the /dev/ output device; and the `sd` parameter is the spool directory that holds the jobs sent to jbunixprt0.

If your Unix users are going to send print jobs larger than one MB to this printer, you need to include the mx flag in the preceding /etc/printcap example. This flag disables the default 1 MB limitation placed on print jobs.

You are now ready to print to the NetWare NFS print server using the remote lp command set. The most frequently used commands are as follows:

✔ **lpr**—Sends the print jobs to the print queue

✔ **lpq**—Enables you to view the status of print jobs

✔ **lprm**—Enables you to remove print jobs from the queue

If you are familiar with the standard Unix printing commands and their associated flags, you need to learn the equivalent commands for the remote lp command set.

Summary

This chapter provided a concise guide to internetworking a typical Unix machine to a NetWare system using the TCP/IP protocol. If you followed the examples in this chapter closely, you should have no problem in transferring files from one system to another and printing in either direction. Recently, the trend toward uniting these two platforms has grown in popularity, and this direction is likely to continue for years to come.

Chapter Snapshot

In 1981, with the advent of the first IBM personal computer, MS-DOS became the operating system of choice for stand-alone business micro computers. Since that date, DOS has become the most widely distributed piece of software in the world, with millions of copies currently in use. Windows, at the present time, is nothing more than an interface graphically presenting options available in DOS. As the world has grown to accept TCP/IP as a networking standard, DOS and Windows have had to grow to implement such. This chapter discusses the topics involved in connecting computers together using TCP/IP over a DOS/Windows platform, including the following:

CHAPTER

Connecting to DOS and Windows

"Education, like neurosis, begins at home."

—Milton Saperstein

4 BSD Unix was widely adopted by workstation and minicomputer vendors, and its networking code went with it. The fact that most vendors shipped it as a no-extra-cost part of the operation system gave TCP/IP a great impetus in the commercial research and engineering sector, moving it out of academia and the government for the first time. Furthermore, because the work was partially DARPA funded, the TCP/IP implementation in 4BSD Unix could be copied freely for both academic and commercial purposes and was ported to many environments other than Unix.

Before the 4BSD TCP/IP existed, a research project led by Professor Jerry Saltzer at the Massachusetts Institute of Technology aimed at proving that TCP/IP could run on platforms as small as the original IBM PC. The original TCP/IP mainframe predecessors were aimed at large systems with abundant memory. Because these systems generally were not efficient enough to take full advantage of LAN speeds, the MIT researchers also planned to use the project as a test bed for innovations in protocol design proposed by Professor Dave Clark. The testing occurred before the introduction of the first PC Ethernet and Token-Ring interfaces, and initially used asynchronous serial lines.

While on sabbatical, Dave Clark wrote a TCP/IP implementation in BCPL, a predecessor to C language. This work was ported to a Xerox Alto, one of the first personal workstations from the mid-70s, and ran over a 3 Mbit/sec Ethernet. Larry Allen ported the code to V6 Unix on a PDP-11 system. The MIT project built on this research, streamlined the code, improved it, and ported it to the Intel architecture.

The body of the programs became known as PC-IP, and served as the basis for a number of follow-up research projects at MIT and elsewhere. Much of the core development was performed by two MIT undergraduate students, John Romkey and Dave Bridgham.

PC-IP was quite successful, both as a research project and as a network protocol stack, and evolved into a package containing several of the standard TCP/IP applications for the PC. MIT released it as freeware, and it became quite popular in the Internet community by 1985. A number of vendors took advantage of its open copyright and offered commercialized versions, slightly modified from the original. One of these vendors was Frontier Technologies Corp., which ported TCP/IP to Windows; whereas Wollongong created Pathway Access for DOS.

Implementing TCP/IP

A number of ways exist to provide a TCP/IP kernel in the PC environment. Of the three primary methods, the VxD is by far the best. The following paragraphs discuss the pros and cons of each method.

TSR

A *TSR* (terminate-and-stay-resident program) is a program that starts up in DOS prior to loading Windows. This program initializes, stays in memory, and returns control to DOS. With this technology, a protocol like TCP/IP is available at all times, enabling it to respond to network traffic very quickly (this is known as *interrupt-level processing*). It also is available for any DOS or Windows program. Unfortunately, a TSR cannot dynamically allocate memory, so when it starts up, it must allocate all the memory it will ever use. A TSR also requires heavy helper *Dynamic Link Libraries* (DLLs) to give Windows applications access to the network. Because a TSR's memory supply is limited and determined at startup, the TSR must make very careful decisions on how to "spend" that allotment of memory. Therefore, if more than one application is utilizing the network, one connection may be favored over the other, or both may suffer. Furthermore, TSRs will be left by the wayside as future versions of Windows eliminate the DOS layer entirely.

Dynamic Link Library

A *DLL* is a 16-bit Windows program helper loaded when its services are needed. This technology enables the protocol to move in and out of the machine's memory and utilize dynamic memory fully when necessary. Therefore, when an application needs to transfer large amounts of data, the TCP/IP kernel can buffer these requests. The drawbacks of DLLs are that they cannot be tied directly to the network card, and they are at the mercy of the Windows scheduler. To talk to the network card, special buffering must be done to ensure that all traffic is received. This buffering will have some limits that may cause the wrong packets to get dropped when on a busy network. Additionally, as a Windows DLL, the TCP/IP kernel relies on all Windows applications to be "nice" and enable it to run often enough to take care of network traffic. If one task performs a long operation without enabling other tasks any time to run, this may mean that the DLL TCP/IP kernel will miss important network traffic, thus requiring retransmissions of the missed data. This limitation tends to make DLLs much less responsive to network demands.

VxD

A *VxD* is implemented in the 32-bit protected-mode layer of Windows, where such critical components as video, mouse, and communications port drivers are implemented. As a VxD, the TCP/IP kernel combines key advantages from TSRs and DLLs while minimizing the disadvantages. Like a TSR, it can respond to the network traffic in response to hardware interrupts and give full access to both Windows and DOS programs. It uses some fixed lower memory, but that memory can be dynamically allocated (as in a DLL) so it can be taken only when it is really needed. Unlike a DLL, a VxD is not at the mercy of other applications running in Windows that tie up the Windows task—it is capable of interrupt-level processing to handle network events as soon as they happen. VxDs fully utilize the 386/486 CPU as full 32-bit drivers. With the advances of *Network Device Interface Specification* (NDIS) 3.0, a 32-bit interface to the network card, the TCP/IP kernel VxD can respond to network traffic without switching the CPU back and forth between real mode and protected mode to interact with 16-bit TSR-based network hardware drivers.

When the TCP/IP kernel is implemented as a VxD, other service VxDs like NFS Client, NFS Server, and NetBIOS can be provided. Typically, these facilities are also very important in a networking environment. With a TSR implementation, each of these can add as much as 200 KB to the DOS memory taken from Windows before Windows starts. With a DLL, these services cannot be fully implemented, as the Windows DOS boxes are left out in the cold. VxD implementations of these important components can provide their services to Windows DOS boxes while using only as much memory as is absolutely necessary.

Table 13.1 lists the comparative differences between the different TCP/IP kernel implementations.

Table 13.1
Differences between TCP/IP Kernel Implementations

	TSR	DLL	VxD
Fixed memory usage	All memory needed by the network is allocated at startup before Windows is run. Memory usage is not related to network usage. Limited to 640 KB available in DOS.	Small amount of fixed memory needed. Only allocated while Windows is running.	Amount used depends on network usage. May use more than the lower 640 KB. Fixed memory may be allocated outside lower 1 MB; only allocated while Windows is running.
Future migration path	Will become obsolete as new versions of Windows supplant the DOS layer.	Usable in 32-bit versions of Windows, but will not take advantage of the 32-bit architecture.	Full 32-bit implementation can take advantage of new 32-bit operating systems.
Handling of network events	Immediate, at interrupt level.	Handled by an intermediate layer, picked up later by the DLL.	Immediate, at interrupt level. Will be handled completely in 32-bit protected mode with NDIS 3.0.
Interface to Windows applications	Winsock DLL must communicate with TCP/IP through software interrupts, causing frequent switches to real mode.	TCP/IP and Winsock can communicate easily, and may even be combined.	TCP/IP and Winsock can communicate easily.

	TSR	DLL	VxD
32-bit	A "thinking layer" passes 32-bit requests through to the 16-bit Winsock DLL, which then has to communicate with the DOS TSR in real mode.	A "thinking layer" passes 32-bit requests through to the 16-bit Winsock DLL.	No "thinking layer" is necessary. A 32-bit Winsock DLL can communicate directly with the 32-bit VxD.

Table 13.2 provides a simple feature comparison between the different methods.

Table 13.2
Feature Comparison

	TSR	DLL	VxD
No DOS memory taken		✔	✔
Interrupt Level Processing	✔		✔
Dynamic Memory Allocation		✔	✔
Available before Windows is run	✔		
Accessible in Windows DOS box	✔		✔
Accessible to Windows programs	✔	✔	✔
Takes advantage of 32-bit processors			✔
Fully-functional NFS	✔		✔
NetBIOS	✔		✔
Runs in protected mode		✔	✔
NDIS 3.0 support			✔

II

Enumeration

Today, TCP/IP kernels, NFS Clients, NFS Servers, and NetBIOS for Windows are typically implemented as either DOS TSRs or as Windows DLLs. The DOS TSRs are typically fast, but can take up more precious DOS memory. Windows DLLs can save on DOS memory, but are usually slower and do not provide TCP/IP and NFS access from Windows DOS boxes. Frontier Technologies' SuperTCP/NFS solves both of these problems. Because the TCP/IP kernel, NFS, and NetBIOS are implemented as Windows VxDs, no DOS RAM is used by SuperTCP/NFS. In addition, because the TCP/IP kernel and the NFS Client/Server are full 32-bit implementations (unlike DOS TSRs or Windows DLLs, which are only 16-bit), they can provide better performance than either DOS TSRs or Windows DLLs.

Pre-Installation

To perform a successful installation of SuperTCP/NFS or any similar Windows-based package, you should carefully review the information provided in this section *prior to* installation.

You need to determine essential network information for your machine, including its IP (Internet) address and name, the IP address of your Domain Name Server (if one is present), and the IP address of your default gateway (if present). Use the following list as a guide to entering appropriate network information before proceeding with installation:

- ✔ Machine name

- ✔ Domain name of your machine

- ✔ IP address of your machine

- ✔ IP address of domain name server (optional)

- ✔ IP address mask of your machine

- ✔ IP address of your default gateway (optional)

- ✔ Hardware driver type and name

- ✔ I/O address

- ✔ Memory address

- ✔ Interrupt

The IP address of your machine translates to its Internet name. A name is easier to remember than an address; therefore, remote users will want to use this name when addressing your PC. The full Internet name is a string of characters, such as

NIC.DDN.MIL, which may contain up to 255 letters, numbers, and the special characters: underscore (_), dash (-), and dot (.). In this example, DDN.MIL is the domain name and NIC is the machine name.

IP addresses are four-part numbers, such as 192.0.0.1, where each part is a number in the range 0-255. Each address must be unique for your network.

If you do not have a domain name server or local gateway, use 0.0.0.0.

Make sure that you know the exact configuration details for the network adapter installed in your PC. You may need to know the I/O address, memory address, and interrupt number for your system. Refer to your network interface manual to obtain this information.

The installation process modifies your AUTOEXEC.BAT, CONFIG.SYS, and Windows system files. Before proceeding with installation, you should create backups of the following Windows system files:

✔ C:\WINDOWS\WIN.INI (Windows configuration file)

✔ C:\WINDOWS\SYSTEM.INI (Windows configuration file)

✔ C:\WINDOWS\PROGRAM.INI (Windows configuration file)

In addition, you may need to create backup copies of the following files:

✔ C:\NET.CFG (ODI configuration file)

✔ C:\LANMAN\PROTOCOL.INI (LAN Manager configuration file)

Understanding Crucial Files

Each TCP/IP software has specific files to be configured for that specific software. A list of these can usually be found in the manuals under the uninstall directions. Some of the files that are affected in SuperTCP/NFS, for example, include the following:

✔ In your AUTOEXEC.BAT file, the following lines and all lines contained between them:

```
REM Frontier Begin Modifications
...
REM Frontier End Modifications
```

✔ If you are using an NDIS driver, the PROTOCOL.INI file and the following lines in your CONFIG.SYS file:

```
DEVICE=C:\SUPERTCP\PROTMAN.DOS /i:C:\SUPERTCP
DEVICE=C:\SUPERTCP\{drivername}.DOS
DEVICE=C:\SUPERTCP\STCPNDIS.DOS
DEVICE=C:\SUPERTCP\NNWNDIS.DOS
```

✔ The following lines in your WIN.INI file, located in your Windows directory:

```
LOAD=C:\SUPERTCP\SUPERTCP.EXE
```

or

```
LOAD=C:\SUPERTCP\MSERVICE.EXE
```

The entire section labeled [FRONTIER TECHNOLOGIES CORPORATION].

(This section will be located near the end of your WIN.INI file.)

Parts of the [Networks], [Printer Ports], and [devices] sections.

✔ The following lines in your SYSTEM.INI file:

```
NETWORK.DRV=NETMUX.DRV
```

(This line will be found under the [BOOT] tag in the SYSTEM.INI file.)

Also under the [BOOT] tag, the following line is present:

```
COMM.DRV=COMM.DRV
```

Under the [BOOT DESCRIPTION] tag, the statement on the NETWORK.DRV line.

Under the [386Enh] section, the following lines:

```
DEVICE=FTCTCPIP.386
DEVICE=FTCNFSC.386
DEVICE=FTCNFSS.386
DEVICE=FTCTCPD.386
DEVICE=FTCSECUR.386
DEVICE=FTCPMAP.386
TRANSPORT=FTCNBD.386
```

✔ All files SUPERTCP.* in the main Windows directory (C:\WINDOWS).

✔ All files FTC*.* in the main Windows directory (C:\WINDOWS).

✔ All files in the C:\SUPERTCP directory (including its subdirectories and their files.

✔ If you are using ODI drivers, the NET.CFG file will be modified.

Using the Network

A number of applications enable users to productively tap the resources on a TCP/IP network and the Internet. The basic applications and the ones that have been around the longest are as follows:

✔ Telnet

✔ FTP

✔ E-mail

These applications provide the basic functionality for TCP/IP connectivity, including the following:

✔ Terminal emulation

✔ File transfer

✔ E-mail

The different services and applications used in a TCP/IP network are defined by documents called *Request For Comments* (RFCs). The RFCs can be written by anyone and are usually discussed at length on Internet mailing lists as they move up the standards track until they become widely used. The Telnet protocol is defined by RFC along with others. The Telnet protocol defines a method to provide terminal support to a Unix-type machine, usually through a DEC VT type (vt100) emulation. Other emulation types include those for IBM connectivity like tn3270. The *File Transfer Protocol* (FTP) is defined by an RFC that provides the capability to move files from one machine to the other. The E-mail protocol is defined by another RFC and provides the capability to send mail messages from one machine to another.

Data communications has become a fundamental part of computing. Worldwide networks gather data about such diverse subjects as atmospheric conditions, crop production, and airline traffic. Groups establish electronic mailing lists so that they can share information of common interest. Hobbyists exchange programs for their home computers. In the scientific world, data networks are essential because they enable scientists to send programs and data to remote supercomputers for processing, to retrieve the results, and to exchange scientific information with colleagues.

From the user's point of view, the Internet appears to be a set of application programs that uses the network to carry out useful communication tasks. The term *interoperability* refers to the capability of diverse computing systems to cooperate in solving computational problems. Internet application programs exhibit a high degree of interoperability. Most users that access the Internet technology or even the path their data travels to its destination rely on application programs to handle such details.

LAN WorkPlace for DOS

LAN WorkPlace for DOS is a suite of TCP/IP applications from Novell that provides a TCP/IP stack, NFS client, and many TCP/IP applications. You implement it as a DOS TSR, with a Windows device driver, and it comes with applications for both DOS and Windows, such as telnet, ftp, rsh, remote printing, and tn3270. It also has its own WINSOCK.DLL for Winsock compatibility.

Because LAN WorkPlace for DOS is a Novell package, it works well with the NetWare client software. It utilizes the Novell ODI (Open Datalink Interface) stack and works with VLMs (Virtual Loadable Modules) or NETX.

The next version, 5.0, will provide additional features, such as X terminal support and dial-up SLIP and PPP.

Installing LAN WorkPlace for DOS

Figure 13.1 shows a sample network that consists of two smaller networks, A and B, connected by a router. Network B has another router that acts as the gateway to the Internet. Network B contains a Domain Name Services (DNS) nameserver and a Unix host named Bob. Network A has two PCs. The diagram in figure 13.1 provides information you need to install LAN WorkPlace for DOS on PC 1.

Figure 13.1
A diagram of a
sample network.

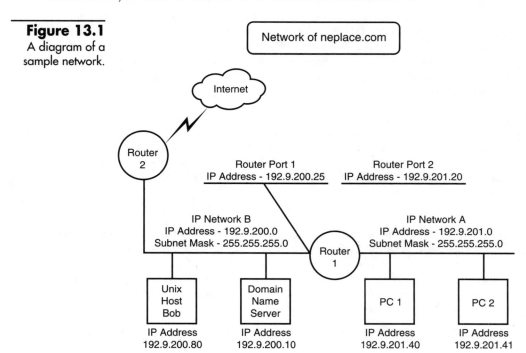

Gathering Network Information

Your first step is to gather the necessary network information. You, as network administrator, should provide the following information:

IP address of the PC

Subnet mask of the local network

Broadcast IP address of the local network

Gateway IP address of the local network

Hostname of the PC, if any

Domain name, if any

Domain Name Server address, if any

Network interface settings, such as IRQ, DMA address, port address and memory base address

You can use a RARP server or a BOOTP server to assign parts of the network information. If so, the network automatically provides some information such as IP address, subnet mask, and local gateway address. When you load the TCP/IP TSR, it sends out a packet requesting information. If the RARP or BOOTP server knows of the PC, it responds with the correct network parameters.

Table 13.3 shows the correct information for the sample network diagrammed in figure 13.1.

Table 13.3
The Correct Information for the Figure 13.3 Network

TCP/IP Network Attribute	Correct Value
IP address	192.9.201.40
Subnet mask	255.255.255.0
Broadcast IP address	192.9.201.255
Gateway IP address	192.9.201.20
Hostname	PC1
Domain name	neplace.com
Domain Name Server address	192.9.200.10
Network interface address	Varies from card to card

Installing

Table 13.4 lists the few requirements for installing LAN WorkPlace for DOS on a PC.

Table 13.4
Requirements for Installing LAN WorkPlace for DOS on a PC

Workstation Attribute	Requirement
System Type	IBM compatible
Microprocessor	Minimum 8088 for DOS applications Minimum 80286 for Windows applications
RAM	512 KB for DOS application 2 to 4 MB for Windows applications
Hard Drive	4.5 MB
Operating System	MS DOS 3.3 or later MS Windows 3.0 or later
Network Connection	Ethernet, token ring, or ARCnet network board and the ODI driver

Using the gathered network information and the setup instructions in the LAN WorkPlace for DOS manuals, installation is a simple matter of changing disks and entering the correct network information at the prompts. Several system files are modified, so you need to reboot the PC after you install LAN WorkPlace for DOS.

Examining the Modified Files

Several files are modified during the installation of LAN WorkPlace for DOS. The following line is added to the C:\AUTOEXEC.BAT file:

```
CALL C:\NET\bin\lanwp.bat
```

The LANWP.BAT contains commands to load the TCPIP.EXE TSR, and its contents are as follows:

```
C:\NET\bin\yesno "Do you want to load the networking software? [y/n] "
if errorlevel 1 goto noload
PATH C:\NET\BIN;%path%
tcpip.exe
```

```
set name=root
break on
:noload
```

When the PC already has the NetWare client software loaded, the final NET.CFG file
looks similar to the following:

```
Link Support
     Buffers 4 1500
     MemPool 4096
Link Driver 3C5X9
     Frame ethernet_802.3
     Protocol ipx 0 ethernet_802.3
NetWare DOS Requester
     FIRST NETWORK DRIVE = F
     USE DEFAULTS = OFF
     VLM = CONN.VLM
     VLM = IPXNCP.VLM
     VLM = TRAN.VLM
     VLM = SECURITY.VLM
     VLM = BIND.VLM
     VLM = NWP.VLM
     VLM = FIO.VLM
     VLM = GENERAL.VLM
     VLM = REDIR.VLM
     VLM = PRINT.VLM
     VLM = NETX.VLM
     SHOW DOTS=ON
```

The following line is added to the NET.CFG file in the Link section:

```
Frame Ethernet_II
```

The following lines are added to the NET.CFG file:

```
Protocol TCPIP
     PATH LANG_CFG     C:\NET\LANG
     PATH SCRIPT     C:\NET\SCRIPT
     PATH PROFILE     C:\NET\PROFILE
     PATH LWP_CFG     C:\NET\HSTACC
     PATH TCP_CFG     C:\NET\TCP
     ip_router          192.9.201.20
     ip_address     192.9.201.40
     ip_netmask     255.255.255.0
```

II

Enumeration

If the network utilizes a RARP or a BOOTP server, the IP_router, IP_address, and IP_netmask entries might be missing. That's normal. The network is telling the TCP/IP TSR to ask the network for this information.

Another file modified is C:\WINDWOS\SYSTEM.INI; the following line is added to the [386Enh] section:

```
device=vtcpip.386
```

Testing the Installation

One of the most useful troubleshooting utilities for TCP/IP networks is the ping command, located in the C:\NET\BIN directory, and using it is very simple. Enter the command **ping <*address | hostname* >**, where *address* is an IP address or *hostname* is a symbolic name, and it responds either, "host is alive" or "host is not responding."

Use the following procedure to test the TCP/IP installation and verify that the network works properly. Make sure each ping works before moving on to the next step.

The first step is to ping 192.9.201.40. If unsuccessful, the TCP/IP installation on PC 1 has a problem: probably TCPIP.EXE isn't loaded. Verify that it *is* loaded and try again.

Next try to ping the router at IP address 192.9.201.20. If this fails, you might have a configuration problem on PC 1 or a general network problem. Verify that the IP_address and IP_netmask fields in the NET.CFG are correct. If so, try to ping another machine on the same network. Here, the only choice is PC2. Remember that TCP/IP must be installed on PC 2 before it can respond to the ping. Also verify that PC 1 is connected to the network. If the router still doesn't respond, verify that the router is up and running.

Now try to ping the other side of the router at IP address 192.9.200.25. If this ping fails, check the IP_router field in the NET.CFG file. It should point to the router on the local network. In this case, the address should be 192.9.201.20. If the NET.CFG file is correct, the router might be the source of the problem. This type of problem requires the network administrator to examine the router's configuration and make the necessary corrections.

If that works, try to ping the Unix host at 192.9.200.80. If the ping fails, the Unix host might be down. Contact the network administrator for assistance at this point.

The next step is to test the Domain Name Service. Instead of entering ping 192.9.200.80, enter **ping bob**. ping should respond "bob is alive." If ping returns an error message, such as "unknown host," check the file C:\NET\TCP\RESOLV.CFG, which should appear as follows:

```
domain          neplace.com
nameserver      192.9.200.10
```

If this file is configured correctly, ask the network administrator to verify that the DNS server knows about Bob.

Using the DOS Applications

Many DOS applications are included with LAN WorkPlace for DOS. Three of the most useful among the many are TNVT220.EXE, FTP.EXE, and NFS, discussed in the following three sections. Refer to the LAN WorkPlace for DOS manuals for descriptions and instructions on using the many others. These DOS applications can work on older PCs, such as those based on the Intel 8088 or 80286 microprocessors.

Using TNVT220

TNVT220 is similar to the Unix telnet command. It enables you to connect to a host, usually a Unix host or a mainframe, and provides terminal emulation. TNVT220 emulates a VT52, VT100, or VT220 terminal. To use it, enter **TNVT220 *hostname*** , where *hostname* represents the name of a host, such as Bob. Alternatively, enter **TNVT220 *IP address*** , where *IP address* is an actual IP address of a host, such as 192.9.200.80.

TNVT220 connects to the host and presents the initial logon screen. After you finish the session and log out, TNVT220 exits back to the DOS prompt.

Using ftp

file transfer protocol (ftp) has been a standard TCP/IP application for many years. Novell has implementation is very similar to the ftp found on Unix hosts and mainframes.

Starting ftp is much like starting TNVT220. Enter **ftp** followed by a host name or an IP address, and it provides a logon prompt for the host. After you log in, you are presented with the `ftp>` prompt. At this point, many commands are available to transfer files. Table 13.5 contains a condensed list of several of the ftp commands.

Table 13.5
Condensed List of FTP Commands

FTP Command	Description
ls	Lists remote directory contents
get	Transfers a file from the remote host
mget	Transfers multiple files from the remote host
put	Transfers a file to the remote host
mput	Transfers multiple files to the remote host

continues

Table 13.5, Continued
Condensed List of FTP Commands

FTP Command	Description
bin	Sets transfer mode to binary, no CR/LF conversion
ascii	Sets transfer mode to ASCII, does CR/LF conversion
bye	Exits from the host and back to the DOS prompt

Using NFS

NFS is a distributed file system that can be used to connect computers that use different operating systems. NFS lets PC mount a Unix file system, which can then be accessed by PC-based applications.

A PC on which both NFS and the Novell client software are running can have drive letters mapped to several Unix file systems and Novell NetWare volumes.

Using the Windows Applications

The Windows application bundled with LAN WorkPlace for DOS provides a comfortable GUI alternative to the DOS applications. The Host Presenter is equivalent to TNVT220, and Rapid Filer is equivalent to ftp. The icons for these applications are located in the Windows group called LAN WorkPlace for Windows. Because Novell has provided the WINSOCK.DLL, you also can use third-party software that conforms to the Winsock standard.

Using the Host Presenter

The Host Presenter provides the same capability as TNVT220, while adding some flexibility. Because it is a Windows application, you can cut and paste between applications. The Host Presenter also allows a higher lever of customization. You can pick and choose colors and fonts to suit your taste.

Because different type of hosts have different terminal preferences, Host Presenter allows different profiles to load when you connect to a host. The profiles can include fonts, colors, and key mappings.

Using the Rapid Filer

The Rapid Filer is an application that incorporates ftp, but you don't need to know the cryptic ftp commands. When you start Rapid Filer, a window appears prompting you to enter host information.

In the **R**emote Host Name text box, enter a name or an IP address. The **U**ser Name and **P**assword boxes are self-explanatory, and you must fill them out. You usually can leave all the other entries at the default values. Although you might need to modify these settings under special circumstances, the default should work most of the time.

After you log in to the remote host, the Rapid Filer provides a listing of files and directories on both the local and remote systems. You can use the mouse to drag a file from one system to the other.

Netscape

Over the past several years, the Internet has become so vast that users need a guide to get around. Information and services abound on the Internet, but finding what you want on it can prove daunting. Development of the World Wide Web (WWW) has simplified access to the Internet.

Netscape is a World Wide Web browser. It provides a graphical interface to the Internet that makes navigating considerably easier. Netscape requires a Winsock-compliant TCP/IP stack to operate.

Installing Netscape

Netscape is available through anonymous ftp from many sites, including the following:

> ftp.netscape.com
>
> ftp2.netscape.com
>
> wuarchive.wustl.edu
>
> ftp.cps.cmich.edu
>
> ftp.utdallas.edu
>
> ftp.micro.caltech.edu
>
> unicron.unomaha.edu
>
> server.berkeley.edu

Uncompress the file into a temporary directory. Choose **F**ile, **R**un from the Program Manager in Windows, then type **setup.exe** in the temporary directory. Use the default values for the questions setup asks.

Setup is now complete. If the network has an Internet connection, Netscape should work fine. However, if there is a firewall setup to access the Internet, the firewall information needs to be entered into the proxies section of the preferences of Netscape.

II

Enumeration

Using Netscape

Netscape is a Windows-based application, and therefore, child's play to use. After you start up Netscape, it connects to a home page at netscape.com. Next, you can bring up an index of useful sites to visit simply by pointing and clicking the mouse.

Summary

Local area *network operating systems* (NOSs) have addressed the problem of interconnecting DOS-based servers and PCs and provided services for sharing access to files and applications. With the implementation of TCP/IP, it is possible to connect to Unix machines, as well as OS/2, NT, and a variety of others—all using the common protocol.

Chapter Snapshot

This chapter explains the process of implementing the TCP/IP protocol in a Microsoft Windows NT network. You learn how to set up your Windows NT Server to use TCP/IP as the transport mechanism. You also learn how to use the TCP/IP applications and utilities provided by Microsoft in Windows NT. The main topics covered are the following:

CHAPTER

Connecting to Windows NT

"In theory, there is nothing to hinder our following what we are taught, but in life there are many things to draw us aside."

—Epictetus

TCP/IP is a powerful transport protocol that gives you access to any number of network resources. Because most major computer platforms support TCP/IP, it should not surprise you that Microsoft has included TCP/IP support in Windows NT right out of the box. Windows NT includes many of the tools common in TCP/IP networks like ftp and telnet, but it also provides tools such as *Dynamic Host Configuration Protocol* (DHCP). The parts that are missing can be filled easily by third-party applications.

Exploring TCP/IP for Windows NT

Because the TCP/IP protocol is the most accepted and complete transport mechanism in the world, Microsoft decided to support it natively. For the user, this means that to use TCP/IP to communicate with other computers requires no additional software. Other products produced by third-party developers might enhance the functionality of TCP/IP on your Windows NT network, but with the tools provided, you can connect to systems using Windows NT, other Microsoft networking products, or with non-Microsoft systems such as Unix.

Windows NT includes many TCP/IP utilities such as telnet, ftp, finger, rcp, rexec, rsh, and tftp. These applications provide users access to resources on non-Microsoft hosts such as Unix. Windows NT also includes a suite of TCP/IP diagnostic tools such as arp, hostname, ipconfig, nbtstat, netstat, ping, and route.

You can use nbstat to check the state of NetBIOS over TCP/IP connections. To find out what name your server registered on the network, type **nbstat -n**. You also can use nbstat to update the LMHOSTS name cache.

tracert is another command you can use to troubleshoot your TCP/IP connections. tracert displays the route taken to a destination, including each router crossed. Type **tracert** *target_name*. The time taken to reach each router along the way also is displayed.

Windows NT also adds a few other utilities that you might not be as familiar with, such as DHCP and *Windows Internet Name Service* (WINS). You learn more about these utilities later in the chapter. All these tools and applications combine to make Windows NT a robust host on a TCP/IP network.

Some tools that Windows NT does not include, but for which third-party support is available, are X Windows, NFS, Gopher, and development tools, such as Xlib and ONC/RPC. If you feel the need to expand your TCP/IP support, check into these products. Luckily, you will find many companies interested in supporting TCP/IP on Windows NT.

Installing TCP/IP on Windows NT

You can install the TCP/IP components of Windows NT when you first set up your system or later as you expand your network. This section assumes that you already installed Windows NT on a machine and that you are adding TCP/IP functionality.

You must be logged in as Administrator or as a member of the Administrators group to install and configure all the elements of TCP/IP mentioned in this chapter.

Begin by opening the Control Panel and double-clicking on the Networks icon. The Network Settings dialog box appears (see fig. 14.1). Click on the Add **S**oftware button to open the Network Software Installation dialog box.

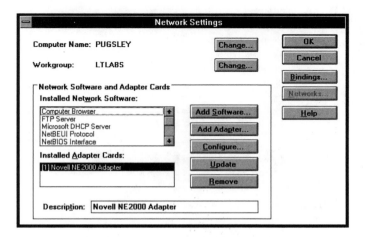

Figure 14.1
The Network Settings dialog box.

II

Enumeration

Scroll through the list of network software components until you see the option TCP/IP Protocol and Related Components. Choose this option, then click on the Continue button.

The Windows NT TCP/IP Installation Options dialog box that appears includes a number of different components (see fig. 14.2). You might want to install all of them eventually, but for now select TCP/IP Internetworking, **C**onnectivity Utilities, and S**i**mple TCP/IP Services.

The TCP/IP Internetworking component installs the TCP/IP protocols, NetBIOS, Windows Sockets, and the TCP/IP diagnostic utilities. The **C**onnectivity Utilities option installs the utilities like telnet, ftp, finger, and so on. S**i**mple TCP/IP Services installs utilities that enable your system to respond to requests from other machines. If you want more information about any of these items, read the hint bar at the bottom of each TCP/IP dialog box or choose the Help button to get more detailed information.

The dialog box shows how much space each component requires. Hopefully, you will have plenty of room for all the components you selected. To see the space required for all the components you selected and the space available on your hard drive, look at the values below the Components box. If you install all the components, you will need about 2 MB of free disk space.

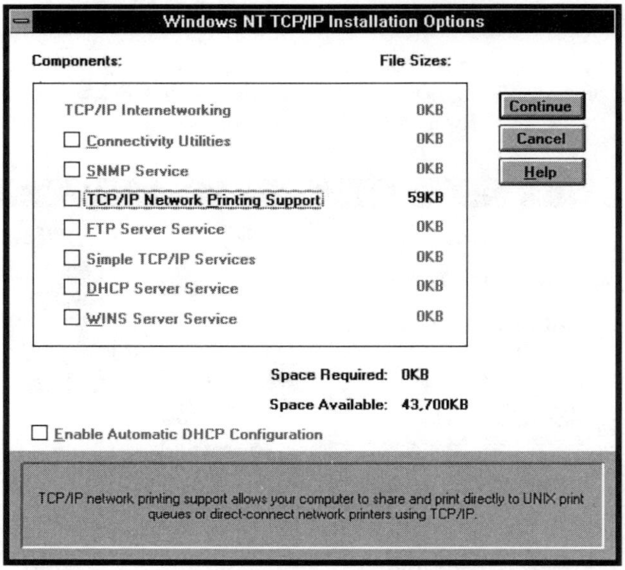

Figure 14.2
The Windows NT
TCP/IP Installation
Options dialog
box.

Windows NT TCP/IP Installation Options	
Components:	**File Sizes:**
TCP/IP Internetworking	0KB
☐ Connectivity Utilities	0KB
☐ SNMP Service	0KB
☐ TCP/IP Network Printing Support	59KB
☐ FTP Server Service	0KB
☐ Simple TCP/IP Services	0KB
☐ DHCP Server Service	0KB
☐ WINS Server Service	0KB

Continue
Cancel
Help

Space Required: 0KB
Space Available: 43,700KB

☐ Enable Automatic DHCP Configuration

TCP/IP network printing support allows your computer to share and print directly to UNIX print queues or direct-connect network printers using TCP/IP.

Once you have selected all the components you want to install, click on OK, and Windows NT starts copying the necessary files.

After the TCP/IP software is installed on your Windows NT computer, you need to provide some configuration information. The first thing Windows NT asks you for is a valid IP address. The easiest way to get a valid address is to use a DHCP server. You learn how to install a DHCP server later in this chapter. For now, you need to insert the IP address information manually. In the TCP/IP Configuration dialog box, enter your machine's IP address, the subnet mask, and the default gateway (see fig. 14.3). The section of the box that deals with WINS is covered later in this chapter. Leave it blank for now.

If your network is already running TCP/IP, make sure that you get a valid IP address from your network administrator. Otherwise, you might accidentally choose an address used elsewhere on the network, which causes all sorts of problems. For more information about IP addressing, see Chapter 3, "Host Names and Internet Addressing."

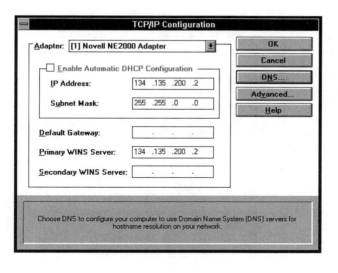

Figure 14.3
The TCP/IP Configuration dialog box.

If you are confused about any part of this dialog box, remember that components are explained in the hint bar. More detailed information is available if you click on the Help button.

Configuring TCP/IP to Use DNS

On the right side of the TCP/IP Configuration dialog box is a button labeled D**N**S (refer to fig. 14.3). DNS (or *Domain Name Service*) is a naming service popular in Unix networks that provides a means of resolving system names with IP addresses. If you have a DNS server on your network and want to use its naming services, Windows NT gives you the option.

The DNS Configuration dialog box is split into three sections (see fig. 14.4). In the uppermost section, you tell Windows NT which naming resources you want to search first. If you have a HOSTS file on your machine, it can use that in conjunction with the DNS server. You can configure TCP/IP to search either resource first.

In the middle section of the DNS Configuration dialog box, you insert the DNS server's IP address. You can include up to three IP addresses, but keep in mind that the order they are listed in this box is the order Windows NT uses to query the name servers. Therefore, you should list first the DNS server you use most often (if there is one). You can use the arrow buttons at the right of the box to change the order.

In the third section in the DNS Configuration dialog box, you can list domain suffixes. This list specifies the DNS domain suffixes to be appended to host names during name resolution. You can add up to six entries in this list. The domain suffixes are used with the host names to create a *fully qualified domain name* (FQDN). A FQDN consists of the host name, followed by a period, followed by the domain name. For example, if *editorial* is the host name and *lantimes.com* is the domain name, the FQDN is *editorial.lantimes.com*.

When you have filled in all the information necessary in the DNS Configuration dialog box, click on OK to return to the TCP/IP Configuration dialog box.

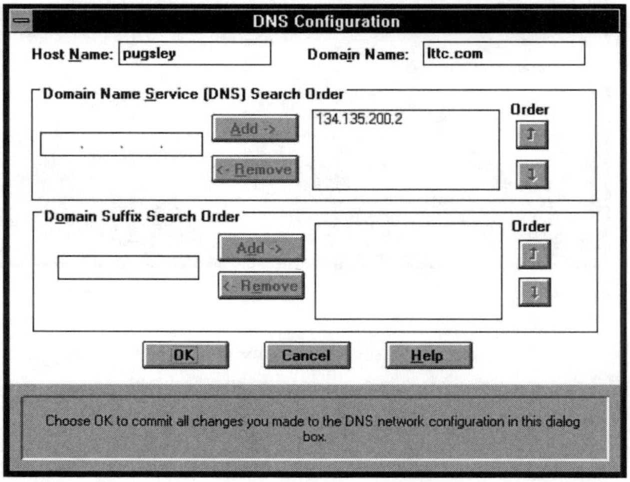

Figure 14.4
The DNS
Configuration
dialog box.

Configuring Advanced TCP/IP Options

Depending on the complexity of your TCP/IP network, you might want to configure the Advanced TCP/IP options of Windows NT. To do this, click on the Advanced button in the TCP/IP Configuration dialog box. The Advanced Microsoft TCP/IP Configuration dialog box appears (see fig. 14.5). At the top of the box, you can select the network adapter for which you want to configure specific options. If you only have one adapter, then this doesn't really matter to you; but if you have two or more adapters, some of the options in this dialog box are of special interest.

Below the Adapter setting is a section of the box in which you can add IP addresses and subnet masks to your machine. You can configure up to five IP addresses for each network adapter on your system. This feature comes in handy if you happen to run multiple IP networks on the same physical segment.

You also can define up to five default gateways for the selected adapter to use. As with the list of DNS servers, the order in which the gateways are listed is important. Windows NT searches the gateway at the top of the list first, and then on down the line.

Two other options deal specifically with Windows networking parameters. Normally, DNS servers are used in host-based TCP/IP environments like Unix. If you select the box next to the option Ena**b**le DNS for Windows Name Resolution, then you can use a DNS server to resolve naming requests for Windows networks also.

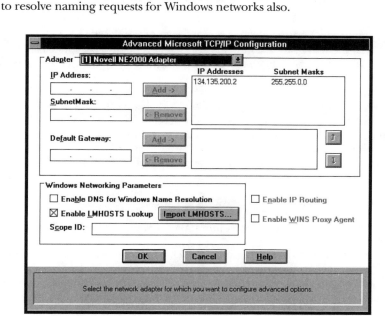

Figure 14.5
The Advanced Microsoft TCP/IP Configuration dialog box.

Another way to resolve naming requests on a Windows network is with an LMHOSTS file. If you aren't familiar with the function of LMHOSTS files, don't worry—you learn about it later in the chapter. The Advanced Microsoft TCP/IP Configuration dialog box also gives you the option of importing an LMHOSTS file.

The final option in this section of the dialog box is to enter a S**c**ope ID. A *scope ID* is a way to group a set of computers so that they only communicate with each other. If you enter a scope ID in this field, your computer will be able to communicate only with other computers on your network that have the exact same scope ID. Usually, you want to leave this value blank.

Finally, you have the option in the Advanced Microsoft TCP/IP Configuration dialog box to enable IP routing. This option is only available to you if you have two network adapters configured for the TCP/IP protocol with their own IP addresses. The WINS Proxy agent field applies only if you have a WINS server on your network.

Configure the options you want to change, then click on OK to return to the TCP/IP Configuration dialog box.

Configuring TCP/IP for Remote Access

Many Windows NT users install *Remote Access Service* (RAS) so that they can use their network from a remote site. Fortunately, this remote access is available for TCP/IP networks as well. Remote users can dial in to an RAS server and have complete remote access to the TCP/IP network as if they were physically connected to the network through a LAN adapter.

RAS has some special considerations in a TCP/IP network, however. For example, how do users resolve naming and address queries—through the RAS server on the LAN or through the remotely attached computer connected with a phone line?

To configure RAS for use on TCP/IP networks, you first need to run the RAS setup program. To get there, follow these steps:

1. Open the Networks icon from the Control Panel.

2. Select Add Software and choose Remote Access Service from the list.

3. In the Remote Access Setup dialog box, click on the **N**etwork button to open the Network Configuration dialog box (see fig. 14.6).

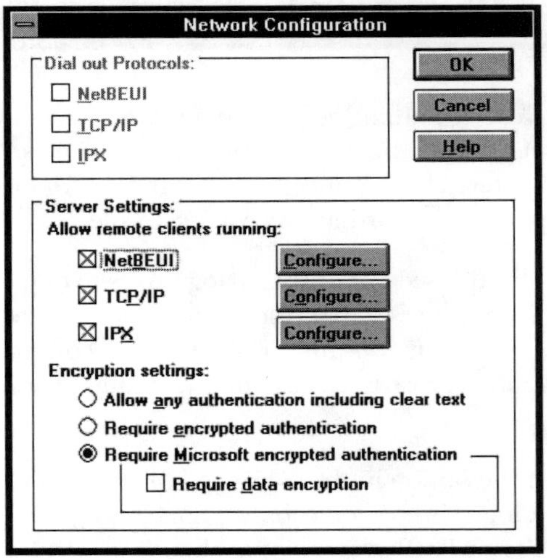

Figure 14.6
The Network
Configuration
dialog box.

4. From this dialog box, select TC**P**/IP and click on the C**o**nfigure button next to it. (If TCP/IP is already installed on your system, that box is checked by default.)

The RAS Server TCP/IP Configuration dialog box appears (see fig. 14.7).

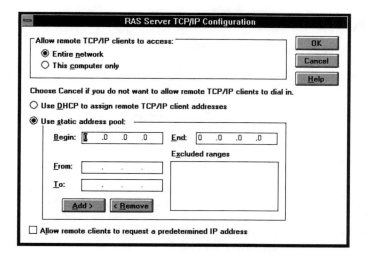

Figure 14.7
The RAS Server TCP/IP Configuration dialog box.

The RAS Server TCP/IP Configuration dialog box enables you to configure the IP address allocation for remote clients using RAS. You can configure remote users to get their IP addresses either from a DHCP server or from a static IP address pool. If you have a DHCP server on your network, it is preferable to use that option. But if you do not use such a server, select the Use static address pool option.

If you select the second option, you need to enter a valid range of IP addresses for remote users. If you want, you also can exclude a range of addresses that remote clients should not have. If your network uses a WINS server or a DNS server for machine name resolution, enter its address in the appropriate field in this dialog box.

All this assumes that the RAS server assigns the IP address. A RAS client can request its own specific address, however. To enable this option, select the check box at the bottom of the dialog box. If a remote client can request its own IP address, it also can request a specific DNS or WINS server for name resolution.

Using TCP/IP Utilities

By this point, you have read about DHCP servers and WINS servers, but you might not fully understand these terms. In this section, you learn about these TCP/IP features as well as HOSTS and LMHOSTS files and *File Transfer Protocol* (FTP) Server services of Windows NT.

Using DHCP

One of the biggest complaints in managing and maintaining a TCP/IP network is the difficulty keeping track of all the addresses and names. DNS servers help by giving clients a central location in which to look for names and addresses, but they still do not solve one problem.

As TCP/IP networking grows more prevalent, it becomes apparent to everyone that IP addresses are limited and sometimes hard to come by. Unfortunately, many of the IP addresses assigned to machines on your network might be used only sporadically, however the addresses are dedicated anyhow.

DHCP was designed to solve this problem while simplifying TCP/IP network administration. A DHCP server makes assigning addresses to machines a dynamic rather than static process. Normally, a new user on the network applies to the manager for a valid IP address. The manager then makes an entry in the HOSTS tables or DNS database. That user might only need that address sporadically or even temporarily; however, while the address is assigned to a machine, no one else can use it.

Another problem arises as users become mobile and take their machines with them. If you take your notebook from one network in your building to another, the old address might not work in the new *local area network* (LAN). To apply to the LAN manager for an address you will use for the afternoon doesn't make sense.

With DHCP, IP addresses are automatically assigned as needed and then released when no longer necessary. The process is quite simple. A DHCP server has a pool of valid addresses it can assign to clients. When a client's system starts, it sends a message on the network requesting an address.

Each DHCP server (several can exist) replies with an IP address and configuration information. The DHCP client collects the offers and selects a valid address, sending the confirmation back to the offering DHCP server. Each DHCP server receives the confirmation from the client. The DHCP server whose address the client selected sends an acknowledgment message back to the client. All the other DHCP servers rescind their earlier offers and put the offered address back into their pool. After the client receives the acknowledgment message from a DHCP server, it can participate in the TCP/IP network.

The DHCP server essentially leases the address to the client. That lease can have time limits so that unused leases are automatically returned to the address pool. If the lease expires, but the machine is still using the lease, the DHCP server can renew the lease so that the client can continue with the same address.

To install a DHCP server on a Windows NT machine, you need to go back to the TCP/IP Installation Options dialog box. If you need to, double-click on the Network icon in the Control Panel. Choose the Add **S**oftware button and select the TCP/IP Protocol and Related Components option in the software list.

Choose the DHCP Server Service from the list and click on OK. Windows NT begins copying the necessary files to your hard disk. That's all there is to the installation.

To configure the **D**HCP Server services, you must use the DHCP Administrator utility. This utility automatically installs when you install the DHCP services. Double-click on the DHCP Administrator icon in the Network Administration group.

The first thing you want to do is to create a DHCP administrative *scope*. A scope is equivalent to a subnet on your network. Highlight the Local Machine entry under the DHCP Servers list. Then select S**c**ope, **C**reate from the menu, and the Create Scope - (Local) dialog box appears (see fig. 14.8).

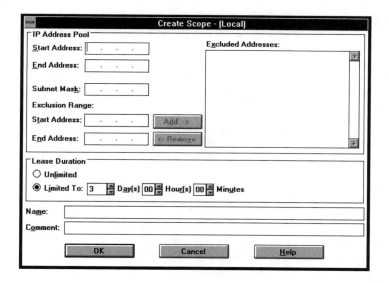

Figure 14.8
The Create Scope - (Local) dialog box.

In this dialog box, you define the pool of addresses DHCP dynamically makes available to DHCP clients. Enter the start and end addresses to define the range. If you want to exclude some addresses that are in that pool, you can either enter an excluded range or an excluded address. To insert an excluded range, enter values in the S**t**art Address and **E**nd Address fields. To exclude a single address, enter the address in the S**t**art Address field. The excluded ranges and addresses should include other DHCP servers, non-DHCP clients, diskless workstations, or RAS clients.

As you insert excluded ranges or addresses, click on the A**d**d button to add them to the list on the right. If you make a mistake or change your mind about an excluded address, highlight it and click on the Remo**v**e button.

The next part of the Create Scope dialog box, entitled Lease Duration, governs the length of time DHCP clients are allowed to keep their addresses. Remember that one of the main reasons for installing a DHCP server is so addresses can be assigned and released dynamically.

If you want your DHCP server to assign addresses as they are requested, but never release them, click on the Unlimited Lease Duration button. More likely, you want to define a duration of a few days or hours. If you specify a duration of three days (the default value), the DHCP server checks to see if the client is still using that address when the lease expires. If the client is still using the address, the lease can be renewed.

If you have a shortage of valid IP addresses on your network and machines go up and down quite frequently, three days might be too long for a lease. You might want to specify a few hours. The only problem with this is the added traffic of negotiating addresses between DHCP servers and DHCP clients so frequently.

If you have plenty of IP addresses for your network, but still want to free unused addresses after a while, it might be more appropriate to assign a longer lease duration (like 30 days).

The only other thing you need to enter in the Create Scope dialog box is a scope name and optional comment. The name can be up to 128 characters and can be any name you want to give the subnet. It can include letters, numbers, and hyphens. Any other information you want to include about the scope can be entered in the Comment field.

When you finish entering all the values in the dialog box, click on OK. Windows NT tells you the scope has been successfully created, but is not yet activated. You then have the option to activate the scope now. Click on Yes if you want to do so.

If you ever need to change the scope properties, you can do so quite easily. Highlight the scope on the left side of the DHCP Manager utility and select Scope, Properties.

Also from the Scope menu, you can select Active Leases to see which computers are using your DHCP server. The Active Leases dialog box appears (see fig. 14.9). If you highlight a client and click on the Properties button, you can see the IP address, when the lease expired, the client name, and the Client Identifier, which is usually the *media access control* (MAC) address of the network adapter on that machine.

Choose the Add Reservations option to bring up the Add Reserved Clients dialog box, in which you can reserve a specific address for a specific client (see fig. 14.10). This option enables you to reserve a specific address for a specific client. You can specify any unused IP address from the address pool. In the Unique Identifier field, enter the MAC address of the network adapter on the client computer.

Next, fill in the computer name for the client to help you remember which client the address is reserved for. You do not have to enter the exact computer name for the client. Any other information you want to enter about the client can be put in the Client Comment field.

The DHCP Manager utility enables you to change the configuration parameters the server assigns to its clients. The options have been given default values based on standard parameters defined by the Internet Networking Group in RFC 1542. You can change these parameters to affect every client the DHCP server services or clients in a certain scope.

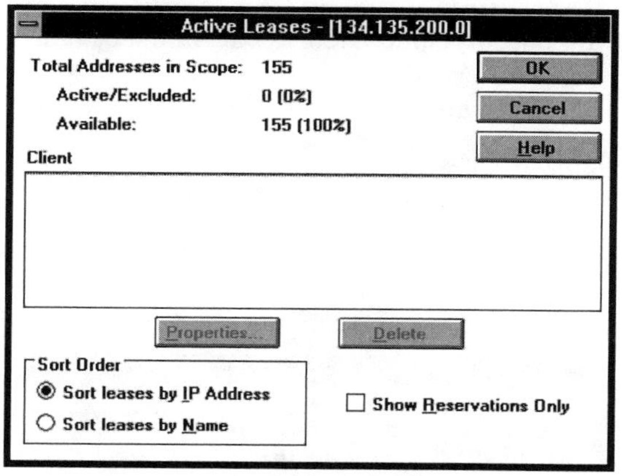

Figure 14.9
The Active Leases dialog box.

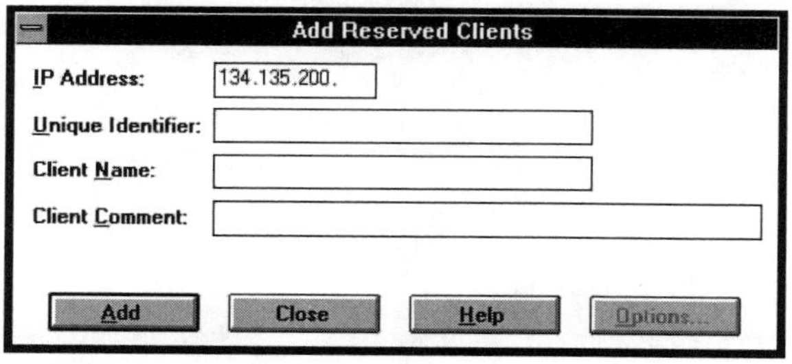

Figure 14.10
The Add Reserved Clients dialog box.

If you want to change the default values, you can do that as well. These TCP/IP networking options are advanced, and unless you know exactly what you are doing, you can degrade performance or make it unusable.

Using WINS

A *Windows Internet Naming Service* (WINS) server maintains a database of computers and their associated IP addresses. It provides dynamic name resolution support, and therefore is suited to work in conjunction with DHCP servers rather than the typical DNS server. In fact, when dynamic address changes are made through DHCP for computers that move between subnets, those changes are automatically made in the WINS database.

Like the DHCP software, WINS has server and client components. WINS name resolution is automatically installed and configured for you when you install DHCP. If you haven't enabled DHCP yet and want to check out WINS, you need to install it manually.

To install WINS, double-click on the Network icon in the Control Panel. After the Network Settings dialog box appears, click on the Add **S**oftware button to bring up the Network Software Installation dialog box. Select TCP/IP Protocol and Related Components from the list and then click on the Continue button.

The Windows NT TCP/IP Installation Options dialog box should be familiar to you by now. Click on the **S**NMP Service and **W**INS Server Service options, then click on Continue. Windows NT copies the necessary files to your hard disk.

When you install WINS, Windows NT adds a utility called WINS Manager in the Network Administration group. Use this tool to manage your WINS server.

On the left side of the WINS Manager application window is a list of WINS servers (see fig. 14.11).

Figure 14.11
The WINS Manager application window.

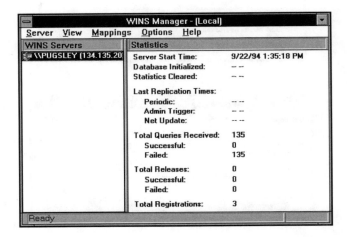

As you highlight a WINS server with a click of your mouse, statistics about that server appear on the right side of the window. Table 14.1 explains what these statistics mean.

Table 14.1
Statistics in WINS Manager

Statistic	Meaning
Total Queries Received	The number of name query request messages received by this WINS server
Total Releases	The number of messages received that indicate a NetBIOS application has shut itself down
Total Registrations	The number of name registration requests accepted by this WINS server

If you want to clear the statistics in this table, select <u>V</u>iew, Clear Statistics from the menu. Because the Statistics table does not dynamically update itself, you might want to refresh the numbers every so often while you have the WINS Manager open. To do so, select <u>V</u>iew, Re<u>f</u>resh Statistics, or press F5.

To add WINS servers to your WINS Manager list, select <u>S</u>erver, <u>A</u>dd WINS Server. Windows NT then prompts you to enter the IP address of the WINS server you want to add. To delete a server from the WINS Manager list, select <u>S</u>erver, <u>D</u>elete WINS Server.

To keep the WINS database on one server doesn't make sense. If that server goes down, someone else needs to handle name resolution on the network. For this reason, consider creating a replication partner for your WINS server. A replication partner helps ensure that the database is always available and also helps balance the job of keeping the database current between more machines.

To set up a replication partner, select <u>R</u>eplication Partners from the <u>S</u>erver menu, and the Replication Partners dialog box appears (see fig. 14.12). In the WINS server list, you should see your own local WINS server. To add other WINS servers to the list, click on the <u>A</u>dd button and enter the address of the WINS server you want to replicate. You can add several WINS servers and set up different relationships with each if you like.

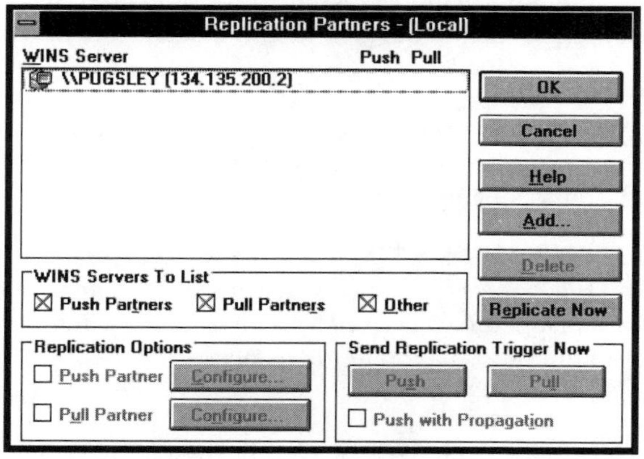

Figure 14.12

Setting up replication partners.

The relationship that can exist between WINS servers is either a Pull or Push relationship. A *Pull Partner* is a WINS server that pulls replicas from its Push Partner. A *Push Partner* is a WINS server that sends replicas to its Pull Partner. Two WINS servers can be both Push and Pull partners with each other.

Because of the extra traffic, you probably do not want the database to replicate every time an entry is made. Click on the Configure buttons under Replication Options to define when and how often the WINS servers share data.

You can configure other aspects of your WINS server by selecting C<u>o</u>nfiguration from the <u>S</u>erver menu. You can adjust the parameters listed in table 14.2.

Table 14.2
WINS Server Configuration

Configuration Option	Meaning
Renewal Interval	Specifies how often a client reregisters its name. The default is 96 hours.
Extinction Interval	Specifies the interval between when an entry is marked *released* and when it is marked *extinct.* The default is 96 hours.
Extinction Timeout	Specifies the interval between when an entry is marked *extinct* and when the entry is finally scavenged from the database. The default is 96 hours.
Verify Interval	Specifies the interval after which the WINS server must verify that old names it does not own are still active. The default is 20 times the extinction interval.

You also can configure Push and Pull parameters of your WINS server. If you want your WINS server to Pull replication information when the server initializes, select the **I**nitial Replication check box. If the servers do not respond immediately, you also can insert a Retry Count.

For Push partners, have your WINS server inform them of the database status when the system is initialized or when an address changes in a mapping record. When you are done configuring the options in this dialog box, click on OK.

To see a copy of the WINS database, select **M**appings, Show **D**atabase from the menu. The Show Database dialog box appears, in which you can see host names and the addresses to which they are mapped (see fig. 14.13). The database can be sorted however you like to make it easier to find information in the database.

Additionally, you can configure this dialog box to show all the mappings in the database or only mappings that relate to a specific WINS server. If you want to view only mappings related to a specific host, you can use the **S**et Filter option to weed unwanted entries from the list.

Your local WINS database should periodically be cleared of unwanted entries. Sometimes entries are registered at another WINS server, but aren't cleared from the local database. The process of clearing unnecessary entries from the database is called *scavenging* and can be started by selecting **In**itiate Scavenging from the **M**appings menu.

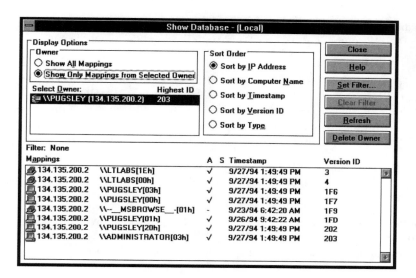

Figure 14.13
Local database mappings.

Using HOSTS and LMHOSTS Files

Although you probably want to use DHCP and WINS for name resolution on your TCP/IP Windows NT network, you also should be aware of a couple of other options Windows NT gives you to resolve host names.

TCP/IP for Windows NT uses two text files to resolve host names with their respective addresses. Both files are found in the \WINNT\SYSTEM32\DRIVERS\ETC directory. One is the HOSTS file; the other is the LMHOSTS file.

If you have any experience with TCP/IP networking on Unix or any other platform, you probably know what a HOSTS file is—a list of IP addresses and host names. If you attempt to use the TCP/IP utilities of Windows NT, you need to specify to which computer you want to attach or log in. You can do this by providing either an IP address, which can be difficult to remember and a pain to type in, or a simple name. If you enabled TCP/IP for Windows NT to use the HOSTS file, it attempts to match the name you type in with an address in the HOSTS file. A HOSTS file is the easiest way to resolve names on an TCP/IP network.

The problem with HOSTS files is that they only work for the computer on which they reside. When your network expands, keeping a current HOSTS file on every computer can be time-consuming and problematic.

LMHOSTS files have many of the same problems as HOSTS files, but they are more flexible. Like HOSTS, LMHOSTS is a simple text file that contains mappings of IP addresses to Windows NT computer names (which are NetBIOS names). LMHOSTS has greater capabilities than the normal HOSTS file because it enables you to include *keywords* that tell the TCP/IP components of your Windows NT server how to handle name resolution.

The keywords that the LMHOSTS file uses are #PRE, #DOM:*domain*, #INCLUDE *filename*, #BEGIN_ALTERNATE, and #END_ALTERNATE. Normally in an LMHOSTS file, anything after the "#" sign is regarded as a remark statement and ignored. If the "#" sign is followed by one of the accepted keywords, however, LMHOSTS treats the statement as a command. Each of these keywords is explained in the following paragraphs.

#PRE following an entry in an LMHOSTS file tells Windows NT to load that entry into the name cache. Loading an entry into cache causes TCP/IP for Windows NT to resolve the name more quickly.

Adding #DOM:*domain* after an entry causes Windows NT to associate that entry with whatever domain you specify. It helps Windows NT resolve the names more efficiently because it does not have to search routing tables to find out to which domain the entry belongs.

An #INCLUDE *filename* entry tells your Windows NT machine where to look for other LMHOSTS files that reside on other servers. When entering the file name, you should use the *Uniform Naming Convention* (UNC)—that is, two \\ (backward slashes), the machine name, another \, and the file name including directory structure. If, for example, you want to include the LMHOSTS file on Windows NT server desdemona, you specify the file name as follows:

```
\\desdemona\winnt\system32\drivers\etc\lmhosts.
```

Before a group of multiple #INCLUDE statements, insert the line **#BEGIN_ALTERNATE**. After you enter the statements, insert the line **#END_ALTERNATE**.

The only other special keyword you can use in an LMHOSTS file is \0x*nn*, which is a hexadecimal notation used to support nonprinting characters in NetBIOS names. You probably do not need to use this keyword unless you have an application that uses special names to function properly in routed topologies.

If you need help creating your HOSTS and LMHOSTS files, see the files themselves in the winnt\system32\drivers\etc directory. The files that Windows NT creates when you install TCP/IP connectivity functions contain sample entries and explanations about their use.

Using FTP Server Services

One of the most commonly used applications in a TCP/IP environment is the *File Transfer Protocol* (FTP). Windows NT includes an FTP client so that you can initiate file transfers between your machine and another on the network. Windows NT also provides an FTP server so that other machines on the network can initiate file transfers.

One problem with using FTP Server services on your computer is that unencrypted passwords can cross the network causing a severe breach in your security. Therefore, you might want to think twice about turning your Windows NT computer into an FTP server.

The security model of the FTP Server service is integrated with Windows NT's own security model. Clients use the Windows NT user accounts and passwords to log into the FTP server through TCP/IP. Access to directories and files on the server is maintained by Windows NT's security structure as well. For this reason, Microsoft recommends that the FTP Server service be installed on an NTFS partition so that the files and directories made available through FTP can be secured.

To install FTP Server services, follow these steps:

1. Choose the Network icon in the Control Panel.

2. In the Network Settings dialog box, click on the Add **S**oftware button. The Add Network Software dialog box appears.

3. Select the TCP/IP Protocol and Related Components entry from the list to bring up the Windows NT TCP/IP Installation options dialog box.

4. Select the **F**TP Server Service option and click on OK.

A security warning similar to the one you read appears. If you still want to install FTP Server services, click on **Y**es. Windows NT copies the appropriate files.

After the FTP Server software is installed on your computer, the FTP Service dialog box appears on your screen (see fig. 14.14). Here you can configure such items as maximum connections and idle timeout periods. You also can specify the home directory FTP clients default to when they first connect.

Another part of this configuration box enables you to configure anonymous connections. If you want, users can log into your FTP Server service with the user name Anonymous. The password is their user account name. By default, the Anonymous FTP account has the same rights and privileges on the Windows NT system as user Guest, but you can change that if you want. You can create a user profile using the User Account Editor of Windows NT to create a default Anonymous user with whatever rights you choose and enter that user name in the appropriate field.

If, for some reason, you have a user name Anonymous on your Windows NT system and that user logs in to your FTP Server, she will receive permissions based on the Guest account, not the native Anonymous account.

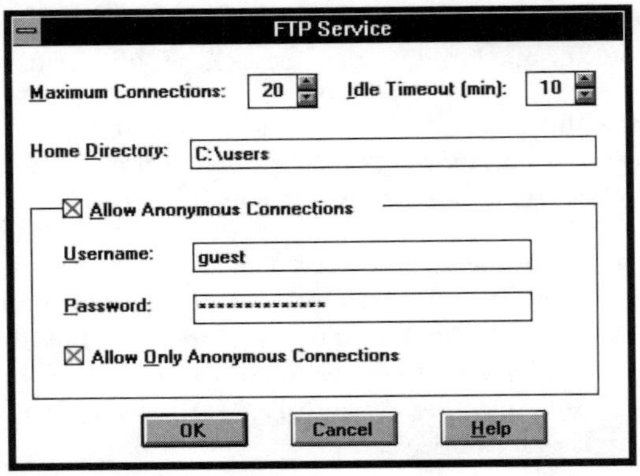

Figure 14.14
The FTP Service
dialog box.

You can set your FTP server to accept Anonymous connections only. If security is an important issue in your network, yet you still want to enable FTP Server services, then perhaps you should select this option. That way, the only passwords that need to travel the wire unencrypted are the user names of the people logging in with the Anonymous account.

To complete the configuration process, click on OK to close the dialog box.

When FTP Server services start, you see a new icon for managing the server in the Control Panel. Double-click on that icon, and the FTP User Sessions dialog box appears. In this box is a list of users connected to your machine through FTP. You can see the user names, IP addresses they are connecting from, and how long they have been connected. If they logged on using the Anonymous account, you can see the passwords they used. You can disconnect all of them if you need to by clicking on the Disconnect **A**ll button at the bottom of the dialog box.

While the box is open, click on the **S**ecurity button to see the level of security that FTP initiates on its own—independent of the Windows NT security architecture. The FTP Server Security dialog box appears (see fig. 14.15).

Figure 14.15
Setting up FTP
server security.

The FTP Server Security dialog box enables you to configure each partition on your system for Read and Write access. One way to add an extra level of security to your system for FTP clients is to place all sensitive files on a separate partition and grant neither Read nor Write access to that partition. Or if you want to allow users to copy files from your server, but not copy files to your server, select the Allow **R**ead check box and leave the Allow **W**rite check box blank. After you configure the security options for each partition, click on OK.

 If you have any questions about the FTP commands that Windows NT uses, select the Windows NT Help icon in the Program Manager Main group. In the Windows NT help window, click on the Command Reference Help button, then click the FTP commands entry in the Commands window. Click on each FTP command name to see a description of the command as well as valid parameters and syntax.

Printing with TCP/IP

With the TCP/IP utilities and resources installed on your Windows NT computer, you now have the ability to print to TCP/IP printers. TCP/IP printers can be connected directly into the network or attached to Unix computers. Furthermore, any Microsoft networking computer can use your machine as a gateway to access the TCP/IP printers—even if they do not have TCP/IP installed.

Follow these steps to configure your Windows NT computer for TCP/IP printing:

1. Double-click on the Network icon in the Control Panel.

2. Select the **A**dd Software button in the Network Settings dialog box.

3. When the Network Software Installation dialog box appears, select the TCP/IP and Related Components entry from the list and click on the Continue button.

4. In the TCP/IP Installation Options dialog box, select the TCP/IP Networking **P**rinting Support option and click on OK. Windows NT then copies the needed files to your hard disk.

With TCP/IP Printing Support installed, you can now use the Print Manager to connect to a TCP/IP printer the same way you connect to any other printer on the network. The only information you need is the DNS name or IP address of the printer, the printer name as it is identified on the host, and the TCP port ID on the host.

To create a printer to use on your Windows NT network, follow these steps:

1. Select Crea**t**e Printer from the **P**rinter menu in Print Manager.

2. Enter the appropriate information for Printer **N**ame, **D**river, and D**e**scription as you would with any printer.

3. Under the Print **T**o field, select Add Other Port from the list. The Print Destinations dialog box appears with a couple of options listed.

4. Select the LPR Monitor from the list, then click on OK. The Add LPR Compatible Printer dialog box appears.

5. Insert the information mentioned earlier to fill in the fields, then click on OK to return to the Create Printer dialog box.

6. If you want to share this printer with other users on the network—even if they don't have TCP/IP installed on their systems—click the check box to **S**hare this printer on the network. You can fill in the Sh**a**re **N**ame and **L**ocation fields to give others an indication of which printer they'll see in a Browse window and where the printer is located.

7. When you are finished, click on OK to close the dialog box.

Managing TCP/IP Computers with Windows NT

With TCP/IP installed on your Windows NT machine, you now have some additional tools available to help you manage the system. These two tools are the SNMP Agent and Performance Monitor. Although Performance Monitor itself is not new with the installation of TCP/IP software, several new monitoring options in that application are now available to you.

Using SNMP Management

Use the following steps to install the SNMP Service option:

1. Double-click on the Networks icon in the Control Panel.

2. In the Network Settings dialog box, click on the Add **S**oftware button. In the Network Software Installation dialog box, choose TCP/IP Protocol and Related Components from the Add Software list.

3. When the TCP/IP Installation Options dialog box appears, select the **S**NMP Service option and click on OK. Windows NT copies the necessary files to your hard disk.

When you return to the Network Settings dialog box, select SNMP Service from the Installed Net**w**ork Software list box. Click on the **C**onfigure button to bring up the SNMP Service Configuration dialog box (see fig. 14.16).

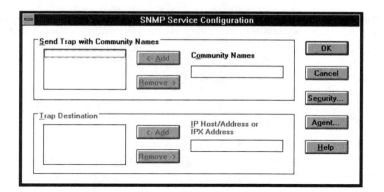

Figure 14.16
The SNMP Service Configuration dialog box.

From this dialog box, you can configure the communities to which you want your computer to send traps, and the hosts for each community to which you send traps. Type the community name or host ID in the field on the right of the box, then click on the **A**dd button.

If you are concerned about the security of your SNMP information, click on the Se**c**urity button to open the SNMP Security Configuration dialog box (see fig. 14.17). You can configure three things about SNMP security from this box.

Figure 14.17
The SNMP Security Configuration dialog box.

The first item—Send A**u**thentication Trap—sends a trap for failed authentications. If you want this option, select the Send A**u**thentication Trap check box.

The next item—Accepted Community **N**ames—enables you to specify from which community names you accept requests. If the host is not on the list, the SNMP service does not accept the request. To add community names to the list, insert the name into the field on the right, then click on the **A**dd button.

The final SNMP security option enables you to specify from which hosts you accept SNMP packets. If you want to accept SNMP packets from any host, click on the Accept SNMP Packets from Any Host radio button. If you want to create a list of valid hosts, select Only Accept SNMP Packets from These Hosts. To add to the list, insert the host name or address in the field to the right, then click on Add.

When you finish configuring SNMP security, click on OK to return to the SNMP Service Configuration dialog box.

To configure the SNMP Agent, click on the Agent button. The SNMP Agent dialog box appears, giving you the option to enter some specific data about your machine (see fig. 14.18). You can insert a contact name and location in the appropriate fields.

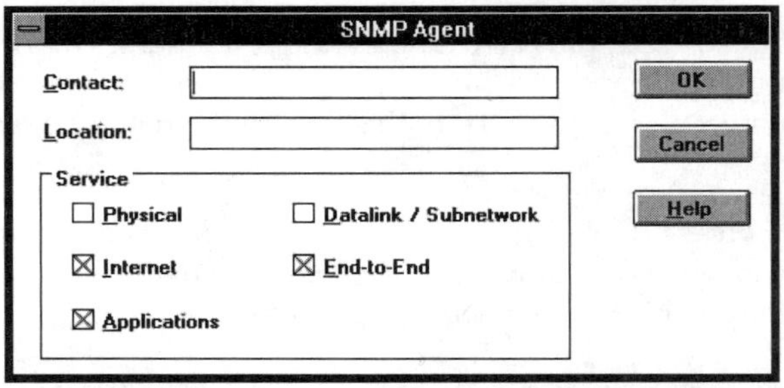

Figure 14.18
The SNMP Agent
dialog box.

In the Service box, you can configure which services to report through SNMP. The services you select depend on the function of your Windows NT machine. Table 14.3 helps you to configure which services to report through SNMP.

Table 14.3
SNMP Agent Services

Option	Meaning
Physical	Select this option if your Windows NT computer manages any physical TCP/IP device, such as a repeater.
Datalink / Subnetwork	Select this option if your Windows NT computer manages a TCP/IP subnetwork or datalink, such as a bridge.
Internet	Select this option if your Windows NT computer acts as an IP gateway.

Option	Meaning
End-to-End	Select this option if your Windows NT computer acts as an IP host. This option should be selected for all Windows NT installations.
Applications	Select this option if your Windows NT computer includes any applications that use TCP/IP, such as e-mail. This option should be selected for all Windows NT installations.

When the agent is configured as you want, click on OK to return to the SNMP Service Configuration dialog box. Then click on OK again to close this box.

Using Performance Monitor

With TCP/IP components installed on your Windows NT computer, you now have a whole new batch of counters to watch from Performance Monitor.

To use the TCP/IP performance counters, you should install the TCP/IP protocols and the SNMP Service.

Additional objects in Performance Monitor are IP performance counters, ICMP performance counters, TCP performance counters, UDP performance counters, FTP Server traffic, DHCP Server performance, and WINS Server performance.

To learn about each of these objects and counters, click on the **E**xplain button in the Add to Chart dialog box from within Performance Monitor. The information you gather here helps you realize when your server is becoming overloaded with process requests. If your machine is very busy as an FTP server, for example, you can move DHCP and WINS server support to another Windows NT machine on the network.

Summary

Windows NT includes most of the TCP/IP tools you need. The things that are missing, like NFS and X Windows support, can be provided by third-party products. Windows NT makes TCP/IP manageable with tools it includes, such as the SNMP agent and the Performance Monitor objects. The best features for managers, however, are the DHCP server for address distribution and the WINS server for name resolution. These two tools eliminate the biggest headache of TCP/IP networks—keeping track of the addresses.

Chapter Snapshot

There is a complete, robust, and easy-to-use TCP/IP package for OS/2. Key TCP/IP functions, including all that you need to access the Internet, are built into the latest version of OS/2. This chapter describes how these packages are used and the features they contain, with detailed information on how to install, configure, and use TCP/IP on OS/2. The following subjects are covered in this chapter:

CHAPTER

15

Connecting to OS/2

"I believe OS/2 is destined to be the most important operating system of all time."

—Bill Gates

BM first released TCP/IP for OS/2 in March of 1990, but the product did not become well known for some time. OS/2 itself was selling slowly, and most of the marketing emphasis within IBM was on the IBM proprietary communications protocols NETBIOS and *Systems Network Architecture* (SNA). IBM also invested heavily in *Open Systems Interconnection* (OSI). At the same time, IBM was a major contributor to the development of the Internet. As TCP/IP has grown in popularity, IBM has put more development and marketing emphasis on its TCP/IP products, and now complete IBM TCP/IP packages exist for each of the operating systems in which IBM has a stake: the mainframe operating systems MVS and VM; the AS/400 minicomputer; AIX, the IBM version of Unix; DOS/Windows; and OS/2.

In the years since its first release, TCP/IP for OS/2 has continued to improve in function, performance, and usability, and the current version is one of the most complete, powerful, and usable TCP/IP packages for the PC.

This chapter describes IBM TCP/IP for OS/2. Other OS/2 TCP/IP packages exist: FTP Inc., Novell, and Wollangong all market good ones. The author believes that the IBM package is the best of the lot—but, as lead developer on the current version of the product, he can hardly be considered an unbiased source. The IBM package has evolved farther than the others because of IBM's big stake in the OS/2 operating system.

Understanding IBM TCP/IP Version 2 for OS/2

The IBM TCP/IP version 2.0 for OS/2 base kit includes the following:

✔ **FTP file transfer, both client and server.** FTP-PM is a graphical user interface for the FTP client. Client and server programs also exist for the older TFTP file transfer protocol.

✔ **Telnet terminal emulation.** The telnet clients emulate VT100, VT220, ANSI, HFT, 3270, and 5250 terminals. The telnet server emulates ANSI or VT100 terminals.

✔ **Remote execution of programs using REXEC or RSH.** REXEC and RSH servers are also provided.

✔ **E-mail using Simple Mail Transfer Protocol (SMTP).** The *Sendmail* program has both client and server functions. *LaMail* is a graphical user interface for editing and sending mail, maintaining address lists, and so on.

✔ **LPR client and LPD server for network printing support.** The LPR client has been integrated with the OS/2 workplace shell so that OS/2 applications can print to network printers transparently.

✔ **SNMP Network Management.** The SNMPD agent is run on user workstations to be managed remotely, and it is an extensible agent—programs can be added to manage additional workstation functions. The *Simple Network Management Protocol* (SNMP) manager program enables a remote network administrator to manage the user workstations.

✔ **TALK and TALKD.** These are for sending and receiving electronic messages.

✔ **ROUTED.** ROUTED enables an OS/2 machine to function as an IP router running the Routing Information Protocol.

✔ **BOOTP client and BOOTPD server.** Configuring many dispersed PCs with IP addresses, net masks, domain names, and the like can be time-consuming. The BOOTP protocol enables TCP/IP to be automatically configured on the machine, using information obtained from the BOOTPD server.

You can use this package to communicate with other computers connected through Ethernet, Token Ring, or FDDI *local area networks* (LANs). A wide variety of LAN cards can be used. The LAN card must have an OS/2 NDIS driver—and most now do. You can also use *Serial Line Internet Protocol* (SLIP) to connect to the Internet or to a remote LAN using a modem and phone line. Support for TCP/IP routing exists over a *wide area network* (WAN), using X.25 or Frame Relay. X.25 support requires the IBM WAC card and two additional software packages—the Extended Networking Kit and IBM X.25 Xpander/2. Frame Relay support requires the IBM WAC card and IBM RouteXpander/2.

In addition to the base, you also can buy some add-on packages for additional functions. These include the following:

✔ **The Network File System (NFS) Kit.** Both NFS server and client programs are included. The NFS server enables a PC to share hard disk drives or directories with other computers on the network. The NFS client enables a PC to access NFS drives and directories made available by NFS servers.

✔ **Ultimedia Mail/2.** This enhanced mail package enables users to exchange multimedia mail. In addition to ordinary text, users can mail with embedded voice messages, graphical images, video clips, binary files (such as programs or spreadsheet files), and "rich" text (a text file format including font and layout information that can be produced with many word processors).

✔ **The Domain Name Server (DNS) Kit.** TCP/IP resolves network names like www.ibm.com into Internet addresses by communicating with a name server. This kit enables an OS/2 machine to be configured as a full function name server.

✔ **The DOS/Windows Access Kit.** This kit enables Windows applications to run in an OS/2 virtual DOS machine on top of TCP/IP version 2 for OS/2. Any Windows applications that comply with the Windows Sockets version 1.0 or 1.1 interface specification will run. DOS TCP/IP applications also can be run, if they are compatible with IBM TCP/IP for DOS.

✔ **The TCP/IP NETBIOS Kit.** A weakness of NETBIOS is that it is intended to run over a single LAN. WANs connected by routers cannot pass NETBIOS packets. One way around this is to encapsulate NETBIOS packets in TCP/IP packets, which is what this package does. With this package, NETBIOS applications like the IBM LAN Server and Requester can be used by PCs connected by routers. All the function of the NETBIOS package is also provided in IBM LAN Services 4.0 for OS/2, which for most uses is a better choice than the TCP/IP NETBIOS Kit.

✔ **The X Windows System Server Kit.** X is the industry standard graphical user interface for Unix systems, and it is gaining popularity on other operating systems as well. With this kit, an OS/2 machine can function as an X Windows terminal.

✔ **The Programmer's Toolkit.** This kit enables users to create client/server TCP/IP applications for OS/2 or to port such applications from Unix. Interfaces include sockets, *remote procedure call* (RPC), FTP, and the SNMP distributed programming interface.

✔ **The X Windows System Client Kit.** This kit enables users to create X Windows applications to be run on OS/2 or to port such applications from Unix. The graphical user interface for an X Client application is displayed on an X terminal or an X Windows System server, which can be on the same PC or elsewhere on the network.

✔ **The OSF/Motif Kit.** Most X applications are not developed from scratch using only the basic X Client functions. Instead, higher level programming interfaces are used, in which the basic graphical controls and windows are already implemented. These higher interfaces are called *widgets*, and the most widely used widget set is OSF/Motif. The X Windows System Client Kit is required for the OSF/Motif Kit. Of course, all the functions of the TCP/IP base kit and the add-on kits listed earlier are implemented in conformity with Internet standards; and as the TCP/IP on Unix, Windows, MVS, VMS, and other platforms adhere to the same standards, OS/2 TCP/IP enables communication and interoperability with all these disparate machines.

TCP/IP on OS/2 Version 3

Included with OS/2 version 3 is the IBM Internet Connection for OS/2. This package provides an easy-to-use and feature-rich way to connect to the Internet using a modem. The package includes e-mail, a news reader for reading and posting to Internet news groups, gopher, FTP file transfer, telnet and 3270 telnet terminal emulation, and dialing and registration utilities. Support for Windows TCP/IP programs is also included: nearly all Windows TCP/IP programs will run unchanged under OS/2 with the winsock library and TCP/IP virtual device driver that are provided. The initial shipment of OS/2 version 3 does not include Web Explorer, but this program is available for use with the Internet Connection Kit by anonymous FTP from software.watson.ibm.com on the Internet. Web Explorer is a World Wide Web client, similar in function to NCSA's MOSAIC.

The Internet Connection Kit can be used to connect to IBM Internet Connection Services or to any of the Internet access providers that support SLIP connections. LAN support is not included with the Internet Connection Kit, nor are any TCP/IP server functions; if you need LAN support, you must buy the OS/2 TCP/IP base package as well. IBM plans a LAN-enabled version of OS/2 version 3 that will include complete TCP/IP LAN support.

Other Software Packages for Client Server Computing

IBM OS/2 TCP/IP provides a comprehensive set of application programming interfaces for creating networked client/server applications, and a number of companies now sell packages that either require or can take advantage of these programming interfaces. These applications include the following:

- ✔ Lotus Notes Release 3.1

- ✔ Oracle SQLNet for OS/2

- ✔ PeerLogic's PIPES Platform

- ✔ SAS/CONNECT Software for OS/2

- ✔ Sybase Net-Library for IBM TCP/IP

IBM also sells several packages to run on top of TCP/IP, including DCE for OS/2, Person to Person/2, Configuration Management Version Control Program, Distributed Data Connection Services/2, and others. Telnet terminal emulation is provided with IBM OS/2 TCP/IP, but more high-function packages can be purchased as add-ons, including Softronics Softerm for OS/2, Software Corporation of America's TalkThru for OS/2, and Wall Data's RUMBA Office.

All these additional software packages and add-on kits extend the power of TCP/IP for OS/2, but plenty of function exists in the TCP/IP base for most users. In general, TCP/IP users can be placed into in one of the following two groups:

- ✔ Those who use TCP/IP primarily for Internet access

- ✔ Those who use it at work or on university campuses, accessing e-mail, data files, and printers on local and wide area networks

Plenty of overlap exists between these two groups, but the IBM Internet Connection package that ships with OS/2 version 3 is designed primarily for the first group of users; and the TCP/IP for OS/2 base kit is designed for the second group. The following sections look at each of these packages.

Using OS/2 TCP/IP to Connect to the Internet

The IBM Internet Connection for OS/2 comes bundled with OS/2 version 3. Given the fact that OS/2 version 3 itself sells for less than the price of some popular Internet access kits, you might expect that the OS/2 version 3 package is just a sampler and that you would have to make an additional purchase to get full function Internet access. The surprising fact is that the Internet Connection is one of the best and most complete products for Internet access.

Although Internet Connection has serious business uses, the marketing focus was on the burgeoning consumer market for Internet access. A goal of the project was to make each function usable by computer novices. Each of the programs has an easy-to-use graphical user interface and ample online help.

Hardware Requirements

To run OS/2 version 3, you need a PC with at least a 386 processor and 4 MB of RAM. The Internet Connection Kit runs well in this environment. The Internet Connection program files occupy 10.5 MB of disk space. A modem supporting 9600 bps or better is recommended; slower modems may be adequate to access CompuServe and America Online, but to take advantage of true TCP/IP access, you really need the additional bandwidth. The Internet is full of multimedia files: pictures, sound bites, video clips, and so on. If your PC has multimedia support, you can view these files; but a multimedia PC is not required to use the Internet Connection Kit.

Installing the Internet Connection

To install the Internet Connection for OS/2, insert the OS/2 version 3 bonus pack installation disk in drive A of your PC and enter the following command:

a:install

The window that appears contains a list of the bonus pack kits. Select the Internet Connection, and you see the window shown in figure 15.1.

Figure 15.1
Installing the
Internet
Connection for
OS/2.

This is a one-button installation, with nothing tricky about it. The only choice you need to make is to pick the disk drive and directory to which you want the files installed. In most cases, you can accept the default installation directory.

While the installation process copies files to your hard disk, a progress window is displayed. Click on the Read Important Information button on the progress dialog box, to read the online introduction to the package. In addition to copying files and creating directories, the installation updates CONFIG.SYS with the following statements:

```
libpath= ... ;C:\TCPIP\DLL;C:\TCPIP\UMAIL;
set path= ... ;C:\TCPIP\BIN;C:\TCPIP\UMAIL;
set help= ... ;C:\TCPIP\HELP;C:\TCPIP\UMAIL;
 ...
SET ETC=c:\tcpip\etc
SET TMP=c:\tcpip\tmp
DEVICE=c:\tcpip\bin\inet.sys
DEVICE=c:\tcpip\bin\ifndisnl.sys
DEVICE=c:\tcpip\bin\vdostcp.vdd
DEVICE=c:\tcpip\bin\vdostcp.sys
RUN=c:\tcpip\bin\cntrl.exe
RUN=c:\tcpip\bin\vdosctl.exe
```

(The old CONFIG.SYS also is saved as CONFIG.001, or if this file already exists, CONFIG.002, CONFIG.003, and so on. After you have TCP/IP running, you will probably want to delete these backups of CONFIG.SYS.) The entries for VDOSTCP.VDD, VDOSTCP.SYS, and VDOSCTL.EXE are needed only if you want to run DOS or Windows TCP/IP programs under OS/2. If not, you can delete these lines. AUTOEXEC.BAT is also updated, with the following lines:

```
PATH=C:\OS2;C:\OS2\MDOS;C:\;C:\WINDOWS;d:\tcpip\dos\bin;
@SET ETC=c:\tcpip\dos\etc
```

Again, these lines are only needed if you plan to run DOS or Windows TCP/IP programs under OS/2.

It is important to shutdown and reboot the machine after installation so that the CONFIG.SYS changes take effect and so that the Internet Connection folder is added to your OS/2 desktop and is completely populated with icons.

For those who are unfamiliar with OS/2, to open an icon or folder, move the mouse pointer to it and double-click on the left mouse button. To select a list box or menu item, move the mouse pointer to it and click once with the left mouse button. To drag an icon or list box item, move the mouse pointer to it and press and hold down the right mouse button; then move the mouse pointer (which now looks like the item you are dragging) to the destination and release the mouse button. It is sometimes necessary to select an item before dragging it. A window is activated by selecting the title bar at the top of the window. To the right of the title bar you usually find two buttons—one to minimize the

continues

II

Enumeration

window, and the other to restore or to maximize it. To the left of the title bar is the system icon; double-click on this icon to close the window. Below the title bar of some windows, you may see a menu bar or icon bar from which various actions can be selected. Most windows and icons also have a context menu, which is displayed by moving the mouse pointer to the window or icon and clicking the right mouse button. The context menu for the desktop contains a menu item to shut down OS/2. At any time, you can press Ctrl+Esc to see the window list from which you can select an entry to activate a particular window. Press the F1 key if you need help.

After you reboot, open the Internet Connection folder, which is inside the IBM Information Superhighway folder. You see the icons shown in figure 15.2.

Figure 15.2
The Internet Connection folder.

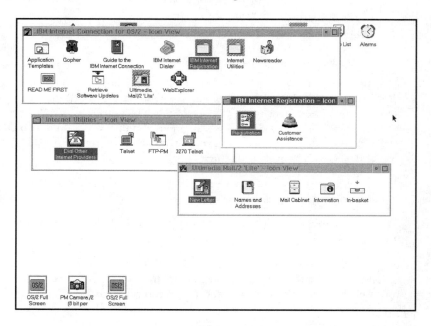

When you install the Internet Connection package, it's a good idea to install another bonus pack kit, the Multimedia Viewer, as well. This package contains multimedia viewers for audio, video, and image files. Many of these types of files are available on the Internet, as you will find in the course of a typical Gopher or Web Explorer session; but the Gopher and Web Explorer programs are dependent upon the viewers in the Multimedia viewer to be capable of displaying images, video clips, and sound bites.

Configuring

Before a SLIP connection to the Internet can be established, a number of steps must occur. The following list may intimidate some users, but fortunately all these steps occur automatically, without user intervention:

1. The com port must be configured.

2. The modem must be initialized with the proper setup strings.

3. The phone number of the Internet provider must be dialed.

4. An Internet access login ID and password must be passed to the provider end of the line for validation.

5. A TCP/IP interface must be configured with a local IP address, a destination IP address, and a net mask.

6. The SLIP protocol must be configured to use or not to use VJ header compression, which is a standard SLIP extension to improve performance. This configuration must match the access provider's.

7. A default route for IP packets must be added to the routing table, so that packets are routed to the other end of the SLIP connection.

8. The RESOLV file in the C:\TCPIP\ETC subdirectory must be updated with the Internet provider's TCP/IP domain name and the IP address of the Internet provider's name server.

All these steps are performed automatically by the dialer programs included in the Internet Connection Kit.

When you use the Internet Connection, you need to choose an Internet access provider. You can choose from quite a few providers, and the list is growing. Typically, you call or fax one of the companies that provides Internet access. They ask you for your name, address, phone number, and credit card; and they fax or mail you the information needed to complete steps 1 through 8 of the preceding list, such as your login ID, password, IP address, and so on.

One Internet access provider is IBM Internet Connection Services, which is run by IBM's Advantis subsidiary. The Internet Connection package includes programs provided by Advantis so that if you choose IBM Internet Connection Services as your provider, the registration procedure described earlier is completely automated. If you choose a different provider, the registration process is not quite as simple, but the end result is the same.

II

Enumeration

Registering with IBM Internet Connection Services

To register with IBM Internet Connection Services, follow these steps (see fig. 15.3):

1. Within the Internet Connection folder is the IBM Internet Customer Services folder. Open this folder, and then open the Registration icon.

2. Click on Open a Personal Account. You are about to contract with Advantis for network services, and a terms and conditions document is presented describing the deal. To continue with registration, click on OK.

3. Now you must enter your name, address, phone number, and credit card number.

4. Click on OK to continue, and a dialog box appears asking which modem you have, which com port you are using, and which 800 number to dial for registration.

   Take some care to choose the correct modem and com port; registration may fail if these are not specified correctly. If your modem is not listed, you can usually choose Default. If that doesn't work, the help for this field explains how you can add your modem type to the list, using the documentation that came with the modem.

5. Click on OK, and you see a dialog panel requesting your preferences for login ID.

6. Fill in this dialog box, and click on OK once more. Make sure your modem is connected to an available phone line, then click on Send Registration to IBM.

   The modem dials the phone and exchanges some information with a registration server. Eventually you see a message stating that your registration is complete and returning your new account, login ID, and password. Write these down—you will need them.

Now you are ready to dial into the Internet. Follow these steps:

1. In the Internet Connection folder is the IBM Internet Dialer. Click on this icon.

2. Before you dial, click on Settings. The Settings pages contain the modem and com port information you have already entered. It's a good idea to turn to the modem page to increase the com port speed, though. The best value to set is usually 57600. Although your modem probably can't send data at this rate, this value enables the best use of the compression capabilities of the modem.

3. Now close the Settings Notebook and click on Dial (see fig. 15.4).

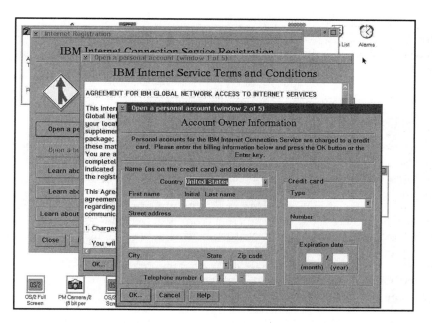

Figure 15.3
Registering with
IBM Internet
Connection
Services.

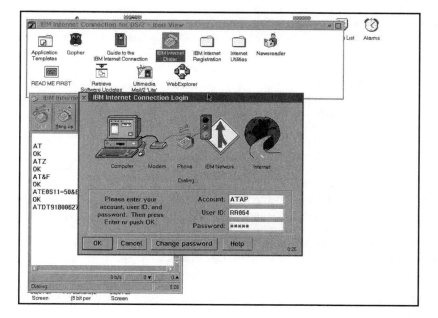

Figure 15.4
Dialing IBM
Internet
Connection
Services.

II

Enumeration

You are prompted for your account, login ID, and password. Even before you enter the password, the dial program begins connecting to the provider, but you don't need to rush; it will wait for you to finish. When the connection is completely established, you can use any of the Internet connection applications. If you try to open an Internet application without dialing first, a message box appears, offering to start the dialer for you.

Registering with Another Internet Provider

In choosing an Internet provider, make sure that you pick a company that provides SLIP access for a real TCP/IP connection to the Internet. Services such as America Online, CompuServe, and Prodigy do not provide this kind of access. Instead, they use private protocols for serial communication. These types of services have advantages, especially if you have a slow modem, but what they provide is not TCP/IP, and your access to Internet resources will be limited. SLIP access to the Internet is provided by companies such as CRL, Colorado Supernet, Internet Express, NetCom, VNET, and many others. Some companies may prefer or require that you use the *Point-to-Point Protocol* (PPP) instead of SLIP. PPP support is available for IBM TCP/IP but was not finished in time to ship with the first release of OS/2 version 3. PPP will be available through anonymous FTP from software.watson.ibm.com in December of 1994.

When you obtain an account from an Internet access provider, you are given information on how to set up the SLIP connection, such as the local and destination IP addresses, the name server domain name and IP address, the subnet mask, and so on. You do not need to know how this information is used. Within the Internet Connection folder is a Dial Other Internet Providers icon. Open this icon, and click on Add Provider. A sequence of four dialog boxes appears that prompts you to enter information about your Internet account: the phone number to dial, the login ID, password, IP address, and so on. If you are confused by a field, click on it and press F1 to get help. Most of the information is optional, such as the default server and mail information, but it is best to enter this information if you know it so that News Reader/2, Gopher, Web Explorer, and other Internet Connection applications are configured to connect to the right Internet hosts.

When you dial an Internet provider, before a TCP/IP connection is made some information is exchanged between your PC and the destination host, typically including your login ID and password. Internet providers vary in how they do this, and some provide the IP address you are to use dynamically when you dial. So, it does not always suffice to fill in the Add Provider panels. A login script may be needed. The online help for Add Provider describes how this can be done, and several sample login scripts are provided with the Internet Connection package. The Dial Other Internet Providers program connects to most Internet access providers without your having to create a login script.

The Add Provider panels of the Dial Other Internet Providers utility also ask for your modem type, com port, and com port speed. If your modem is not among those listed, try Hayes Compatible, or specify your own modem setup strings according to the information provided with your modem documentation. In most cases, the best value for com port speed is 57600 because, although the modem may not be able to pass data at that rate, the compression capabilities of the modem will be fully used.

After completing the Add Provider panels, click on OK, and an entry for the provider appears in the list box of the Dial Other Internet Providers. Now you are ready to dial the Internet. Click on the provider entry you just created, and then click on Dial. You will be connected to the Internet.

No other configuration is required to begin using the Internet Connection. After you register with an Internet provider and dial the connection, you can begin using the applications.

Although the target audience of the Internet Connection Kit is the growing number of home users who want access to the "Information Superhighway," it is also a valuable tool for professional people who need access to office or campus computer networks when they are at home or traveling. A LAN-attached PC running OS/2 and TCP/IP can be set up with a modem configured to answer incoming calls and a SLIP interface to that modem. This PC can be configured to route IP packets from the SLIP interface to the LAN and vice versa. (Some details on how this is done are provided later in this chapter.) You then can use the Dial Other Internet Providers program in a way that its name might not suggest: to dial a connection with the LAN-attached PC. Then you can use the Internet Connection applications for full TCP/IP remote access to the LAN: e-mail, terminal access, file transfer, and so on. All the applications of the Internet Connection Kit can be used when dialed into the LAN. In this case, the IP addresses, the subnet mask value, and the other configuration parameters of the Dial Other Internet Providers program are assigned by the LAN network administrator.

Using the Applications

The dialer and registration utilities of the Internet Connection Kit are just a means to an end—a way to establish a connection. The real value is using that connection to access the vast store of information available on the Internet. If you are new to the Internet, begin with Gopher. This application is extremely easy to use, and—at the same time—is a powerful and fast way to obtain information.

Gopher

Gopher is a program to access text files, telnet servers, graphics images, news groups, and other types of information that the plethora of Internet hosts makes available (see fig. 15.5). One of the most troublesome characteristics of the Internet is that it is hard to find your way through the maze of information. Gopher makes this task much easier.

Figure 15.5
Using Gopher.

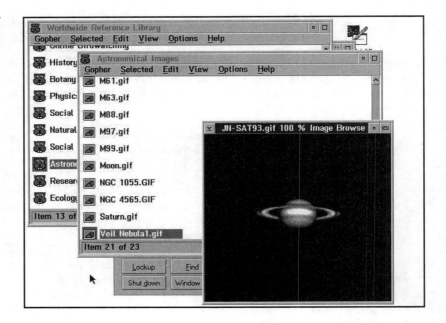

Open the Gopher icon in the Internet Connection folder. (If you are not already dialed into the Internet, a message box appears with an option to start the dialer.) Gopher connects to a default Gopher server. If the default server is not one you would choose or if the connection fails for some reason, you can change to a different server by selecting the Specify Gopher Item option from the **G**opher menu on the menu bar. Give the name of the Gopher server to which you want to connect, and click on Open. If you don't know the names of any Gopher servers, select the Well Known Gopher Servers menu item from the **G**opher menu on the menu bar, and pick from the list. After you are connected, a menu appears with various icons. The Gopher icons represent links to other Gopher menus, but most menus also contain icons representing text files, telnet sessions, graphics images, search utilities, and so on.

The items on a Gopher menu may actually reside on many different Gopher servers widely dispersed throughout the network. Hundreds of Gopher servers are on the Internet, and it is not at all obvious where the items in a given menu actually reside—but you do not need to know. If you are ever curious, select **V**iew, Details view from the menu bar; information about each menu item, including the name of the host on which it resides, is displayed. Click on any of the icons to view the menu, text file, or image it represents.

Gopher is easy to use, but the following three problems are commonly experienced:

✔ After making your way through dozens of menus, you may reach one that is really interesting and have no idea how you got there. Select Bookmark this menu from the **G**opher menu to mark your place. The Open Bookmark window option of the **G**opher pull-down menu displays all the bookmarks you have saved. If you click on a bookmark, the corresponding menu opens. You can also view a history of all the Gopher windows you have opened since the start of your session. Select **G**opher, Open history window from the menu bar to view the history window.

✔ It is not uncommon to click on a **G**opher menu item only to find that the requested information is never returned from the server; the window that appears stays blank. This happens because Gopher servers change frequently over time and are sometimes unavailable. Press Esc to close the blank window and try another item.

✔ Sometimes when you try to open certain items, a message box appears with the message `No viewer is registered for objects of this type. Get the file anyway?`. You have encountered an item that Gopher does not know how to view. Press Esc to close the message box, and select **V**iew, Details view, to determine the object type. Many viewers for various object types are available for download from the Internet as freeware or shareware. After you have such a viewer, you can configure Gopher to use it. Select **O**ptions, Configure from the Gopher menu bar. A list of object types is presented, and for many of these associated viewer programs exist. You can modify any of the entries, or create new ones, to enable Gopher to invoke the appropriate viewer program. The Multimedia Viewer included in the OS/2 bonus pack provides support for most of the image and multimedia files that can be viewed with Gopher.

When Gopher obtains an item to be viewed by a viewer program, the file is not deleted after the viewer is closed. Your hard disk can fill up with many Gopher files, and some of the image and multimedia files are quite large. The **O**ptions, Configure dialog box enables you to specify a drive and directory for each of the object types, and it is wise to delete old files from these directories periodically.

Mail

Mail is a popular topic with TCP/IP, often linked in the minds of most who discuss it. The following packages are the most common implementations.

Ultimedia Mail/2 Lite

The e-mail package included with the Internet Connection for OS/2 is called Ultimedia Mail/2 Lite (nicknamed Ultimail). The "lite" is intended to distinguish it from the Ultimedia Mail/2 product, but it may be an inappropriate word for a mail package as complete in function as Ultimedia Mail/2 Lite—and in any case, this "lite" program occupies 4.5 MB of disk space.

Internet Mail Protocols

The Internet standard way to send mail is *Simple Mail Transfer Protocol* (SMTP). SMTP is the protocol used by Ultimail to send mail. SMTP can be configured to send mail directly to the destination Internet host, but it is usually not wise to set it up this way. If the destination host is not up the mail is not sent, the e-mail notes queue up, and periodically a retransmission is attempted. The job of queuing and retransmitting the mail is best done by a mail gateway host that is connected to the Internet all the time. Ultimail sends mail via such a gateway if one has been configured.

Mail can be received using SMTP too, but this is not the best approach for the reason mentioned previously: If the destination host is not up or not connected, the mail gateway must queue the mail and attempt periodic retransmission, and the retransmission rarely succeeds if the destination host is actually connected to the Internet only a small percentage of the time. Also, some Internet providers, IBM Internet Connection Services for one, assign IP addresses dynamically when the user dials in—so PCs connected in this way have no fixed address that SMTP can use.

To receive mail, Ultimail uses the *Post Office Protocol*, or POP. Mail is sent through SMTP to a POP server on which the user has an account. Probably all Internet access providers provide POP mail accounts to their customers. E-mail messages are sent using SMTP to the POP server, which keeps them in a mail box for the user until she requests them using a POP client like Ultimail. Ultimail can be configured to receive mail in other ways, but POP is the default.

Ultimail Configuration

To send and receive mail, you need to configure Ultimail with the host name of your mail gateway, host name of your POP server, your POP login ID and password, your name, signature lines, reply ID, and reply domain. This chapter has already explained how the gateway name and POP information are used. Your reply ID and reply domain make up the return address for your e-mail messages. Typically, your reply ID is the same as your POP login ID and your Internet login ID, and your reply domain is the Internet domain name of your Internet provider's name server—but not necessarily. You may prefer to use a different reply address so that e-mail replies to your messages come to some other Internet mailbox on the network. When you first run Ultimail, you are prompted to enter your name, and this is added to headers of your messages.

If you connect to IBM Internet Connection Services, the gateway, POP, and reply information are configured automatically, although in some cases you may want to override this configuration. If you use a different Internet provider, you can type this information in the Add Provider and Modify Provider dialog boxes of the Dial Other Internet Providers program.

To start Ultimail, follow these steps:

1. Open the Ultimail Lite folder that appears inside the Internet connection folder.

2. Open the Mail Cabinet icon.

3. Select Cabinet, Settings from the menu bar, and when the settings notebook comes up, check that the configuration is to your liking.

   A number of options affect the appearance of your e-mail, and you will certainly want to customize the signature line. Pages 4 and 5 of this settings notebook are quite confusing; these pages exist in part to enable extensions to Ultimail so that it can be used to display, edit, and mail all sorts of multimedia objects.

4. If you want to use your favorite editor instead of the Ultimail text editor, turn to page 5 of the settings notebook, select the text object type from the list box at the top, and specify E.EXE (or whichever editor you prefer) as the object handler.

Using Ultimail

Open the Address Book icon to create addresses and address lists. Open the In Basket icon to retrieve your mail. To view a letter, double-click on the icon for the letter.

To create a new e-mail message, open the New Letter icon (see fig. 15.6). Ultimail is an implementation of the *Multimedia Internet Mail Extensions* (MIME) standard. MIME letters are composed of one or more parts. A plain text part, created with an ordinary text editor, almost always exists. In addition to the text, some letters may contain image files or binary files. For example, programs and spreadsheets can be sent as binary files. The easiest way to add image and binary parts to a letter is to open a directory folder in the Drives icon and drag the file to be mailed to the list bar on the lower left side of the letter window. A copy of the file is added to the letter. Similarly, if binary and image files appear in a MIME e-mail message that you receive, you can drag and drop the icons for these parts to any desktop or Drives folder. A good source of image files is Web Explorer, which enables the user to drag images and other objects out of the Web Explorer window. You can drag these directly to an Ultimail letter and mail them, which may have little practical value, but is kind of cool.

Across the top of the letter window are icons representing various actions: Send, Save, Delete, Print, and so on. Clicking on the Names icon brings up a list of names from your address book, which can be selected as destinations for the letter.

Whenever you start Ultimail, it prompts you to connect to the Internet if you are not already connected. You don't need to connect to view mail you have already received and to create new letters and replies. You do need to connect to the Internet when you actually send the mail or when you view your in-basket.

II

Enumeration

Figure 15.6
Creating an
e-mail message
using Ultimail.

Web Explorer

Web Explorer is used to navigate Internet resources using a graphical interface. In Gopher, you navigate the World-Wide Web through a series of menus. In Web Explorer, you are guided by hypertext documents (see fig. 15.7).

As you move the mouse pointer across the Web Explorer window, the mouse pointer changes shape to indicate hot spots on the page. If you click on one of these hot spots, another hypertext document from the Internet server is presented. Like Gopher, Web Explorer enables you to save the location of any hypertext document or other resource by placing a bookmark. An information line at the bottom of the window gives some details about the document link underneath the mouse pointer. If you move the mouse pointer across the icon bar at the top of the window, the information line indicates what each icon does.

Web Explorer is an all-purpose client. It can be used to access not only *HyperText Markup Language* (HTML) servers, but also FTP, Gopher, and news servers as well. HTML is a language used to create Web documents.

Web Clients are becoming very popular. Press attention has focused on the MOSAIC Web Clients, which are based on source code from the NCSA corporation. Web Explorer does not derive from MOSAIC, but it has the same function and a very similar look and feel.

One common problem in using Web Explorer is getting started. Web Explorer accesses network resources by *Uniform Resource Locator* (URL) name, as follows:

```
explore http://www.ibm.com
```

Figure 15.7
Using Web Explorer.

In the preceding command, `http` specifies the access method (hypertext), and `www.ibm.com` is the host name. The preceding command gets you to the IBM home page, which is all right if you like reading advertisements, but after you tire of this, it is not obvious where to go next. Whereas Gopher servers are numerous on the Internet and their menus are all linked together, Web servers are not as numerous or closely linked. So, it is useful to understand the URL syntax.

Each URL specification begins with an access type, depending on whether hypertext, Gopher, FPT, or news reader access is requested. For hypertext, the access type is http. You specify the following:

        `http://hostname:port/path?search`

The URL is typed as one word with no embedded spaces or square brackets. The italic parts in the preceding example are optional. For example, you might specify

        `http://www.openlab.advantis.net/fun`

to get to the www.openlab.advantis.net hypertext server. The port defaults to an appropriate value, and `/fun` is specified as the path. Gopher URL syntax is similar, as follows:

        `gopher://hostname:port/path?search`

For FTP, you use the following:

```
ftp://userid:password@hostname/path!transfertype
```

The transfer type is *A* for ASCII or *I* for binary (image) transfers. For news reader access, you must first configure a news server using the Configure, Configure servers option of the menu bar. Then specify the following:

```
news:newsgroup
```

Two other access methods are telnet and file. Telnet is not very useful—it is usually better just to start the telnet program. But file is useful when using Web Explorer to view local image and hypertext files. You use the following syntax:

```
file:///filename
```

Web Explorer has comprehensive online help that explains how to specify the URLs for resources you want to view, and it also suggests a few likely sites.

Hypertext documents can, and usually do, contain many pretty graphics. They may also contain multimedia objects like sound and video clips. The graphics make the documents nice to look at and sometimes convey useful information. But image files are voluminous, so it can take a long time to receive all the data needed to display a hypertext page. This makes navigation with a Web client very slow. The Options, Load graphics entry on the Web Explorer menu bar can be used to disable the display of hypertext graphics; the result is not as pretty but much faster.

Any of the objects (image files, sound clips, HTML documents, and so on) displayed by Web Explorer can be saved on your PC hard disk. Move the mouse pointer to the object and click and hold down the right mouse button. Then drag the mouse to any desktop folder and release the mouse button. A copy of the object is saved in the folder.

Like Gopher, Web Explorer sometimes finds objects it does not know how to view; and like Gopher, Web Explorer enables you to register external viewers for such objects. Select Configure, Viewers from the menu bar to register an external viewer program. The same external viewers can be used for both Gopher and Web Explorer.

News Reader/2

Internet newsgroups are a kind of online public forum. Each newsgroup is devoted to an interest area. Thousands of newsgroups exist: on politics, the arts, scientific topics, television, jokes, and so on. Like caller remarks on talk show radio, Internet news articles vary in quality: some articles are thoughtful, considered, and even carefully researched; others are boring or even offensive. Using News Reader/2, you can connect to a news server to browse any of these newsgroups. You also can contribute your own articles by posting to one or more groups, or e-mail a private response to another contributor (see fig. 15.8).

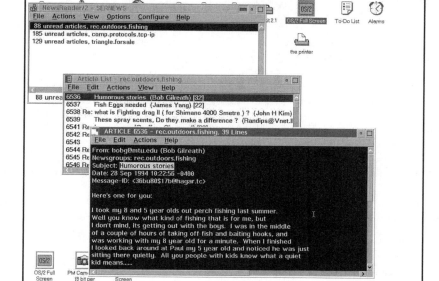

Figure 15.8
Using News Reader/2.

News Reader/2 must be configured with the host name of a news server. This configuration can be done using the Dial Other Internet Providers program, and it occurs automatically when connecting to IBM Internet Connection Services. The news server name can also be set using the Actions, Choose news server entry on the News Server/2 menu bar.

Before you can post to a newsgroup, you must also configure the from address for your posts. This line includes your e-mail address and usually your name as well. After the from address is configured, that line appears in the header of articles posted to newsgroups. You may also want to configure a signature, which consists of one or more lines appended to each article before it is posted. The signature is configured by selecting Options, Signature from the News Reader/2 menu bar.

The first time you use News Reader/2, a message box appears that asks if you want to download the list of all newsgroups from the server. This download can take several minutes because thousands of newsgroups exist, but you cannot do much without this list. From the list of all groups, you choose the ones to which you want to subscribe by clicking on them with the mouse. When you close the All Groups window, the newsgroups you selected are added to your subscriptions list. News Reader/2 then retrieves the article headers for each of the groups to which you have subscribed. You can then double-click on one of the entries in your subscription list to open the Article List window. All the article headers for that newsgroup are displayed. At this point, News Reader/2 manifests a peculiar quirk: you can't have more than one Article List window open at once; and after you open this window, you can close it only by ending News Reader/2. You can change the contents of the Article List window by clicking on a different entry in your subscription list.

An active newsgroup typically has many discussions on different subjects going on at once. Before you start viewing articles, you may want to sort by subject: select View, Sort from the menu bar. Then double-click on a header to view the article. The default configuration only shows one article window at a time, but the Options, Article entry in the News Reader/2 menu bar enables you to configure the program to display simultaneously as many article windows as you want. When an article window is active, you can press N to go to the next article; P to go to the preceding article; or Esc to close the window and return to the Article List window.

To post an article on a new subject, select **A**ctions, Post from the menu bar of the Article List window. To post a reply to an article, select **A**ctions, Post reply from the menu bar of the Article window; or select **A**ctions, Mail reply from that menu bar to send an e-mail reply to the article author. The mail will be sent using the same configuration values used by Ultimail.

Some newsgroups are moderated by an owner who selects from among the inbound posts, discarding the ones that are inappropriate, boring, or not to his liking, and publishing the rest. Others are not moderated at all—whatever articles are posted appear in the newsgroup—and because the people who contribute to Internet news are a cross section of the population, among them is a sprinkling of boors, bigots, and cretins. Fortunately, you can create a block list of authors and subjects, and the articles you see will exclude any by the authors or subjects in the block list. (This is one reason why Internet news is better than talk radio.) To edit the block list, select Edit, Block from the menu of the News Reader/2 Article List window.

A few functions would be very nice additions to News Reader/2. Reading newsgroups takes time, and paying an Internet provider and a phone company for all that time can get expensive. It would be good to be able to download entire groups for later viewing, and also to be able to compose news articles offline for posting at the time of the next connection. These functions are not available—at least, not yet.

FTP-PM

FTP-PM is a graphical user interface that enables you to access files on FTP servers on the Internet. Many such servers exist, and they contain documents, programs, images, and other useful files. FTP-PM needs no configuration. Inside the Internet Connection folder is an Internet Utilities folder, and inside that is the FTP-PM icon. When you open this icon, you are prompted for the host name of an FTP server, your user id, your password, and your account. A good source of OS/2 files is ftp-os2.cdrom.com. For this server and for most of the FTP servers you will access on the Internet, you may use a user id of "anonymous" and a password that is the same as your e-mail address. Servers that permit anonymous FTP access do not require an account. The user id, password, and account values are case-sensitive, meaning that "anonymous" may work, but "ANONYMOUS" and "Anonymous" do not.

When you start a FTP-PM session, you see the window shown in figure 15.9.

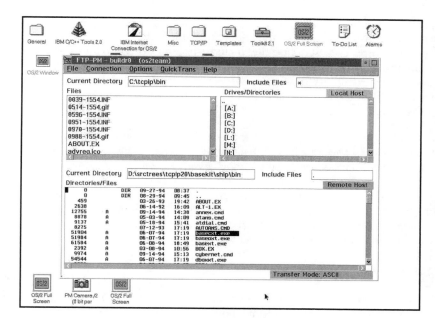

Figure 15.9
Using FTP-PM.

The list box at the bottom of the FTP-PM window shows the files on the remote host. This window has a few clumsy features. Typically, you must use the scroll bar at the bottom of the list box to scroll the file names into view. Some of the files listed are directories; when you double-click on the directory name, FTP-PM switches to that directory. To transfer a file from the remote host, you click on the file name to select it (it must not be a directory), and then press and hold down the right mouse button to pick up the file with the mouse. You can then drag it to your desktop or to the folder of your choice, and the transfer begins. If the server permits files to be uploaded, you can transfer files to the remote host by dragging them with the mouse from the folder or drives icon to the list box of files on the remote host.

When you transfer a file, you need to specify whether you want ASCII transfer (the default) or binary; this selection is done with the **O**ptions, Transfer mode menu. ASCII transfer is used for text files. Binary transfer is used for images, programs, and archives in zip format—in general, for files that are not readable. If you specify the wrong transfer format, the file is not usable. When a file is transferred from one system to another, it is often necessary to change the file name because of the difference in file systems. A Unix or OS/2 system might have a file called "this.is.too.long.for.DOS," whose name would certainly have to be truncated, not only for DOS, but also for OS/2 systems that use the FAT file system (as opposed to HPFS, which supports such names). The application prompts you, before the transfer occurs, to confirm that the way the file name is truncated is to your liking.

FTP-PM has many other features, and the online help explains each of them well, but it has one very clumsy feature. The list of host files includes not only the file name, but also the size, date, and other attributes. If you click on one of these parts of an entry, the program makes a witless attempt to transfer the date or size entry under the mouse—which of course fails with an error. Make sure that the selected area contains only the name of the file you want to transfer.

You may find that you connect to a few of the servers on the Internet again and again. You can create a customized copy of FTP-PM that connects automatically to a server you choose, with a preferred directory and transfer mode already established. To do this, open the Application Templates folder inside the Internet Connection folder and use the mouse to drag an FTP-PM template to the desktop. A settings notebook appears, and you can enter your preferences for destination host user id, password, and the like in the pages of that notebook. When you close the notebook, an FTP-PM icon appears, and you can open this icon whenever you want to connect to that particular server.

telnet and 3270 telnet

telnet and 3270 telnet are terminal emulation programs—that is, they enable you to log in to an Internet host as if your PC were a terminal on the remote computer. You can start a telnet session in several ways. First, you can use Gopher or Web Explorer to bring up a menu on which an icon for the telnet session appears. When you click on that icon, Gopher or Web Client starts a telnet session automatically. If you already know your destination host, you can start the telnet program directly. Icons for telnet and 3270 telnet are in the Internet Utilities folder. Templates for telnet and 3270 telnet also are inside the Application Templates folder, so you can create customized icons to connect to specific hosts.

In general, if an Internet host supports both telnet and 3270 telnet, you should use 3270, because it is much faster. When you use non-3270 (ASCII) telnet, typing seems very slow and clumsy, because every character you type must be sent to the remote host and echoed back by that host before it appears on your screen. Select Options, Line mode from the telnet menu bar to work around this problem. In Line mode, you type an entire line before it is sent to the computer, your keystrokes are displayed immediately, and you can edit mistakes before the line is sent.

Problem Diagnosis and Network Utilities

If you fail to connect to the Internet, possible reasons for the failure include the following:

✔ The com port was not configured correctly.

✔ The modem was not initialized correctly.

✔ The modem was not plugged in.

✔ The Internet provider did not answer the phone call, or the line was busy.

When you run either the IBM Internet Dialer or the Dial Other Internet Providers program, a list box displays the information exchanged with the modem, and error messages explain what went wrong.

After you are connected, you may experience some other kinds of problems. When you connect to IBM Internet Connection Services, configuration information is downloaded to your machine from a central server. This server might be down. You can still run all the Internet Connection applications, but each application may need to prompt you for the missing information; otherwise connection to a specific host may fail. Possible reasons for the failure are the server program on the host is down or busy, or the host is down; your Internet provider's name server is unable find the Internet address of the host; or a link to that host is down. Included with the Internet Connection are several programs to help diagnose the problem, but as they are rarely used, you won't find them as icons in the Internet Connection folder. These programs are started from an OS/2 command window.

Suppose that you are unable to connect to a host called ftp-ser.loc.com. You could enter the following:

ping ftp-ser.loc.com

The ping program sends probe packets to that host, and if a response is returned, the round-trip time is displayed. If ping packets are returned, the remote host is up and connected, but the FTP, Gopher, or other server program that it runs may be down or busy. If ping does not display anything, end it with a Ctrl+Break. Then enter the following to see if your name server can find the address for that host:

host ftp-ser.loc.com

If not, the name server may be down. Press Ctrl+Break again, if necessary, and then enter the following to see the contents of the resolv file:

type %etc%\resolv

This file should look something like this:

```
domain openlab.advantis.net

nameserver 192.147.13.10

nameserver 192.124.113.30
```

The domain names and IP addresses differ depending on your Internet provider. One or several name server lines may exist, but each should have an IP address. This file is typically created by one of the dialer programs. If the resolv file does not exist, or does not look like the one in the preceding example, TCP/IP on your machine cannot communicate with a name server to get IP addresses for host names. It is possible to limp along without a name server, if you have a hosts file. This file contains a list of IP addresses and the corresponding host names. But this approach won't work for applications like Gopher and Web Client, which access many more hosts than would ever appear in your hosts file.

If the resolv file looks OK, enter the following (substitute the IP address of your name server) to see if the name server is up:

ping 192.147.13.10

Even if the name server is working OK, the host name you give it may be incorrect or unknown, so it may not be able to find the corresponding IP address.

Suppose that the following command returns an IP address, but that host still does not send any PING packets:

```
host ftp-ser.loc.com
```

A link or router may be down between that host and your PC. Enter the following to check out the route:

tracerte ftp-ser.loc.com

If a name server, router, or link is down, you cannot do much about it but wait or, when patience runs out, call your Internet provider.

A few other command-line utilities are of interest. The netstat command gives some statistics about IP traffic, routes, and the like. Also included are some text mode versions of standard TCP/IP applications: telnet, FTP, and finger. These basic TCP/IP applications were discussed in an earlier section, and the OS/2 versions are basically the same in appearance and function as the versions for Unix and many other platforms.

Running Windows TCP/IP Applications on OS/2

Although a rich set of TCP/IP applications are available for OS/2, you may find some Windows TCP/IP applications that you like and that you want to run under OS/2. Almost all Windows TCP/IP applications run unchanged with OS/2 TCP/IP, and the Internet Connection includes Windows support. Windows TCP/IP applications are typically written to use standard Windows Sockets programming interfaces, which are implemented in a winsock.dll file. OS/2 TCP/IP supports Windows Sockets and provides a winsock.dll. The TCP/IP communication is routed from Windows sessions to the OS/2 TCP/IP protocol stack through a virtual device driver.

Configuration files for OS/2 TCP/IP are found in the subdirectory that the ETC environment variable specifies—typically this is C:\TCPIP\ETC. Configuration files for Windows TCP/IP programs under OS/2 are found in a separate subdirectory, typically C:\TCPIP\DOS\ETC. When you use the IBM Internet Connection for OS/2, the only configuration file likely to be important is the resolv file discussed earlier. Because Windows and OS/2 programs use different copies of this file, there is a chance that the two may get out of synch. If you have trouble running Windows programs, check to see if the two resolv files differ.

Coexistence Issues

The Internet Connection can be installed on machines along with other communications programs without any conflict. The only limitation is that only one communications program at a time can use a particular com port and the modem attached to it. If you use a communications program from CompuServe, Prodigy, America Online, or others, then select the Hang Up function from the Internet Dialer before you start the other program.

Some coexistence issues arise if you try to run the Internet Connection at the same time you are using TCP/IP services on your LAN. The next section discusses these issues.

Using OS/2 TCP/IP on a LAN

All the programs described in the preceding section (telnet, FTP, Gopher, News Reader/2, Ultimail, and Web Explorer) are usable and useful in the LAN environment. The IBM TCP/IP version 2 for OS/2 base package contains several of the applications discussed in the preceding section: telnet and 3270 telnet, FTP and FTP-PM, and News Reader/2. Gopher is not included, but the same Gopher program is available on the Internet through anonymous FTP from software.watson.ibm.com, and Web Explorer also is available from the same site. The TCP/IP base kit contains SLIP support and can be used to dial in to the Internet, but the dial support is not as polished as that in the Internet Connection Kit.

Along with these programs are some additional ones primarily useful on the LAN. These include the following:

✔ **LPR, LPRMON, LPQ, and LPRPORTD** —Enables printing of PC files on TCP/IP print servers

✔ **LPD**—Enables the OS/2 PC to be set up as a TCP/IP print server

✔ **Telnetd**—The telnet server program that enables a user to log in to the OS/2 machine from a remote PC

✔ **FTPD**—The FTP server program

✔ **REXEC and RSH clients**—For remote execution of commands

✔ **REXECD and RSHD**—The server programs for REXEC and RSH, so that commands can be invoked on an OS/2 machine from a remote PC

✔ **TALK and TALKD**—Client and server programs for the TCP/IP Talk protocol, enabling electronic messaging

✔ **The Simple Network Management Protocol agent (SNMPD)**—Enables the PC to be managed by a network administrator on a remote workstation

✔ **The SNMP manager program**—Enables the management of other machines from an OS/2 PC.

An e-mail package, LaMail, is also included. LaMail differs from the Ultimail package found in the Internet Connection Kit.

Installing the TCP/IP Base Package

The package can be installed from a floppy disk or from a network drive. The process in either case is to enter the following command:

a:\tcpinst

If you're installing from a network drive, type that drive letter instead of a. The window shown in figure 15.10 appears.

The Select components for installation section contains a long list of components that can be installed, but of these components, only Base TCP/IP for OS/2, Publications for Base TCP/IP for OS/2, LaMail, and the IBM Library Reader are actually part of the base kit. The other items in the list are included in kits sold separately. If you bought NFS, the X Windows Server Kit, or one of the other kits, you can select these items in the list and install all of them in one step. If you did not buy any other kits, it does no good to select components you do not have—think of them as an advertisement and skip ahead. It is best to install the online publications because the hard copy documentation that comes with the kit is limited. When you install the publications, you should also install the IBM Library Reader because these publications are in Bookmanager format and are not readable without the Library Reader. You can specify the drive and base directory in which you want these components installed, and whether you want your CONFIG.SYS updated automatically.

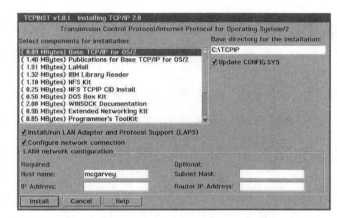

Figure 15.10
Installing the TCP/IP base kit.

When you select to install Base TCP/IP for OS/2 , some other options are made active. The first of these is for *LAN Adapter and Protocol Support,* or LAPS. Whenever you first install TCP/IP for use with a LAN adapter, you must install and run LAPS to configure the TCP/IP protocol to use that LAN card. (It is not necessary to run LAPS if TCP/IP is only to be used over a SLIP interface.) The LAPS program is described in more detail later. Optionally, at installation time you can configure the TCP/IP network connection. It is not necessary to configure the network connection when installing—a configuration tool is provided—but TCP/IP is not usable until this configuration is done. The four items in the network configuration are as follows:

✔ Host name, which is the name by which your machine is known to other machines on the network

✔ IP address for your machine

✔ Subnet mask

✔ Router IP address

You get IP addresses from your network administrator. Typically, she gets a range of addresses from the *Internet Network Information Center,* or InterNIC. Do not invent an address; it may not work and will cause problems if someone else already has that address.

A computer that is never to be connected, directly or indirectly, to the Internet can use an address that the InterNIC has not assigned; but if you use TCP/IP, you probably will want to connect to the Internet sooner or later. You also get the subnet mask and router IP address from your network administrator. Some networks do not use subnetting and require no subnet mask. The router IP address is the address of a gateway machine, which routes your IP packets beyond your local network. Some networks do not have these either.

Configuring Ethernet or Token Ring Cards

When TCP/IP communicates with a LAN card, the following device drivers must be loaded:

- ✔ The TCP/IP device drivers INET.SYS and IFNDIS.SYS

- ✔ A *Medium Access Control* (MAC) driver, provided by the company that makes the LAN card

- ✔ PROTMAN.OS2

OS/2 TCP/IP communicates with MAC drivers written to the *Network Device Interface Specification* (NDIS). Other kinds of MAC drivers are available—Novell promotes an alternate specification called ODI, used by Novell NetWare—but OS/2 TCP/IP requires NDIS; and to run it on a LAN, you must have a LAN card with an OS/2 NDIS driver. (If your LAN card does not have an OS/2 NDIS driver, a workaround is available—provided that the card has an OS/2 ODI driver.) Other NDIS-based products are OS/2 LAN Services, Communications Manager/2, and Banyan VINES. PROTMAN is a part of NDIS that initializes the MAC driver and binds it to the protocols. The LAPS program is used for NDIS configuration.

When LAPS runs, you see a window with buttons for Install, Configure, Remove, Exit, and Help. Select Configure. The window shown in figure 15.11 appears.

Figure 15.11
Configuring
network adapters
with LAPS.

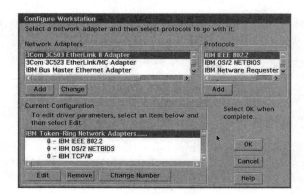

The Network Adapters section of this window contains a list box of some commonly used network adapters. If, as is often the case, your LAN card is not in the list, configuration of your LAN card requires an additional step. When you bought the LAN card, you should have received a floppy disk with device drivers for the card. Select Cancel in the LAPS Configure Workstation window. Now put the device driver disk for the card in the A drive and click on Install. In most cases, the NDIS driver for the card is installed, and you can return to the configuration step.

In a few cases, the device driver disk has an OS/2 NDIS driver, but the disk does not include a NIF file for the driver. (The NIF file contains information so that LAPS can configure the MAC driver.) If this problem occurs, complete LAPS configuration by choosing some other card from the Network Adapters list. After LAPS configuration is completed, you must copy the OS/2 NDIS driver for the card from the device driver disk to your \IBMCOM\MACS subdirectory; this directory is typically on the same drive as your OS/2 system files. Then use an editor like the OS/2 system editor to modify the \IBMCOM\PROTOCOL.INI file. Documentation on the device driver disk should tell you how to do this. Manual editing of PROTOCOL.INI is complicated and subject to error; but fortunately this step is not necessary for most network cards, and the card providers give pretty good instructions in the exceptional cases.

After the NDIS driver for your card has been installed by LAPS, select Configure, and then select that card from the Network Adapters list. Click on the Add button below this list. An entry for your card is added to the Current Configuration list box. In most cases, this entry ends with an ellipsis (...), and you can double-click on the entry to bring up a configuration dialog box. In this configuration dialog box, you specify the interrupt level, I/O address, buffer size, and so on used by your card. Usually, the default values work well, but sometimes it is necessary to modify these, and in this case the card manufacturer will provide appropriate information. Some online help is also available for this configuration dialog box. When configuring a Token Ring card for TCP/IP, it is usually best to set the transmit buffer size to the largest value the card supports.

Now you must specify the protocols you want to use on the card. Select the entry for your card in the Current Configuration list box and select the protocols you want from the Protocols list; click on the Add button below this list after each selection. The list of protocols you see depends on what is installed on the machine. You may see IBM IEEE 802.2, which is used by Communications Manager/2, or IBM OS/2 NETBIOS, which is used by the IBM LAN Services programs. When you start LAPS as part of TCP/IP installation, always select the IBM TCP/IP protocol.

Coexistence of IBM TCP/IP for OS/2 with Other Protocols

When LAPS is used to configure the TCP/IP protocol to use a LAN card, applications like the IBM OS/2 LAN Server and Requester programs and Communications Manager/2 also can be installed on the same machine to use the same LAN card. No danger of conflict exists. If you are using IBM LAN Services version 4.0 for OS/2, you should install it after TCP/IP because that program contains a TCP/IP protocol stack newer than the one in the TCP/IP base.

NetWare is one exception. NetWare requires that an ODI MAC driver for the LAN card be used, whereas other applications use NDIS. An easy resolution exists for this apparent incompatibility: install NetWare first; then in the LAPS Configure Workstation window, add IBM NetWare Requester Support from the list of protocols. After this entry is added, LAPS modifies CONFIG.SYS so that the real ODI MAC driver used by OS/2 does not talk to the LAN card. Instead NetWare communicates with a fake ODI driver called ODI2NDI, which interacts with NetWare just as a real ODI MAC driver would—except that ODI2NDI converts the ODI calls to NDIS and uses the NDIS MAC driver. NetWare runs every bit as fast with ODI2NDI as it does with a real ODI driver, but ODI2NDI enables coexistence with protocols like TCP/IP. ODI2NDI was only recently added to TCP/IP version 2 for OS/2, and was not included in the initial shipments of this product. If you don't have this driver, you can get it through anonymous FTP from the Internet. The file is included on the Etherstreamer device diskette, which can be downloaded from ftp.pcco.ibm.com.

A few LAN cards have OS/2 ODI drivers but no NDIS drivers. You can run NDIS protocol stacks like OS/2 TCP/IP on such cards, using a wedge program called *ODINSUP*, developed by Novell. ODINSUP converts NDIS calls to ODI and uses an ODI MAC driver. Unfortunately, ODINSUP has some side effects. NDIS-based protocols like TCP/IP run about 30 percent slower with ODINSUP. Also, ODINSUP Token Ring support is not so good; packets from NDIS protocols are not formatted to cross source route bridges. Configuring ODINSUP is not so easy either, but Novell provides some documentation for this, as does IBM. The IBM book, *TCP/IP V.20 for OS/2 Installation and Interoperability*, discusses TCP/IP and ODINSUP and can be ordered with the publications number GG24-3531-02.

Completing the Installation

After you complete the LAPS Configure Workstation dialog box, click on OK. In the next window, click on Exit. In the next window, click on Continue; then click on OK once more. (LAPS is a somewhat skeptical program; it wants to be absolutely sure.) Finally, you see an Exiting LAPS dialog box that advises you to shut down OS/2 and restart your workstation. If you are running LAPS as part of TCP/IP installation, DO NOT DO THIS. Instead, just click on Exit and return to TCP/IP installation, and let it run to completion. Then shut down OS/2 and reboot.

LAPS adds the following statements to CONFIG.SYS:

```
DEVICE=C:\IBMCOM\PROTMAN.OS2 /I:C:\IBMCOM
RUN=C:\IBMCOM\PROTOCOL\NETBIND.EXE
```

```
DEVICE=C:\IBMCOM\MACS\IBMTOK.OS2
DEVICE=C:\IBMCOM\PROTOCOL\INET.SYS
DEVICE=C:\IBMCOM\PROTOCOL\IFNDIS.SYS
```

In this example, LAPS is installed on drive C, and the IBM Token-Ring MAC driver is used; with these exceptions, the statements that LAPS adds will be similar for all machine configurations. LAPS may add other statements to CONFIG.SYS if other protocols like NETBIOS and IEEE 802.2 are loaded.

LAPS also creates a file \IBMCOM\PROTOCOL.INI, which appears something like the following:

```
[PROT_MAN]

    DRIVERNAME = PROTMAN$

[IBMLXCFG]
    TCPIP_nif = TCPIP.NIF
    IBMTOK_nif = IBMTOK.NIF

[TCPIP_nif]

    DriverName = TCPIP$
    Bindings = IBMTOK_nif

[IBMTOK_nif]

    DriverName = IBMTOK$
    ADAPTER = "PRIMARY"
    MAXTRANSMITS = 6
    RECVBUFS = 2
    RECVBUFSIZE = 256
    XMITBUFS = 1
    XMITBUFSIZE = 4456
```

Of course, the exact contents of this file depend on which network cards are used and how many, and on which protocols are used. OS/2 TCP/IP can be configured to use as many as eight LAN cards simultaneously.

TCP/IP installation also modifies CONFIG.SYS, adding the following statements:

```
LIBPATH=... ;C:\TCPIP\DLL
SET PATH=... ;C:\TCPIP\BIN
SET HELP=... ;C:\TCPIP\HELP
```

```
SET BOOKSHELF= ...;C:\TCPIP\DOC
SET READIBM= ...;C:\TCPIP\DOC
SET ETC=C:\TCPIP\ETC
RUN=C:\TCPIP\BIN\CNTRL.EXE
```

TCP/IP won't run correctly if any of these are missing.

After you shut down and restart your machine, you find a TCP/IP folder on your OS/2 desktop (see fig. 15.12).

Figure 15.12
The TCP/IP folder.

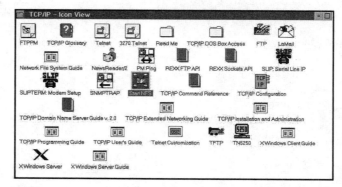

Inside the OS/2 System folder is the Startup folder, which contains a list of programs to be started when OS/2 starts. TCP/IP installation adds an icon for TCP/IP startup to this folder, so that it is started automatically when OS/2 starts. If you do not want TCP/IP to be started automatically, you can drag this icon out of the Startup folder. The Start TCP/IP icon invokes TCPSTART.CMD, which configures the network interface and starts the TCP/IP servers you choose to run.

Configuring TCP/IP

Open the TCP/IP folder. Inside is an icon called TCP/IP Configuration. When you click on this icon, the TCP/IP Configuration Notebook appears.

Network Interfaces

The first pages of the TCP/IP Configuration Notebook are used to configure network interfaces. Included are entry fields for the IP address and subnet mask, discussed earlier. A number of other entry fields and check boxes are on this page, but the purpose of each is somewhat technical and obscure. Almost all users should use default values. In most cases, the additional options are for rarely used standards for TCP/IP encapsulation that are now obsolete.

The eight network pages enable configuration of up to eight network adapters. Unless you are setting up your machine as an IP router, you will probably only configure one adapter. If you do configure more than one adapter, be aware of the following limitations:

✔ Each adapter must have a unique IP address. When packets are routed, an internal routing table based on the IP addresses of each adapter keeps track of the network interface used to reach each host and network in the table.

✔ Each adapter should use the same subnet mask (this is a limitation of IBM TCP/IP for OS/2). (If you never intend to configure a router, skip the following technical explanation.)

Typically, different networks use different subnet masks, and a router is attached to several networks, so the restriction that all masks must be the same length is somewhat onerous. However, it is OK to use two different subnet masks on different adapters so long as the longer subnet mask is on the FIRST adapter. If the adapters are not configured in this way, a possibility exists that packet destinations may be misrouted. The routing function does a logical AND of the destination address and the subnet mask for the first interface. If the result matches the subnet address of the first interface, the packet will be routed to that interface unless a host route exists for the destination address. If the second LAN interface uses a shorter mask, the packet may be misdirected.

Routing

Following the Network Configuration section in the TCP/IP Configuration Notebook is the Routing page. If your PC only communicates with other hosts on the same LAN, you do not need to define any routes. TCP/IP can send packets directly to hosts on the same LAN by putting the LAN hardware address of the host in the Ethernet or Token Ring header of the packet. The hardware address is determined using the *Address Resolution Protocol* (ARP). If your PC communicates with hosts on other LANs (this is certainly the case when you are connected to the Internet), you need to define a default route, which is the IP address of a gateway machine, to which packets are sent for all IP addresses beyond your LAN. Sometimes you may use several gateways. You can only have one default route in OS/2 TCP/IP, but you can also define network routes so that all packets destined for a particular network are sent to the corresponding gateway; you may also have routes for particular subnets or for individual hosts.

Automatic Starting of Services

When your machine is to be used as a telnet, FTP, or print server, typically you want the server function to be started whenever the machine is started. Also, you may want NFS file sharing and other functions to be active as soon as the machine starts. The Autostart section of the configuration notebook is used to set up these services to be automatically started. Suppose that you want the same machine to be a telnet, FTP, REXEC, RSH, TFTP, and LPD server. OS/2 is a wonderful multitasking environment, and you can configure your machine to start up the server programs for each of these services at boot time. However, a super server program called INETD can be started instead and configured so that whenever a host on the network requests a telnet, FTP, or other connection, INETD starts a session of the requested type. Other services you may want to start automatically include the following:

- ✔ **NFS server**

- ✔ **The lprportd daemon process**—Used to integrate TCP/IP printing with the OS/2 desktop

- ✔ **ROUTED**—Enables the PC to act as a router using the RIP dynamic routing protocol

- ✔ **Sendmail**—Enables your machine to receive mail from other machines

- ✔ **Portmap**—Needed if the PC is running server applications that use Remote Procedure Call, including the NFS server

- ✔ **SNMPD**—Used when the workstation is to be managed remotely using Netview or other SNMP manager programs

Changes to the Network, Routing, and Autostart pages of the Configuration Notebook do not have an immediate effect. These changes only become active when the PC is restarted. To cause these changes to take effect immediately, enter **TCPSTART** at an OS/2 command line.

Configuring Serial Line Connections

The SLIP page of the Configuration Notebook is used to configure the SLIP interface. To configure this interface, you must specify a com port, whether *Van Jacobsen* (VJ) compression is to be used, the *maximum transmission unit* (MTU) of the interface, and the local and destination IP addresses of the interface. VJ compression and MTU size must be configured to match the values for the other end of the SLIP connection; if you do not know those values, use the defaults. The SLIP configuration page cannot be used to configure the modem. To do that, you must either write a script file using the OS/2 REXX language; or you must set up the modem manually, using the SLIPTERM modem setup program from the TCP/IP folder. All this is pretty clumsy by comparison to the straightforward dialing utilities of the Internet Connection Kit; but if you have enough patience, and if you follow the directions for modem setup in the pamphlet that came with your modem, you can establish a SLIP connection to the Internet or to another TCP/IP host running SLIP.

You may intend to use the TCP/IP base kit without any LAN card for SLIP-only connections. In this case, LAPS is not run at TCP/IP installation time, and therefore LAPS does not add the TCP/IP device driver statements to CONFIG.SYS. Unfortunately, the TCP/IP installation program does not either, which is definitely a program defect. So, if you are setting up the TCP/IP base for SLIP-only connections, you must first add the following statements to CONFIG.SYS:

DEVICE=C:\TCPIP\BIN\INET.SYS

DEVICE=C:\TCPIP\BIN\IFNDISNL.SYS

These statements should be added above the RUN statement for CNTRL.EXE.

Another curious fact about the SLIP-only environment is that loopback (sending IP packets to another application on the same machine) is not automatically enabled. The loopback interface is actually quite useful for interprocess communication on a TCP/IP host—for example, when X Client applications are run on a machine and their user interface is provided by an X Windows server on the same machine. To enable the loopback interface, enter the following command:

ifconfig lo 2.2.2.2

You can create a file, TCPEXIT.CMD, in the C:\TCPIP\BIN subdirectory, and enter this statement. This command file is run whenever TCP/IP is started. Again, these steps are necessary only if no LAN interface is enabled.

One common way of using SLIP in combination with a LAN connection is to set up a desktop machine as a router. You can dial in to the desktop machine from home, using another PC running TCP/IP to establish a SLIP connection. Through that connection you have complete TCP/IP access from the remote machine to LAN resources. It is not difficult to set up the desktop machine to route packets from the SLIP interface. Follow these steps (call the desktop OS/2 machine A, and the remote PC B):

1. Machine A must have two IP addresses—one for the LAN interface and one for the SLIP interface; B must also be assigned a network address. Each of these addresses must be assigned by the network administrator and must belong to the same network and subnet as the IP address of A's LAN interface. The IP address for B is the destination address of the SLIP interface for A and vice versa.

2. Route entries must be configured on both A and B. On A, a host route must be configured. The destination address of the route is B's IP address; the router address is A's SLIP interface address; and the hop count for the route is 0. On B, a default route must be configured. The router address is A's SLIP interface address, and the hop count is 1.

3. An ARP table entry for B must be created on A. The ARP protocol is a way of determining the LAN hardware address for a given IP address, and a TCP/IP host does this by broadcasting an ARP request for the destination IP address to all the other TCP/IP hosts on the network. The host that has the IP address in the ARP request replies with a packet that contains its LAN hardware address. Machine B is connected by a SLIP line and has no LAN hardware address; so A is configured to respond to ARP requests on B's behalf. If B's IP address is 9.67.111.80, and A's LAN hardware address is 1000545a6c6c, enter the following ARP command on A to create the new ARP table entry:

   arp -s 9.67.111.80 10:00:54:5a:6c:6c pub

   Responding to ARP requests for another machine is known as *proxy ARP*.

Frequently, you will not know the hardware address for your LAN adapter. At an OS/2 command line, enter **netstat -n** to see information on the various TCP/IP interfaces, including the hardware address of each.

4. The modem of the desktop machine must be set for auto answer on ring so that it answers the incoming call.

This same basic configuration can be used to extend TCP/IP services to a machine without a LAN adapter. The com ports of the two machines are connected with a NULL modem cable. Typically, the speed of this connection is 57600 bps—not as fast as a LAN connection, but certainly much cheaper.

Configuring TCP/IP Services

The Services pages of the TCP/IP Configuration Notebook contain information affecting name resolution, FTP, telnet, printing, REXEC, and RSH. The items on these pages are described in the following sections.

Codepage Issues

The PC presents text to the user using an ASCII *codepage*. In OS/2, these codepages have numbers like 437 or 850. Unfortunately, computers vary in how they represent ASCII text. Although reasonable uniformity exists in the use of ASCII codes 0 through 127, ASCII codes 128 through 255 appear on-screen as different characters depending on which computer is used. U.S. English speakers rarely notice this problem, because all the characters of U.S. English are included in ASCII 0 through 127. However, the written languages of Western Europe require characters with umlauts, circumflexes, cedillas, and the like; and computers vary on how these are represented in ASCII, so a document on one computer may be partly converted to random punctuation when it is moved to another machine.

To solve this problem, the *International Organization of Standards* (ISO) defined standards for the network representation of ASCII. The standard is ISO 8859, and the languages of Western Europe can all be represented in the ISO 8859-1 codepage. Therefore, when a computer puts ASCII text on the network, it must first be translated into a standard network codepage such as ISO 8859-1. The codepage entry of the Configuration Notebook enables you to specify the translation table FTP and telnet client and server programs are to use. The three choices are as follows:

- ✔ **TCP8859**—For ISO 8859-1

- ✔ **TCPDECMU**—For DEC multinational, a codepage commonly used by VAX machines

- ✔ **No translation**—Convenient if both the client and server ends of the connection are OS/2 machines

Japan, China, and Korea use double-byte codepages, and an Asia/Pacific version of the TCP/IP base kit is enabled for double-byte codepages.

FTP Server Access

FTP server access is controlled by the \TCPIP\ETC\TRUSERS file. The FTP Access Protection list on the first Service page of the TCP/IP Configuration Notebook enables the user to customize this file. Each user is assigned a password and a list of directories for which read or write access is permitted. The special FTP user ID "anonymous" does not require any password.

Domain Name Services (DNS)

The Domain Name Services section is used to configure the machine's host name and domain name. For example, the host name might be eeyore and the domain name raleigh.ibm.com. When other hosts communicate with the eeyore machine, they do not need to use the IP address. Hosts in the same domain can use eeyore, and hosts in a different domain can specify the fully qualified domain name of eeyore.raleigh.ibm.com.

Usually, a host name is resolved to an IP address by a name server. This page of the Configuration Notebook enables the user to configure the IP address of one or more name servers.

Other Services

The rest of the Services pages of the Configuration Notebook can be used to configure passwords for the REXEC and telnet servers, define a default destination for TCP/IP network printing, specify a default news server to which News Reader/2 connects, and so on. A hosts file can be created to resolve host names to IP addresses if a name server is not used, or if the name server cannot resolve certain host names. If both a name server and a hosts file are configured, the name server is queried first when a host name is resolved. All this configuration is straightforward.

 After the telnet server function is started and a telnet password is configured, the OS/2 machine can function as a telnet server. Remote users logging in to the PC through telnet can perform many of the same functions as the user at the PC keyboard, with one important restriction: the remote user can only run OS/2 text mode programs. He can cause DOS, Windows, and Presentation Manager programs to start, but cannot type into a DOS, Windows, or Presentation Manager session; nor can he see the screen output from such a session.

SNMP Configuration

The SNMP configuration pages control the behavior of the SNMP agent, which is run to enable the machine to be remotely managed by a network administrator. You must configure the following:

- ✔ **SYSCONTACT**—The name (and perhaps the phone number) of someone to contact if the network administrator observes a problem with the machine

- ✔ **SYSLOCATION**—The physical location of the machine

- ✔ **Trap destination list**—A list of IP addresses of hosts to which SNMP messages called *traps* are sent if a troublesome event occurs on this machine

- ✔ **Community names file**—A list of passwords

Each password in the community names file is associated with an IP address and a bit mask. When an SNMP management request is received, the SNMP agent compares the IP address in the received packet with addresses in the community names file. Bits that are not part of the bit mask do not count in this comparison. If a match is found, the community name is compared, and if it matches, the request is honored. If the community name does not match, the request is not honored, and an SNMP trap is sent to each of the trap destinations, reporting the invalid access.

The configuration notebook writes the community name entries in a file called PW.SRC in the \TCPIP\ETC directory. However, this file is not what the SNMP agent reads. You must enter **make_pw** at an OS/2 command prompt to generate the file snmp.pw from the pw.src file. Because the file contains passwords, make_pw is used to encode the passwords so that they cannot be read easily.

The MIB_2.TBL file also can be configured with the configuration notebook. This table is only important if the PC is to be used as an SNMP network manager. Usually, it is best to leave this file alone.

Mail

The mail program included with the TCP/IP base kit is LaMail, which uses the *Simple Mail Transfer Protocol* (SMTP) to both send and receive mail. LaMail is a good tool, but is not as capable as Ultimail; and you might reasonably conjecture that Ultimail will soon replace LaMail for LAN-based mail. Sendmail is the SMTP program. Sendmail must run continuously as a server to send or to receive mail, and the Sendmail program is called to send mail. A connection must be made with the host that is the mail destination address to actually send the mail message. If this connection is not made, the message is queued, and retransmission is periodically attempted until a timeout interval elapses. Then the message is discarded from the outbound queue. Incoming mail is stored in the \TCPIP\ETC\MAIL directory; outbound mail is stored in \TCPIP\ETC\MQUEUE.

The problem with this approach is that if both the source and destination machines are not up, connected to the network, and running sendmail, the mail may not get through. A solution is to send all outbound mail to a mail gateway and to receive inbound mail from a mail server using the POP protocol. This is the approach used by the Ultimail package of the Internet Connection Kit. You can to configure LaMail to do this as well. You must obtain the LAMPOP package, which can be downloaded from the Internet from software.watson.ibm.com. You must also configure the Sendmail program to use a mail gateway.

The Sendmail configuration file is \TCPIP\ETC\SENDMAIL.CF. Sendmail and sendmail.cf both derive from Unix. Unix manuals describe what the lines in sendmail.cf mean; these manuals can be used for the OS/2 sendmail.cf file as well. Now for those who find the Rosetta stone easy reading, sendmail.cf is not too tough to decipher; but for the rest of us, this file is somewhat opaque. One of the big advantages of Ultimail is that it does not use this file. Fortunately, after you have used the Configuration Notebook to set the host and domain name, sendmail.cf is basically usable as is. It is only necessary to alter it if a mail gateway and POP server are to be used. The recommended changes are in the next paragraph, but most users can skip it and use Ultimail or LaMail as is.

Sendmail.cf must be edited with an editor that preserves tab characters. The OS/2 system editor does preserve tabs, but EPM, the OS/2 enhanced editor, does not. It is wise to back up the file before you change it. Lines beginning with a # are comments and are ignored by the Sendmail program. The lines are listed following this paragraph. (Incidentally, these lines originate from the Ultimail file SENDMAIL.UML, which comes preconfigured with POP and gateway support.) The first group of lines is automatically updated by the TCP/IP configuration notebook:

```
# Lines that define your host name
```

```
Dwyour-host-name
Cwyour-host-name

# A line that defines your mail domain
DDyour.domain.name

# The location of the mail alias file
OAc:\tcpip\etc\aliases

# The location of the mail help file, for messages displayed when
# a client program connects to the Sendmail server
OHc:\tcpip\etc\sendmail.hf

# The location of the Sendmail log file and mail queue
OHc:\tcpip\etc\mqueue

# The location of the Sendmail status file
OSc:\tcpip\etc\sendmail.st

# The local mailer specification
Mlocal, P=c:\tcpip\bin\mail.exe, F=lsDFP, S=10, R=20,
A=C:\tcpip\etc\mail $u

# The following lines are not added by the configuration notebook.
# These must be added manually, but they are only important if a mail
# gateway or hub is to be used.

# The unqualified (domain-less) name of the mail gateway
DVYourMailRelay

# The fully-qualified domain name of the mail hub. This is typically
# the name of the pop server
DHYour.Mail.Hub

# S0 stands for rule 0, and S3 stands for rule 3.  To use mail gateways
# and hubs, you would replace the SO and S3 of sendmail.cf with the
# following. Where you see (tab) you must type a tab.

# Throw all mail to relay
S0
R$*(tab)(tab)(tab)$#relay $@$V $:$1
```

```
# Rewrite local addresses so they look like they are from the hub
S3
R$*<$*<$*>$*>$*(tab)$3(tab)(tab)denest
R$*<$+>$*(tab)$2(tab)(tab)basic RFC822 parsing
R$*<>$*(tab)(tab)$n(tab)(tab)RFC1123 <>
R$-(tab)(tab)$@ $1 @ $H(tab)user => user@hub
R$+@$+(tab)(tab)$: $1 @ $[$2$](tab)canonify the hostname
R$+@$w(tab)(tab)$@ $1 @ $H(tab)user@thishost => user@hub
R$w!$+(tab)(tab)$@ $2 @ $H(tab)thishost!user => user@hub
R$*%$w(tab)(tab)$@ $>3 $1 @ $2(tab)handle % hack thishost
R$*(tab)(tab)$@ $1(tab)(tab)default, unchanged
```

Printing

The TCP/IP base kit provides three client programs that enable printing to TCP/IP network printers. The first is *lpr*, a program that can be invoked at the OS/2 command line to print a file. The destination host, destination printer, and printing mode must be specified. The two printing modes are ASCII and binary. ASCII mode is used to print ordinary text files to dissimilar machines. Using ASCII mode, you can have a text file printed on a printer attached to a Unix print server, and line breaks and other basic formatting is preserved. Binary mode is used to print postscript files and other files that are not ordinary text files.

The second printing program in the TCP/IP base is *lprmon*. Lprmon intercepts all output directed at a printer port such as LPT1 and redirects it to a network printer. When lprmon is running, TCP/IP network printing can be done seamlessly from OS/2, DOS, and Windows applications.

The third client program is *lprportd*. This program runs in the background, without an obvious user interface, but it enables seamless printing from OS/2 Presentation Manager programs. To set this up, you first configure the program to start automatically whenever the PC is started; this is using one of the Autostart pages of the TCP/IP Configuration Notebook. Next, a printer icon for TCP/IP network printing must be created on the OS/2 desktop. Open the templates folder, and drag a printer template to the desktop. Configure the printer icon to use a print driver that matches the destination printer, and then select an output port. Output ports for printing typically include com1, lpr1, and so on, but when lprmon is running, you also see output ports named \pipes\lpr0, \pipes\lpr1, and so on. Select one of these with the mouse. Then click on the right mouse button to bring up the context menu for the icon and select settings. The settings page that is presented enables you to specify the host name of the print server and the name of the destination printer. You should also give the printer icon a descriptive name. Click on Create to complete the creation of the printer icon.

After a printer icon is configured to use lprportd, you can print files on that printer by dragging the icon for the file from a desktop folder to the printer icon. The printer also appears as a print destination for OS/2 Presentation Manager programs like Lotus AMI Pro and DeScribe. Printer icons can only be used to print in binary mode. One more interesting option is available. If the print server is configured with fax support, then the lpr printer port used by the printer icon can be configured with a filter so that the file is not actually printed by the print server, but instead is sent directly to any fax machine. The filter program prompts you to enter the phone number of the fax machine and the name of the fax recipient.

LPD, a program to enable an OS/2 machine to function as a print server for TCP/IP network printing, is also included in the TCP/IP base kit.

Automatic Host Configuration

The TCP/IP base kit includes support for the *Bootstrap Protocol* (BOOTP). Both client and server programs are provided. The idea behind BOOTP is that users should not have to configure TCP/IP on their machine and should not need to know how. This configuration information is stored on a central server, and is transmitted to client machines when they are started. When the BOOTP client program runs, a message is broadcast on the network that solicits network configuration information from the BOOTP server. The message contains the LAN hardware address of the client machine. The BOOTP server looks up the client's address in a table, and if it finds a match, returns configuration information to the client, including the client's IP address, netmask, name server address, domain name, and routing information. When the reply is received at the client, the client is automatically configured. If the client hardware address is not in the table it will be added and automatically assigned an IP address and netmask.

The Installation and Administration manual that comes with the product contains information on how to configure a client machine to use BOOTP, and on how to configure a BOOTP server.

Coexistence with the Internet Connection for OS/2

The TCP/IP for OS/2 Base Kit and the Internet Connection Kit can coexist on the same machine, running simultaneously and both using the same TCP/IP protocol stack. Some care is required in getting this to work. It is important that the installed version of the TCP/IP base kit has all the latest service (through August 1994). The TCP/IP Base Kit must be installed first because the Internet Connection has the latest version of the applications. Both the TCP/IP Base Kit and the Internet Connection Kit must be installed in the same drive and directory.

When you install the Internet Connection Kit on top of the TCP/IP Base Kit, the installation program displays a warning message that problems can occur with this combination of packages. That is true—but this section explains those problems and how to work around them, so you can ignore this message and continue with the installation. Of course, when the LAN-enabled version of OS/2 version 3 comes out, these package conflicts will have been resolved.

Two kinds of problems can occur. The first has to do with routing. When a connection with the Internet is established, a default route to a gateway machine on the Internet is set up. If you already have a default route defined to a gateway machine on your LAN, it is deactivated for the duration of your connection to the Internet. To get around this problem, you can typically define network and host routes to your LAN gateway machine, using the routing page of the TCP/IP Configuration Notebook. For example, suppose that you have a machine on a LAN with a class A network address of 9.67.111.80, with a subnet mask of 255.255.240.0, and with a default router at address 9.67.96.4. The default route becomes inactive while this machine is connected to the Internet, so additional routing statements are needed, one for each subnet accessed through the 9.67.96.4 router. To reach a host at 9.67.245.3, you add a route for the 9.67.240.0 subnet, with 9.67.96.4 as the router address.

The second problem is in resolving host names to IP addresses. While the PC is connected to the Internet, TCP/IP uses an Internet domain name, and a name server on the Internet is used for host name resolution. The LAN name server is not used, so LAN host names cannot be resolved. You can work around this by using the Configuration Notebook to create a hosts file, with entries for each of the hosts you regularly access on the LAN. The domain name and name server IP address are stored in the resolv file in the \TCPIP\ETC subdirectory. When you disconnect from the Internet, the file is restored to the state it was in before the Internet connection was made. The file restoration may fail, so back up this file. If you have name resolution problems after a session with the Internet, copy your backup version over the resolv file.

Finally, one security issue exists. By default, the OS/2 TCP/IP protocol stack routes IP packets whenever the PC has two TCP/IP interfaces active. Therefore when both the LAN connection and the Internet connection are active, the possibility exists that a rogue on the Internet could gain access to your LAN through your PC. To eliminate this possibility, enter the following at an OS/2 command prompt:

    ipgate off

OS/2 TCP/IP and Wide Area Networking

In the preceding sections, two types of connectivity for TCP/IP for OS/2 were discussed: SLIP and PPP links using modems and phone lines, and LAN connectivity using Ethernet or Token Ring LANs. (FDDI LANs also are supported.) Geographically separated LANs can be joined into a single WAN in various ways. One approach is to attach dedicated routers to each of the LANs and connect those routers with a backbone network. TCP/IP for OS/2 provides other options. The following are two possibilities:

- ✔ **Frame Relay.** The OS/2 machine is configured with an IBM *Wide Area Connection* (WAC) card and IBM RouteXpander/2. *RouteXpander/2* is a general-purpose software router that can route IPX and SNA traffic as well as IP packets and also operates as a bridge for NETBIOS.

✔ **X.25.** The OS/2 machine is configured with a WAC card and IBM X.25 Xpander/2. The Extended Networking kit for OS/2 TCP/IP also is required.

A third possibility exists for users who already have an SNA network. AnyNet for OS/2 can be installed on the machines that run TCP/IP. *AnyNet* for OS/2 converts IP packets to SNA APPC packets so that they can pass over an SNA network. Another function of AnyNet for OS/2 is to encapsulate SNA APPC packets inside IP packets, so that they can pass over an IP router network.

In any of these cases, an OS/2 machine can be configured as a router with a wide area connection and one or more LAN adapters. Thus configured, it will route packets between any of its network interfaces. By default, the OS/2 TCP/IP protocol stack has routing enabled. In most cases, static routing is used, which means that each of the routing statements is manually configured. OS/2 TCP/IP also supports the RIP protocol for dynamic routing. The ROUTED program, included in the TCP/IP Base Kit, is an implementation of RIP.

A PC running OS/2 TCP/IP provides excellent performance as a router, but it cannot support the volume of traffic that a dedicated router can. Dedicated routers also have more routing functions. Most routers support OSPF, which is becoming more common than RIP as a dynamic routing protocol; and OS/2 TCP/IP does not support OSPF. On the other hand, using an OS/2 machine as a router has some advantages. An OS/2 machine does not have to be dedicated to routing, and can double as a print server or name server—and it's tough to beat the price.

Connecting with Unix Machines

A very common reason for installing TCP/IP is for interoperability with Unix machines, some of which support no other networking protocol. In addition to the basic TCP/IP applications already discussed, two more are of special importance when communicating with Unix: NFS and X Windows.

Network File Sharing

In general, Unix machines do not use NETBIOS. NETBIOS-based file servers on OS/2 or DOS cannot be accessed from a Unix machine. The file sharing protocol with the widest use in the Unix world is the *Network File System* (NFS). An NFS kit for OS/2 TCP/IP is available, and it includes both an NFS client and an NFS server. The client is used to access files on NFS servers, which may or may not be Unix machines. The server program enables local files to be accessed by NFS clients.

Interoperability with Unix is by no means the only reason for using NFS. NETBIOS is not routable, so it is clumsy to access NETBIOS-based servers on a WAN. NFS can be used instead. It is also possible for an OS/2 machine configured as an NFS server to use LAN requester or NetWare Requester to access a network drive, which is then shared with other TCP/IP hosts on the network using NFS.

The NFS protocol uses the *User Datagram Protocol* (UDP). UDP is an *unreliable* protocol, which may discourage some from using NFS for important data. Actually, NFS is quite reliable. First, OS/2 TCP/IP does perform checksums on all UDP packets to ensure data integrity. Not all versions of TCP/IP perform UDP checksums, and some permit UDP checksums to be disabled; but without this checksum UDP really is unreliable, and data integrity may be threatened. Second, although the UDP protocol does not provide for guaranteed delivery of packets, retransmission of missing data, and so on, NFS does.

TCP/IP packets are routable, and NETBIOS packets are not. The routing layer has a price: IP is not as fast as NETBIOS on a LAN, and NFS is not as fast as LAN Requester, although the performance difference is narrowing. The LAN Requester file system is a very close approximation of the native OS/2 file system, but in some respects NFS is not. For example, when a file is transferred from one OS/2 machine to another using NFS, the extended attributes of the file are not preserved.

One common access control mechanism for NFS is PCNFSD. PCNFSD support is included in the NFS kit, and both the server and the client can be configured to use it.

The X Windows System

The dominant graphical user interface for Unix is the X Windows system, and it is used in other operating environments as well. The IBM X Window Server Kit for OS/2 TCP/IP has been available for several years now. The latest version of this kit conforms to the X11 release 5 standard, and it is all implemented in 32-bit code. The Hummingbird company recently released an X Windows server for OS/2 TCP/IP, but they are relative newcomers to the OS/2 market.

An X Windows server is called a server because it provides presentation services to an X Windows client program. Despite the name, the X Windows server is always running on the user's desktop workstation when X is used, whereas X client programs may run on a remote machine. The X Windows server for OS/2 runs as a seamless part of the OS/2 desktop. For example, you can copy text or graphic data from an X window to the OS/2 Presentation Manager clipboard and paste it into a standard Presentation Manager application or vice versa. This integration of the X server into the Presentation Manager desktop has the side effect that the OS/2 desktop is the window manager for the OS/2 X server. This means that X applications that require a particular window manager, such as the OSF Motif window manager, will not work correctly with the OS/2 X Windows server. Arguably, such applications do not conform with X Window standards, but fortunately they are few in any case.

To display an X client application on an X server, the client application must be started, and the display variable for the client program must be set to point to the OS/2 X server. The way the display variable is set depends on the version of Unix and on the Unix command shell used. The client application is typically started using telnet or rexec.

Most of the OS/2 TCP/IP kits are quite compact, using very little disk space or memory. The X Windows server kit is not. It requires 11.7 megabytes of disk space. If you do not plan to use the X server to display double-byte character sets like Japanese, Korean, and Chinese, it is possible to reclaim some disk space by deleting the double-byte font files, which are each about 0.5 megabytes in size. These files are located in the \TCPIP\X11\MISC subdirectory and have the file extension PCF. Although the TCP/IP base will run with OS/2 version 3 in 4 megabytes of memory, the X Windows server must be run on a machine with 8 megabytes of memory. Until recently the X Windows server for OS/2 was somewhat slow in displaying text data, but this performance problem was fixed in the latest service update for the package, and it is now competitive even with dedicated X servers.

Client/Server Computing and OS/2 TCP/IP

IBM TCP/IP for OS/2 includes programming interfaces to enable the creation of client/ server applications. Many such applications, including order management, database, and interactive multimedia applications, have been created. Because TCP/IP is an open protocol, the server and the client workstations do not need to be the same kind of machine. Company, government, and college networks are usually a mix of various kinds of computers and operating systems. TCP/IP is a common denominator in such environments.

OS/2 provides an operating environment that is powerful, robust, and easy to use. TCP/IP for OS/2 adds a rich set of programming interfaces that makes OS/2 a client/ server environment to match or exceed any in the PC world.

The TCP/IP base contains REXX programming interfaces for sockets and FTP, to enable easy development of simple applications. To develop more complicated applications, you need the TCP/IP programming tool kit. Each of the available interfaces is reviewed in the following sections.

TCP/IP Sockets Programming

Sockets programming originates with Unix and is the standard way to create TCP/IP applications. OS/2 TCP/IP has full 32-bit support for all the standard sockets functions; the sockets code itself derives from Berkeley Unix. In most cases, socket functions in OS/2 are syntactically the same as they are in Unix, making it relatively easy to port TCP/IP applications to OS/2 from Unix.

Remote Procedure Call

Remote Procedure Call (RPC) is a higher level interface that is implemented using sockets. Using RPC, a program on a client machine can call a function on a server machine. During the call, data is sent or received, and *external data representation* (XDR) functions are provided so that the data is represented on the network in a standard way and is readable at both ends.

Two common versions of RPC are SUN RPC and OSF DCE. The OS/2 TCP/IP programming tool kit contains support for SUN RPC. IBM also sells DCE for OS/2. Both of these versions of RPC are 32-bit programming interfaces. DCE has a built-in security function called *Kerberos* to protect the data exchanged between client and server.

X Windows Programming and OSF/MOTIF

Client/server applications built using sockets and RPC tend to have some similarities. Often, the client half of the application, including much of the application logic, resides on the end user's workstation; and the server half runs on some central host, where most of the data resides. One disadvantage of this structure is that the client machines must be kept current with the latest level of application code. Moreover, client workstations may vary in the capabilities of the hardware and the installed operating system.

The X Windows formula is different. The server part of the application runs on the end-user machine, and it provides only the graphical user interface for the application. Application logic and application-specific programs do not need to reside on the end-user workstation. All X Windows servers support a common set of presentation services. The client end of the application contains all the application code. Application code does not need to be distributed, or in some cases ported, to dispersed and various end-user machines. The X graphical user interface is rich in function, and X servers have been implemented on many different platforms.

IBM sells an X Client kit and an OSF Motif kit to be used with TCP/IP for OS/2. These are programming tool kits, and the actual programming interfaces are built into OS/2 dynamic link libraries that ship with the kits. X Client and OSF Motif programming interfaces originate on Unix. In almost all cases, the OS/2 versions of the function calls are syntactically identical to the Unix versions, making the task of porting X Client and OSF Motif applications to OS/2 very easy.

SNMP Distributed Programming Interface

The SNMP *Distributed Programming Interface* (DPI) is in a special category. This interface is not used to create client/server applications, but to extend the management functions of the SNMP agent so that additional functions of the OS/2 machine can be remotely managed. DPI applications are SNMP subagents. Special subagents have been developed to manage the APPC interface, the OS/2 desktop, and other functions.

II

Enumeration

Exploring the Future of OS/2 TCP/IP

As the preceding sections have shown, IBM TCP/IP for OS/2 both provides a valuable collection of application programs and makes OS/2 a base for client/server applications as good as any in the PC world. However, TCP/IP continues to evolve, with new applications and connectivity options being added all the time. This overview of IBM TCP/IP for OS/2 concludes with a brief discussion of a few likely areas of enhancement.

ISDN Support

The *Integrated Services Digital Network* (ISDN) is a class of telephone service that provides a fast digital line for computer access. Standard phone lines and modems can communicate at speeds of up to 28800 bps—if the phone line and modem are very high quality. The typical ISDN service provides two channels, each capable of 64000 bps speeds. Telephone companies in the United States are starting to provide ISDN service very cheaply (the price is close to the cost of an ordinary telephone line), and phone companies in Europe have been providing ISDN service for some time. Unfortunately, little standardization exists in ISDN hardware.

The ISDN adapter cards available for PCs today simulate a com port. Many communications programs run over such cards unchanged, and this may be true of the Internet Connection kit, although the author has not had the opportunity to try it. When the ISDN adapter is used in this way, the SLIP or PPP protocols are used to encapsulate packets. There is also an Internet standard way of putting IP packets on ISDN connections, but it is not widely implemented. ISDN will be an important area of growth for computer networking.

Dynamic Host Configuration Protocol

The BOOTP protocol is a way of automatically configuring TCP/IP network interfaces when the computer is started, but it has limits. The *Dynamic Host Configuration Protocol* (DHCP) is gaining acceptance as a much more powerful replacement for BOOTP and is being promoted by Microsoft and many other companies as a solution to host configuration problems. IBM now has available a test (beta) version of the DHCP client for OS/2, and a product level version is in the works.

Asynchronous Transfer Mode

Asynchronous Transfer Mode (ATM) is a new standard for high-speed communication and routing for WANs. ATM will be widely used to connect routers on backbone networks, and it also has important advantages for multimedia applications. IBM and a number of other companies are betting heavily on ATM and plan to extend ATM communications to the desktop, using it as a transport for TCP/IP and other protocols.

Summary

A fundamental change is occurring in the way people use personal computers. Until recently, PCs were detached machines used primarily for word processing and games, and for those purposes the DOS operating system with a Windows graphical user interface was adequate. Now computers are used to access and exchange information over worldwide networks, and the largest and most important network is the Internet. Ever more powerful client/server applications are being created, and these are used not only in universities but also in homes, government agencies, and businesses of every size.

This process has only begun. As more and more people use the worldwide networks, and as they become dependent on client/server applications for more of what they do, the old DOS/Windows environment is becoming inadequate, lacking the power, robustness, and multitasking capabilities that are now needed. OS/2 has that power, robustness, and multitasking. It also has excellent Internet access programs built in. TCP/IP version 2 for OS/2 provides a complete application suite for client/server computing on local and wide area networks. OS/2 is not the only candidate to replace DOS-based Windows, but right now it is arguably the best—and OS/2 TCP/IP is a major reason why.

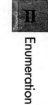

II

Enumeration

Chapter Snapshot

Over the last few years, the number of Unix workstations installed in businesses and institutions has grown dramatically. With very few exceptions, these workstations are all attached to larger networks via TCP/IP. In this chapter, you learn to do the following:

Connecting to Unix

"No man was ever wise by chance."

—*Seneca*

U nix and TCP/IP have been interrelated for almost as long as networks have existed. Today, Unix workstations can be found in many corporate offices and virtually every college campus. With the affordability and powerful capabilities of Intel-based personal computers, public domain and commercial implementations of Unix are even finding their way into households and small businesses. So what's the attraction?—Unix's powerful networking connectivity featuring TCP/IP.

History of Unix

As with many technological advances, the creation of the Unix operating system would not have been possible without federal support. In the 1960s, the *Department of Defense Advanced Research Projects Agency* (DARPA) wanted an information system capable of handling the many echelons of governmental security clearances. They contracted a team consisting of researchers from AT&T's Bell Labs, Honeywell, and General Electric. In addition, the project known as *Multiplexed Information and Computing Service* (Multics) also included scientists from the Massachusetts Institute of Technology. Multics was design-ed to be a time-sharing system that would enable many users to work concurrently and share their work with selected colleagues while preventing others similar access.

Unfortunately, because of all the features promised with Multics, the development of the project quickly fell behind schedule. In 1969, Bell Labs decided to pull out of the project, which may have further hindered the work on Multics but, as it turned out, was beneficial to the creation of Unix. One of the former members of the Multics project, Ken Thompson, decided to try and implement some of the Multics concepts on a used Digital Equipment (DEC) PDP-7. He and another Multics project refugee, Dennis Ritchie, began work on a new system, Unix. Unix was designed to be a much simpler system capable of running on smaller computers. Soon others added their own contributions as Unix was adopted throughout Bell Labs. In 1973, Ken Thompson decided to rewrite Unix, this time using a new language called C, created by Dennis Ritchie. The C language included many of the features expected in high-level programming languages and also incorporated the concept of portability. A *portable program* can be written on one machine, and then compiled and run on others. The concept of portability was later expanded to Unix itself, as Thompson and company began porting Unix to other computers.

While Unix was being developed at AT&T's Bell Labs, DARPA was involved in another project concerning communications. The results of this research led to the establishment of a network known as the *Advanced Research Project Agency Network* (ARPANET). The original goal of the network was to interconnect computers at research institutions as well as military installations. All information transmitted through this network was unclassified. The method by which information went from one computer to another was actually based on work done by Paul Baran of the Rand Corporation. Concerned by the potential breakdown in telephone communication resulting from a nuclear war, he worked on a concept that would disassemble electronic messages into small parts called *packets*. These packets could then be sent along the most efficient path to their destination, and when all the packets arrived, they could be reassembled into the original message.

As access to the ARPANET grew, so did the popularity of Unix. The University of California at Berkeley became the first institution to purchase Unix. Unlike many of today's operating systems, when Berkeley bought the operating system, they got everything, including source code. Several years later, *Berkeley Software Distribution* (BSD) Unix was born. Two graduate students, Bill Joy and Chuck Haley, began to add some of their own enhancements to the Unix code. This BSD flavor of Unix was then given to others. The modifications continued, supported by funding from DARPA.

DARPA recognized the popularity of Unix and, having already adopted TCP/IP as the communication protocol of the ARPANET network, decided that adding network support to Unix would encourage universities to accept TCP/IP. They accomplished this by first contracting Bolt, Beranek, and Newman, Inc., the creators of TCP/IP, to build TCP/IP for use with the Unix operating system. They then worked with Berkeley to make TCP/IP a part of the BSD Unix distribution. Berkeley did and, true to history, they added utilities to take advantage of the new connectivity. The electronic freedom to communicate and share information with others added to the general acceptance of Unix and lead to the large-scale expansion of networks like ARPANET into the Internet of today.

Installing TCP/IP

Most BSD-based implementations of Unix already include TCP/IP networking support as part of the operating system. Usually, when you first boot a new Unix workstation, a program runs asking if the workstation is to be used on a network. If you answer yes, the program prompts you for information it needs to get all the networking features correctly configured. At times, however, your workstation may not initially be installed on a network, or you may need to change the configuration. This section describes the configuration files and programs that involve networking your Unix workstation.

Initial Planning

Before installing a network that includes Unix workstations, you must consider several things. Often, if you are adding a new workstation to a preexisting network, the network administrator can already provide you with most of the information you need.

IP Addresses and Host Names

Every machine on a TCP/IP network must have its own *Internet Protocol* (IP) address, and that address must be unique. Similarly, every machine should have its own name. This name is used to differentiate one machine from another within your network. Chapter 3, "Host Names and Internet Addressing," covers these two topics in detail.

Making a New Kernel

The Unix *kernel*, or operating system, is a little different from most other operating systems. The kernel knows about every supported piece of hardware and how to use it. Fortunately, many types of hardware, such as hard disks or tape drives, conform to a standard already supported by the kernel, but sometimes this is not the case. If you were adding a new device to an MS-DOS personal computer, all you would need to do is run the supplied program or include the new device driver in the system's CONFIG.SYS file. Not so with Unix workstations. If you want to add a new device to a Unix workstation not already supported by the kernel, you have to create a new one. This is not as bad as it sounds and usually the documentation that accompanies the new device includes all the steps necessary to install it.

The steps for creating a new kernel depend on whether your version of Unix is based on Berkeley's BSD 4.3 (soon 4.4) or Novell's (formerly AT&T's) System V Release 4. If you are uncertain which type you have, check your documentation or contact the vendor from which you purchased your workstation. Typically, BSD versions already include support for TCP/IP networking, and most System V versions install the TCP/IP software as part of the initial boot-up installation program.

BSD Kernel Configuration

When you create a new kernel, what you are actually doing is compiling a series of C language programs. Normally, this requires that you edit a number of files, which could quickly become tedious. Fortunately, BSD versions of Unix include a program called /etc/config that makes the changes for you. To determine what changes are necessary, /etc/config reads a configuration file that is usually stored in the /usr/sys/conf directory.

If the kernel has never been modified, there is a basic configuration file called GENERIC. This file was used to create the kernel your workstation is currently running. Typically, when creating a new configuration file, give it the same name you selected for your machine.

The easiest thing to do when creating a new configuration file is to copy one that already exists, as in the following example:

```
# cd /usr/sys/conf
# cp GENERIC JUPITER
# chmod u+w JUPITER
```

A new kernel file, JUPITER, is created by copying one that already includes all the devices supported by the system.

It is best to copy the configuration file used to create the most recent version of the kernel. This ensures that all the changes made since the initial installation of the workstation are included.

Several statements need to be included in the kernel configuration file for the workstation to be networked. Most BSD Unix workstations come preconfigured for use in TCP/IP-based networks, so the configuration file may already include these options:

```
options         INET

pseudo-device   loop
pseudo-device   ether
pseudo-device   pty

device          qe0 at uba0 csr 0174440 vector qeintr
device          le0 at SBus slot 0 csr 0xc00000 pri 5
```

INET is a mandatory entry. By including this option, the kernel supports networking protocols. Specific hardware requirements however, are not required until later.

Pseudo devices are device drivers without corresponding pieces of hardware. The pseudo-device loop creates a loopback network device. The purpose of this device is covered later. The *ether pseudo-device* provides support for Ethernet connectivity. *Ethernet* is a low-level networking scheme through which most TCP/IP networks run. *Pty pseudo devices* enable users to connect through the network as if they had a direct terminal connected to the Unix workstation.

The last two lines in the preceding listing are the configuration information about the actual network device. Note there is some variance in the information. The first device is a Digital Q-Bus network adapter used in a MicroVAX II. The second entry is a LANCE Ethernet adapter commonly installed in most Sun Sparcstations. Documentation for newly installed network interfaces includes specific information on how to configure devices.

Note that these statements are not the only ones that appear in the configuration file. Entries for hard disk and tape controllers, keyboards, file system storage methods like *Network File System* (NFS) and *Remote File System* (RFS), and miscellaneous hardware devices also are included by the manufacturer.

After the configuration file is edited, the kernel files can be modified appropriately. The program that handles this is /etc/config. The following example shows the syntax for using /etc/config:

```
# /etc/config JUPITER
```

/etc/config reads the configuration file and creates a new directory (if it doesn't already exist) in /usr/sys. This directory uses the same name as the configuration file. C language files necessary for creating the kernel are then copied into this directory for compilation. The kernel is created using a program called /bin/make. /bin/make reads its own configuration file (created by /etc/config) and begins compiling the code. Assuming that no errors occur, a new file, vmunix, is created. This is the new kernel program, as shown in the following example:

```
# cd /usr/sys/JUPITER
# make
   ... (Actual Compile Commands) ...
# ls vmunix
vmunix*
#
```

All that remains is to install it. BSD Unix expects the kernel file to be in the root directory. It's a good idea to back up the original kernel program first in case problems occur with the new kernel. After this is done, the new kernel can be copied to the root directory and is ready for testing:

```
# mv /vmunix /vmunix.old
# cp /usr/sys/JUPITER/vmunix /vmunix
```

System V Kernel Configuration

Unlike the BSD kernel that comes preconfigured for networking, System V kernels typically come configured with the bare minimum. When the system is first booted, a program is run that prompts you to enter information about which options you want to include. After this process is complete, a new kernel is created. This same program also is used later when devices are added or changed. The name of this configuration program varies among vendors; consult your documentation for details. As mentioned previously, before installing a new kernel, back up the old one first.

Configuring the Network Interface

Even though the device drivers needed for networking are loaded when the Unix workstation kernel is booted, the network interface still needs to be configured. The utility ifconfig provides this function. With ifconfig you can turn the interface on or off, assign an IP address to the interface, or define the network subnet mask and broadcast address.

The common usage of ifconfig is as follows:

```
ifconfig interface address netmask address broadcast address
```

The `interface` is the network device defined in the kernel. If you want to configure multiple network devices, you need to use ifconfig once for each interface. To apply a setting to every network interface, you can replace the interface name with the -a flag instead.

The `address` is the IP address of the workstation. You can either supply the numerical IP address or enter the host or machine name. If you choose the latter, ifconfig consults the /etc/hosts file to extract the machine's IP address. The /etc/hosts file is discussed later.

`netmask` refers to the subnet mask. Large networks are broken into smaller networks or subnetworks. The subnet mask is a 32-bit number that enables you to isolate only those machines on your subnet. If the bit is one, that bit corresponds to the network address. Otherwise, the bit is part of the host machine's address on the subnet. This entry can be entered in one of the following three ways:

✔ A hexadecimal number starting with 0x

✔ An IP address

✔ A network name corresponding to an entry in /etc/networks

The `broadcast address` is the address used to send messages to every machine on the subnet. Typically, the host portion of the broadcast address is 255.

In the following example, the Lance Ethernet adapter, `le0`, is being configured on a workstation named jupiter. This machine is on a Class C network with a domain IP address of 134.68.7. Broadcast messages are read if the message is sent to IP address 134.68.7.255.

```
ifconfig le0 jupiter netmask 255.255.255.0 broadcast 134.68.7.255
```

To see what the current setting of an interface is, use ifconfig *interface*:

```
# ifconfig le0
le0: flags=63<UP,BROADCAST,NOTRAILERS,RUNNING>
    inet 134.68.7.8 netmask ffffff00 broadcast 134.68.7.255
    ether 8:0:20:19:e3:bc
```

The last line displays the Ethernet address of interface le0. Unlike the IP address of the interface, the Ethernet address is set by the manufacturer of the interface and cannot be changed. The first three sets of numbers (8:0:20) indicate which manufacturer made the interface. In this case, it was Sun Microsystems. The remaining sets of numbers (19:e3:bc) form an internal number used by the manufacturer. The Ethernet address must be unique.

One of the first flags displayed is UP. With ifconfig, you can also enable or disable the interface:

```
# ifconfig interface down
# ifconfig interface up
```

II

Enumeration

Standard Networking Configuration Files

Several configuration files also provide networking information. Two have already been mentioned, /etc/hosts and /etc/networks. Others include /etc/ethers, /etc/services, and /etc/protocols. Each of these files consists of one entry per line. All text that follows the # is ignored as comments.

/etc/hosts

/etc/hosts is a database of networked machine names and their corresponding IP addresses. This file is consulted by a number of programs including ifconfig and ping, which is discussed later. An example of an /etc/hosts file follows:

```
#
# Host Configuration File
#
127.0.0.1          localhost
#
# New Riders Publishing Accounting Department Host Addresses
#
134.68.7.1     earth
```

continues

```
134.68.7.2      venus
134.68.7.3      mercury
134.68.7.4      mars
134.68.7.5      saturn
134.68.7.6      neptune
134.68.7.7      uranus
134.68.7.8      jupiter
134.68.7.9      pluto
134.68.7.100         acct-gw
```

In addition to the machines found on the network, there is an entry for `localhost`.
127.0.0.1 is a special address referred to as a *loopback address*. This address can be used to
test the network settings installed in the kernel.

/etc/ethers

Like /etc/hosts, /etc/ethers is a database of machine names and addresses. The difference is that this file includes Ethernet addresses. An example of an /etc/ethers file
follows:

```
#
# New Riders Publishing Accounting Department Ethernet Addresses
#
8:0:20:23:3a:45     earth
8:0:20:78:36:19     venus
8:0:20:d4:62:7b     mercury
8:0:20:37:97:31     mars
8:0:20:40:e5:c9     saturn
8:0:20:1f:53:68     uranus
8:0:20:52:70:83     neptune
8:0:20:19:e3:bc     jupiter
8:0:20:81:88:3f     pluto
0:0:c:0:41:ba           acct-gw
```

/etc/networks

/etc/networks is an optional file that associates names with subnet mask values or domain
network addresses. For larger networks with several subnets, using names makes it easier
to remember which IP addresses and subnet masks are defined for which networks. An
example of an /etc/networks file follows:

```
#
# New Riders Publishing Accounting Dept. Subnet Masks
#
acct.nrp.com    134.68.7
nrp-acct-mask   255.255.255.0
```

In this example, only one netmask for a Class C network is defined.

/etc/protocols

A number of protocols make up the TCP/IP suite. When a packet arrives, the host machine first checks to see if the packet is meant for it. If so, the machine next checks to see which upper level protocol can process it further. The machine determines this by extracting a protocol number from the packet and comparing it to the entries in /etc/protocols:

```
#
# Internet (IP) protocols
#
ip      0       IP      # internet protocol, pseudo protocol number
icmp    1       ICMP            # internet control message protocol
igmp    2       IGMP            # internet group multicast protocol
ggp     3       GGP             # gateway-gateway protocol
tcp     6       TCP             # transmission control protocol
pup     12      PUP             # PARC universal packet protocol
udp     17      UDP             # user datagram protocol
```

The first field is the official protocol name followed by the protocol number. The third field is an alias for the protocol.

/etc/services

One of the popular networking features of Unix is the capability to run a program on one machine and have information or services provided on another. This forms the basis of client/server computing. The client machine informs the server of which service it wants to access by including a port number within the packet requesting the service. After processing the packet, the server routes the request to the process that handles that port.

This assumes that the server uses the same port numbers as the client. That's the purpose of /etc/services. This file includes the process name along with the port and protocol associated with it:

```
#
# Network services, Internet style
#
tcpmux          1/tcp                   # rfc-1078
echo            7/tcp
echo            7/udp
systat          11/tcp                  users
daytime         13/tcp
daytime         13/udp
netstat         15/tcp
chargen         19/tcp                  ttytst source
```

continues

```
chargen          19/udp              ttytst source
ftp-data         20/tcp
ftp              21/tcp
telnet           23/tcp
smtp             25/tcp              mail
time             37/tcp              timserver
time             37/udp              timserver
name             42/udp              nameserver
whois            43/tcp              nickname       # usually to sri-nic
domain           53/udp
domain           53/tcp
hostnames        101/tcp             hostname       # usually to sri-nic
#
# Host specific functions
#
tftp             69/udp
rje              77/tcp
finger           79/tcp
link             87/tcp              ttylink
supdup           95/tcp
iso-tsap         102/tcp
x400             103/tcp             # ISO Mail
x400-snd         104/tcp
csnet-ns         105/tcp
pop-2            109/tcp             # Post Office
uucp-path        117/tcp
nntp             119/tcp             usenet         # Network News Transfer
ntp              123/tcp                            # Network Time Protocol
NeWS             144/tcp             news           # Window System
#
# Unix specific services
#
# these are NOT officially assigned
#
exec             512/tcp
login            513/tcp
shell            514/tcp             cmd            # no passwords used
printer          515/tcp             spooler        # line printer spooler
courier          530/tcp             rpc            # experimental
uucp             540/tcp             uucpd          # uucp daemon
biff             512/udp             comsat
who              513/udp             whod
syslog           514/udp
talk             517/udp
```

```
route          520/udp        router routed
new-rwho       550/udp        new-who        # experimental
rmonitor       560/udp        rmonitord      # experimental
monitor        561/udp                       # experimental
pcserver       600/tcp                       # ECD Integrated PC board srvr
ingreslock     1524/tcp
```

As you can see, a large number of network resources are available. You may notice that some process names have several entries. This is because in some cases, different protocols can be used to request the same service. Sometimes ports are also referred to as sockets even though sockets typically include the IP address in addition to the port number.

Starting the Internet Daemon

A number of client/server applications are included in Unix. Some of these programs, called *daemons*, are running all the time, but most are not. If you were to continuously run every daemon, you would have little computer resources left to do anything else. So how do these daemons service requests?

A special daemon, known as the *internet daemon* or *inetd*, "listens" to many ports (mentioned earlier) for incoming service requests. If a request is received, inetd starts the appropriate daemon to handle it. After the service is provided, inetd shuts down the daemon. inetd knows which daemons it supports by reading /etc/inetd.conf when it is initially started, typically when the workstation boots.

/etc/inetd.conf contains a number of fields for each entry. Like the other files discussed, text following # is ignored as comments. The format is as follows:

```
service-name  socket-type  proto  wait-status  user  server-pathname
args
```

service-name is the name of the service listed in /etc/services.

socket-type describes what sort of socket the service uses. Valid entries include stream, dgram (datagram), raw, and rdm (reliably delivered message).

When installing a new service entry in /etc/inetd.conf, the documentation for the software includes the /etc/inetd.conf entry that needs to be added.

proto is the protocol used by this service. Valid protocols include those listed in /etc/protocols.

`wait-status` is kind of like a traffic cop for that service. If the status is set to *wait*, inetd must wait until the server releases the socket before listening for another request for that server. For *no-wait* status servers, inetd can continue to listen for more server requests without interruption. Usually, *stream* socket servers don't require inetd to wait, but many *dgram* servers do.

`user` is the name of the user who owns the server process when it runs. The effective permissions of the server are those assigned to that user.

`server-pathname` is the actual name of the server program to be run. To ensure that the correct program is selected, the full path is included with the name. Some entries have *internal* in the field instead. In these cases, inetd itself services the request because it would be more efficient than to start a separate daemon.

`args` include any command-line arguments needed to process the request correctly. At a minimum, the command name is entered in this field.

Unless you add a new service or disable a currently active one (putting # at the beginning of the entry), you shouldn't need to edit /etc/inetd.conf. If you do, you need to restart inetd to activate your changes. The following shows the commands needed to restart inetd. Note that the # character denotes the root command prompt.

```
# ps -acx ¦ grep inetd
  131 ? IW    0:04 inetd
# kill -HUP 131
```

A sample listing of /etc/inetd.conf follows. You may notice that some services have two entries. As noted when discussing /etc/services, some services can be requested through different protocols.

```
#
# inetd.conf - Configuration file of inetd
#
# Ftp and telnet are standard Internet services.
#
ftp     stream    tcp    nowait    root    /usr/etc/in.ftpd      in.ftpd -l
telnet  stream    tcp    nowait    root    /usr/etc/in.telnetd   in.telnetd
#
# Tnamed serves the obolete IEN-116 name server protocol.
#
name    dgram   udp   wait    root    /usr/etc/in.tnamed            in.tnamed
#
# Shell, login, exec, comsat and talk are BSD protocols.
#
shell   stream    tcp    nowait    root    /usr/etc/in.rshd      in.rshd
```

```
login   stream        tcp     nowait      root      /usr/etc/in.rlogind    in.rlogind
exec   stream        tcp     nowait      root      /usr/etc/in.rexecd     in.rexecd
comsat       dgram        udp         wait      root   /usr/etc/in.comsat      in.comsat
talk  dgram   udp    wait       root       /usr/etc/in.talkd      in.talkd
#
# Run as user "uucp" if you don't want uucpd's wtmp entries.
#
uucp   stream        tcp  nowait      root     /usr/etc/in.uucpd     in.uucpd
#
# Tftp service is provided primarily for booting.  Most sites run this
# only on machines acting as "boot servers."
#
#tftp  dgram   udp     wait    root    /usr/etc/in.tftpd        in.tftpd -s /tftpboot
#
# Finger, systat and netstat give out user information which may be
# valuable to potential "system crackers."  Many sites choose to disable
# some or all of these services to improve security.
#
finger       stream       tcp     nowait      nobody      /usr/etc/in.fingerd in.fingerd
#systat       stream       tcp     nowait      root      /usr/bin/ps         ps -auwwx
#netstat      stream       tcp     nowait      root      /usr/ucb/netstat    netstat -f inet
#
# Time service is used for clock synchronization.
#
time   stream    tcp     nowait       root    internal
time   dgram     udp     wait         root    internal
#
# Echo, discard, daytime, and chargen are used primarily for testing.
#
echo   stream    tcp     nowait      root    internal
echo   dgram     udp     wait        root    internal
discard      stream      tcp     nowait    root    internal
discard      dgram       udp     wait      root    internal
daytime      stream      tcp     nowait    root    internal
daytime      dgram       udp     wait      root    internal
chargen      stream      tcp     nowait    root    internal
chargen      dgram       udp     wait      root    internal
#
#
# RPC services syntax:
# <rpc_prog>/<vers> <socket_type> rpc/<proto> <flags> <user> <pathname> <args>
#
```

continues

```
# The mount server is usually started in /etc/rc.local only on machines that
# are NFS servers.  It can be run by inetd as well.
#
#mountd/1      dgram      rpc/udp      wait   root    /usr/etc/rpc.mountd    rpc.mountd
#
# The rexd server provides only minimal authentication and is often not run
# by sites concerned about security.
#
#rexd/1        stream     rpc/tcp      wait   root    /usr/etc/rpc.rexd      rpc.rexd
#
# Ypupdated is run by sites that support NIS updating.
#
#ypupdated/1   stream     rpc/tcp      wait   root    /usr/etc/rpc.ypupdated rpc.ypupdated
#
# Rquotad serves UFS disk quotas to NFS clients.
#
rquotad/1      dgram      rpc/udp      wait   root    /usr/etc/rpc.rquotad   rpc.rquotad
#
# Rstatd is used by programs such as perfmeter.
#
rstatd/2-4     dgram      rpc/udp      wait   root    /usr/etc/rpc.rstatd    rpc.rstatd
#
# The rusers service gives out user information. Sites concerned
# with security may choose to disable it.
#
rusersd/1-2    dgram      rpc/udp      wait   root    /usr/etc/rpc.rusersd   rpc.rusersd
#
# The spray server is used primarily for testing.
#
sprayd/1       dgram      rpc/udp      wait   root    /usr/etc/rpc.sprayd    rpc.sprayd
#
# The rwall server lets anyone on the network bother everyone on your machine.
#
walld/1        dgram      rpc/udp      wait   root    /usr/etc/rpc.rwalld    rpc.rwalld
#
```

Connecting to Larger Networks

If your network is isolated, you should have no difficulty communicating with other hosts. But if your network is connected to a larger one like the Internet, you need to configure your workstation to communicate through a special machine known as a *gateway* to be able to access machines outside your local network.

/etc/routed, which is run during boot up, is a special program that handles communication to other machines through a gateway. routed learns about the gateway it should use by using /usr/etc/route to define it. The following example demonstrates the use of the /usr/etc/route commands. Note that # denotes the root command prompt.

```
# route -f add default acct-gw
```

In the preceding example, the routing table is erased through the -f option. A new default route, acct-gw, is then established. In large organizations, you can minimize confusion by selecting the same host number for every network interface used by the gateway. From the sample /etc/hosts file, acct-gw has an IP address of 134.68.7.100. If the gateway also connects to network 134.68.6, then the interface on that network should use 134.68.6.100.

To view the currently configured routes, you can use the netstat command, as follows:

```
# netstat -r
Routing tables
Destination          Gateway           Flags    Refcnt Use
Interface
localhost            localhost         UH       3      1332
lo0
default              acct-gw           UG       5      168358
le0
134.68.7.0           jupiter           U        11     42227
le0
```

Netstat is discussed again later in this chapter.

Advanced Networking Features

As Unix evolved, new features were added to further networking capabilities. By incorporating them, you can install workstations that can act as servers to provide access to shared disk storage, network configuration files, and domain name databases. Although some implementations of Unix may not include any or some of these enhancements, it's worth mentioning them here.

Network Information Services

One of the most difficult tasks that faces network administrators is keeping networking information consistent on every host machine on a network. For example, if you were to add a new host to your network, you would have to edit /etc/hosts on every machine already on the network. By using *Network Information Services* (NIS), this problem can be greatly minimized. Formerly known as *Yellow Pages*, NIS enables one machine to maintain configuration files such as /etc/passwd and /etc/hosts for all other machines on your network. Now, you only need to make changes on one machine, and those changes take effect almost immediately.

Domain Name Services

For networks not connected to larger ones such as the Internet, NIS is a good way to maintain a database of all reachable machines. However, with networks as large as the Internet, thousands of machines are interconnected, and changes occur daily. There is no way you could keep track of all the changes. This is where *Domain Name Service* (DNS) servers help out. Typically, when you request a domain name from NIC, you create a DNS server. The purpose of this server is twofold. It maintains a database of all machines on your network as well as forwards queries for addresses of machines it does not know about. Client machines automatically connect to the name server through the resolve daemon when they need addresses. The whole process is transparent to the end user. For more information on DNS, see Chapter 8, "Domain Name System."

Network File System

Storage of user files can be another source of frustration for network administrators. With many machines on a network, a user can have files in numerous home directories. Backups become increasingly complex, not to mention inconsistent duplicates of information can quickly spread. A solution to this problem is to have a central server store all the users' files no matter to which network machine they connect. The *Network File System* (NFS) provides just that feature. To the client machines, the server's shared directories appear to be on the local machine. Only one machine needs to be backed up, and users have all their files available to them. For more information on NFS, see Chapter 3, "Host Names and Internet Addressing."

Testing the Network Setup

Now that the kernel and all the network files have been configured, it's time to test the network. It's important to be systematic when doing this sort of troubleshooting. Otherwise, a simple problem can be confusing and difficult to isolate. Fortunately, Unix provides a couple of utilities for this purpose.

ping

Similar to the sonar "pings" used by naval vessels to determine the location of submarines, the Unix command *ping* checks to see if other machines on the network are reachable. The first goal is to check the networking capability of the kernel. This is accomplished by "pinging" the loopback interface, localhost:

```
# ping localhost
localhost is alive
```

Although no physical hardware corresponds to the loopback interface lo, when a request to localhost is sent, the kernel processes the request without sending anything out through the network. If the kernel is not properly configured for networking, you might see a message like this instead:

```
# ping localhost
No answer from localhost
```

Assuming that the network portion of the kernel works, you can now check to see if you can ping your machine by either its IP address or its host name as listed in /etc/hosts, as in the following example:

```
# ping jupiter
jupiter is alive
```

If ping fails to reach your machine through the network, check to see that the interface is set up correctly. To do this, use the ifconfig command discussed earlier. Modify the interface configuration if it is incorrect and try again. If it continues to fail, check the machine's physical connection to the network.

When you can ping your machine, it's time to try reaching another one. As before, use the name of a machine found in /etc/hosts. Typically, if you can ping your machine, you should have no difficulty pinging another one. At this point, more detailed information also can be obtained. You can have ping attempt to reach another host once every second and display statistics. This is done by adding the -s option, as in the following example:

```
# ping -s saturn 64 5
PING saturn: 64 data bytes
72 bytes from saturn (134.68.7.5): icmp_seq=0. time=1. ms
72 bytes from saturn (134.68.7.5): icmp_seq=1. time=1. ms
72 bytes from saturn (134.68.7.5): icmp_seq=2. time=1. ms
72 bytes from saturn (134.68.7.5): icmp_seq=3. time=1. ms
72 bytes from saturn (134.68.7.5): icmp_seq=4. time=1. ms
----saturn PING Statistics----
5 packets transmitted, 5 packets received, 0% packet loss
round-trip (ms)  min/avg/max = 1/1/1
```

In this example, several arguments are entered after the hostname. 64 is the amount of data, in bytes, sent to saturn, and 5 is the number of times the data is sent to saturn. Without this last option, ping continues to transmit until Ctrl + C is pressed. For each attempt, ping displays the sequence number and amount of time in milliseconds it took the packet to get to the destination and back. After all repetitions are completed, a summary is included.

On some versions of Unix, the default option for ping is equivalent to ping -s.

netstat

After you know that the workstation can communicate through the network, you need to know how well it is communicating. *netstat* is a utility designed to display statistics about each workstation's network interfaces. The amount of information displayed depends on what command-line options are included. To get a one-line entry per interface summary, you can use the -i option, as follows:

```
#netstat -i
Name  Mtu   Net/Dest     Address      Ipkts   Ierrs Opkts  Oerrs Collis Queue
le0   1500  acct.nrp.com jupiter      695753  5     578323 0     1298   0
lo0   1536  loopback     localhost    68723   0     68723  0     0      0
```

Even though two interfaces are displayed, lo, the loopback interface, doesn't provide any useful information because no network traffic travels through it. The three fields you should be most concerned with are Queue, Ierrs, and Oerrs. If Queue is a non-zero number, then packets can't be transmitted out. This is symptomatic of a network cabling problem. Ierrs (Incoming packet errors) and Oerrs (Output packet errors) need not be zero, but the value should be very low. Values greater than 100 may indicate a problem such as numerous collisions of the network. Studying the percentage loss and round-trip time statistics generated by ping -s may assist in isolating this sort of problem.

On occasion, you may want to have detailed statistics on your workstation's network communication. This can be provided by using netstat -s, as the following code illustrates:

```
# netstat -s
udp:
        0 incomplete headers
        0 bad data length fields
        0 bad checksums
        0 socket overflows
tcp:
    345743 packets sent
        230978 data packets (24536791 bytes)
        1646 data packets (429969 bytes) retransmitted
        49946 ack-only packets (34452 delayed)
        25 URG only packets
        148 window probe packets
        50131 window update packets
        12869 control packets
    433439 packets received
        220994 acks (for 24541178 bytes)
        9023 duplicate acks
        0 acks for unsent data
        354661 packets (167477101 bytes) received in-sequence
        3248 completely duplicate packets (158506 bytes)
```

```
            6 packets with some dup. data (731 bytes duped)
            5289 out-of-order packets (74066 bytes)
            3 packets (1 byte) of data after window
            1 window probe
            1472 window update packets
            2 packets received after close
            0 discarded for bad checksums
            2 discarded for bad header offset fields
            0 discarded because packet too short
        5273 connection requests
        1580 connection accepts
        6138 connections established (including accepts)
        6878 connections closed (including 35 drops)
        732 embryonic connections dropped
        214259 segments updated rtt (of 220663 attempts)
        2886 retransmit timeouts
            0 connections dropped by rexmit timeout
        14 persist timeouts
        1393 keepalive timeouts
            119 keepalive probes sent
            420 connections dropped by keepalive
icmp:
        253 calls to icmp_error
        0 errors not generated 'cuz old message too short
        0 errors not generated 'cuz old message was icmp
        Output histogram:
            echo reply: 844
            destination unreachable: 253
            address mask reply: 8
        0 messages with bad code fields
        0 messages < minimum length
        0 bad checksums
        0 messages with bad length
        Input histogram:
            echo reply: 30107
            destination unreachable: 338
            source quench: 1
            echo: 844
            time exceeded: 7
            address mask request: 8
        852 message responses generated
ip:
        766386 total packets received
```

continues

```
0 bad header checksums
0 with size smaller than minimum
0 with data size < data length
0 with header length < data size
0 with data length < header length
2119 fragments received
0 fragments dropped (dup or out of space)
0 fragments dropped after timeout
0 packets forwarded
1 packet not forwardable
0 redirects sent
0 ip input queue drops
```

Using the Network

When your workstation is networked and configured correctly, you can take advantage of a number of features. From your workstation, you can run programs on other workstations, transfer files among them, and even communicate directly with other users no matter how physically far away they are. This section briefly describes several of these utilities.

Remote Logins

In the early days of Unix, you had to have access to a terminal directly connected to the Unix machine to use it. The only remote computing possible required a modem and telephone access. Networks changed everything. Now, you connect to any network machine (assuming that you have an account on it) and can work on distant machines at a much faster rate. The program that provides this access is called *telnet*.

To connect to another machine, you simply include the address of the machine you want to use. If the machine is installed on your network, you can use the name of the machine as listed in /etc/hosts. Otherwise, you have to enter either the machine's fully qualified domain name or IP address:

```
% telnet saturn.acct.nrp.com
Trying 134.68.7.5 ...
Connected to saturn.acct.nrp.com
Escape character is '^]'.
SunOS Unix (saturn)
login: scott
password:
Last login: Mon Sep 12 10:34:24 from mars
SunOS Release 4.1.3 (SATURN) #1 Mon Aug 15 14:44:35 EST 1994
```

```
You have new mail
Mon Sep 12 11:55:40 EST 1994
%
```

The first thing telnet does is try and convert the entry on the command line to an IP address. /etc/hosts is checked for a match, and if it is not found there, telnet queries the DNS server, if available. Telnet discovers that 134.68.7.5 corresponds to saturn and attempts to connect to it. If telnet can connect to that address, telnet displays a message indicating success and prompts you to enter your login name and password. Notice that the password you type in is not displayed. This is to prevent someone from looking over your shoulder and stealing your password. Assuming that everything is correct, you are notified of when you last logged in and from where, and if mail has arrived since the last time you logged in. Now you can work on the remote machine.

Suppose that after you start telnet, you realize that you selected the wrong machine. If you have a valid account on that machine, you can log in then immediately log out, or you can wait for the login process to time out (60 seconds). Telnet provides better ways to end your login session.

When at the login prompt, you can press Ctrl+D. This is the control character Unix uses to mean End of File or <EOF>. When the login process encounters an <EOF>, it closes the session. This is demonstrated in the following code. Note that Ctrl+D is pressed at the login prompt.

```
% telnet mars
Trying 134.68.7.5 ...
Connected to mars.
Escape character is '^]'.
SunOS Unix (mars)
login: Connection closed by foreign host.
% telnet saturn
```

By entering Ctrl+D, the telnet session is immediately closed, and you can start another one from the Unix prompt. Another way to accomplish the same thing is to use the escape sequence to get to the telnet command prompt. Notice that telnet tells you what this sequence is as soon as you connect to the remote machine. By using Ctrl+], you can close the connection and start again. This is demonstrated in the following:

```
% telnet mars
Trying 134.68.7.4.
Escape character is '^]'.
SunOS Unix (mars)
login:
telnet> close
Connection closed.
% telnet saturn
```

II

Enumeration

Another time that this feature comes in handy is when the program you are running has locked your session. By using Ctrl+], you can close the session; then use telnet to reconnect to the remote machine. Only do this as a last resort.

Although used primarily for running remote login sessions, you also can use telnet to directly connect to other remote services. Standard port numbers are listed in /etc/ services. To connect to a specific port, enter the port number as a second argument to telnet, as shown in the following example:

```
% telnet saturn 23
Trying 134.68.7.5 ...
Connected to saturn.
Escape character is '^]'.
SunOS Unix (saturn)
login:
```

In the preceding example, telnet is used to connect to port 23 of saturn. By searching /etc/services, port 23 corresponds to telnet. This is the same port that the telnet program uses by default.

When using telnet to connect to other ports, you must know what information you need to supply to get the desired results. Some ports may provide online help, but many do not. It is best to use Unix utility programs to extract service information instead of trying to do it manually. The only time you should use telnet to connect to a port is if a special program uses its own port for remote user access. *Multi User Dungeon* (MUD) games often work this way.

Transferring Files

Files can be transferred from one machine to another through the *File Transfer Protocol* (ftp) program or anonymous ftp. For more information on this, see Chapter 3, "Host Names and Internet Addressing."

Using the Remote Commands

In addition to telnet and ftp, a common set of powerful networking utilities is included with virtually every implementation of Unix. These Unix-specific commands enable you to run programs to log into remote machines, copy files back and forth through the network, and even provide information about which users are currently logged into a networked machine. These tools are commonly referred to as *remote* or *r commands* because each command starts with the letter *r*.

/etc/hosts.equiv and rhosts files

One of the most popular features of the r commands is that they can be configured so you do not need to enter your password when using them. This assumes a level of trust. All that is required is an entry in either /etc/hosts.equiv or a rhosts file in the user's home directory.

The entries in /etc/hosts.equiv are names of machines and users that are trusted. Trusted machines are typically on the same network and administered by the same group. In addition, these network administrators may have accounts on multiple machines and set them up so that they could log in from anywhere without needing to enter their passwords. A sample /etc/hosts.equiv file follows:

```
#
# hosts.equiv file for jupiter.acct.nrp.com
#
saturn
mars-jon
mercury+jon
-pluto
+ scott
```

Not only can you grant free access through /etc/hosts.equiv, but you also can deny it. The characters + and - provide this service, respectively. In the sample /etc/hosts.equiv file presented earlier, every user on saturn is granted free access; the same goes for mars, except for jon. However, only jon is granted free access from mercury. pluto is not a trusted host, so no one is granted free access. Finally, scott is granted free access to this machine, no matter which machine he is using remotely.

This free access extends beyond the local account bearing the same name. A user can gain access to any account, except for root. In the last entry, anyone with the user name *scott* on any machine can gain free access to saturn.

In addition, users can define their own access list. By creating a file called rhosts in their home directories, they can grant access to their account to any or all users on a particular remote host. All that they need to include is the remote machine and user login name:

```
#
# User scott's .rhosts file
#
saturn
mercury
mars scott
mars -jon
venus orr
```

With this rhosts in scott's home directory, anyone can freely access scott's account from machines saturn and mercury. scott also can gain password-free access from mars, but jon is denied the same privilege. scott would also like to be granted free access from venus on which his user name is orr.

When a user on a remote machine attempts to use an r command, the daemon that services that r command searches /etc/hosts.equiv to determine if the user of the remote machine is granted free access. Most of the r commands require that the user name be the same on both the local and remote machine. If access cannot be granted through /etc/hosts.equiv, the user's home directory is checked for the existence of a rhosts file. This file also is searched to determine if free access should be granted.

In the early days of networking, security wasn't a major concern. Networking encouraged the sharing of information, and a level of trust was associated with users and machines on a local network. That was, of course, until some users took advantage of the laxity of security and compromised many systems. Probably the most significant event was the Internet Worm incident of 1988. In less than a day, this specialized program completely shut down much of the Internet. One of the security holes it exploited was the open access granted through use of /etc/hosts.equiv and user rhosts files.

Today, security is taken much more seriously. Many sites do not even allow /etc/ hosts.equiv and rhosts files. Unfortunately, some of the popular r commands depend on the existence of at least one of these files to function.

Remote Login

The *rlogin* utility is very similar to telnet. Both enable you to log in to a remote machine. The only differences are in how access is granted. As mentioned earlier, telnet requires that you enter both your user name and password before access is granted. However, when using rlogin, access can be granted without even including the user name:

```
% rlogin jupiter
Last login: Mon Sep 12 19:30:56 from mercury
SunOS Release 4.1.3 (JUPITER) #1 Mon Aug 15 14:44:35 EST 1994
You have new mail.
Mon Sep 12 19:44:30 EST 1994
%
```

Because no user name was supplied, rlogin used the same user name as on the local machine. Sometimes, you may have different user names on different machines. To specify a different user name, include -l *remote_user_name* as an argument to rlogin:

```
% who am i
venus!orr      ttypb    Sep 12 19:23
% rlogin jupiter -l scott
Last login: Mon Sep 12 19:44:30 from saturn
```

```
SunOS Release 4.1.3 (JUPITER) #1 Mon Aug 15 14:44:35 EST 1994
You have new mail.
Mon Sep 12 19:53:17 EST 1994
%
```

Unlike most of the r commands, which display an error message and exit, if access cannot be granted through /etc/hosts.equiv or the user's rhosts file, you are prompted to enter your password before you can access the remote system.

Remote Shell

rsh (or remsh) is similar to rlogin, except that only one command is run on the remote machine and not an actual login session. In addition, rsh also includes the -l option. If free access cannot be granted, the command fails.

```
% rsh saturn date
Mon Sep 12 20:12:21 EST 1994
%
```

Remote Copy

rcp works exactly like its standard Unix counterpart, /bin/cp. You can copy one file, multiple files using wild cards, and even entire directory trees from one machine to another. One or both the machines can be remote. The remote file is referenced as *hostname:file*. If the file does not include a full path, rcp uses the user's home directory. rcp doesn't support the -l option. Instead, you can switch between users by replacing the host name field with user@hostname. Like rsh, rcp must be granted free access or it will fail. An example of remotely copying a file from one machine to another is shown in the following:

```
% ls test
test not found
% rcp orr@venus:test .
% ls test
test
%
```

Remote Users

Unlike the previously discussed commands, rusers doesn't require any entries in either /etc/hosts.equiv or a user's rhosts. Its function is to list which users are currently logged into remote machines. If run without any command-line arguments, it queries every machine on your network and displays user names in a space-separated list, one machine per line. By including a host name on the command line, only that host is queried:

```
% rusers jupiter
jupiter        scott scott jon damon scott damon debbie
%
```

If you want more information, include -l as a command-line argument, and rusers displays information similar to /usr/bin/who. You can see who is logged in, when and from where the user logged in, and how long it's been since he or she typed anything, as in the following example:

```
% rusers -l jupiter
scott     jupiter:console       Sep  3 18:33    0:02
scott     jupiter:ttyp0         Sep  3 18:34    0:02 (:0.0)
jon       jupiter:ttyp1         Sep  3 18:34    0:50 (:0.0)
damon     jupiter:ttyp2         Sep  3 18:34    8:06 (saturn)
scott     jupiter:ttyp3         Sep  3 18:34    2:23 (:0.0)
damon     jupiter:ttyp4         Sep  3 18:34    5:10 (mars)
debbie    jupiter:ttyp5         Sep  6 10:02    8:15 (mercury)
```

The same functionality also can be provided through the *rwho* command. The rwho command is not discussed here because the rwho daemon server, rwhod, often utilizes a great deal of cpu time, and many sites choose to disable it.

Remote Up

rup is another remote query program. rup reports the amount of time remote machines have been operational. If you run rup without any command-line arguments, rup queries every machine on your network. In addition to the active time, rup also reports each machine's current cpu load. If you want this information for only one host, include the host name as a command-line argument. The following is an example of using rup:

```
% rup
  mercury    up 24 days,   7:29,    load average: 0.29, 0.27, 0.00
    venus    up 55 days, 13:58,    load average: 0.00, 0.00, 0.00
    earth    up 65 days, 10:04,    load average: 0.10, 0.02, 0.01
     mars    up  9 days,   5:53,    load average: 0.40, 0.37, 0.03
  jupiter    up 14 days, 10:17,    load average: 0.46, 0.39, 0.01
   saturn    up  3 days,   8:28,    load average: 0.00, 0.00, 0.01
   uranus    up 25 days, 14:37,    load average: 1.51, 1.41, 1.04
  neptune    up  4 days,   1:53,    load average: 0.25, 0.32, 0.00
    pluto    up 32 days, 14:06,    load average: 3.48, 3.66, 3.47
%
```

finger—The Network Phonebook

Although originally designed for use on a local machine, the vast amount of information finger can provide about the users on a system has made it very popular among network users as well. Suppose that you want to send some e-mail to a person you met at a conference. You forgot to ask for his e-mail address, but you do know his last name. With finger, you can query his system for the information you seek. An example of using finger to gain information about a user is shown in the following:

```
% finger orr@jupiter.acct.nrp.com
[jupiter]
Login name: scott                      In real life: Scott Orr
Directory: /home/users/scott           Shell: /bin/csh
Last login Mon Sep 12 11:37 on ttyp7 from saturn
Mail last read Mon Sep 12 15:27:35 1994
No Plan.
```

Notice that the last name *orr* was the only information provided to jupiter. Jupiter searches for orr in /etc/passwd and discovers that user scott's last name is Orr. scott's user name, full name, home directory, and default shell are all extracted from his /etc/passwd entry. In addition, jupiter consults /etc/utmp to determine when scott last logged in and checks the permissions on scott's mail file to see when it was last read. All this information is then provided to the remote user.

Some users create files named .plan and .project in their home directories to give remote users additional information. If either file exists, finger also displays the contents of the file along with the other information.

Finger also can be used to provide much the same information that rusers -l does. You can see who is logged in, their full names, when and on which terminal they logged in, where they logged in from, and how long since they typed anything on the keyboard. Some people use this information to see if a coworker is logged in before trying to contact them. An example is shown in the following:

```
% finger @jupiter
[jupiter]
Login     Name            TTY Idle    When      Where
scott     Scott Orr       co 3:24 Sat 18:33
jon       Jon Burgoyne    p0    4d Sat 18:34    :0.0
scott     Scott Orr       p1    4d Sat 18:34    :0.0
scott     Scott Orr       p3 4:48 Sat 18:34     :0.0
jon       Jon Burgoyne    p4 2:45 Sat 18:34     :0.0
damon     Damon Beals     p5 5:10 Tue 10:02     mars
debbie    Debbie Smith    p6 5:12 Sat 12:50     mercury
```

Many security-conscious sites often choose to disable fingerd, the server daemon. With finger, a remote user can gain information about every account on a system, including those that have not been used for a while. People attempting to break into a system target these inactive users first.

E-Mail

No network system is complete without a method of sending messages from one user to another. Unix is no exception. E-mail has been part of the Unix operating system since the very beginning. Users all accessed the same machine, and mail messages were just files copied from one location to another. Then, with the inclusion of TCP/IP networking with BSD Unix, mail was revised to provide network support.

To send mail to a remote user, you include the user's name along with the fully qualified domain name of the machine on which the user has an account. The @ character separates the two, and together they form what's known as an e-mail address. A sample e-mail address is scott@jupiter.acct.nrp.com. When an e-mail address is used, the mail program copies the message to a special directory, such as /var/spool/mqueue, to await the e-mail delivery daemon to send it to the remote machine. The daemon that handles this transfer of mail is known as *sendmail* and is discussed further in Chapter 9, "sendmail and SMTP."

Summary

The merger of Unix and TCP/IP contributed much to the popularity of networking in today's workplace. What started as a convenient method for researchers to collaborate on projects has now become the backbone of many organizations. This chapter focused on installing a Unix workstation on a network and demonstrated several of the common features. It's important to realize that this functionality is only the tip of the iceberg. New resources are being developed and used on the Internet everyday.

Chapter Snapshot

This chapter covers how to configure Windows 95 to use TCP/IP. One section discusses TCP/IP in a LAN environment, and the next shows how to set up TCP/IP for use over a modem connection. The chapter also covers the TCP/IP applications that come with Windows 95. These topics are presented in the following order:

CHAPTER

Connecting to Windows 95

"Minnesota is the leading producer of turkeys in the U.S."

—1995 Farmers' Almanac

Today, nearly every major operating system for the PC platform comes with TCP/IP support built in. Windows 95 is no exception. Windows 95's TCP/IP implementation follows the 32-bit VxD driver architecture. Microsoft has included several commonly used TCP/IP utilities such as telnet, ftp, arp, ping, route, netstat, nbstat, ipconfig, tftp, rexec, rcp, rsh, and traceroute. 32-bit and 16-bit support for the Windows Sockets API allows for numerous third-party applications such as Netscape and Mosaic.

Windows 95 Networking Benefits

Compared to Windows 3.1 and Windows for Workgroups, Windows 95 is much more network-aware. If an organization has more that one computer, then that organization probably has a network in place to connect these computers together. Most organizations typically have more than one operating system and network protocol deployed. Windows 95 was built with multiprotocol network environments in mind. Instead of loading a complicated list of network drivers before starting Windows, Windows 95 loads all the appropriate drivers for the network as they are needed.

Windows 95 virtually eliminates the need for any terminate-and-stay-resident (TSR) device drivers. The majority of these device drivers, including network drivers, can be replaced with 32-bit protected mode virtual device drivers (VxDs) that come with Windows 95. These protected mode drivers run in extended memory and, therefore, require zero bytes of conventional memory. With the Windows 95 architecture, the protected mode drivers provide a more reliable and faster network platform that is less prone to resource conflicts and system crashes.

The new Windows 95 user interface is much easier to work with and configure compared to Windows 3.1 or Windows for Workgroups. The network control panel allows for point-and-click configuration of all network components. Adding or removing drivers for network protocols, network cards, or network clients all can be done from one dialog box.

During the installation process of the TCP/IP protocol and Dial-Up Networking, Windows 95 will need to copy several files to your computer from the installation source media. Insert the source media, CD-ROM or disk, when prompted to do so.

Configuring TCP/IP with a Local Area Network

This section assumes your computer already has a network interface card installed and is connected to a network configured to support TCP/IP. If this is not the case, additional installation and configuration steps beyond the scope of this chapter will be necessary before you proceed.

Before you begin, you need to know the proper values for the following TCP/IP parameters for your network:

    ✔ IP address

    ✔ Subnet mask

✔ Domain name

✔ Domain name server address(es)

✔ Gateway address(es)

If your network uses the Dynamic Host Configuration Protocol (DHCP), most of these values can be left blank and resolved through the DHCP server. In either case, if you do not know the proper values for these parameters, contact your network administrator to get them.

Adding the TCP/IP Protocol

The first step in adding TCP/IP to Windows 95 is to add the TCP/IP protocol to your network configuration. To do this, open the Network folder from the Windows 95 Control Panel (see fig. 17.1).

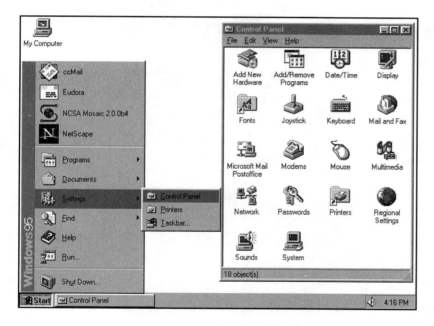

Figure 17.1
The Windows 95 Control Panel.

II

Enumeration

To open the Network folder, double-click on the Network icon in the Control Panel window. Figure 17.2 shows an example of a Windows 95 network configuration for a PC on a Novell network.

To add the TCP/IP protocol, click on the **A**dd button. In the Select Network Component Type dialog box, click on the Protocol icon, then click on the **A**dd button. The Select Network Protocol dialog box opens (see fig. 17.3).

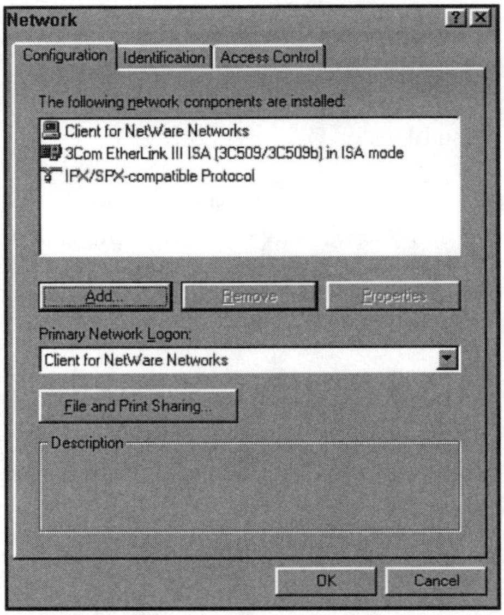

Figure 17.2
The Configuration tab of the Network dialog box—LAN example.

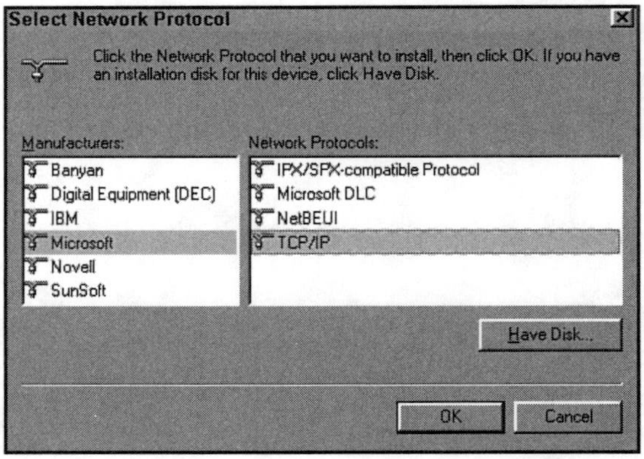

Figure 17.3
The Select Network Protocol dialog box.

From the **M**anufacturers list, select Microsoft, select TCP/IP from the Network Protocols list, then click on the OK button. The TCP/IP protocol now appears in the list of components of the Network dialog box's Configuration tab.

If your network has a DHCP server you can use, no additional configuration is required. If you are unable to use DHCP, you need to configure your TCP/IP properties manually (see the following section).

Configuring TCP/IP Properties

After the TCP/IP protocol has been added to your network configuration, the last step is to configure the protocol for use in your network. In the Configuration tab of the Network dialog box, double-click on the TCP/IP protocol icon. The TCP/IP Properties dialog box contains all the parameters you need to set for use on the network. The individual tabs are covered in the next sections.

IP Address

To set the IP address of your PC, click on the IP Address tab in the TCP/IP Properties dialog box. Click on **S**pecify an IP address, then type the appropriate values for your **IP** Address and S**u**bnet Mask. Figure 17.4 shows an example for a PC on a Class C network 198.70.150.0. The IP Address is 198.70.150.10 and the Subnet Mask is 255.255.255.0.

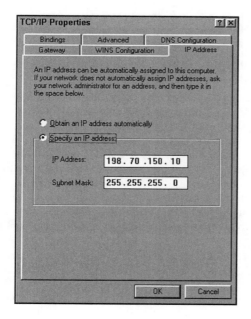

Figure 17.4
The TCP/IP Properties dialog box showing the IP Address tab.

DNS Configuration

If your PC will be using Domain Name Service to resolve host names into IP Addresses, you will need to configure a few parameters. Click on the DNS Configuration tab in the TCP/IP Properties dialog box (see fig. 17.5).

Figure 17.5
The TCP/IP
Properties dialog
box—DNS
Configuration tab.

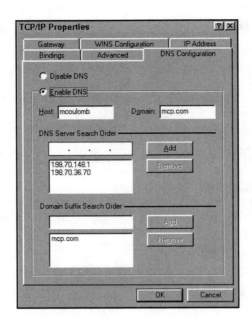

Figure 17.5
The TCP/IP
Properties dialog
box—DNS
Configuration tab.

Click on **E**nable DNS. Type the name of your PC in the **H**ost field and its domain name in the D**o**main field. Type the addresses of any Domain Name servers in the DNS Server Search Order section of the dialog box. For each address, click on the **A**dd button to add the address to the list box. You must specify at least one server address. By having more than one server address, your PC can query other servers if one goes down.

To add a domain to the Domain Suffix Search Order list box, type the domain name in the field next to the A**d**d button and click A**d**d. This section enables you to shortcut host names. If your PC were in the foo.com domain, for example, and you wanted to access the machine named marketing1, the fully qualified domain name would be marketing1.foo.com. If you were to add foo.com in the Domain Suffix Search Order, you would only need to type **marketing1** for the host name to access the machine.

Figure 17.5 shows a DNS configuration for a PC named "mypc" in the mcp.com domain. The domain name servers for this domain are 198.70.148.1 and 198.70.36.70. The domain name mcp.com appears in the Domain Suffix Search Order to simplify the typing of host names within the mcp.com domain.

Gateway

To configure the TCP/IP gateway address, click on the Gateway tab in the TCP/IP Properties dialog box (see fig. 17.6).

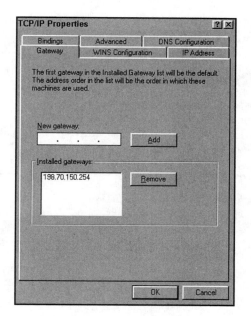

Figure 17.6

The Gateway tab of the TCP/IP Properties dialog box.

Type the gateway address in the field next to the **A**dd button, then click on **A**dd. If your network has more than one gateway, you can specify additional gateway addresses.

WINS Configuration

Windows Internet Naming Service (WINS) is a dynamic host name service that works in conjunction with DHCP. With DHCP, IP addresses are assigned dynamically as needed, which means that a PC's IP address might not be the same each time the system is turned on. WINS tracks the assignment of IP addresses to host names so that the correct IP address is resolved for a computer configured with DHCP. It is best to let DHCP configure these values instead of specifying them manually. If DHCP is not used on your network, you can leave WINS resolution disabled. To enable WINS, click on the WINS Configuration tab of the TCP/IP Properties dialog box, then click on Use D**H**CP for WINS Resolution. If WINS resolution is not used, click on **D**isable WINS Resolution.

Configuring TCP/IP with a Dial-Up Connection

This section covers how to configure a stand-alone computer to use TCP/IP over a modem connection. Before you can proceed here, you need a modem installed and functional, and a SLIP or PPP connection available to you. The following explains how to setup TCP/IP to work via a PPP connection.

Installing Dial-Up Networking

If Dial-Up Networking was not selected during Windows 95 installation, you have to install it now. Begin by double-clicking the Add/Remove Programs icon from the Windows 95 Control Panel (refer to fig. 17.1). Click on the Windows Setup tab and double-click on the Communications component (see fig. 17.7).

Figure 17.7
The Communications dialog box after the Communications component is chosen in the Add/Remove Programs Properties dialog box.

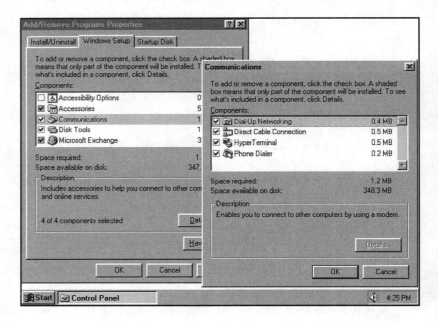

If there is a check in the box next to Dial-Up Networking, you can click on the Cancel buttons to exit—Dial-Up Networking is already installed. If not, click the box next to Dial-Up Networking and click on the OK button to close the Communications dialog box. Click on the OK button again to close the Add/Remove Programs Properties dialog box. Windows 95 should now install Dial-Up Networking.

Adding the TCP/IP Protocol

After Windows 95 has installed Dial-Up Networking, you must add the TCP/IP protocol to the Network Configuration dialog box. To do this, you need to open the Network folder from the Windows 95 Control Panel. To open the Network folder, double-click on the Network icon in the Control Panel window. To add the TCP/IP protocol, click on the <u>A</u>dd button. In the Select Network Component Type window, click on the

Protocol icon, then click on the **A**dd button. The Select Network Protocol dialog box opens (refer to fig. 17.3). From the **M**anufacturers list, select Microsoft, select TCP/IP from the Network Protocols list, then click on the OK button. The TCP/IP protocol appears in the list of components of the network configuration dialog box. Figure 17.8 shows an example of a Windows 95 network configuration for a stand-alone PC using TCP/IP over a modem.

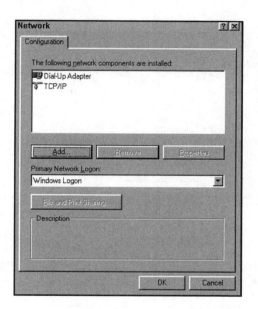

Enumeration

Figure 17.8
A dial-up example in the Configuration tab of the Network dialog box.

If you are not using your modem for any other networking protocols, highlight any other network clients or protocols that were installed by default and click on the **R**emove button. This reduces the number of drivers that Windows 95 loads for the modem network connection. Figure 17.8 shows the Configuration tab for a PC that is only using the TCP/IP protocol for Dial-Up Networking. For a PPP connection, the TCP/IP protocol is configured at login—no additional configuration is needed.

Adding a Dial-Up Connection

After installing Dial-Up Networking and TCP/IP, you need to add a dial-up connection. To open the Dial-Up Networking dialog box, click on Dial-Up Networking from the Accessories section of the Start menu (see fig. 17.9).

Begin by double-clicking on the Make New Connection icon. After typing a name for the connection and selecting a modem, click on the Next button. Type the A**r**ea code and **T**elephone number of the remote service, then click on the Next button. Click on the Finish button to close the Make New Connection dialog box.

Figure 17.9
The path to Dial-Up Networking.

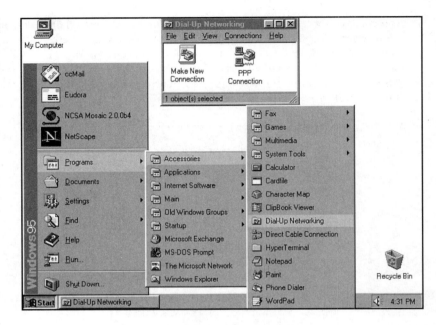

Before you can use the new connection, a few more parameters should be set to make network access as easy as possible. Open the connection properties dialog box (fig. 17.10) by clicking once on the newly created PPP Connection icon and choosing P**r**operties from the **F**ile menu of the Dial-Up Networking dialog box.

Figure 17.10
The Dial-Up Networking connection properties dialog box.

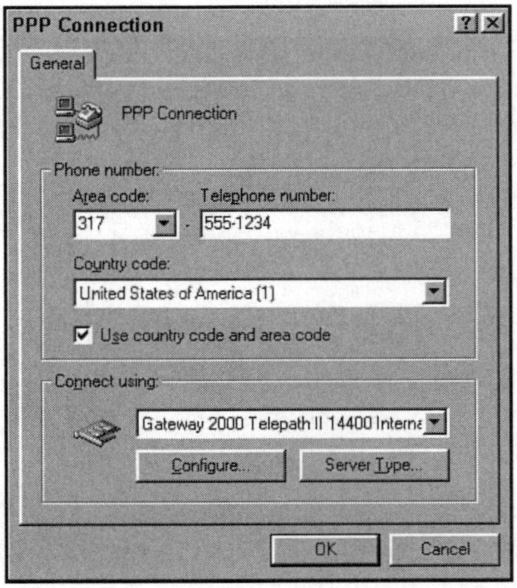

Server Type Configuration Parameters

From the connection properties dialog box, click on the Server **T**ype button. Select "PPP: Windows 95, Windows NT 3.5, Internet" as the Type of Dial-Up **S**erver. For a PPP connection to a TCP/IP network, you should only need to check Enable software **c**ompression under Advanced options, and **T**CP/IP under Allowed network protocols (see fig. 17.11).

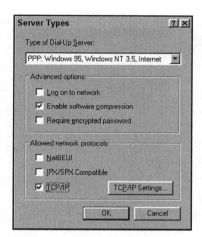

Figure 17.11
The Server Types dialog box.

Now click on the TC**P**/IP Settings button. Make sure that **S**erver assigned IP address is selected and that Use IP header **c**ompression and Use default **g**ateway on remote network are both checked. If you want to use Domain Name Service over this connection, you need to specify the IP address of at least the Primary **D**NS server in the TC**P**/IP Settings dialog box. Get these addresses from your service provider. Click on the OK buttons to close the TCP/IP Settings and the Server Types dialog boxes.

Other Connection Configuration Parameters

In the connection properties dialog box (refer to fig. 17.10) click on the **C**onfigure button. This opens a dialog box for modem properties related to the new connection you are configuring (see fig. 17.12).

The first two tabs of this box deal with connect speeds, data bits, stop bits, parity, and time-out values. Typically, the defaults for all these are sufficient. The last tab, Options, has several features you might need to use. The first section, Connection control, deals with manual commands you might have to give to your modem or service provider before or just after the connection is established. If you need to send any special commands to the modem that are not in the initialization string, you can check Bring up terminal window **b**efore dialing, and do so at that time. By default, Windows 95 expects login and password prompts from your service provider immediately after the modem connects. After login, Windows 95 attempts to start the PPP connection. If your service provider requires other steps before a login, or if you have to select PPP from a menu after login, you need to check Bring up terminal window **a**fter dialing. This allows you to perform whatever steps are necessary with your service provider to start PPP after the modem has connected. If you need to dial the phone number manually, you can do so by checking the Operator assisted or **m**anual dial box. With this option, you can dial the phone number, and, when you hear the modem connect, you can click the connect button and hang up the phone.

Figure 17.12

Modem
Connection
Properties dialog
box.

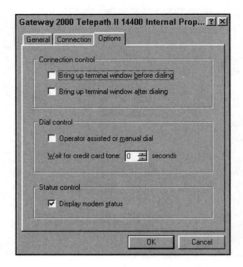

Configuring any dial-up connection is usually a trial-and-error process. Do not be too disappointed if the connection does not work the first time. Depending on your provider, you might have to use the Terminal window option discussed previously. This also is a good way of debugging what happens during the connection sequence. If all else fails, contact your service provider for support.

Simple shareware or freeware modem dialing software programs are available for Windows 95 that support scripting. With a scripting feature, you could program the steps necessary to connect with your service provider into a script, and the dialer software would handle the rest. This again is a trial-and-error setup process, but it can make your login process much easier in the long run.

Using a Dial-Up Connection

After you set all your parameters and click on OK to close the dialog boxes, you are ready to dial. To connect, open the Dial-Up Networking folder from the Accessories section of the Start Menu (refer back to fig. 17.9). Click one time on your Connection icon. Select Co**n**nect from the **F**ile menu. The Connect To dialog box opens (see fig. 17.13).

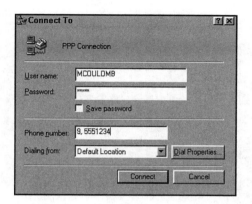

Figure 17.13
The Connect To
dialog box.

Type the user name and password for your dial-up account. If you are completing the login process through the Terminal window, these values are not used; they are only used if Windows 95 logs in for you. Click on the Connect button to dial the modem and initiate the connection. After the modem connects and logs in, the PPP protocol starts. After the protocol has started, your PC becomes a node on the TCP/IP network you have just dialed. Any TCP/IP applications installed on your computer now run.

Windows 95 TCP/IP Applications

After TCP/IP is running, either after you log in to a local area network or a dial-up network, Windows 95 has a few bundled TCP/IP applications you can run.

ping

The first program you should use to test your new TCP/IP connection is ping. ping sends a test packet of data to whatever machine you specify. That machine then sends a data packet back in response. If the result packet comes back, you know the connection works. If it does not, you know there is a problem. The ping program should be run from the DOS Prompt. Figure 17.14 shows the results of ping.

ping reported four packets sent and received. The second to last column of output is the time in milliseconds taken for each packet to return. Both machines in this example are on the same LAN. If you were to ping a machine over a 14.4 Kbps modem connection, a typical response time would be around 250 ms. If you cannot ping a machine by name, you might want to try its IP address instead. If the ping works with the IP address and not by name, then your Domain Name resolution is not working. Either your Domain Name Server is down, or it is not configured properly. When troubleshooting a TCP/IP connection with ping, IP addresses of your Domain Name Server or Gateway are always good choices to use.

Figure 17.14
A ping example.

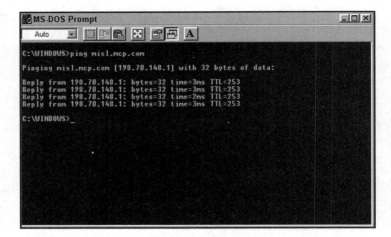

```
C:\WINDOWS>ping misl.mcp.com

Pinging misl.mcp.com [198.70.148.1] with 32 bytes of data:

Reply from 198.70.148.1: bytes=32 time=3ms TTL=253
Reply from 198.70.148.1: bytes=32 time=3ms TTL=253
Reply from 198.70.148.1: bytes=32 time=2ms TTL=253
Reply from 198.70.148.1: bytes=32 time=3ms TTL=253

C:\WINDOWS>_
```

Traceroute

Another excellent program by which to test TCP/IP connectivity is traceroute (TRACERT.EXE). Traceroute shows the path data must take to get from your computer to the given destination. Run the TRACERT.EXE program from the MS-DOS Prompt. Figure 17.15 shows a traceroute from a PC (mcoulomb.mcp.com) to www.iquest.net.

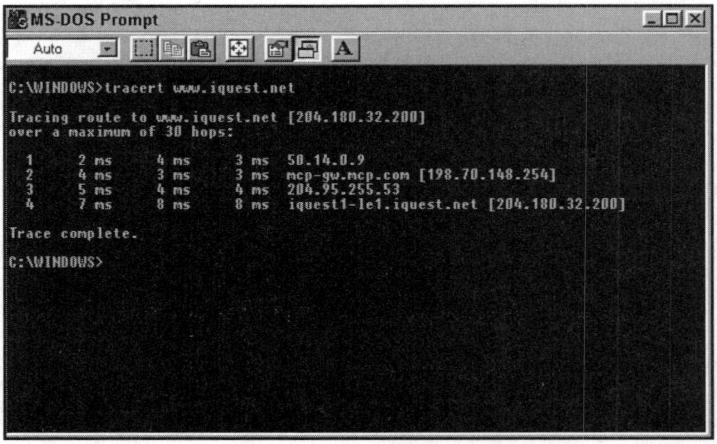

Figure 17.15
A traceroute example.

```
C:\WINDOWS>tracert www.iquest.net

Tracing route to www.iquest.net [204.180.32.200]
over a maximum of 30 hops:

  1     2 ms     4 ms     3 ms  50.14.0.9
  2     4 ms     3 ms     3 ms  mcp-gw.mcp.com [198.70.148.254]
  3     5 ms     4 ms     4 ms  204.95.255.53
  4     7 ms     8 ms     8 ms  iquest1-le1.iquest.net [204.180.32.200]

Trace complete.

C:\WINDOWS>
```

Traceroute also shows the time taken along each link of the route to the destination. If traceroute stops along the way, that could be an indication that a network link is down.

telnet

telnet enables you to log in to a remote machine through the TCP/IP network. The remote machine must accept incoming telnet connections. Typically, these machines run Unix or some other multiuser operating system. Windows 95 does not support incoming telnet connections. telnet is a Windows program; it will not, however, appear in your Start menu by default. To run telnet, choose **R**un from the Start menu, type **telnet** in the dialog box, then click on the OK button. To log in to the remote computer, choose **R**emote System from the **C**onnect menu and type the name or address of the remote computer. Figure 17.16 shows an example of a telnet login to a Unix workstation.

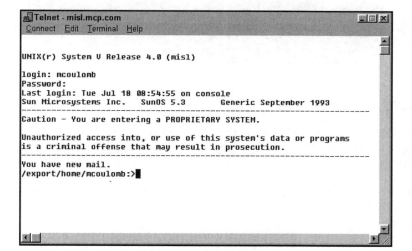

Figure 17.16
A telnet example.

ftp

FTP (File Transfer Protocol) is an application that gives you a text command-line interface to upload and download files to and from a remote computer. The remote computer must be running an ftp server program that accepts incoming connections. ftp server software can be found for MS-DOS, Windows 3.*x*, Windows 95, Windows NT, Unix, and other platforms. For a detailed explanation of how to use ftp to transfer files, see Chapter 4, "Remote Access and Network File Transfer." To run the Windows 95 ftp program, choose **R**un from the Start menu, type **ftp hostname** in the dialog box(where *hostname* is the name or IP address of the machine you want to transfer files with), then click on the OK button. Figure 17.17 shows an ftp session with ftp.mcp.com (Macmillan Publishing's ftp server). The login name is "anonymous" and the password is your e-mail address.

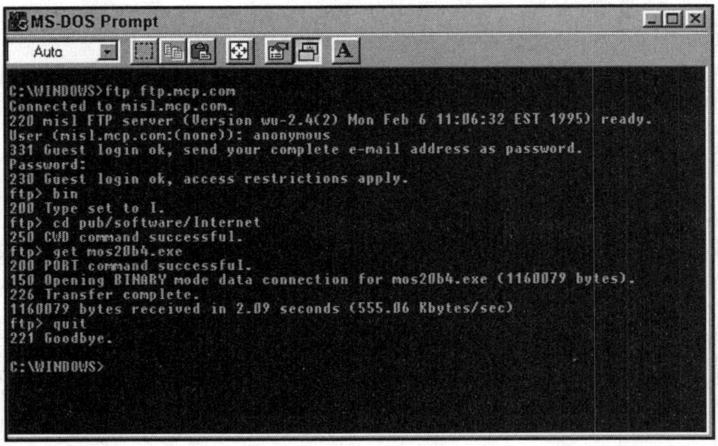

Figure 17.17
An ftp example.

```
C:\WINDOWS>ftp ftp.mcp.com
Connected to misl.mcp.com.
220 misl FTP server (Version wu-2.4(2) Mon Feb 6 11:06:32 EST 1995) ready.
User (misl.mcp.com:(none)): anonymous
331 Guest login ok, send your complete e-mail address as password.
Password:
230 Guest login ok, access restrictions apply.
ftp> bin
200 Type set to I.
ftp> cd pub/software/Internet
250 CWD command successful.
ftp> get mos20b4.exe
200 PORT command successful.
150 Opening BINARY mode data connection for mos20b4.exe (1160079 bytes).
226 Transfer complete.
1160079 bytes received in 2.09 seconds (555.06 Kbytes/sec)
ftp> quit
221 Goodbye.

C:\WINDOWS>
```

Summary

Microsoft's Windows 95 TCP/IP easily integrates with the rest of the Windows 95 networking architecture. The same TCP/IP stack works with a direct local area network connection or through a modem. The 32-bit VxD implementation allows for fast network performance with zero conventional memory utilization. Microsoft also includes a suite of utilities for basic TCP/IP communication and troubleshooting. Support for the Windows sockets API provides a foundation that third-party TCP/IP applications can build on.

Chapter Snapshot

The Internet offers almost instantaneous globe-spanning e-mail communication, archives of powerful free software, powerful online information access tools and data repositories, and about 4,500 ongoing discussion newsgroups. This chapter introduces you to the Internet and discusses the following topics:

18

CHAPTER

Accessing the Internet

"Whatever needs to be maintained through force is doomed."

—Henry Miller

The Internet—the most widespread computer network on the planet—is the most obvious example of the information realm in which so many white-collar professionals evidently wish to spend all their time. The Internet is a seductively attractive realm, with sound and pictures and powerful free software whizzing around, all just waiting to be invited into your own environment. However, you must find your place in the Internet and see how to make it work for you. This chapter looks at some of the tools and practices currently on the Internet.

Internet = Protocols + Culture

The Internet is a community of people who do things their way because, for better or worse, that is what they want. A well-known example of this is the Internet's pronounced antipathy to direct advertising. Even the creator of the Internet worm has never been vilified to the degree that some hapless marketeers have been who send out the e-mail equivalent of junk mail. Sometimes the Internet is the world's biggest small town, with its own narrow way of doing things. But the Internet persists and thrives because of the tyranny of the useful. Its protocols and way of doing things are so useful that people carry on, constantly trying to refine and improve it. Have a look and see if it works for you.

Protocols

Internet Protocols (IPs) are the low-level tools that bind the machines on the Internet into a useful whole. IPs specify the kinds of communications that can occur between machines and how connections can be made to enable those communications. To be on the Internet, a machine must support the IP. One of the most important of these is the *Transmission Control Protocol* (TCP, hence the often-used abbreviation TCP/IP). Among the many others are the *Simple Mail Transport Protocol* (SMTP), *file transfer protocol* (ftp), and *User Datagram Protocol* (UDP).

A *protocol* is an agreement about how something will work. When you see children jumping rope, the rope handlers agree to the speed and intensity with which they will spin the rope. The other kid, the one who gets to jump up and down and have all the fun, is the one who enjoys the benefit of this agreement or protocol. That's you! Because the machines on the Internet use these protocols, you are able to use the following services:

- ✔ E-mail

- ✔ Directories similar to "white pages"

- ✔ Information access tools

- ✔ Database queries

- ✔ Executable program archives

The Internet basically treats all its communications as packets of data, each of which has an address. Machines (or their routers) on the Internet maintain tables that describe addresses of local and remote machines and routes for packets. They deliver packets to addresses by looking up the address and using the route described in the table. (You can use the command netstat to see information about your system's routing table.) Needless to say, with millions of users on the Internet, many complications can arise, but this is the simple version of what happens: packets with addresses get passed from sender to addressee.

For some insight into how the Internet might work, imagine a paper-and-pencil system that people seated in a room might use to send messages to each other. Imagine that each person has two neighbors, one in front and one behind, except for the lucky person who gets to sit up front near the door and who always gets a whole graham cracker and the unlucky person who sits in the back and has to erase rude remarks in math books whenever he has a spare minute. To begin with, participants need a unique name to differentiate themselves from each other, so they write down their unique names on pieces of paper that they can keep.

Each participant can get pieces of paper from each other and read them. To make it easy to read and process each piece of paper, they all agree to put the name of the addressee at the top of the paper. Furthermore, they agree to write their messages with a particular alphabet in blocks of a particular size, say, 64 letters. Now to create a network communications system, they all agree to reach out to their two neighbors every once in a while to see if there are any pieces of paper for them to process. If they get a piece of paper, they read its address. If it is addressed to them, they read the message. If it is not for them, they look up the name of the addressee and the route to use to relay the paper to that name and pass it on.

Imagine that there are many rooms with people doing these paper-shuffling routines. One person from each room is designated as a router to the other rooms. Messages bound for another group are accumulated by the router and periodically handed over to the designated router in one of the other rooms. Of course, the router must keep another table which says what addresses are in use in other rooms. This process continues and the next thing you know, you have an information superhighway.

In our example, each "room" needs its own name in order to be uniquely identified. So all machines and groups of machines on the Internet need unique identifiers. If it were just up to computers, machines would be happy with such memorable labels as "254.253.0.17". Humans prefer names like "whitehouse.gov" and "mit.edu". Tables, such as the file /etc/hosts, contain lists of names and matching Internet addresses. Machines and groups of machines are assembled into a hierarchy described by the *Domain Name System* (DNS). The various levels of the hierarchy are separated by the period (.) in a name, like crl.ucsd.edu. The letters after the last period are one of the following:

com	commerce
edu	education
gov	government
mil	military
net	network
org	other organizations

How the Internet Handles the Changing Network Environment

The Internet has its roots in a networking initiative and associated protocols created by the United States Department of Defense. Since then, new network issues have arisen—new data types like audio and video, new requirements like real-time response, new hardware, new software, and so forth. How have the protocols used on the Internet kept up?

The Internet and its protocols grow and evolve in response to user needs and currently available resources. Unlike a piece of commercial software that is designed from the top down to accomplish specific things in specific ways, the Internet is adapted to the needs of its users by the users themselves. It grows from the bottom up. Certain ways of doing things prove to be useful and become candidates for the IPs. For instance, the Kerberos protocol enables authentication of packets on a network. That is, it can assure a user, process, or machine that users, processes, or machines are who they say they are. Since its formulation at MIT many years ago, it has been used at many different sites and added to and resold in various commercially available products. The base source code is freely available through ftp from MIT and other sites. Not all machines on the Internet use Kerberos; many machines not on the Internet do. So there is not a necessary relationship between Kerberos use and Internet participation.

Mechanisms are available for formalizing, altering, and replacing IPs. The protocols themselves are stated in documents freely available from various sites on the Internet. You can see a list of the ones used on your machine by entering the command:

    % cat /etc/protocols

The proposal and review process uses a document called a *Request for Comment* (RFC) which describes the protocol. As one RFC puts it, "[An] RFC specifies a standard for the... Internet community. Hosts on the... Internet are expected to adopt and implement this standard."

The Internet Society—a voluntary association—has an Architecture Board and an Engineering Task Force that review and approve technologies as Internet standards. Compliance is voluntary in the sense that if you use the IPs you are on the Internet, and if you don't you are not. But note that different protocols for networking can coexist with IPs and communicate through gateways. It is not an either/or choice.

Layers and the TCP/IP Stack

The IP is sometimes referred to as the TCP/IP stack because the various constituent protocols are clustered in layers that specify different kinds of interrelated services. Layers are relatively independent of each other. For example, the application layer, which bundles text into a piece of e-mail, does not really know or need to know how the network layer routes the e-mail packets to the destination machine. Similarly, the network layer does not know about the voltage levels that different pins on different connectors use in either machine's hardware.

Classifying Users, Machines, Connections, and Communications

How can users and machines connect and communicate? Some of the most important issues to consider when hooking up people and computers are the following:

✔ How many different machines will each person or machine be connected to?

✔ How much information will be transmitted?

✔ How much autonomy does each user or machine have when connected?

All the different types of connections between machines and users have their own costs and benefits, and each has a place on the Internet.

One familiar connection type is from a mainframe computer over a serial line to a simple terminal and keyboard. In this setup, the only machine with any smarts is the mainframe. The terminal can only send and receive characters—letters, numbers, and a few other symbols. This is referred to as *character-based communication.* The user types text that appears on the screen. In response, the mainframe computer at the other end of the connection types back some text to the user's screen or performs some other function such as making an entry in a database. The mainframe runs its operating system and other programs and is responsible for all communication. Such a system, for instance a point-of-sale terminal, restricts users to a limited range of interactions.

In Unix systems, terminals such as the vt100 are typical of terminals used in such a setup. In fact, vt100 has come to be synonymous with *dumb terminal.* Emulation of the vt100 has come to be the sine qua non of dumb terminals, not because dumb terminals are especially backwards, but because they are simply exceedingly numerous. Unfortunately, dumb terminals can only render about a hundred blocky and hard-to-read characters. Furthermore, they do so in colors that give a vivid visual impression of the words "occupational hazard." Such terminals have some virtues—they are inexpensive, do not require a high bandwidth connection to their computer, and can present readable text.

The Internet version of the dumb terminal is *telnet*, and it shares one of the virtues of its hardware cousin—it requires a relatively low bandwidth connection. *Bandwidth* is a measure of a transmission channel's capacity to carry information. For example, letters carried by post are of quite low bandwidth; they carry only a few hundred or thousand words and can require several days to deliver. Stepping up another level, telephones transmit sound in real-time, that is, without any appreciable delay, from sender to receiver. Up one more level is television, which carries both sound and pictures. A transmission channel with a given capacity can carry more low-bandwidth than high-bandwidth connections. In other words, it is cheaper to run a low-bandwidth connection.

Using telnet on the Internet, it is also possible to have character-based, peer-to-peer connections in which there are machines on both ends of the line. These machines can communicate in their own rights and "discuss" what functionality they will mutually support. The users of the machines are more autonomous than the users on the point-of-sale terminal example because they can choose from a much wider range of useful commands and actions. Though telnet is still limited to using a bidirectional stream of eight-bit bytes, users can chat in real-time using the *talk* command or its multiuser client/server counterpart, *Internet Relay Chat* (IRC).

Another connection type is peer-to-peer in which two machines have equal access to resources such as data on a hard disk or printers. These machines are workstations, each with the capability to run its own operating system and other programs. Personal computers in office networks are typically configured as peers. News groups (Netnews or Usenet) are distributed across many different computers. That is, they are not supported or sustained by any single machine anywhere. Any machine which subscribes to them can participate in them.

Client/server connections combine elements of both these types. Autonomous users instruct their workstations to perform a wide range of functions; some of these functions are performed by the workstation itself. The workstation, for instance, accepts information from an input device such as a keyboard, mouse, or other pointing device. It also displays information on its screen. However, other instructions are relayed to other machines on the network, which then perform the work that the user wants done. For example, one can instruct a television set-top switching box to display a movie. The box relays the request to another machine which bills the user for the movie and returns an "OK" to the set-top box to show the movie. The machine that initiated the request for a service is the client; the machine that provided the service is the server. The automated teller machine, a low-bandwidth example, performs some functions on its own (the desirable ones, like dispensing twenty-dollar bills); whereas another machine on its network performs other functions (undesirable ones mostly, like debiting your checking account).

Other client/server relationships on the Internet range from the *Network File System* (NFS), which allows a machine to access files elsewhere on its network, to the Domain Name System (DNS), which specifies the correspondence of machine IP addresses to machine names. Typically, Unix systems run their servers as *daemons*, processes which are always running and are not attached to a particular user or terminal.

Security

The security of Unix systems on the Internet is a specialized and complicated topic. Because of the easy access that the Internet allows, potential threats can occur that may be new to sites accustomed to allowing more limited access. Many sites have developed security policies for themselves by which they assess risks and develop methods for minimizing them.

Following are some places to look for more information about security issues.

See the Network Working Group document called *For Your Information (FYI) 8, Site Security Handbook*. This is a text file located on the machine named nic.merit.edu in the directory /documents/fyi.

The Editors' Note from that document reads:

"This FYI RFC is a first attempt at providing Internet users guidance on how to deal with security issues in the Internet. As such, this document is necessarily incomplete. There are some clear shortfalls; for example, this document focuses mostly on resources available in the United States."

The preceding Network Working Group document also contains a bibliography.

The Network Working Group document *For Your Information (FYI) 3, A Bibliography of Internetworking Information*—a bibliography of information about TCP/IP internet-working—mentions the following:

U.S. General Accounting Office, Computer Security—Virus Highlights Need for Improved Internet Management, 36 pgs., United States General Accounting Office, Washington, DC, 1989.

"This report (GAO/IMTEC-89-57) describes the worm (the Internet worm of 1988) and its effects. It gives a good overview of the various U.S. agencies involved in the Internet today and their concerns vis-a-vis computer security and networking. The report is vailable on-line on host nnsc.nsf.net, directory pub, file name GAO_RPT, and on nis.nsf.net, directory nsfnet, file name GAO_RPT.TXT."

Several Netnews groups discuss security issues. Some of these groups are the following:

Newsgroup	Topic
alt.security	Security issues on computer systems
alt.security.index	Pointers to good stuff in alt.security (Moderated)
comp.security.announce	Announcements from the *Computer Emergency Response Team* (CERT) about security (Moderated)

continues

Newsgroup	Topic
comp.security.misc	Security issues of computers and networks
comp.virus	Computer viruses and security (Moderated)
comp.security.Unix	Discussion of Unix security

File Encodings

A file might be encoded on the Internet for different reasons: to assure its privacy, to encapsulate it in an archive, to compress it, or to send a binary file using an ASCII transmission method like mail or Netnews. The first issue—privacy—is not covered in this book. The tar, cpio, and bar commands handle the second issue—encapsulation. The *compress* program handles file compression. This chapter addresses the last issue—sending binary files through ASCII channels.

Binary files represent different kinds of data than plain text. Pictures, sounds, executable programs, the save state of a game, and so on are all different kinds of binary files. They can be transferred around the Internet with a program like ftp. But what if the file's sender or would-be receiver does not have access to ftp? As long as the sender has e-mail or a Netnews feed, the binary files are available by using the uuencode and uudecode commands. These programs convert an arbitrary stream of bytes into ASCII and back again.

To use uuencode, type the following:

    % uuencode *file label* > out_file

file is the file to be encoded and *label* is the name the file will have when it is decoded with uudecode.

uuencode will first write a header into the encoded version of the file which is being written to the file out_file. The header contains the label specified on the command line and the ownership and permissions of the original file. uudecode will later produce its output file with that same ownership and permissions.

Once you have the ASCII-encoded version of the binary file, you can send it as an e-mail message or post it to a news group. Anyone who wants to have the file can then copy it to a local disk and type the following:

    uudecode file

uudecode then discards anything that the mail or news program has added to the file and writes a new file. The new file will have the name specified when it was originally uuencoded. It will also have the original file's permissions and ownership, so be sure to use uudecode in a directory in which that user ID will have write permission.

Using ping

ping provides the Internet version of a "Hello, are you there?" query. ping sends network packets to a machine on the Internet which you designate either by name or by address. Use this command when a machine you believe should be present and available on the Internet does not respond to you.

Consider, for example, the following scenario. You try to send e-mail to someone whose address you jotted down on the back of a business card. Unfortunately, you were standing in a crowded shuttle bus at the time and some parts of the address are unclear. You formulate your carefully considered letter (in a word processor, not your mail program, just in case there are problems delivering it later) and send it off. Almost instantly, you receive a message that until you reformulate the address portion of your mail, it cannot be sent. You take a second look at the wrinkled and smeared business card and ask was that "whitehouse.gov" or "whitehouse.gof" you wrote? You can use ping to untangle this mail delivery problem by typing the following command:

   % **ping whitehouse.gov**

You see the result:

```
Source: [137.110.108.25] —> Destination: whitehouse.gov
[198.137.240.100]

RESULT     PKT#     TIME     LENGTH
success     1        23        56
success     2        22        56
success     3        22        56
success     4        22        56
success     5        21        56
Packets out/in/bad/%loss = 5/5/0/0
Round Trip Time (Ticks) min/avg/max = 21/22/23
~~~~~~~~~~~~~~~~~~~~~~~~~~~~~~~~~~~~~~~~~~
```

On BSD versions, if you use ping without any options, ping will return a message that the destination machine is either alive or unreachable. To get the output shown here, you must use ping -s.

Ⅱ

Enumeration

Though most of this output from ping is self-explanatory, a few comments are in order. ping sent five packets (at the rate of one per second) and each one arrived at its destination successfully. (Note that you can send as many packets as you wish, but five is probably about right. Sending more than five would not really tell you anything more and would definitely use up some of the network's second most precious commodity: bandwidth.) The % loss in this example is 0, but even if it was something like 20, you don't need to worry. After all, the IP was designed to accommodate packet loss. All the packets seem to take approximately the same amount of time (measured in arbitrary "ticks") to make their trip, and they were all the same length.

If you had typed the following line:

> % **ping whitehouse.gof**

you would have seen something similar to the following message:

```
whitehouse.gof —> Host not responding (Cannot resolve name)
```

Usage

ping requires the name or IP address of a host. ping accepts a few options to change the rate at which it sends out packets and how those packets are routed to the destination machine (see table 18.1). The syntax for using ping to detect an Internet machine is as follows:

```
ping host packetsize count.
```

Table 18.1
Using ping to Detect an Internet Machine.

Option	Effect
host	Specifies the name or Internet address of the machine to be ping'ed.
packetsize	Specifies the number of bytes in the transmitted packet. The default is 64, which is fine for most uses. Larger packets can hold routing information.
count	Specifies the number of packets to send. Be sure to include this number. Otherwise, ping will emit packets until you press Ctrl+D.

ping sends a special type of packet called ECHO_REQUEST to the host you specify on the command line. You can use a name for a host (such as whitehouse.gov) rather than the IP address (198.137.240.100) as long as you have a table on your machine which translates from the name to the number.

The ECHO_REQUEST packet is part of the *Internet Control Message Protocol* (ICMP), which is in turn part of the IP itself. Because a machine (or its gateway) can't be on the Internet without supporting these protocols, you can rely on ping to positively identify whether or not a machine is accessible.

Using the finger Command

The finger command can be used over the Internet to show you information about users on other machines. The exact information you receive depends on the command options you use and what the user you are asking about has made available in their plan and project files. As long as you can overcome any squeamishness you may have about issuing a command like finger bobr@mrktng.bigbiz.com or finger ritaz@finance.soho.com, you should be able to find out some combination of these information tidbits:

✔ Login name

✔ Actual name

✔ Whether or not you can use the write command to write to the user's terminal

✔ Length of time since the user last issued a command

✔ Length of time since the user logged in

✔ The user's home directory and which login shell is being used for the login

✔ Any information the user wrote in the plan file in the home directory

✔ Any information the user wrote in the project file in the home directory

✔ Local location and phone number

You may already be familiar with this command from using it on your own system. The only significant addition of which you need to be aware is that you can include an Internet host name or IP address as part of the user's name you give on the command line.

For example, say you want to see who is currently logged on a machine (called bigbiz.com, for example) on the Internet. You can type the following:

    % **finger @bigbiz.com**

(Note that you need to include the at sign (@) before the machine name; otherwise your local finger process will look for a user named (bigbiz.com) and come up empty-handed.) The output will be a list that looks something like the following:

```
[bigbiz.com]

Login        Name               TTY Idle    When      Where
buff         Robin Buffy        p2    1 Tue 19:26   bigbiz.com
bigbiz       Big Business       q3   21: Mon 08:54   bigbiz.com
jps          Jean-Paul Sartorial q4  20: Mon 15:43   bigbiz.com
```

A few words about the column labeled `Idle`. User `buff` has been idle for 1 minute while users `bigbiz` and `jps` have been idle for 21 and 20 hours respectively. Hey, it may not be big-league industrial espionage but at least you get some idea of what is going on over at BigBiz. Note that for a machine with many users, typing finger can yield a long list.

Using finger To See Information about a Specific User

finger can also show information about a specific user whether or not that user is currently logged in.

Typing the following command:

finger buff@bigbiz.com

might show the following:

```
[bigbiz.com]

Login name: buff                    In real life: Robin Buffy
Directory: /user/mngmnt/buff          Shell: /bin/csh
On since Jan 26 14:31:05 on ttyrc
4 days 23 hours Idle Time
New mail received Tue Jan 30 10:39:23 1994;
   unread since Tue Jan 30 09:37:16 1994
Plan:
Manager, Big Biz Businesses
Mail Code:   2741
Extension:   1212 (phone: 307-555-1212)
Office:      HQ, 200B
Motto: "If it's big business, it's our business!"
```

Here we see some information about user `buff`. Everything after the word `Plan:` is what user `buff` wrote in a file called plan. Your site may support the use of a finger daemon (there are some that don't—the White House, for example). You can edit your plan file to contain the information you would like others to see when they use finger on your account name.

A Noteworthy New Use for finger

As you can see, finger is a tidy, easy-to-use and understand Internet utility. Some sites use pseudo-users with names like "help" and "info" to enable commands such as the following:

> % **finger help@***such-and-such.org*

This command allows for the dissemination of small amounts of information which are not necessarily about an individual user. For instance, typing the following command should show information about a soft drink vending machine in the Computer Science House of Rennselaer Institute of Technology:

> % **finger graph@drink.csh.rit.edu**

Usage

finger requires the name or IP address of a remote host machine. Additionally, you can provide a valid user name at the remote machine (see table 18.2). It uses the following syntax:

```
finger options [user_name OR @machine_name] ...
```

Table 18.2
Using finger to Get Information about Remote Machines

Option	Effect
user_name	Specifies a specific user at a remote machine. Must be in the form user_id@machine name.
@machine_name	Specifies a specific remote machine and all users currently logged in to that machine.
-l	Shows long version of information about the user including login name, name, login shell, how long the user has been logged in or the last time the user was logged in, when the user last read e-mail, and optional information such as location, phone number, and the contents of the plan and project files.
-s	Shows short version of information about the user including login name, name, the tty connection being used, and when and from where the login session began.
-p	Does not include information from the user's plan file when showing long version.

When used with a remote machine, finger actually connects you with a finger daemon running on the remote machine. Your finger process passes the information from your command line along to the remote finger process. The remote finger process gathers the information requested and passes it pack to your local finger, which then displays it to you.

E-Mail on the Internet

Sending and receiving messages electronically is certainly one of the most visible and attractive benefits of computer networking. Electronic mail occupies a useful niche midway between the telephone call and physical mail. Now if only you knew or could find out anybody's e-mail address! And if only e-mail never bounced!

Whereas the next chapter covers the mail utility, this section covers the role of the Internet in sending mail among various systems. Because there are different addressing schemes in common use, some of them quite complex, not all e-mail gets where it is intended to go. This section also provides some starting points in the search for the complete directory of all e-mail addresses everywhere.

Handling E-Mail

The propagation of e-mail requires different mechanisms than the creation and use of e-mail. Just as with physical mail where all letter writers are on one side and various national postal services are on the other, e-mail has both user front ends and behind-the-scenes mail transport programs and protocols.

Electronic mail can originate from hand-held computers, home computers, desktops, terminals, mainframes, workstations, fax machines, and possibly the soft drink vending machine at Rennselaer that is on the Internet. Furthermore, all these machines can be on networks other than the Internet, such as BITNET or CompuServe. Certainly each one of the machines does not use Unix and mail. Each uses its own mail programs; some have several from which to choose. That makes the business of addressing and delivering mail quite complex. Even within the Unix community in the last few years there have been two different methods for addressing mail—the "bang path" and the "domain-based" address (currently the preferred one).

Because of the ever-swelling ranks of Internet users who use domain-based addresses of the form userID@machine_name.domain, other networks can sometimes accommodate such addresses directly. To send e-mail from a Unix system to either CompuServe or America Online, two popular online services, you can use addresses such as the following in which userID_string is converted from the CompuServe ID number by making the comma after the first four digits into a period.

userID@aol.com

or

userID_string@compuserve.com

To send to someone on MCIMail, use an address with the following form:

accountname@mcimail.com

or

mci_id@mcimail.com

or

full_user_name@mcimail.com

In other cases, you must explicitly include the gateway between the two networks that you want to use. A *gateway* is a system that understands and communicates with both networks and can translate messages between them. For example, to send e-mail to a user on the BITNET network, use this style of address:

userID%site_name.BITNET@BITNET_gateway

Two BITNET gateways are UICVM.UIC.EDU and CUNYVM.CUNY.EDU.

Though it is tempting to imagine that anyone on any computer network can receive e-mail that originates on the Internet, it just isn't so. In that regard, e-mail distribution still lags behind the ubiquitous and easy-going telephone.

Internet E-Mail

Within the Internet, e-mail moves according to the *Simple Mail Transport Protocol* (SMTP). A letter writer uses a program such as elm or mail to create a message. If the address includes a machine.domain part, the mail program hands over the message to SendMail or to some other mail transport program. SendMail interprets the address as written by the user and produces the appropriate IP address. It then relays the e-mail to another mail program for delivery and display to the recipient. However, because of the complexity of generating a valid IP address from whatever the user's mail program hands it, SendMail can have difficulties. Furthermore, e-mail from one point to another may take different routes. If an e-mail address that worked last week suddenly fails this week, this may be part of the explanation.

If It Talks, Is It Still E-Mail?

As long as e-mail consists of nothing more than text, many different machines can read it. But as new data types such as graphics and sound appear in e-mail, incompatibilities can arise. *Multipurpose Internet Mail Extensions* (MIME) describes some extensions to the earlier standard Internet e-mail. Hardware to enable technologies such as fax, video- and whiteboard-conferencing, and audio is not yet standardized.

E-Mail Address Directories

No single directory can be searched for an individual's e-mail address. Two resources on the Internet might help you locate an e-mail address. They are the *whois* program and the *Knowbot Information Service* offered by the *Corporation for National Research Initiatives* (CNRI).

Using whois

The whois program searches in a database for matches to a name you type at the command line. The database to be searched is kept at a *network information center* (NIC). By default, whois looks up records at the machine specific to your site. You can specify another host with the -h option. (The RFC that describes this service is entitled NICNAME/Whois.)

For instance, what if you meet someone on a bus, but all you can remember is the person's last name. You recall that you were talking about e-mail, so you feel certain that the person has an e-mail address. To search for all records that match the string boulanger, type the following:

> **% whois boulanger**

The result is the following:

```
% whois boulanger

using default whois server rs.internic.net

Boulanger, Nadia (NB76)            nadboul@SOUTHSTAR.COM
+1 xxx xxx xxx

Boulanger, Paul (PB61)            pwb@FIRST.UP.COM
(xxx) xxxx-xxx

The InterNIC Registration Services Host ONLY contains Internet
Information
```

```
(Networks, ASN's, Domains, and POC's).
```

```
Please use the whois server at nic.ddn.mil for MILNET Information.
```

(I have deleted the telephone numbers from the output.) Perhaps this is a start in your search for the person. The NIC that provides directory services has the address internic.net. To get help on the current state of the whois command, type the following:

> **% whois help**

The preceding command produces a long display of information about whois. You can also call the InterNIC at (800) 444-4345 or the registration services group at (703) 742-4777.

Using CNRI's Knowbot

The whois program can look up records in any database that conforms to the format it expects. It's possible to type the target string for which you seek matches just once and have many different databases searched. As CNRI says in the Knowbot manual page, "By submitting a single query to KIS [Knowbot Information Service], a user can search a set of remote 'white pages' services and see the results of the search in a uniform format."

Start up a telnet session. At the prompt, enter the Knowbot IP address.

> **% telnet**
>
> **telnet> open info.cnri.reston.va.us 185**

At the KIS prompt (>) type the following:

> **> query boulanger**

You see the output shown previously and much more because KIS searches many different databases.

Mail Lists

The Internet supports sending mail to whole groups of users at once. This service differs from Usenet news groups because the recipients have the mail list distributions delivered by mail and read them with their mail reader. Typically, a mail list consists of users with a common interest in some topic and a strong desire to read everything that other people have to say on that topic. Of course, some lists are private but many are open to anyone who wishes to join. Most work in the same way.

The contents of the mail list—the e-mail messages—are sent to everyone on the list.

Administrative matters such as subscribing and unsubscribing are communicated only to the list administrator.

You subscribe to the mail list by e-mailing the list administrator and saying that you want to be added to the distribution list. List administrators sometimes use a program to assist in managing their mail list, so you may want to keep your subscription request rather terse. If your mail program provides a subject line, type in the word **subscribe**. You might type the same word as the body of the message and include your name. Your e-mail address will already be part of the message. If you do not know the e-mail address to use for the list administrator, try the name of the list with **-request** appended to it; for example, **games-scores-request@sports.report.com**. If you want to start your own mail list, the source code for list server programs is available and free.

Mail Servers

Mail servers are programs that distribute files or information. They respond to e-mail messages that conform to a specific syntax by e-mailing files or information requested in the message back to the sender. The information on demand can be program archives, documents, digests, indices to other documents, and so on. If, for example, you have an Internet e-mail address, you can request copies of IP RFCs by sending a mail message to mailserv@ds.internic.net. The body of the message can include the following:

`rfcnnn`	*nnn* is the RFC number. (You receive the text of the RFC.)
`file /ftp/rfc/rfcnnnn.yyy`	*nnnn* is the RFC number and *yyy* is either txt for the plain text version or ps for the PostScript printable version.
`help`	You receive information about using the mail server.

Using mail servers is a convenient way of getting many forms of information, even if you do not have direct ftp or telnet access to it.

Special Text Conventions in E-Mail

In an effort to overcome the drab appearance of text in messages sent through e-mail and to newsgroups, some writers use special configurations of alphabetic characters and punctuation, either in their writing or appended to messages as fanciful signatures.

Smileys, Abrvtns, and Signatures

Viewed sideways, in-line combinations such as :-{) (smiler with mustache) or :-D (laugher) can add emotional overtones to plain text messages that might otherwise be unclear.

Possibly their only downside is the pains you develop trying to puzzle out *-) (happy Cyclops) or :-& (cigarette smoker).

Cn u rd ths? If you can, you are a candidate for using such abbreviations as btw (by the way) and fyi (for your information) in your own messages. Guess they save some bandwidth.

Finally, some e-mail writers like to append signatures to their messages. Created with the same character set as smileys, these semi-graphics add something of the character of a handwritten name to the end of a letter or newsgroup posting.

Understanding Usenet and Netnews

Usenet is a network of people and machines that propagate Netnews. Some Internet machines use Usenet and some do not. Similarly, some Usenet systems are not part of the Internet. Usenet works on networks other than the Internet; for instance, the educational and professional network called *Bitnet*. Usenet is a happy overlap of network news and protocols. TCP/IP now includes the *Network News Transfer Protocol* (NNTP).

Netnews transmits discussions about three-dimensional imaging; movies from Hong Kong, Taiwan, and China; pornographic photographs; and chinchilla farming. And that's just newsgroups that start with the letter "a." Netnews consists of opinions, facts, and rumors, all floating like clouds through cyberspace. Sometimes the range of subject matter in Netnews is so wide that it is hard to remember that most participants in news groups share a common interest—ready access to discussion of topics that are important to them.

You read and write messages to news groups with programs like rn and tin.

Using rn

The very first time you use rn or any newsreader, the database file newsrc is initialized for you. The newsrc file is a resource configuration file that lists, in plain ASCII text, your newsgroups and which messages from the newsgroup you have already read, if any. (Of course, the first time you start reading news, you won't have read any messages.) A default set of newsgroups will be entered, and you can begin reading them:

```
(crl) rn
Trying to set up a .newsrc file—running newsetup...
Creating .newsrc in /user/mbd to be used by news programs.
Done.
```

If you have never used the news system before, you may find the articles in news.announce.newusers to be helpful. A manual entry for rn is also available.

To get rid of newsgroups you aren't interested in, use the u command.

```
Type h for help at any time while running rn.
(Revising soft pointers—be patient.)
Unread news in campus.bulletins                2 articles
Unread news in campus.buy+sell                18 articles
Unread news in campus.cs                       1 article
Unread news in campus.cs.grads                 2 articles
Unread news in campus.grads                    2 articles
etc.
********   2 unread articles in campus.bulletins—read now? [ynq]
```

When you read an article, the newsrc file is updated to reflect this. For example, you might have just started rn for the first time. A new newsrc file has been created for you. You can look at this file with any text viewing program such as more or head, as is shown in the following example:

```
(crl) more .newsrc
to: 1-270
campus.bad-attitude: 1-9
campus.bulletins: 1-71
```

After you read an article, the database changes. For example, you might see the following:

```
to: 1-270
campus.bad-attitude: 1-9
campus.bulletins: 1-72
Note that the last message read in the newsgroup
  ***campus.bulletins*** is now 72.
```

Every time you type in the command rn, there is a pause. The more newsgroups you subscribe to, the longer the pause because rn is reading the newsrc file.

First, you see a list of unread messages and a prompt line which asks if you want to begin reading your news:

```
(crl) rn
Unread news in misc.kids                      25 articles
Unread news in sdnet.jobs                      7 articles
Unread news in misc.jobs.offered             285 articles
```

```
Unread news in misc.jobs.contract                    178 articles
Unread news in alt.support.big-folks                   5 articles
etc.
********  25 unread articles in misc.kids—read now? [ynq]
```

Typing **q** quits without any changes being made in your newsgroups database file. Note that what you type in response to these prompt lines does not echo on your screen. Whatever action you specify simply happens.

Responding **y** shows the first unread article in the group:

```
Article 72 (1 more) in campus.bulletins (moderated):
From: Jan Malden
Subject: (none)
Date: 23 Aug 1994 18:40:23 -0700
Organization: campusgw
Lines: 2
NNTP-Posting-Host: network.campus.edu
jobs
Another test from malden
(Mail) End of article 72 (of 73)—what next? [npq]
```

It is important to note two things about the newsrc file. First, it grows larger as you add more newsgroups to your list because there will be one new line added for every added newsgroup. Second, it is a single file and should not be subjected to the strain of being used by two programs at once. Only have a single instance of a newsreader at any one time.

The Culture of Netnews

Like any community, even one with such widely varying interests as Usenet, certain standards of behavior evolve by mutual practice and come to be, if not enforced, at least expected. Some groups answer the question of how participants will interact by moderating their newsgroup. A few people read all submissions to the group and decide what will be put in it. Still, many groups are free-for-alls.

As Chuq Von Rospach says in *A Primer on How to Work With the Usenet Community,* "It is the people on these computers that make Usenet worth the effort to read and maintain, and for Usenet to function properly those people must be able to interact in productive ways." A modest guide to newsgroup etiquette follows.

Do participate in your newsgroup when you are pretty certain many other people in the group want to know what you have to say. If you have some thoughts that would be most appreciated by one or two individuals in the group, why not just e-mail them directly?

In most newsgroups, the unmoderated ones anyway, there are the good, the bad, and the rest of us. A large number of newsgroup readers simply *lurk* (Internet jargon for "silently watch"), rarely, if ever, posting messages of their own. For example, in groups such as misc.jobs that describe job opportunities, most postings are from job providers, not job seekers.

Many newsgroups have questions that are asked every time a new member joins. Most groups have produced a *FAQ*, a list of frequently asked (and answered) questions. These are usually produced as a public service by some long-time participant for whom the pain of maintaining the FAQ is just slightly less than seeing a question about what :-) means. (You already know of course that this is a *smiley*, a sideways collection of keyboard characters organized into a little drawing.) It is always proper to ask for a group's FAQ if you don't see it posted.

Besides civility, another important quality to preserve is bandwidth. The Internet, though it may seem to have almost limitless resources, can definitely get clogged up at times. So keep your postings to the point.

Newsgroups are all people talking to people. Though there is little face-to-face communication, participants on the Internet offer ideas and emotions that they care about.

Maximing telnet and ftp

telnet and ftp are both commonly used on the Internet. With telnet, you can log in to other machines on the network on which you have an account. With ftp, you can copy files back and forth between machines. Both ftp and telnet are programs as well as protocols, and detailed completely in Chapter 4, "Remote Access and Network File Transfer."

Mastering archie

archie is a database search server. The archie database lists files that are available through anonymous ftp from machines on the Internet. You give archie search instructions—text strings or regular expressions that can be expanded to text strings. These strings should be keywords from your topic of interest.

archie Servers

The list of archie servers in table 18.3 is current as of 1994:

Table 18.3
archie Servers

Machine Name	IP Address	Location
archie.au	139.130.4.6	Australia
archie.edvz.uni-linz.ac.at	140.78.3.8	Austria
archie.univie.ac.at	131.130.1.23	Austria
archie.uqam.ca	132.208.250.10	Canada
archie.funet.fi	128.214.6.102	Finland
archie.univ-rennes1.fr	129.20.128.38	France
archie.th-darmstadt.de	130.83.128.118	Germany
archie.ac.il	132.65.16.18	Israel
archie.unipi.it	131.114.21.10	Italy
archie.wide.ad.jp	133.4.3.6	Japan
archie.hama.nm.kr	128.134.1.1	Korea
archie.sogang.ac.kr	163.239.1.11	Korea
archie.uninett.no	128.39.2.20	Norway
archie.rediris.es	130.206.1.2	Spain
archie.luth.se	130.240.12.30	Sweden
archie.switch.ch	130.59.1.40	Switzerland
archie.nctuccca.edu.tw		Taiwan
archie.ncu.edu.tw	192.83.166.12	Taiwan
archie.doc.ic.ac.uk	146.169.11.3	United Kingdom
archie.hensa.ac.uk	129.12.21.25	United Kingdom
archie.unl.edu	129.93.1.14	USA (NE)
archie.internic.net	198.49.45.10	USA (NJ)
archie.rutgers.edu	128.6.18.15	USA (NJ)

continues

Table 18.3, Continued
archie Servers

Machine Name	IP Address	Location
archie.ans.net	147.225.1.10	USA (NY)
archie.sura.net	128.167.254.179	USA (MD)

Connecting to archie

You can connect to archie through telnet and conduct sessions interactively. You can e-mail instructions to archie and have any results e-mailed back to you. Also, archie client programs exist that enable direct interactive connections to archie servers.

The telnet interface enables you to type commands at the archie prompt, which looks like `archie>`, and see the results. Connect by typing the following command:

> % **telnet** *archie_server*

In the preceding command, *archie_server* is a machine listed in the table. When you are prompted for a user name, type **archie**. No password is required. You can then enter commands at the prompt. Typing **help** will get you started.

To use the e-mail interface, you mail instructions to the following address:

> archie@*archie_server*

In the preceding example, *archie_server* is a machine listed in the table. To get a list of servers, type the word **server** as the body of the message. To get help, type **help** as the body of the message.

Free specialized archie clients are available. You can ftp source code for them from the servers listed in the table. The code is in the archie/clients of pub/archie/clients directories. Character-based and graphical versions are available.

Finding Files with archie

To find a file when connected to archie through telnet, type the following:

> archie> **find** *string*

In the preceding example, the variable *string* is a string of alphanumeric characters that you are interested in. The string can be a regular expression as described in the Unix ed command. Regular expressions can include pattern matching and wild-card expansion. For example, type the following:

> archie> **find philately**

You then see the following result:

```
archie> find philately
# Search type: sub.
# Your queue position: 2
# Estimated time for completion: 33 seconds.
working... O
# No matches were found.
```

The following instruction yields about 40 files:

> archie> **find oxygen**

Here are the first three of about 40 files produced by the preceding command:

```
# Search type: sub.
# Your queue position: 1
# Estimated time for completion: 1 minute, 28 seconds.
working... O
Host ftp.iro.umontreal.ca    (132.204.32.22)
Last updated 05:12  6 Sep 1994
    Location: /lude-iro/lynx
2.0.11/run/iro/sun4.1_sparc/samples/elements
FILE    -rw-r—r—    185 bytes  20:00 13 Jul 1993  Oxygen
    Location: /lude-iro/lynx-2.0.11/src/iro/samples/elements
FILE    -rw-r—r—    169 bytes  20:00 13 Jul 1993  Oxygen.Z
    Location: /lude-iro/lynx-2.0.11/src/iro_sol/samples/elements
FILE    -rw-r—r—    169 bytes  20:00 13 Jul 1993  Oxygen.Z
```

Notice that the list of code includes sufficient information for you to access the files using ftp. You cannot view them or download them directly using archie.

How Many Files Does archie Know About?

At press time, the archie database lists more than two million files at more than 900 anonymous ftp sites on the Internet.

Getting Information about archie

You can get information about topics within archie using the help command. To see the status of all the variables that you can set within a session, type the following:

archie> **show**

There is much more. You can get started by addressing an e-mail message to the following:

mail archie@*archie_server*

Type the word **manpage** in the body of the message and send it off. You should receive your reply within a day or two.

archie searches within its huge database of Internet-accessible files to find matches to keywords you type. If any of the found files look interesting, you can copy them using ftp or use an ftp-by-mail service that sends them to you through e-mail.

Comprehending gopher

gopher displays documents, retrieves files, looks up items in databases, plays sounds, shows pictures, runs other gophers—it sings! it dances! It is a very flexible information access tool that uses TCP/IP to create what users call *gopherspace*, the sum of all the documents that gopher can use. gopher has both client and server parts. The clients attach to the servers and request documents. You control what the client "points at" with simple nested menus.

Using gopher

When you use gopher, you see a sequence of menus and submenus. You select a menu item using whatever capabilities your gopher access machine (and you thought it was just a computer!) allows. Character-based terminals can select an item by typing the number of the item and pressing Enter. Graphical user interfaces enable point-and-click access. You start a gopher by typing the following:

% gopher

You see the beginning menu screen that looks something like this:

```
                    Internet Gopher Information Client v1.12S
                          CIS: Campus Information Service
        —>  1.  About CIS/
            2.  What's New (February 7, 1994).
            3.  Campus Information/
            4.  The World/


        Press ? for Help, q to Quit, u to go up a menu        Page: 1/1
```

Notice the arrow pointing at menu item 1. You can select another menu item by typing a new number or using the Up or Down arrows. After making your new selection, press Enter. gopher shows you your choice. For example, if you select 1, you see the next screen for the item About CIS. You can tell that About CIS will offer further choices because there is a forward slash (/) after it.

Next you see the following:

```
                    Internet Gopher Information Client v1.12S
                    About CIS
  —>  1.   What is CIS.
      2.   How to Access CIS.
      3.   General Internet Access Topics/
      4.   What's New with CIS.
      5.   Send suggestions or comments <TEL>




      Press ? for Help, q to Quit, u to go up a menu        Page: 1/1
```

Now if you select 5. Send suggestions or comments <TEL>, you go to an interactive dialog box in which gopher prompts you to type answers to questions.

```
                    Internet Gopher Information Client v1.12S
                    Comments or Suggestions about CIS
      Please enter your remarks here. When you are finished, enter 2
      blank lines to send your message to the CIS staff. Thanks!
```

gopher is actually using the mail program to enable you to enter text and then to send it off to someone who will read it. It does not replicate the functionality already available in the mail program. It uses the other program in the context of a menu-driven interaction guided by you.

Adding to gopherspace

gopher conceals many details of file format, type of machine and operating system, and so on from the user. This enables users to focus on the way their particular user interface works and the information they want, not on the mechanics of access and manipulation. Furthermore, it is quite straighforward to add your own documents to gopherspace. Client versions of gopher are available for the following platforms:

Unix curses and emacs

X Windows (athena, Tk, Xview)

Macintosh Hypercard

Macintosh

DOS with Clarkson Driver

NeXTstep

VM/CMS

VMS

OS/2 2.0

MVS/XA

Microsoft Windows

Server versions are available for the following:

Unix

VMS

VM/CMS

MVS

Macintosh

DOS PC

OS/2

Specifying Helper Programs for gopher

You can set environment variables to instruct gopher to use particular programs for particular purposes.

Variable	Result
GOPHER_MAIL	Sends mail with this program
GOPHER_TELNET	Provides telnet services with this program
GOPHER_PLAY	Plays sound with this program
GOPHER_PRINTER	Prints with this program

gopher uses a client/server relationship and the IPs to make a wide array of information and types of data available to users on many different types of machines.

Using the World Wide Web

The *World Wide Web* (or WWW or W3) is considered either a hyperlink, a multimedia client/server information access system, or the universe of network-accessible information, that is, an embodiment of human knowledge. Though the first definition may seem prosaic, realize that WWW uses TCP/IP and other pieces of technology that are more than 20 years old. If the second definition seems outlandish, remember that the Internet is the largest computer network ever and that you can now use it to transfer music, video, text, executable programs, and real-time data feeds.

The Web consists of resources that have addresses. *Browsers*—programs that can look at a resource and use it—run on systems from character-based terminals to point-and-click graphical user interfaces. A *Uniform Resource Locator* (URL) describes how to find a resource. Resources range from files to commands that access newsgroups, copy files, play sounds, show pictures, and so on. A Web page, written in a plain ASCII language called *hypertext markup language* (html) links resources. Web server software, also available for many different platforms, handles requests for the resources it knows about.

Using the Mosaic Browser

The Mosaic client displays a screen image on a graphical terminal. Words and pictures contain links to other resources. By default, Mosaic starts up connected to a home page on a machine at the *Center for High-Energy Physics* (CERN), the home of the WWW, in Switzerland.

When you start Mosaic, you see a large logo-like graphic and text that occupy most of the page. Some text is underlined. This represents the presence of a link. If you click on the underlined text, you summon whatever the original author of the document thought you should see. This could be more text, making the link like a footnote, or it could be more elaborate like an entirely different Web page. In the bar above the page, you see several icons and fields that contain text. For example, immediately to the left of the globe are two arrows and a stylized picture of a house. These buttons take you back and forth on the trail of links that you traverse in the current Mosaic session. To the left of these is a small window that shows the text NCSA Home Page. The *National Center for Supercomputing Applications* (NCSA) maintains its home page at the *Uniform Resource Locator* (URL) shown as http://www.ncsa.uiuc.edu... and so on. The pointing finger cursor hovers over the link to this URL; it is where you will go if you click the finger down on the link. (By the way, the window next to the button labeled Search is not active now because there is nothing to search.) The globe in the upper left corner rotates when Mosaic loads images, text, or other resources over the network.

If you ever tire of waiting for Mosaic to load a massive color image, just click on the globe to interrupt the loading process.

The program HyperCard on the Macintosh and the Help program on Microsoft Windows are examples of this kind of interface to resources. These programs work only on their own platforms, whereas Mosaic and WWW can work across many different platforms anywhere on the Internet.

html Authoring

Users can author their own Web pages in hypertext markup language. An html document looks like the following:

```
<TITLE>My Local Home Page</TITLE>
<H1>My Local Home Page</H1>
This is a sample page. You may wish to edit this page to
customize it for your own use. This can be done by editing the
file with a word processor, making the desired changes and saving
the file as text only.
<H2>Your Own Stuff</H2>
......
<H2>Places to Surf</H2>
<UL>
<LI> <A
HREF="http://www.ncsa.uiuc.edu/General/NCSAHome.html">NCSA Home
Page</A>
```

html interleaves plain text with *tags* (the text between the < and the >). The tag <L1> introduces a hypertext link to the NCSA home Web page. Mosaic displays the text on the screen and performs whatever action is specified by the hyperlink. The NCSA home page has links to information about html and authoring so you can get to it right away if you want.

Though the World Wide Web does not magically configure all the information you have on your machine by itself, it does provide the tools for you to configure it if you wish.

Summary

The Internet offers almost instantaneous globe-spanning electronic mail communication, archives of powerful free software, powerful online information access tools and data repositories, and something like 4,500 ongoing discussion newsgroups. This chapter introduced you to the Internet and some of its key features.

Chapter Snapshot

Troubleshooting a TCP/IP network is a complex subject. What it amounts to, however, is common sense and a thorough knowledge of all the protocols in use. Explaining each of the protocols well enough to find and repair problems could easily fill many books. Furthermore, although the protocols themselves are standardized, the implementation is not. That is to say, the name of the programs and command-line switches and options vary from installation to installation. If your implementation does not work like the examples provided here, check your documentation to note the differences.

In this chapter, you learn about the following:

Troubleshooting

"When people stop complaining, they stop thinking."

—*Anonymous*

What does it take to be a "Super-Tech" in the TCP/IP networking environment? The answer to this question is simple; you must have the following:

✔ A great deal of common sense

✔ A systematic and logical approach to troubleshooting

✔ A solid knowledge of each protocol in use on your network

Examining the Six-Step Troubleshooting Procedure

Common sense, of course, cannot be provided in a book; either you have it or you don't. Most do, but some people do not think it applies to computers. This book does not have enough space to provide the third requirement—knowledge of each protocol. The second requirement, a systematic and logical approach, is what this chapter provides, starting with the following six-step troubleshooting procedure:

1. Recognizing symptoms

2. Elaborating on symptoms

3. Listing probable faults

4. Localizing the faulty function

5. Localizing and repairing the actual problem

6. Analyzing the failure

First, you need some general advice: **Write Everything Down!** Take notes as you proceed through the troubleshooting steps, not after the fact. Taking notes helps keep you on track and also provides a record of what has been done—for both yourself and anyone who steps in to help. Pay attention to details. The smallest detail can sometimes put the whole problem into perspective. More often than not, overlooking a seemingly minor indication doubles your troubleshooting time.

Recognizing Symptoms (Step One)

Knowing something is wrong and recognizing the problem are the most important steps to successful troubleshooting. If you are to be an effective troubleshooter, you must be able to recognize a problem in the first place. You first need to establish a starting point. A doctor must know a patient's symptoms before treating an illness; similarly, you must know what is wrong with your network before you can fix it.

You must know how the system is supposed to operate. If you do not know how the system works under normal circumstances, you cannot possibly recognize a problem. Therefore, a good working knowledge of your network and the hosts and programs on it is essential to troubleshooting a potential problem. Again, you have to know the normal operating characteristics before you can recognize a trouble symptom.

Some of the questions you should ask at this stage of the operation include the following:

- ✔ What was being done at the time the noted "symptom" occurred?

- ✔ Has this procedure ever been done before?

- ✔ Was the procedure successful in the past?

- ✔ When was the last time the procedure was successful?

- ✔ What has changed since that time?

Elaborating on Symptoms (Step Two)

In this phase of the troubleshooting operation you further define the symptoms. Symptom elaboration is particularly important when troubleshooting a problem reported by another user. Run the program yourself. Note any error messages and look them up in the user manuals for a more detailed explanation of the problem. For instance, a user of your system tells you, "I can't ftp to novell.com!" Often this amount of information is the most that can be obtained. Further inquiries frequently result in answers like, "I don't know! It just doesn't work!" Try the operation yourself. Note the error messages. Does the ftp program report back with `connection timed out` or `unknown host`, for example? Error messages such as these give you much valuable information for localizing the problem. If you do not recognize the error message, look it up. Running the operation yourself also gives you the opportunity to check that the various options were specified correctly. If the operation works for you, it was probably operator error. Have the user try again while you watch and look to see that all operating controls and options are set correctly.

Another function of this phase of the operation is the actual elaboration of the noted symptoms. Jot down some notes about the indications noted thus far. What do they actually indicate? How do the symptoms relate to each other? Answering questions may point out even more symptoms. Before you begin troubleshooting, perform these steps:

- ✔ Gather information about the symptoms

- ✔ Elaborate on the problem and symptoms

- ✔ Pay attention to detail

- ✔ Write everything down

- ✔ Don't jump to conclusions

Listing Probable Faults (Step Three)

Now stop and reread the information you gathered in steps one and two. That's right, you should have taken notes so that you can reread. Next, list any and all things that might cause the symptoms noted thus far—for example, a bad network connection, a down gateway, or improper configuration of the host, the client, or a gateway, and so on. Don't try to figure out which one it is. Just write down everything you can think of that might cause the problem. You might consider prioritizing them based on likelihood of the error, but don't eliminate any of them yet.

Narrowing the Search (Step Four)

Use the tools available to you (discussed later in this chapter) to begin eliminating the various possible faults. Test each of the faults listed in step three. Don't rely on only one test to prove that an area is or isn't working. Most importantly, don't stop at the first fault you think you have proven. You may be mistaken or more than one fault might exist. Test them all in as many ways as you can. Again, write down your tests and results—this cannot be stressed enough. Taking notes makes things simpler for you and anyone who has to take over the operation, help with it, or repeat it later.

Isolating the Fault (Step Five)

By this time, you should have determined which machine on the network is causing the problem and quite possibly which program. Now start checking configuration files, log files, route tables, other protocols, background processes, and anything else related to the known symptoms. If you have followed the regimen thus far, this is the easiest step. By now, you should have a pretty good idea of what went wrong. All that remains is repairing the fault. But don't quit, yet—one more very important step still remains.

Analyzing the Failure (Step Six)

What is left to do after you fix the problem? In this phase of the operation, you must determine how the fault was introduced. What caused the configuration file to change and why? Why was the background process (daemon) not running? Did the route tables change or did the connections change without updating the route tables? Why? These are the questions that must be asked. You may have to make policy changes to avoid future trouble, or you may also find another fault that caused the fault you just repaired.

A review of all the symptom and testing information gathered thus far helps to isolate other possible faults. Would the malfunction you found and repaired directly or indirectly cause all the symptoms noted in steps one and two? If not, you must begin the operation again because you may have multiple faults. Also, retesting the system after repair of the fault can lead to more information about the fault and its overall effect on your network.

This procedure may sound a little silly. For some very simple and obvious problems maybe it is. If you want to be a super-tech, though, you have to "Do it right the *first* time!"? This procedure helps you do exactly that. One more time, *Write everything down!*, and keep your notes. You may run into a similar problem later, and referring back to your old notes can greatly reduce your troubleshooting time and increase your accuracy.

Deciding What To Check

Every problem is unique, and each requires that you check different things. As mentioned earlier, implementations vary. Some items are fairly common though. This section discusses some of the more common things to check.

Network Connectivity

Do any other protocols work? For example, if you are checking a problem with ftp, try telnet. If telnet works, then you know the cabling and other hardware are not the problem. If one protocol works, then they all should. This narrows your search and points to the server daemons on the target host. The odds are good that something is wrong with the configuration files or the daemons on the server.

Use ping for a better test of connectivity. With the ping program you can test for percentage of packet loss. Intermittent problems can cause some, but not all, of the network packets to be lost. One of the gateways between your host and the target server, for instance, might be overloaded and dropping packets. Most protocols work around this problem, but may time out before receiving the data they expect.

If no other protocols work and ping reports 100-percent packet loss, check the cables and gateways. Are all the cables plugged in? Are all the intermediate gateways up and operational? Are the local and remote interfaces up? Some network cards must be initialized by the operating system before they can operate. Check your startup files and use netstat to ensure that all interfaces are operational.

Configuration Files

Read through the configuration files. Almost all the TCP/IP programs store configuration information in plain, or mostly so, English. Read through the files related to your problem to make sure that they are correct. Check the last modified date on the files to see if they have changed recently. It is a good idea to document in the file, using comment lines, any changes made, who made the change, and why. Sometimes correcting one problem here can cause other problems.

Check all the configuration files; some common files are shown in table 19.1. Because the protocols and services are so interrelated, the problem may be in a different service. An unknown host error, for instance, in any service is probably a problem with the domain name service. Here again, you must know your system. As many different configurations exist as do implementations. Solid notes in the configuration files and in your system log will help here.

Table 19.1
Typical Configuration Files

File Name	Description
/etc/syslog.conf	Defines message types and log file paths.
/etc/bootptab	Defines addresses and load files.
/etc/snmp.conf	Defines communities and allowable addresses; may also define hosts to receive trap messages.
/etc/inetd.conf	Defines servers to be run by inetd.
/etc/resolv.conf	Name service; defines local domain name and next name server in chain.
/etc/named.boot	Defines location of databases, other nameservers, and domains served for named.
/usr/local/domain/named.fwd	Name server database for normal requests; NOTE: path/name may be different. Check in named.boot for proper path/name.
/usr/local/domain/named.rev	Name server database for IN-ADDR.ARPA requests; NOTE: path/name may be different. Check named.boot for proper path/name.
/usr/local/domain/named.ca	Name server database to prime the cache. NOTE: path/name may be different. Check named.boot for proper path/name.
/etc/services	Database for service name/number translation.
/etc/protocols	Database for protocol name/number translation.
/etc/networks	Database of network name/address. Not needed if using named.
/etc/hosts	Database of host name/address. Not needed if using named.

Log Files

Check the various log files; some common files are shown in table 19.2. Log files often provide important clues to the problem. Most programs written for TCP/IP create a log file of various information about the operation of the program. The service *providers* are especially noted for their log files. Most of the client programs provide diagnostic information directly to the screen when using the appropriate option (usually -d). Server programs, however, run in the background and save diagnostic information to a file.

Table 19.2
Typical Log Files

File Name	Description
/etc/bootplog	Log of bootp transactions.
/usr/adm/errlog	Log of hard disk errors.
/usr/adm/messages	Default name of syslog data file; check your syslog configuration file discussed earlier for file name(s).
/usr/adm/sulog	Log of super user or root logins.
/usr/lib/cron/log	Log of commands executed by cron; shows who, what, and when; may also show error messages.
/usr/spool/mqueue/syslog	Log of sendmail transactions and error messages.

Routing

Check the routing information on the gateway(s) in your system. If you are using TCP/IP, you more than likely have gateways between various networks. When a change is made to the networks, the routing information frequently is not forwarded to all the gateways in a timely manner. Protocols exist specifically for promulgating the routing changes automatically, but it takes time. In some cases, by the time you begin troubleshooting, the problem has already been solved.

Sometimes, the routing updates never occur at all. In some cases, the administrator has to enter the routing information manually. Not all gateways use the route update protocols. So check the tables on as many gateways as you can to make sure that they point to the right places for your eventual destination.

Every gateway should have a default route. When no specific route exists for the network or host you are trying to reach, the gateway forwards to the default. The gateway that receives the forwarded packets then checks its own routing table, and the process repeats until the data is delivered. Follow this chain of routes and watch for loops and misdirection.

Most transfers should reach their destination with less than twenty gateway hops, even on the Internet. If your chain of gateways goes over twenty, you probably have a misdirected route. The data may make it to the target eventually, but odds are that the time will be too great. Check also, if possible, for *Internet Control Message Protocol* (ICMP) redirect messages. Such a message is sent when a gateway forwards packets to a route when a shorter route is available.

A loop in the routing of packets ruins any chance of accessing your target host. For example, gateway A forwards data to gateway B; gateway B forwards to gateway C; gateway C forwards back to gateway A which, of course, forwards to gateway B again; and so on and so on. This eventually ends when the *Time To Live* (TTL) field in the IP header expires. TTL was added to IP headers specifically to help with this routing loop problem. Watch for ICMP TTL Expired messages and look for loops in your gateway routing.

Name Service

People like to think in terms of names because they are easier to remember. Computers, however, were designed to work with numbers. They refer to each other using numeric addresses even though people refer to them with names (albeit they are not always nice names). Within TCP/IP networking is a protocol to resolve this problem. Because millions of addresses can be used, especially if attached to the Internet as many TCP/IP installations are, it would be impractical to manually keep the names and addresses on each and every computer. The name service sometimes falls behind, though, on updates. Furthermore, you may have connectivity to the machine you're trying to get to, but not to your name server. Try running your program with the numeric address instead of the name if you can and if you know the numeric address. Also, try looking up the numeric address with a program that queries the name server.

Daemons Running

Are the daemons running on the machine to which you are trying to connect? If you have access to or control of the machine that is supposed to be providing service, check to make sure that they are doing so. Sometimes the background job is not running for one reason or another. If you do not control the machine in question, you have to contact the system administrator of that system if possible. In this case, it should probably be a last resort. Remember, he probably has troubles of his own to troubleshoot.

Protocol Enabled

Is the protocol you are trying to use enabled on the target host? For example, if trying to use ftp to reach a given host, you must ensure that that host is in fact an ftp server. Not all hosts run daemons for all protocols. Check with the system administrator for the target host to ensure that the protocol you are trying to use is enabled. It may well be that the administrator, not you, needs to do some troubleshooting. Be careful, however, not to get into a finger-pointing game. At least, check the more obvious possible faults on your system before calling to check someone else's host.

If you are the administrator of the server in question, check that the daemons are running and that the configuration files are correct. In some cases, you might need to check that inetd is running and that the problem protocol is enabled in the inetd configuration file.

Packet Trace

Last but not least, you might need to check the actual packets going across the network. To do this, you need some specialized tools or programs to present the packets as they move across the net. You also need to know exactly what these data packets should look like, which is when a thorough knowledge of the protocols is absolutely necessary. You cannot possibly know if a problem exists with the data packets if you do not know how to read them. The better varieties of packet trace tools format the headers to make them easier to read, but you must know what the fields are supposed to contain.

Using Troubleshooting Tools

Many tools are at your disposal. TCP/IP has been in use for many years, and the protocols are very well documented. Because the standards are openly available rather than being proprietary, many people have written programs that take advantage of the network. Most of these programs should be included with your TCP/IP implementation. Some are public domain and can be obtained through the Internet or Bulletin Board Systems. A few, usually very powerful, must be purchased, but generally do not save that much time. The commonly available tools should be enough to troubleshoot almost any problem on your network.

ping

The quickest and easiest way to determine if network connectivity is a problem is to use the ping utility. The ping program simply sends a network packet using the ICMP protocol to request an echo. The target host, upon receipt, echoes back the same data

II

Enumeration

received, again using ICMP. Most implementations of this useful utility report the round trip times for each packet sent and received. It usually, after sending several packets, also reports the percentage of packets not echoed. This feature is useful for checking the high packet-loss problem mentioned earlier. The following shows an example of using the ping utility:

```
$ ping admin
No response from xyp_admin.bar.com after 4 seconds
No response from xyp_admin.bar.com after 8 seconds
No response from xyp_admin.bar.com after 16 seconds
No response from xyp_admin.bar.com after 32 seconds
----admin.bar.com PING Statistics----
6 packets transmitted, 0 packets received, 100% packet loss


$ ping r-2
r-2.bar.com is alive
```

For a simple test of network connectivity, enter **ping <*hostname*>**. The program sends echo requests until either a response is received or the timer expires. If successful, the program notifies you with a message such as <*hostname*> is alive!

For more control over the program, you may enter some options on the command line. The usual format for the command is ping [hostname] <# of databytes> <# of echo requests>. The hostname is mandatory. <# *of databytes*> enables you to vary the size of the echo request packet. Be careful with this option. Some hosts do not answer large packet echo requests. You should never request packets of more than 512 data bytes because this often requires fragmenting, which does not work well with ICMP. Normally, the size of the packet is not a concern, and the default size is perfectly acceptable. Also, sending ping requests across someone else's network, through the Internet for example, with large packets, wastes bandwidth and annoys system administrators. The following shows an example of using ping with size and number specified. Notice that more specific information is returned than in the previous example.

```
$ ping xyp_r-2 56 10
PING xyp_r-2(193.114.36.137): 56 bytes      min/avg/max/mdev
Type ^A (decimal 1) <CR> to return to NetBlazer
56 bytes from 193.114.36.137 icmp_seq=0 time=10 ms  10/10/10/0
56 bytes from 193.114.36.137 icmp_seq=1 time=1 ms  1/9/10/2
56 bytes from 193.114.36.137 icmp_seq=2 time=1 ms  1/8/10/4
56 bytes from 193.114.36.137 icmp_seq=3 time=1 ms  1/7/10/5
56 bytes from 193.114.36.137 icmp_seq=4 time=1 ms  1/6/10/5
56 bytes from 193.114.36.137 icmp_seq=5 time=1 ms  1/5/10/5
56 bytes from 193.114.36.137 icmp_seq=6 time=1 ms  1/4/10/5
```

```
56 bytes from 193.114.36.137 icmp_seq=7 time=1 ms  1/4/10/5
56 bytes from 193.114.36.137 icmp_seq=8 time=1 ms  1/4/10/5
56 bytes from 193.114.36.137 icmp_seq=9 time=1 ms  1/4/10/5
----xyp_r-2 PING Statistics----
10 packets transmitted, 10 packets received, 0% packet loss
round-trip (ms)  min/avg/max/mdev = 0/4/10/5
```

Notice the times reported in the preceding example. This sample was taken from two hosts on the same Ethernet backbone. Do not expect your delivery times to be this small if pinging through gateways or across *Serial Line Interface Protocol* (SLIP) or *Point to Point Protocol* (PPP) interfaces. Delivery times greater than 1000 ms are not unheard of in these cases and should not cause a major problem.

Notice *icmp_seq*=# in the preceding example. The ICMP protocol puts a sequence number on each echo request it sends. The responding system should send back an echo response with the same sequence number. Ping programs use this to determine which packets were lost. As you can see in the following example, sequence numbers 1-6, 9, 13, and 14 were never echoed.

```
$ ping xyp_admin 56 20
PING xyp_admin.bar.com (193.114.36.138): 56 data bytes
64 bytes from 193.114.36.138: icmp_seq=0
64 bytes from 193.114.36.138: icmp_seq=7
64 bytes from 193.114.36.138: icmp_seq=8
64 bytes from 193.114.36.138: icmp_seq=10
64 bytes from 193.114.36.138: icmp_seq=11
64 bytes from 193.114.36.138: icmp_seq=12
64 bytes from 193.114.36.138: icmp_seq=15
64 bytes from 193.114.36.138: icmp_seq=16
64 bytes from 193.114.36.138: icmp_seq=17
64 bytes from 193.114.36.138: icmp_seq=18
64 bytes from 193.114.36.138: icmp_seq=19


----xyp_admin.bar.com PING Statistics----
20 packets transmitted, 11 packets received, 45% packet loss
```

<# of echo requests> is useful for checking intermittent problems. Specifying a number here causes the program to send one echo request per second until that number is reached. When finished, ping should report the number of packets sent, the number received, and the percentage of loss. A high percentage of loss causes many protocols to time out even though the data eventually gets through.

hopcheck

Another utility similar to ping is *hopcheck*. This utility is not generally packaged with TCP/IP implementations, but is available as public domain software—which means that its program implementation varies widely. Hopcheck is great for checking routing because it either uses ICMP echo requests, like ping, with a *record route* option in the IP header or it modifies the Time to Live field in the IP header. The method depends both on the implementation and your needs. Some gateways and hosts do not implement the Record Route option in IP headers. The modified TTL version of hopcheck, therefore, is more reliable. The following is an example of the hopcheck utility:

```
hopcheck rs.internic.net
Trying 198.41.0.5
    Address            Domain Name                         Time
 1. 193.114.36.8       nb-ny.bar.com                     (275 ms)
 2. 138.146.25.2       ***                               (549 ms)
 3. 26.29.0.207        OAKLAND-IP.DDN.MIL                (659 ms)
 4. 137.209.18.1       AMES-IP.DDN.MIL                   (659 ms)
 5. 192.52.195.253     en-0.enss144.t3.ans.net           (769 ms)
 6. 140.222.8.4        t3-3.cnss8.SanFrancisco.t3.ans.net (824 ms)
 7. 140.222.25.4       t3-3.cnss25.Chicago.t3.ans.net    (824 ms)
 8. 140.222.40.1       t3-0.cnss40.Cleveland.t3.ans.net  (769 ms)
 9. 140.222.48.2       t3-1.cnss48.Hartford.t3.ans.net   (769 ms)
10. 140.222.32.3       t3-2.cnss32.New-York.t3.ans.net   (769 ms)
11. 140.222.56.2       t3-1.cnss56.Washington-DC.ans.net (769 ms)
12. 140.222.56.194     mf-0.cnss58.Washington-DC.ans.net (769 ms)
13. 140.222.136.1      t3-0.cnss136.t3.ans.net           (824 ms)
14. 192.221.252.8      sura8-ext-cf.sura.net             (714 ms)
15. 128.167.212.2      wtn8-sura8.c3.sura.net            (824 ms)
16. 128.167.24.4       ***                               (824 ms)
17. 192.221.22.2       netsol-wtm4-cl.sura.net           (824 ms)
18. 198.41.0.5         rs.internic.net                   (824 ms)

hopcheck complete
```

In the preceding example, number 1 is the first gateway, which receives data from your host. Number 2 is the gateway to which number 1 forwards the data. In some cases, gateways are not listed in the domain name system. hopcheck normally displays *** when it cannot retrieve a name.

netstat

The netstat program can provide plenty of useful information from systems that you control or at least to which you have access. Using netstat, you can check the routing tables on your host, how many IP packets have been sent and received and how many error packets. As usual, implementations vary, but options should be available to enable you to check the route table and the interface(s).

The -r option on most implementations reports the contents of the route table. Compare the address of your target to the host, network, and subnet addresses in the route table. At least one entry must match, and it must point to a gateway that can reach the target. If none of the entries match exactly, check the "default" entry to make sure that the gateway it specifies can reach the target.

The -i option reports the statistics related to each of the interfaces on the host you are checking. The use of netstat -i should report the number of packets sent and received on each packet and the number of errors encountered on each interface. A high number of errors can indicate a problem either with the cabling, the interface card, or perhaps the network driver software. The following is an example of using the netstat utility to check utilities:

```
$ netstat -i
Name    Mtu     Network  Address  Ipkts   Ierrs  Opkts   Oerrs  Collis
ether   1500    none     none     50291   412    45241   0      0
ether1  0       none     none     0       0      0       0      0
ether2  1500    none     none     46675   0      21342   0      0
ether3  0       none     none     0       0      0       0      0
serial  0       none     none     0       0      0       0      0
loop    65535   none     none     490     0      496     0      0
```

Next is an example of using the netstat utility to view the routing table:

```
$ netstat -rn
Routing tables
Destination      Gateway          Flags   Interface
default          193.114.36.8     UG      ether
102              102.0.0.3        U       ether2
127.0.0.0        127.0.0.1        UH      loop
193.114.36       193.114.36.3     U       ether
193.114.36.3     127.0.0.1        UH      loop
```

Appending a -n option to this command reports a numeric address rather than the default of reporting by name. It also increases the speed of the command because name service lookup is not required. Read through the documentation on your implementation of netstat for other options. Several are available, but the preceding two are the most useful and most common.

nslookup

Almost any service can report an unknown host error, which is usually caused by a typographical error on the part of the user. A problem may exist, however, with the domain name service. The nslookup program is a simple utility to retrieve information from the name service. Use nslookup to verify the name of the host you are trying to reach. If the specific name you enter shows up as unknown, try an ls command within nslookup to retrieve the names of all hosts for a given domain. By scanning this list, you can check for misspelled names. As you can see in the following example, if you try to snyb, you won't have any luck because there is not one in the name server database.

```
$ nslookup
>ls bar.com.
[ns.bar.com.]
Host or domain name              Internet address
 bar                              server = ns.sys.com
 bar                              server = ns.bar.edu
 bar                              server = ns2.sys.com
 nb-ny                            193.114.36.8
 david1                           142.156.95.142
 novell1                          193.114.36.16
 snya                             193.114.36.3
 snyc                             193.114.36.4
 R-2                              193.114.36.137
 Admin                            193.114.36.138
 me                               127.0.0.1
```

SNMP

If your site implements the *Simple Network Management Protocol* (a misnomer if I have ever heard one because SNMP is anything but simple), then an SNMP management station can be an invaluable tool for monitoring or troubleshooting networks. SNMP reports on all the statistics related to all the protocols used within your network. From one machine, you can check the operation of every server on your system (every server that reports through SNMP, that is). This program is usually implemented with a graphical user interface such as that displayed in figure 19.1. Generally, the administrator must set up configuration files to allow access from the management station. Select the host you want from those displayed, then select the *Management Information Base* (MIB) you want to display (see fig. 19.2). Some SNMP systems also enable you to change various options. You can do things like add route table entries or even reboot a remote system with some clients and servers.

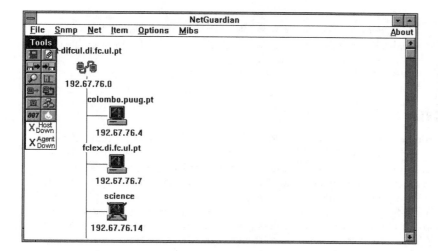

Figure 19.1
The opening window of Public Domain MS-Windows SNMP manager (NetGuardian).

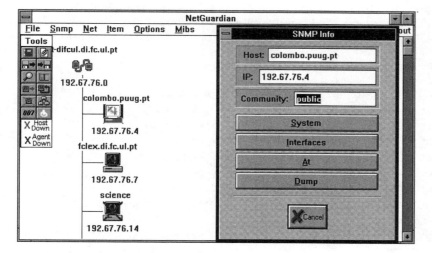

Figure 19.2
The MIB information selection window for NetGuardian.

syslog

Another very useful monitoring and troubleshooting protocol is *syslog*, which enables you to maintain all your log files for your entire network in one place. Run the syslog daemon on your most reliable host and configure your gateways and secondary hosts to report to the primary. When you have to troubleshoot or are monitoring the net, you can sit down at one host to check the error and diagnostic logs for all your systems. Syslog is a great time saver; moving from system to system, even using telnet from the same terminal is very time-consuming and sometimes completely impractical.

II
Enumeration

If the system on which you are maintaining all your log files crashes completely, you will not be able to check the logs. You should probably run the syslog daemon on more than one system.

Daemons

The method for checking the serve daemons varies, depending on the operating system. If you are using *nix, as most TCP/IP installations do, then the command to use is ps. This reports back every process running on the system. Look to see that the daemon for the problem protocol is running. For example, if you are checking for an ftp problem, make sure that the ftpd program is running on the server. Also, check the CPU time column for unusually high or low numbers. As mentioned earlier, you have to know your system. You cannot know what is wrong unless you know how it is supposed to work, and it is different on every system. Another item to check on *nix systems is the inetd program and configuration. Is inetd running and is the protocol you are having problems with configured correctly in the inetd.conf configuration file? Use ps, as mentioned earlier, to check to see if inetd is running and consult your implementation documentation to check the configuration. The following is an example of the ps command on a *nix system:

```
$ ps -ef
  UID   PID PPID  C    STIME TTY      TIME COMMAND
  root     0    0  0   Sep 30 ?       4:30 sched
  root     1    0  0   Sep 30 ?       1:40 /etc/init
  root     2    0  0   Sep 30 ?       0:00 vhand
  root     3    0  0   Sep 30 ?       0:01 bdflush
  root 24047    1  0 11:51:28 console 0:00 /etc/getty console console
  root   181    1  0   Sep 30 ?       0:12 /usr/netbin/inetd
  root   186    1  0   Sep 30 ?       0:04 /usr/netbin/named /etc/
     named.boot
  root   486    1  0   Sep 30 ?       0:00 /etc/getty contty contty
  root   206    1  0   Sep 30 ?       0:05 /usr/lib/sendmail -bd -q30m
  root   213    1  0   Sep 30 ?       0:18 /etc/cron
  root   235    1  0   Sep 30 ?       0:00 cat -u /dev/osm.all
  root   239    1  0   Sep 30 ?       0:30 /usr/lib/lpsched
  root   251    1  0   Sep 30 ?       0:00 /usr/net/netbios/nblisten
  root   487    1  0   Sep 30 ?       0:01 /etc/hdelogger
  root   503  499  0   Sep 30 ?       0:00 /usr/netbin/syslogd -f/etc/
     syslog.conf
  root   499    1  0   Sep 30 ?       0:11 /usr/netbin/syslogd -f/etc/
     syslog.conf
```

To check for background processes or *terminate-and-stay resident* programs (TSRs) on an MS-DOS system, run mem /c. This command does not prove conclusively that the program is actually running, but if the program is listed here, it is more than likely enabled. Some third-party utilities also are available that check interrupts and report which program has "hooked" them. Checking the interrupts is much better proof that the TSR is actually running.

If your server is implemented within Microsoft Windows or OS/2, the simplest way to check that the daemon is running is to look at the task manager (or use the OS/2 pstat utility). Double-click on the desktop background and check the pop-up list for the daemon program.

How do you check the name server problem? You can do two things: "ping" the name server to ensure connectivity and—more importantly, because you do not always know which name server answers for the name address pair in question—run nslookup and set the debug mode. Use this procedure to look up the name in question and check for irregularities in the resulting debug output.

Packet Trace

For some very difficult problems, you need to check the individual packets on the network, and you need some advanced tools. Some are provided as hardware and are generally referred to as *network sniffers* or *analyzers*. Others are provided as programs run on hosts and gateways, such as *trace*. In general, they provide a formatted output of the packets moving across your network or at least through the gateway or host. Most also enable you to limit the output to only the types of packets you are interested in. You can block out everything except the ftp protocol to or from the addresses in question, for example. This enables you to examine the actual data and headers for implementation problems. Remember also to watch for ICMP packets. ICMP is the network control protocol and will tell you about problems such as bad routes and down services.

ifconfig

The last tool discussed is *ifconfig*. Ifconfig is not so much a troubleshooting program as a configuration utility. It is how most host computers configure the network interfaces. Ifconfig is usually implemented in the network startup code and can sometimes cause problems—especially after reconfiguring any part of the net. Ifconfig is used to set the host address, subnet mask, broadcast address, and so on. If your startup files have been modified recently, look very closely at the ifconfig lines.

Troubleshooting Protocol-Specific Problems

As protocols vary, so do the common difficulties. This section discusses the problems and solutions specific to the protocols discussed throughout this chapter.

FTP and RCP

Although slightly different in method, the ftp and rcp protocols serve the same purpose. The common errors and the troubleshooting of these commands therefore are very similar. The most common problems in both protocols are `foo.bar.edu: unknown host`, `connection timed out`, or `connection refused`, and corrupted files. Only the last of these errors implies a different problem for each protocol.

The `unknown host` error message implies that a problem with the name server exists. This message tells you that the name requested by the user does not correlate to a numeric address. The human user of the system uses the name, but computers use only numeric addresses. The ftp program, therefore, uses the name server or the /etc/hosts file to convert the given name to a numeric address. If you are not using the name server system, troubleshooting this problem is simple. Just check the file /etc/hosts to ensure that an entry for the hostname is reported in the error message. If, on the other hand, your system does use the name-server-distributed database, you need to use nslookup as described earlier to check the name-to-address conversion.

The message `connection timed out` or `connection refused` can be caused by any number of problems. Both ftp and rcp employ the use of a timer to determine if the connection to the server is lost. If a packet of data is not received in a reasonable amount of time, the client program assumes that the connection has been lost and reports the error to the user. To find out if a connection problem exists, try "pinging" the server or perhaps a different protocol, such as telnet. Check all your cables and gateways, too. To find out if ftp (or rcp) is supported by the server, try using nslookup with querytype set to WKS and look for port/protocol 21. WKS stands for *Well-Known Services*. A WKS query should report back which services, such as ftp or telnet, are supported by the host. Unfortunately, nslookup usually reports these services as numbers. You have to look up the numbers in your /etc/services file or the Internet Assigned Numbers RFC. An example follows:

```
$ nslookup
Default Server:  snya.bar.com
Address:  193.114.36.3

> set querytype=WKS
> ftp.bar.com
Server:  snya.bar.com
Address:  193.114.36.3
```

```
ftp.bar.com    inet address = 127.0.0.1, protocol = 17
 42
ftp.bar.com    inet address = 127.0.0.1, protocol = 6
 21 23 25 42
```

In the preceding example, the server, snya.bar.com, claims that it provides service 42 for protocol 17, and services 21, 23, 25, and 42 for protocol 6. Checking the /etc/protocols file reveals that 17 is UDP and 6 is TCP. Checking the /etc/services file shows that 42 is named; 21 is ftp; 23 is telnet; 25 is SMTP; 42 is again named. You can, therefore, expect to be able to use name service, telnet, ftp, or mail to this host.

You might also have to call the system administrator of the server and ask if the ftp daemon is enabled. Perhaps a problem exists on the other end. Remember also that a listing in the name service, or lack thereof, is not conclusive proof of availability of a service. WKS records are not automatically inserted when a daemon starts up nor deleted on shutdown. The administrator must manually enter these records in the name service database.

Corrupted files from the ftp program are more than likely caused by setting the wrong mode. The ftp protocol is designed to be used to transfer files between various operating systems and to convert the data *on-the-fly*. The three basic modes of operation are as follows:

✔ Binary

✔ ASCII

✔ Tenex

ASCII should be used for transfer of text files. *Binary* mode is used for most transfers of non-text files such as executable programs or compressed files. *Tenex* mode must be used if transferring files from a system that uses a different number of bits per computer word than your system. For instance, if you are using a Unix system, which normally has 8 bits in a computer word to transfer files from a Simtel system, which has 30 bits in a computer word, you must use Tenex in place of Binary mode. Make sure that the proper mode was used to transfer the file. If so and the file is still corrupted, check with the system administrator of the server to make sure that it was not already corrupted before the transfer.

Another common problem with ftp is *anonymous ftp setup*. The ftp daemon changes the root directory to the home directory of the ftp user for security purposes. Directories normally available to the system, therefore, must be reproduced as subdirectories of the ftp home directory. Make sure that you have reproduced /bin, /etc, and /dev. The /ftp/ bin directory must contain the ls program. /ftp/etc must contain a copy of /etc/groups and /etc/passwd. Most important, /ftp/dev must contain links to the device entries for the TCP/IP networking implementation.

II

Enumeration

The passwd file in the ftp/etc subdirectory need not contain passwords and in fact should not. This file is only used for showing ownership of files. Do not include passwords in this copy of the passwd file because it can be downloaded by anyone.

The rcp protocol has no facility for conversion of data between operating systems. If files are corrupted after an rcp download, they were either corrupted on the server or you need to use ftp due to differing operating systems. This error is actually not very common for rcp. Usually, if rcp is supported at all by a server or client, it transfers files in a format common to the Unix operating system. If either the server or the client is not a *nix system, the protocol converts the data as it is transferred. This may end up as a double conversion, but it does solve the problem before it develops.

Routing

As mentioned earlier, loops and misdirected routes are the biggest problems with gateways. Any host that has more than one network interface may act as a gateway and must maintain a table to determine which network addresses are on which interface. Because other gateways can be on any of the attached networks, this table can be quite complex. Gateways are frequently added and deleted from various networks, especially if connected to the Internet, and the table must be changed accordingly. Often the routing tables are not changed for some time after the physical changes. Adding or deleting a gateway generally entails changes to many routing tables and occasionally some of the gateways go unnoticed until a problem develops.

Updating all the gateways is often too complex. So many gateways exist on a complex internetwork that few people can remember them all. Luckily, several protocols were developed to automate this procedure. RIP, GGP, EGP, IGP, and RDP—just to name a few—help to promulgate the routing table updates. If you are running any of these protocols on your network your job will be greatly simplified. You must be running the same protocol on each machine, however, because they are not compatible with each other. Also, do not expect the updates to take place immediately. To reduce the amount of network traffic, they are normally designed to send the information on an infrequent basis. Furthermore, the information may have to travel through several gateways before updating the one you are currently using.

Using a default route greatly simplifies the routing tables. Only listings for the directly attached networks must be maintained in the routing table. Packets for any address that does not fit one of the specific network or host entries are forwarded to the gateway in the default entry. With a default route in place, forgetting an update normally does not have a major impact on the net. The data may take the long way around, but it still gets where it is going.

Route table entries may be either for a single host or for an entire network. Each entry consists of an address, subnet mask, interface, and possibly another gateway attached to the interface that forwards data. In this situation, the subnet mask specifies how much of the given address to compare with for forwarding decisions. The following is a simple routing table for a gateway with three interfaces:

```
193.114.36.0    255.255.255.0    en0
139.23.0.0      255.255.0.0      en1
10.0.0.0        255.0.0.0        en1    139.23.12.4
default                          sc0    138.145.25.2
```

The first entry specifies that any packet with an address that starts with 193.114.36 should be sent to the network attached to the en0 interface. The next entry shows that data destined for address 139.23.<anything> will be routed on the en1 interface. The third entry tells the system to send data addressed to the network address starting with 10 to the gateway address of 139.23.12.4, which is attached to en1 interface. Finally, if none of these entries matches the address on the packet, it is sent to the gateway address of 138.145.25.2 through the sc0 interface.

Routing conflicts such as loops and misdirections result in ICMP warning messages. Depending on your gateway implementation, these messages may be acted upon automatically or they may be reported to the administrator. Watch for ICMP Redirect messages and ICMP TTL Expired messages. The first implies that your data is taking the long way around. If a gateway receives a packet that it must transmit to a gateway that it knows is attached to the sending gateway it sends back a redirect message. Check your routing table to make sure an entry exists for the new gateway. ICMP TTL Expired messages are most likely a result of a loop. Each time a packet passes through a gateway, the TTL field is decremented by one. When this number reaches 0, the packet is discarded and an ICMP TTL Expired message is sent back to the source. In a loop condition, the packet is sent through the loop until the TTL reaches 0. Under normal circumstances, the TTL is set high enough that it does not time out, so an Expired TTL implies a loop in the routing chain.

The hopcheck utility discussed earlier is an excellent tool for checking the routing tables. You may not know all the gateways that must be traversed, nor control any or all of them. Hopcheck quickly determines the route and shows if a loop or a down gateway exists. A quick glance at the following example shows that a loop condition obviously exists. Check the gateways on lines 2 through 5:

```
hopcheck rs.internic.net
Trying 198.41.0.5
     Address           Domain Name                         Time
  1. 193.114.36.8      nb-ny.bar.com                       (275 ms)
  2. 138.146.25.2      ***                                 (549 ms)
  3. 26.29.0.207       OAKLAND-IP.DDN.MIL                  (659 ms)
  4. 137.209.18.1      AMES-IP.DDN.MIL                     (659 ms)
```

II

Enumeration

```
 5. 192.52.195.253    en-0.enss144.t3.ans.net          (769 ms)
 6. 26.29.0.207       OAKLAND-IP.DDN.MIL               (659 ms)
 7. 137.209.18.1      AMES-IP.DDN.MIL                  (659 ms)
 8. 192.52.195.253    en-0.enss144.t3.ans.net          (769 ms)
 9. 26.29.0.207       OAKLAND-IP.DDN.MIL               (659 ms)
10. 137.209.18.1      AMES-IP.DDN.MIL                  (659 ms)
11. 192.52.195.253    en-0.enss144.t3.ans.net          (769 ms)

...
```

SNMP

Security is a major concern with SNMP. This protocol provides much information about your network. It also can allow an SNMP management station to control your network. Naturally, passwords and management station address control are implemented to determine who can access this information.

Security functions are designed to stop those who should not access the data. Unless configured correctly, however, these functions also stop those who should be accessing the information. When a problem develops while someone is trying to access an SNMP agent, one of the first things to check is the configuration files on both machines. Is the agent configured to allow access from the address of your management station? Are the "communities" the same on both machines? SNMP uses communities as passwords. If your management station is part of the "public" community, but the agent is only in the "myspecial" community, access will be denied.

Another problem with SNMP is version conflict. Using an SNMP v1 management station to access an SNMP v2 agent causes various conflicts—not the least of which may be complete lack of access. Check closely the version of SNMP on both machines. Note, too, that some SNMP implementations support either or both versions.

Last, but certainly not least, make sure that you have the appropriate *Management Information Bases* (MIBs) enabled on both machines. A Management Information Base enables the SNMP protocol to specify what information it will provide and how to ask for that information. At least 20 different MIBs are available for various machines, networks, and operating systems. Any SNMP implementation, though, should at least support the System, IP, and TCP MIBs. If these three work, but a specialty MIB does not, make sure that the extra MIB is supported by both the agent and management stations.

DNS

The *Domain Name Service* (DNS) is a distributed database system. DNS has several servers, each of which maintains a small portion of the complete list of names and addresses. Not only must you have connection between your host and the default name server, but the default name server must be able to connect with other name servers. If the name/ address pair you are looking for is not contained in the database on the default server, it must ask the next server in the tree of the distributed system. To troubleshoot a timeout problem like the one shown in the following example, you must determine where the connectivity is being lost. Try to look up a name that you know is contained in the default name server. If it does not work, the problem is probably connectivity with that machine. If it does work, the problem is most likely connectivity between the servers.

```
$ nslookup
> set debug
> foo.bar.com.
Server:  snya.bar.com
Address:  193.114.36.3

Local datagram port number: 1440
Timeout 1
Local datagram port number: 1440
Timeout 2
Local datagram port number: 1440
Timeout 3
Local datagram port number: 1440
Timeout 4
*** Request to snya.bar.com timed-out
```

Often the connectivity between servers is lost because of a down gateway or misdirected route. Sometimes your host can talk to either of the servers, but they cannot talk to each other. To help narrow the search for the connectivity problem use set recurse, as in the next example, to determine which server should have the answer to your query. Then set the default server within nslookup to that host and try your query again. If it works, a route problem or down gateway probably exists. If this procedure does not result in an answer, unfortunately, it does not provide you with much information. Perhaps there is still a down gateway, and your host must use it as well to get to the name server.

```
$ nslookup
> set norecurse
> www.town.hall.org.
Server:  snya.bar.com
Address:  193.114.36.3

Name:    www.town.hall.org
Served by:
- NS.INTERNIC.NET
   198.41.0.4
```

```
- AOS.ARL.ARMY.MIL
  128.63.4.82, 192.5.25.82

- NS1.ISI.EDU
  128.9.0.107

- C.NYSER.NET
  192.33.4.12

- TERP.UMD.EDU
  128.8.10.90

- NS.NASA.GOV
  128.102.16.10, 192.52.195.10

- NIC.NORDU.NET
  192.36.148.17

- NS.ISC.ORG
  192.5.5.241

- NS.NIC.DDN.MIL
  192.112.36.4
```

When troubleshooting with nslookup as with almost any command, set the debug mode. This causes the program to provide extra information.

The following is an example of the nslookup utility in debug mode:

```
$ nslookup
> set debug
> rs.internic.net.
Server:  snya.bar.com
Address:  193.114.36.3

Local datagram port number: 1445
-----------
Got answer:
    HEADER:
opcode = QUERY, id = 6, rcode = NOERROR
```

```
header flags:  response, want recursion, recursion avail.
questions = 1,  answers = 1,  auth. records = 3,  additional = 3

    QUESTIONS:
rs.internic.net, type = A, class = IN
    ANSWERS:
    ->  rs.internic.netinet address = 198.41.0.5
    AUTHORITY RECORDS:
    ->  INTERNIC.netnameserver = RS.INTERNIC.NET
    ->  INTERNIC.netnameserver = IS.INTERNIC.NET
    ->  INTERNIC.netnameserver = NOC.CERF.NET
    ADDITIONAL RECORDS:
    ->  RS.INTERNIC.NETinet address = 198.41.0.5
    ->  IS.INTERNIC.NETinet address = 192.153.156.15
    ->  NOC.CERF.NETinet address = 192.153.156.22


- - - - - - - - - - -
Non-authoritative answer:
Name:    rs.internic.net
Address:  198.41.0.5
```

The domain name service uses a human-readable (and writeable) text file to convert names to numeric addresses. What, then, do you suppose is the most common error within this file of names and addresses? Typographical errors, of course. Make certain that all the host names are spelled correctly.

A Note from the Author

When I set up my first name server, I mistyped the name of my main mail server. It was just a simple typographical error. I entered **syna** instead of the proper **snya**. I had not followed my own advice about triple checking the database before implementation. Because it was a Friday afternoon, the error wasn't caught until Monday morning. The error was caught because a 50 character e-mail message had bounced back and forth across the Internet so many times that it had turned into a 1 megabyte message. All from a simple mistyped name. I learned the triple check rule the hard way, and I'll never forget it!

Make sure that you have not forgotten the trailing period at the end of a domain name to prevent appending the default domain name. The name service daemon is *very* particular about this file. Forgetting the period on an entry could result in the name foo.bar.com.bar.com in place of foo.bar.com. Even though the computer will catch this missing period in an instant, it may take you hours to catch it. Take your time when making changes to the file and triple check everything you enter.

Most name server programs load the database into memory upon initialization and do not refer back to the disk file. If you have just entered the problem host name into the database, make sure that you restart the name server daemon to pick up the change. You may need to verify by dumping the database from memory to a disk file. On *nix implementations, you can usually use the kill command to send a signal to cause this. Other systems probably will have a menu option. Consult your documentation and try it. Then read the resulting file. It probably will be slightly different from the original. All the abbreviated entries will be expanded to their full form. This may in itself help for checking your entries. The abbreviations do not always work as expected.

sendmail/SMTP

Because sendmail is normally implemented as a background daemon, it reports its error messages directly to the user with e-mail. It also sends error information to the log file, but your first contact with the error will probably be from the user reporting a message from MAILER-DAEMON or POSTMASTER. The daemon returns the original message along with error information and the headers placed on the message as it travels through the network. The message may move smoothly through several systems before the error develops. Read the headers closely to determine where the error was caught.

The most common errors are host unknown and user unknown. These errors are usually the result of a typographical error on the part of the user sending the message. Check the To: field on the message header to make sure that everything was spelled correctly. Because you undoubtedly will not know every user name on every system, you probably need the user's help with this. You can check for obvious errors, though, such as blank spaces within the address.

To verify the host name exists, use the nslookup procedures described earlier. If it does exist, try nslookup from the system that sent the error message. If it still works, try sending the message again. A gateway probably was down when the message was originally sent.

Verifying the existence of a user is a little more tricky. If the target host implements the finger protocol, you can try finger user@host.domain. Many hosts do not implement a finger server though because of security precautions. An alternative is to telnet to port 25 of the target host and send a VRFY command. Failing this, you must call the system administrator or send a message to POSTMASTER@target.host to ask if the user exists. The following example shows this procedure:

```
$ telnet foo.bar.com 25
Trying...
Connected to foo.bar.com.
Escape character is '^]'.
220 foo.bar.com Sendmail 5.60/25 ready at Sat, 1 Oct 94 12:04:27 EDT
```

```
VRFY srimbey
250 Stephen Rimbey <srimbey>
VRFY jones
550 jones... User unknown
VRFY Executive_List
550 Executive_List... User unknown
EXPN Executive_List
250-John Smith <jsmith>
250-Mike Burns <mburns>
250-Bill Green <bgreen>
250-Emery Wilhelm <ewilhelm>
250-Anthony Jones <ajones>
250 Peter Cain <pcain>
QUIT
221 foo.bar.com closing connection
Connection closed.
Connection closed by foreign host.
```

Not all mail servers have designated an alias for POSTMASTER. The RFC concerning e-mail recommends it, but it is not built into most mail implementations. If the administrator does not create an alias for POSTMASTER, your query will be returned with a user unknown error. The only alternative is to try calling the administrator.

The domain name service can also cause problems for sendmail. A special type of record in the name service specifies what host will manage e-mail for which networks. Check your name service for MX records that pertain to the target host from the To: address field.

MX records were designed into the domain name service to allow hosts to act as intermediate mail gateways for hosts not directly connected to the network. For instance, if you want to send mail to a host that is not connected to the network (hostA), but hostB can reach hostA through a different protocol, an MX record—such as in the following example—should be in the domain name system to redirect hostA's mail to hostB:

```
hostB     IN    MX     3 hostA.bar.com.
```

The name service also implements MB records and MG records for the e-mail system. Most mailer daemons, however, ignore these records. They were introduced in the domain name service standards, but have never been very popular. Error messages sometimes develop because a system administrator relied on MB or MG records and the mailer neither recognizes nor uses them.

Avoiding Trouble and Being Prepared

Preventing problems from the beginning makes you look (and feel) great. The best way to avoid problems is to monitor the network, even when it is (supposedly) working correctly. Keeping a written log of events also helps to ensure that all runs smoothly, particularly in a multiperson AOP center.

System Log

A log or diary of all events related to your system can be an invaluable resource when troubleshooting. This is especially true of large sites in which several people in the ADP center are responsible for the system in question. In this log, you should record any and all changes to the configuration files, the startup files, and the protocols supported by the system. In short, any change to the system should be written down along with the date, time, reason, person making change, and projected impact. When a problem develops, check the log first for recent changes that might cause the problem. You might cut your troubleshooting time down to five minutes. This also helps to ensure that you do not solve one problem only to create another; such as reenabling a protocol that was intentionally disabled because of a bug in the system or for security purposes.

Configuration File Hard Copies

Maintain a printed copy of each configuration file on your system. Backup tapes are great, but they can be damaged just as easily as the hard drive. Configuration files for TCP/IP protocol implementations are almost always normal human-readable text files. It also helps to use the remarks feature in most of these files. Leave many comments in your configuration files explaining exactly what each line does. Along with your system log, this helps to remind you and others of what you had in mind when you last changed the file.

Monitoring

Troubleshooters never seem to be noticed until the system goes down. When you are noticed, it is usually not in a good light. It is, therefore, usually best to maintain a low profile and not be noticed at all. How do you do this? Monitor your network and catch problems before the users do. Check your online log files frequently. Obtain an SNMP client and monitor the error statistics. Run netstat to check the interfaces regularly. Even try the various protocols you offer to your users every so often to make sure that they are working properly. In short, use the troubleshooting techniques outlined in this chapter even when no known problem exists. Find the errors before they find you!

Summary

Knowing something is wrong and recognizing the problem are the most important steps in troubleshooting. This chapter outlined a six-step troubleshooting procedure that, if followed, can help you quickly diagnose any problem you might encounter on your network. The chapter also discussed common problems encountered on TCP/IP networks and the tools that you can use to most efficiently troubleshoot these problems. The ping and netstat programs were discussed, and use of the domain name system and SNMP also were covered. As always, preventing problems in the first place is important, and this chapter also offered tips, such as monitoring your network and taking notes, to help you find and fix the problems before they find you.

Part III

Appendixes and Glossary

APPENDIX

Current Vendors

The following is a current list of TCP/IP software vendors, presented in alphabetical order. Important things to note are the operating systems supported and protocols.

Cykic Software

(619) 297-0182
(800) 544-4620

Product	Multibase-Telnet Server
OSs supported	DOS, Windows 3.1, Windows NT, Macintosh, OS/2, VMS
NOSs supported	Any NOS that supports TCP/IP
Transport protocols available	IP, TCP, UDP
E-mail protocols available	Proprietary MultiMail
File-transfer protocols supported	ftp

D-Link Systems

(714) 455-1688
(800) 326-1688

Product	TCP/IP for DOS
OSs supported	DOS
NOSs supported	OS/2 LAN Manager, NetBIOS, NetWare 3.x, NetWare 4.0
Transport protocols available	IP, TCP
E-mail protocols available	SMTP
File-transfer protocols supported	ftp

Distinct

(408) 366-8933

Product	Distinct TCP/IP for Windows— Software Developers Kit
OSs supported	Windows 3.1, Windows NT
NOSs supported	LAN Server, NetWare 3.x, NetWare 4.0, Pathworks, VINES, Windows for Workgroups
Transport protocols available	IP, TCP, UDP
E-mail protocols available	None
File-transfer protocols supported	ftp, tftp

Distinct

(408) 366-8933

Product	Distinct TCP/IP Tools for Windows
OSs supported	Windows 3.1, Windows NT
NOSs supported	LAN Server, NetWare 3.x, NetWare 4.0, Pathworks, VINES, Windows for Workgroups, LANtastic
Transport protocols available	IP, TCP, UDP
E-mail protocols available	None
File-transfer protocols supported	ftp, tftp

Eicon Technology

(514) 631-2592
(800) 803-4266

Product	Access for OS/2 3270; Access for OS/2 5250
OSs supported	OS/2
NOSs supported	NetBIOS, NetWare 3.x
Transport protocols available	IP, TCP
E-mail protocols available	None
File-transfer protocols supported	IND$File, PS/CICS, DISOSS; None

Eicon Technology

(514) 631-2592
(800) 803-4266

Product	Access for Windows 3270; Access for Windows 5250
OSs supported	Windows 3.1
NOSs supported	NetBIOS, NetWare 3.x, VINES
Transport protocols available	IP, TCP
E-mail protocols available	None
File-transfer protocols supported	IND$File, PS/CICS, DISOSS; AS/400

Esker

(415) 341-9065
(800) 883-7537

Product	TUN*PLUS; TUN*TCP
OSs supported	DOS, Windows 3.1
NOSs supported	NetWare 3.x, NetWare 4.0, VINES, Windows for Workgroups
Transport protocols available	IP, TCP, UDP
E-mail protocols available	SMTP, POP2, POP3
File-transfer protocols supported	ftp, rcp

Firefox

(408) 321-8344
(800) 230-6090

Product	NOV*IX for NetWare
OSs supported	DOS, Windows 3.1, VMS
NOSs supported	NetWare 3.x, NetWare 4.0, Windows for Workgroups
Transport protocols available	IP, TCP, SPX/IPX
E-mail protocols available	SMTP, POP2, POP3
File-transfer protocols supported	ftp, tftp, rcp, NVTCP, NVftp

Frontier Technologies

(414) 241-4555

Product	Super TCP for Windows; Super TCP/NFS for Windows
OSs supported	Windows 3.1
NOSs supported	LAN Server, NetBIOS, NetWare 3.x, NetWare 4.0, VINES, Windows for Workgroups, DECnet, 10Net
Transport protocols available	IP, TCP, UDP
E-mail protocols available	Rules-based messaging (TCP), SMTP, POP2, POP3, MIME
File-transfer protocols supported	ftp, tftp, rcp

FTP Software

(508) 659-6458
(800) 282-4387

Product	PC/TCP
OSs supported	DOS, Windows 3.1, OS/2
NOSs supported	OS/2 LAN Manager, NetBIOS, NetWare 3.x, NetWare 4.0, Pathworks, VINES, Windows for Workgroups

Transport protocols available	IP, TCP, UDP
E-mail protocols available	SMTP, POP2, POP3
File-transfer protocols supported	ftp, tftp, rcp

Hughes LAN System

(415) 996-7300
(800) 395-5267

Product	ProLinc Multi-Protocol Software
OSs supported	DOS, Windows 3.1
NOSs supported	OS/2 LAN Manager, LAN Server, NetBIOS, NetWare 3.x, NetWare 4.0, Pathworks, VINES, Windows NT, Windows for Workgroups
Transport protocols available	IP, TCP, UDP
E-mail protocols available	SMTP, POP2, POP3
File-transfer protocols supported	ftp, tftp, rcp

IBM Corporation

1-800-IBM-CALL

Products	TCP/IP for DOS/Windows, TCP/IP for OS/2, TCP/IP for MVS, TCP/IP for VM,
OSs supported	DOS. Windows 3.1, OS/2, VM, MVS, AIX, RS/6000, OS/400
NOSs supported	OS/2, LAN Manager, LAN Server, NetBIOS, NetWare, Windows for Workgroups, CM/2
Transport protocols available	IP, POP2, POP3, MIME
E-mail protocols available	SMTP, POP2, POP3, MIME
File transfer protocols supported	FTP, TFTP, RCP

III

Appendixes and Glossary

InterCon Systems

(703) 709-5500
(800) 468-7266

Product	TCP/Connect II for Windows; TCP/Connect II for Macintosh
OSs supported	DOS, Windows 3.1, OS/2, Power Macintosh with Soft Windows, Macintosh
NOSs supported	OS/2 LAN Manager, NetWare 3.x, VINES, Windows for Workgroups; None
Transport protocols available	IP, TCP; None
E-mail protocols available	MIME (Windows), SMTP, POP2, POP3
File-transfer protocols supported	tftp (Windows), rcp (Windows), ftp

Interlink Computer Sciences

(510) 657-9800
(800) 422-3711

Product	SNS/TCPaccess
OSs supported	MVS
NOSs supported	None
Transport protocols available	IP, TCP, UDP
E-mail protocols available	SMTP
File-transfer protocols supported	ftp

Ipswitch

(617) 246-1150

Product	Acadia/VxD; Piper/IP
OSs supported	Windows 3.1, DOS (Piper)
NOSs supported	OS/2 LAN Manager, LAN Server, NetBIOS, NetWare 3.x, NetWare 4.0, Pathwork, VINES, Windows for Workgroups
Transport protocols available	IP, TCP, UDP

E-mail protocols supported	SMTP, POP3, MIME
File-transfer protocols supported	ftp, tftp, rcp

Ipswitch

(617) 246-1150

Product	Catipult
OSs supported	OS/2
NOSs supported	LAN Server, NetWare 3.x, NetWare 4.0
Transport protocols available	IP, TCP
E-mail protocols available	SMTP
File-transfer protocols supported	ftp, tftp, rcp

Ipswitch

(617) 246-1150

Product	Vantage/IP
OSs supported	OS/2
NOSs supported	OS/2 LAN Manager, LAN Server, NetBIOS, NetWare 3.x, NetWare 4.0, VINES
Transport protocols available	IP, TCP, UDP
E-mail protocols supported	SMTP, POP3
File-transfer protocols supported	ftp, tftp, rcp

James River Group

(612) 339-2521

Product	ICE.TCP
OSs supported	DOS, Windows 3.1, Windows NT
NOSs supported	OS/2 LAN Manager, LAN Server, NetBIOS, NetWare 3.x, NetWare 4.0, Pathworks, VINES, Windows NT, Windows for Workgroups, LANtastic

Transport protocols available	IP, TCP, UDP
E-mail protocols supported	None
File-transfer protocols supported	ftp, tftp

NetManage

(408) 973-7171

Product	Chameleon
OSs supported	Windows 3.1
NOSs supported	LAN Server, NetWare 3.x, NetWare 4.0, Pathworks, VINES, Windows for Workgroups, Microsoft LAN Manager
Transport protocols available	IP, TCP, UDP
E-mail protocols available	SMTP, POP2, POP3, MIME
File-transfer protocols supported	ftp, tftp

NetManage

(408) 973-7171

Product	Chameleon 32; Chameleon 32 NFS
OSs supported	Windows NT
NOSs supported	Windows NT
Transport protocols available	None
E-mail protocols available	None
File-transfer protocols supported	ftp, tftp

NetManage

(408) 973-7171

Product	Chameleon NFS; Chameleon NFS/X
OSs supported	Windows 3.1

NOSs supported	LAN Server, NetWare 3.x, NetWare 4.0, Pathworks, VINES, Windows for Workgroups, Microsoft LAN Manager
Transport protocols available	IP, TCP, UDP
E-mail protocols supported	SMTP, POP2, POP3, MIME
File-transfer protocols supported	ftp, tftp

NetManage

(408) 973-7171

Product	Chameleon/D NFS; Chameleon/X
OSs supported	DOS, Windows 3.1; Windows 3.1
NOSs supported	LAN Server, NetWare 3.x, NetWare 4.0, Pathworks, VINES, Windows for Workgroups, Microsoft LAN Manager, NetBIOS (/D NFS)
Transport protocols available	IP, TCP, UDP
E-mail protocols available	SMTP, POP2, POP3, MIME
File-transfer protocols supported	ftp, tftp

NetManage

(408) 973-7171

Product	Internet Chameleon
OSs supported	Windows 3.1
NOSs supported	LAN Server, NetWare 3.x, NetWare 4.0, Pathworks, VINES, Windows for Workgroups, Microsoft LAN Manager
Transport protocols available	IP, TCP, UDP
E-mail protocols available	SMTP, POP2, POP3, MIME
File-transfer protocols supported	ftp, tftp

III

Appendixes and Glossary

Process Software

(508) 879-6994
(800) 722-7770

Product	TCPware for OpenVMS
OSs supported	VMS
NOSs supported	NetWare 3.x, Pathworks
Transport protocols available	IP, TCP, UDP
E-mail protocols available	SMTP, POP3
File-transfer protocols supported	ftp, tftp, rcp

Qualcomm

(800) 238-3672

Product	Eudora
OSs supported	Windows 3.1, Windows NT, Macintosh (System 7), OS/2, VMS, VMS/CMS
NOSs supported	AppleShare, OS/2 LAN Manager, LAN Server, NetBIOS, NetWare 3.x, NetWare 4.0, VINES, Windows NT
Transport protocols available	IP, TCP, serial dial-up
E-mail protocols available	SMTP, POP3, MIME
File-transfer protocols supported	ftp

Relay Technology

(703) 506-0500
(800) 795-8674

Product	Relay/PC Gold for DOS LAN 5.1
OSs supported	DOS
NOSs supported	OS/2 LAN Manager, LAN Server, NetBIOS, NetWare 3.x, NetWare 4.0, VINES, Windows NT, Windows for Workgroups

Transport protocols available	IP, TCP
E-mail protocols available	N/A
File-transfer protocols supported	XYZ Modem, Kermit, CompuServe, ASCII Capture

Relay Technology

(703) 506-0500
(800) 795-8674

Product	Relay/PC Gold for Windows 6.0
OSs supported	Windows 3.1
NOSs supported	OS/2 LAN Manager, LAN Server, NetBIOS, NetWare 3.x, NetWare 4.0, VINES, Windows NT, Windows for Workgroups
Transport protocols available	IP, TCP
E-mail protocols available	N/A
File-transfer protocols supported	XYZ Modem, Kermit, CompuServe, ASCII Capture

Shany

(415) 694-7410

Product	AlertView
OSs supported	DOS, Windows 3.1, OS/2
NOSs supported	OS/2 LAN Manager, LAN Server, NetBIOS, NetWare 3.x, NetWare 4.0, Pathworks, Windows for Workgroups
Transport protocols available	IP, TCP
E-mail protocols available	None
File-transfer protocols supported	None

III

Appendixes and Glossary

Spartacus Technologies

(617) 487-2700
(800) 937-5638

Product	KNET TCP/IP Network Software
OSs supported	MVS and VM
NOSs supported	Mainframe
Transport protocols available	IP, TCP, UDP
E-mail protocols available	SMTP
File-transfer protocols supported	ftp, tftp

Spider Software

011-44-31-556-5166

Product	SpiderTCP
OSs supported	Windows 3.1, Windows NT, VRTX, P505, VxWorks
NOSs supported	None
Transport protocols available	IP, TCP, UDP
E-mail protocols available	SMTP
File-transfer protocols supported	ftp, tftp, rcp

Spry

(206) 447-0300
(800) 777-9638

Product	The Air Series
OSs supported	Windows 3.1, Windows NT
NOSs supported	NetBIOS, NetWare 3.x, NetWare 4.0, Pathworks, VINES, Windows NT, Windows for Workgroups, LAN Manager
Transport protocols available	IP, TCP UDP
E-mail protocols available	SMTP, POP3
File-transfer protocols supported	ftp

Synergy Software

(610) 779-0522
(800) 876-8376

Product	VersaTerm, VersaTerm Pro; Versa Tilities
OSs supported	Macintosh
NOSs supported	AppleShare; AppleShare, Pathworks
Transport protocols available	IP, TCP
E-mail protocols available	SMTP, POP3
File-transfer protocols supported	ftp

TGV

(408) 457-5200
(800) 848-3440

Product	MultiNet
OSs supported	Windows 3.1, Windows NT, VMS
NOSs supported	NetWare 3.x, NetWare 4.0
Transport protocols available	IP, TCP, UDP
E-mail protocols available	SMTP, POP2, POP3, All-in-1
File-transfer protocols supported	ftp, tftp, rcp

Visionware

(415) 325-2113
(800) 949-8474

Product	Xvision5
OSs supported	Windows 3.1, Windows NT
NOSs supported	NetWare 3.x, NetWare 4.0, Pathworks, Windows NT, Windows for Workgroups
Transport protocols available	TCP
E-mail protocols available	None
File-transfer protocols supported	ftp

WallData

(206) 883-4777

Product	Rumba for the Mainframe (OS/2); Rumba Office
OSs supported	OS/2; Windows 3.1
NOSs supported	OS/2 LAN Manager, NetBIOS, NetWare 3.x, NetWare 4.0, LAN Server (Office), Windows for Workgroups (Office)
Transport protocols available	None
E-mail protocols available	None
File-transfer protocols supported	Kermit, IND$File

The Wollongong Group

(415) 962-7100

Product	Pathway Access
OSs supported	DOS, Windows 3.1, Macintosh, OS/2, VMS
NOSs supported	AppleShare, OS/2 LAN Manager, LAN Server, NetBIOS, NetWare 3.x, NetWare 4.0, Pathworks, VINES, Windows for Workgroups, LANtastic
Transport protocols available	IP, TCP, UDP
E-mail protocols available	SMTP, POP2, POP3, NNTP, IMAP
File-transfer protocols supported	ftp, tftp, rcp

WRQ

(206) 217-7100
(800) 872-2829

Product	Reflection Network Series for DOS
OSs supported	DOS, Windows 3.1

NOSs supported	OS/2 LAN Manager, NetBIOS, NetWare 3.x, NetWare 4.0, Pathworks, VINES, Windows NT, Windows for Workgroups
Transport protocols available	IP, TCP, UDP
E-mail protocols available	None
File-transfer protocols supported	ftp, IND$File, proprietary to HP 3000, VAX, Unix

WRQ

(206) 217-7100
(800) 872-2829

Product	Reflection Network Series for Macintosh
OSs supported	Macintosh
NOSs supported	AppleShare
Transport protocols available	IP, TCP, UDP
E-mail protocols available	None
File-transfer protocols supported	ftp, proprietary to HP3000, VAX, Unix

WRQ

(206) 217-7100
(800) 872-2829

Product	Reflection Network Series for Windows
OSs supported	Windows 3.1
NOSs supported	OS/2 LAN Manager, NetWare 3.x, NetWare 4.0, Pathworks, VINES, Windows NT, Windows for Workgroups
Transport protocols available	IP, TCP, UDP
E-mail protocols available	None
File-transfer protocols supported	ftp, IND$File, proprietary to HP3000, VAX, Unix

III

Appendixes and Glossary

Obtaining RFCs

Most information pertaining to TCP/IP and related protocols is included in documents called *Request for Comments,* or RFCs. In contrast to most documents regarding standards, RFCs are more "open," with less restrictions. These documents contain information and suggestions helpful to system administrators who deal in any way with TCP/IP.

RFCs are located around the world on various hosts. Table B.1 reflects a partial list of RFC repositories. In lieu of requiring a user account at every location, RFCs are most commonly obtained via "anonymous ftp."

Table B.1
RFC Locations

Location	Host Name
Western U.S.	ftp.nisc.sri.com
Eastern U.S.	nic.ddn.mil
Eastern U.S.	nisc.junc.net
Eastern U.S.	nnsc.nsf.net
Australia	munnari.oz.au

Within each of these RFC repositories is a rfc subdirectory and three helpful files. These files—rfc-index.txt, rfc-sets.txt, rfc-by-title.txt, and rfc-by-author.txt—reflect what they suggest: an index of RFCs indexed upon the RFC number, RFCs grouped by major topics, RFCs listed alphabetically by title, and RFCs listed alphabetically by author.

To obtain a list of RFCs held within any repository (or RFCs themselves), after you attach to the site through ftp you port the rfc-index.txt to your local host. You then sort (or grep) for any information you want locally, ftp back to the site, and again port (or receive) the specific TCP/IP data to your local host.

RFCs follow a naming convention of seven-dot-three. The first three letters of the prefix are rfc, the next four characters are the RFC number, and the suffix is either txt or ps (reflecting whether the file is in text or postscript format). RFCs are added as the protocols change or as a need arises. Many popular RFCs are listed in Table B.2.

Table B.2
RFC Descriptions

RFC Number	Title
Parameters, Requirements, and Useful Information	
rfc1340	Assigned numbers
rfc1360	IAB official protocol standards
rfc1208	Glossary of networking terms
rfc1180	TCP/IP tutorial
rfc1178	Choosing a name for your computer

RFC Number	Title

Parameters, Requirements, and Useful Information

RFC Number	Title
rfc1175	A bibliography of internetworking information
rfc1173	Responsibilities of host and network managers
rfc1166	Internet numbers
rfc1127	Perspective on the Host Requirements RFCs
rfc1123	Requirements for Internet hosts—application
rfc1122	Requirements for Internet hosts—communication
rfc1118	Hitchhikers guide to the Internet
rfc1011	Official Internet protocols
rfc1009	Requirements for Internet gateways
rfc980	Protocol document order information

Lower Layers

RFC Number	Title
rfc1220	Point-to-Point Protocol extensions for bridging
rfc1209	Transmission of IP datagrams over the SMDS Service
rfc1201	Transmitting IP traffic over ARCNET networks
rfc1188	Proposed standard for the transmission of IP datagrams over FDDI networks
rfc1172	Point-to-Point Protocol (PPP) initial configuration options
rfc1171	Point-to-Point Protocol (PPP) for the transmission of multi-protocol datagrams over PPP links
rfc1055	Nonstandard for transmission of IP datagrams over serial lines: SLIP
rfc1042	Standard for the transmission of IP datagrams over IEEE 802 networks
rfc1027	Using ARP to implement transparent subnet gateways
rfc903	Reverse Address Resolution Protocol (RARP)

III

Appendixes and Glossary

continues

Table B.2, Continued
RFC Descriptions

RFC Number	Title
Lower Layers	
rfc895	Standard for the transmission of IP datagrams over experimental Ethernet networks
rfc894	Standard for the transmission of IP datagrams over Ethernet networks
IP and ICMP	
rfc1112	Host extensions for IP multicasting
rfc1088	Standard for the transmission of IP datagrams over NetBIOS networks
rfc950	Internet standard subnetting procedure
rfc932	Subnetwork addressing scheme
rfc922	Broadcasting Internet datagrams in the presence of subnets
rfc919	Broadcasting Internet datagrams
rfc886	Proposed standard for message header munging
rfc815	IP datagram reassembly algorithms
rfc814	Name, addresses, ports, and routes
rfc792	Internet control message protocol
rfc791	Internet protocol
rfc781	Specification of the Internet protocol
Routing Protocols	
rfc1267	Border gateway protocol 3
rfc1222	Advancing the NSFNET routing architecture
rfc1195	Use of OSI IS-IS for routing in TCP/IP and dual environments

RFC Number	Title

Routing Protocols

rfc1074	NSFNET backbone SPF-based Interior Gateway Protocol
rfc1058	Routing Information Protocol (RIP)
rfc823	DARPA Internet gateway
rfc1136	Administrative Domains and Routing Domains: A model for routing in the Internet
rfc911	Exterior Gateway Protocol (EGP) under Berkeley Unix 4.2

Routing Performance and Policy

rfc1254	Gateway congestion control survey
rfc1245	OSPF protocol analysis
rfc1125	Policy requirements for inter-Administrative Domain routing
rfc1124	Policy issues in interconnecting networks
rfc1104	Models of policy based routing
rfc1102	Policy routing in Internet protocols

TCP and UDP

rfc1072	TCP extensions for long-delay paths
rfc896	Congestion control in IP/TCP internetworks
rfc879	TCP maximum segment size and related topics
rfc813	Window and acknowledgment strategy in TCP
rfc793	Transmission Control Protocol (TCP)
rfc768	User Datagram Protocol (UDP)

File Transfer and File Access

rfc1094	NFS: Network File System Protocol specification
rfc1068	Background File Transfer Program (BFTP)

III

Appendixes and Glossary

continues

Table B.2, Continued
RFC Descriptions

RFC Number	Title
File Transfer and File Access	
rfc959	File Transfer Protocol (FTP)
rfc949	FTP unique-named store command
rfc783	TFTP Protocol (rev. 2)
rfc775	Directory oriented FTP commands
Terminal Access	
rfc1205	Telnet 5250 interface
rfc1198	FYI on the X window system
rfc1184	Telnet Linemode option
rfc1091	Telnet terminal-type option
rfc1080	Telnet remote flow control option
rfc1079	Telnet terminal speed option
rfc1073	Telnet window size option
rfc1053	No description available
rfc1043	Telnet Data Entry Terminal option: DODIIS implementation
rfc1041	Telnet 3270 regime option
rfc1013	X Window System Protocol
rfc946	Telnet terminal location number option
rfc933	Output marking Telnet option
rfc885	Telnet end of record option
rfc861	Telnet extended options: List option
rfc860	Telnet timing mark option

RFC Number	Title
Terminal Access	
rfc859	Telnet status option
rfc858	Telnet Suppress Go Ahead option
rfc857	Telnet echo option
rfc856	Telnet binary transmission
rfc855	Telnet option specification
rfc854	Telnet Protocol specification
rfc779	Telnet send-location option
rfc749	Telnet SUPDUP-Output option
rfc736	Telnet SUPDUP option
rfc732	Telnet Data Entry Terminal option
rfc727	Telnet logout option
rfc726	Remote Controlled Transmission and Echoing Telnet option
rfc698	Telnet extended ASCII option
Mail	
rfc1090	SMTP on X.25
rfc974	Mail routing and the domain system
rfc822	Standard for the format of ARPA Internet text messages
rfc821	Simple Mail Transfer Protocol (SMTP)
Domain Name System	
rfc1035	Domain names—implementation and specification
rfc1034	Domain names—concepts
rfc1032	Domain administrators operations guide

III

Appendixes and Glossary

continues

Table B.2, Continued
RFC Descriptions

RFC Number	Title
Domain Name System	
rfc1101	DNS encoding of network names and other types
rfc974	Mail routing and the domain system
rfc920	Domain requirements
rfc799	Internet name domains
Other Applications	
rfc1196	Finger User Information Protocol
rfc1179	Line printer daemon protocol
rfc1129	Internet time synchronization: The Network Time Protocol
rfc1057	RPC: Remote Procedure Call Protocol specification: Ver. 2
rfc868	Time Protocol
rfc867	Daytime Protocol
rfc866	Active users
rfc865	Quote of the Day Protocol
rfc864	Character Generator Protocol
rfc862	Echo Protocol
Network Management	
rfc1231	IEEE 802.5 Token Ring MIB
rfc1230	IEEE 802.4 Token Bus MIB
rfc1228	SNMP-DPI: Simple Network Management Protocol Distributed Program Interface
rfc1227	SNMP MUX protocol and MIB
rfc1224	Techniques for managing asynchronously generated alerts

RFC Number	Title
Network Management	
rfc1215	Convention for defining traps for use with the SNMP
rfc1214	OSI internet management: Management Information Base
rfc1213	Management Information Base (MIB) for network management of TCP/IP-based internets: MIB-II
rfc1187	Bulk table retrieval with the SNMP
rfc1157	Simple Network Management Protocol (SNMP)
rfc1155	Structure and identification of management information for TCP/IP-based internets
rfc1089	SNMP over Ethernet
Security	
rfc1244	Site Security Handbook
rfc1115	Privacy enhancement for internet electronic mail: Part III—algorithms, modes, and identifiers
rfc1114	Privacy enhancement for Internet electronic mail: Part II—certificate-based key management
rfc1113	Privacy enhancement for Internet electronic mail: Part I—message encipherment and authentication procedures
rfc1108	Security Options for the Internet Protocol
Tunneling	
rfc1241	Scheme for an internet encapsulation protocol: Ver. 1
rfc1234	Tunneling IPX traffic through IP networks
rfc1088	Standard for the transmission of IP datagrams over NetBIOS networks
rfc1002	Protocol standard for a NetBIOS service on a TCP/IDP transport: Detailed specifications

continues

Table B.2, Continued
RFC Descriptions

RFC Number	Title
OSI	
rfc1001	Protocol standard for a NetBIOS service on a TCP/UDP transport: Concepts and methods
rfc1240	OSI connectionless transport services on top of UDP: Ver. 1
rfc1169	Explaining the role of GOSIP
rfc1142	OSI IS-IS Intra-domain Routing Protocol
rfc1086	ISO-TP0 bridge between TCP and X.25
rfc1070	Use of the Internet as a subnetwork for experimentation with the OSI network layer
rfc1008	Implementation guide for the ISO Transport Protocol
rfc1006	ISO transport services on top of the TCP
rfc941	International Organization for Standardization; ISO Addendum to the network service definition covering network layer addressing
Miscellaneous	
rfc1251	Who's who in the Internet: Biographies of IAB, IESG, and IRSG members
rfc1207	FYI on Questions and Answers: Answers to commonly asked "experienced Internet user" questions
rfc1206	FYI on Questions and Answers: Answers to commonly asked "new Internet user" questions

APPENDIX

Registering Your Site

There are several forms that need to be sent to NIC in order to connect your local network to the Internet and obtain a registered address. This appendix contains portions of these forms and related RFCs, as well as some of the information needed for the forms' completion. Use the questions printed here as guides to alert you to the information you will need in order to fill out the actual forms.

If you have access to the Internet, these forms can also be obtained via anonymous ftp. Just connect to rs.internic.net. When you've completed the forms, you can send the applications via e-mail to hostmaster@internic.net.

IP Network Number Request

```
[ templates/internet-number-template.txt ]                    [ 04/94 ]
This form must be completed as part of the application process for
obtaining an Internet Protocol (IP) Network Number.  To obtain an
Internet number, please provide the following information on-line, via
electronic mail, to HOSTMASTER@INTERNIC.NET.  If electronic mail is not
available to you, please mail hardcopy to:
```

```
                          Network Solutions
                          InterNIC Registration Services
                          505 Huntmar Park Drive
                          Herndon, VA 22070
                               — OR —
                          FAX to (703) 742-4811
```

Once Registration Services receives your completed application we will
send you an acknowledgment, via electronic or postal mail.

NOTE: This application is solely for obtaining a legitimate IP network
number assignment. If you're interested in officially registering a
domain please complete the domain application found in templates/
domain-template.txt. If FTP is not available to you, please contact
HOSTMASTER@INTERNIC.NET or phone the NIC at (800) 444-4345 or (703)
742-4777 for further assistance.

ATTENTION:

----

1) European network requests should use the European template (tem-
plates/european-ip-template.txt). Please follow their instructions for
submission.

2) Networks that will be connected/located within the geographic region
maintained by the Asian-Pacific NIC should use the APNIC template
(templates/apnic-001.txt). Please follow their instructions for submission.

```
*******************************************************************
                    *** NON-CONNECTED NETWORKS ***
```

If the networks you are requesting address space for will NEVER BE
CONNECTED TO THE INTERNET, YOU ARE REQUIRED TO REFER TO AND ADHERE TO
THE GUIDELINES SET FORTH IN RFC 1597, UNDER SECTION 3 "PRIVATE ADDRESS
SPACE". This RFC contains important information regarding the Poli-
cies/Procedures that are to be implemented when IP address space is
requested for networks that will NEVER be connected to the Internet. A
large portion of address space (one (1) class A, sixteen (16) class Bs
and two-hundred fifty-six (256) class Cs) has been reserved for address
allocation for non-connected networks. Please obtain the IP address
space you require by utilizing the IP address range(s) that have been
reserved by the IANA for use by all non-connected networks specified in
this RFC. RFC 1597 may be obtained via anonymous FTP from
DS.INTERNIC.NET (198.49.45.10).

```
*******************************************************************
```

YOUR APPLICATION MUST BE TYPED.

1) If the network will be connected to the Internet, you must provide
the name of the governmental sponsoring organization or commercial
service provider, and the name, title, mailing address, phone number,
net mailbox, and NIC Handle (if any) of the contact person (POC) at

that organization who has authorized the network connection. This person will serve as the POC for administrative and policy questions about authorization to be a part of the Internet. Examples of such sponsoring organizations are: DISA DNS, The National Science Foundation (NSF), or similar government, educational or commercial network service providers.

NOTE: IF THE NETWORK WILL NEVER BE CONNECTED TO THE INTERNET, PLEASE UTILIZE THE ADDRESS SPACE RESERVED FOR NON-CONNECTED NETWORKS THAT IS SPECIFIED IN RFC 1597. IF YOU INTEND TO CONNECT THIS NETWORK TO THE INTERNET BUT HAVE NOT YET CHOSEN A SERVICE PROVIDER, LEAVE THIS SECTION BLANK, BUT INDICATE THE APPROXIMATE DATE OF YOUR INTERNET CONNECTION IN SECTION 9 OF THIS TEMPLATE. IF YOU INTEND TO CONNECT TO THE INTERNET AND HAVE ALREADY CHOSEN A PROVIDER, YOU ARE REQUIRED TO SUBMIT THIS REQUEST TO YOUR SERVICE PROVIDER FOR PROCESSING. SERVICE PROVIDERS ARE ALLOCATED BLOCKS OF ADDRESSES TO SUPPORT THE NETWORKING NEEDS OF THEIR CUSTOMERS. THIS PROCEDURE WILL ENSURE THAT THE NUMBER OF ENTRIES ADDED TO THE INTERNET ROUTING TABLES IS KEPT TO A MINIMUM, AND CIDR IS USED AS EFFICIENTLY AS POSSIBLE. THE ABOVE PROCEDURES PERTAIN EXCLUSIVELY TO REQUESTS FOR CLASS C ADDRESS(ES).

```
    1a.  Sponsoring Organization:
    1b.  Contact name (Lastname, Firstname):
    1c.  Contact title:
    1d.  Mail Address :
    1e.  Phone :
    1f.  Net mailbox :
    1g.  NIC handle (if known):
```

2) Provide the name, title, mailing address, phone number, and organization of the technical Point-of-Contact (POC). The on-line mailbox and NIC Handle (if any) of the technical POC should also be included. This is the POC for resolving technical problems associated with the network and for updating information about the network. The technical POC may also be responsible for hosts attached to this network.

```
    2a.  NIC handle (if known):
    2b.  Technical POC name (Lastname, Firstname):
    2c.  Technical POC title:
    2d.  Mail address :
    2e.  Phone :
    2f.  Net Mailbox :
```

3) Supply the SHORT mnemonic name for the network (up to 12 characters). This is the name that will be used as an identifier in internet name and address tables. The only special character that may be used in a network name is a dash (-). PLEASE DO NOT USE PERIODS OR UNDERSCORES. The syntax XXXX.com and XXXX.net are not valid network-naming conventions and should only be used when applying for a domain.

```
    3.  Network name:
```

4) Identify the geographic location of the network and the organization responsible for establishing the network.

    4a. Postal address for main/headquarters network site:

    4b. Name of Organization:

5) Question #5 is for MILITARY or DOD requests, ONLY.

If you require that this connected network be announced to the NSFNET please answer questions 5a, 5b, and 5c. IF THIS NETWORK WILL BE CON-NECTED TO THE INTERNET VIA MILNET, THIS APPLICATION MUST BE SUBMITTED TO HOSTMASTER@NIC.DDN.MIL FOR REVIEW/PROCESSING.

    5a. Do you want MILNET to announce your network to the NSFNET? (Y/N):

    5b. Do you have an alternate connection, other than MILNET, to the NSFNET? (please state alternate connection if answer is yes):

    5c. If you've answered yes to 5b, please state if you would like the MILNET connection to act as a backup path to the NSFNET? (Y/N):

6) Estimate the size of the network to include the number of hosts and subnets/segments that will be supported by the network. A "host" is defined as any device (PC, printer etc.) that will be assigned an address from the host portion of the network number. A host may also be characterized as a node or device.

Host Information

    6a. Initially:

    6b. Within one year:

    6c. Within two years:

    6d. Within five years:

Subnet/Segment Information

    6e. Initially:

    6f. Within one year:

    6g. Within two years:

    6h. Within five years:

7) Unless a strong and convincing reason is presented, the network (if it qualifies at all) will be assigned a single class C network number. If a class C network number is not acceptable for your purposes, you are required to submit substantial, detailed justification in support of your requirements.

****

THE NIC WOULD STRONGLY SUGGEST YOU CONSIDER SUBNETTING CLASS C AD-DRESSES WHEN MULTIPLE SEGMENTS WILL BE USED TO SUPPORT A MINIMAL AMOUNT OF HOST ADDRESSES. MULTIPLE CLASS C NUMBERS SHOULD BE UTILIZED WHEN IT

IS NECESSARY TO SUPPORT MORE THAN 256 HOSTS ON A SINGLE NETWORK. YOU
MAY WISH TO CONFER WITH A NETWORK CONSULTANT AND ROUTER VENDOR FOR
ADDITIONAL INFORMATION.
****

(Note: If there are plans for more than a few local networks, and more
than 100 hosts, you are strongly urged to consider subnetting. [Refer-
ence RFC 950 and RFC 1466])

    7. Reason:

8) Networks are characterized as being either Research, Educational,
Government - Non Defense, or Commercial, and the network address space
is shared between these four areas. Which type is this network?

    8. Type of network:

9) What is the purpose of the network?

    9. Purpose:

For further information contact InterNIC Registration Services:
        Via electronic mail: HOSTMASTER@INTERNIC.NET
        Via telephone: (800) 444-4345
        Via postal mail: Network Solutions
                      InterNIC Registration Service
                      505 Huntmar Park Drive
                      Herndon, VA 22070

Internet Domain Name Registration

<templates/domain-templates.txt>   [07/94]

To establish a domain, the following information must be sent to the
InterNIC Registration Services (HOSTMASTER@INTERNIC.NET). Either this
template, or the "short form" following this template may be used.

(1) The name of the top-level domain to join (EDU, GOV, COM, NET, ORG).

    1. Top-level domain:

(2) The name of the domain (up to 24 characters). This is the name
that will be used in tables and lists associating the domain with the
domain servers addresses. While domain names can be quite long, the
use of shorter, more user-friendly names is recommended.

    2. Complete Domain Name:

(3) The name and address of the organization for which the domain
is being established.

    3a. Organization name:

    3b. Organization address:

(4) The date you expect the domain to be fully operational.

    4. Date operational:

NOTE: The key people must have electronic mailboxes (even if in the
domain being registered) and "handles" (unique InterNIC database

identifiers). If you have access to "WHOIS", please check to see if
the contacts are registered and if so, include only the handle and
changes (if any) that need to be made in the entry. If you do not have
access to "WHOIS", please provide all the information indicated and a
handle will be assigned.

(5) The handle of the administrative head of the organization in (3)
above or this person's name, postal address, phone number, organization, and network e-mailbox. This is the contact point for administrative and policy questions about the domain.

Administrative Contact

        5a. Handle (if known):
        5b. Name (Last, First):
        5c. Organization:
        5d. Postal Address:
        5e. Phone Number:
        5f. Net Mailbox:

(6) The handle of the technical contact for the domain or this
person's name, mailing address, phone number, organization, and network
mailbox. This is the contact point for problems and updates regarding
the domain or zone.

Technical and Zone Contact

        6a. Handle (if known):
        6b. Name (Last, First):
        6c. Organization:
        6d. Postal Address:
        6e. Phone Number:
        6f. Net Mailbox:

NOTE: Domains must provide at least two independent servers for trans-
lating names to addresses for hosts in the domain. The servers should
be in physically separate locations and on different networks if
possible. The servers should be active and responsive to DNS queries
BEFORE this application is submitted. Incomplete information in
sections 7 and 8 or inactive servers will result in delay of the
registration.

  (7) The primary server information.

        7a. Primary Server Hostname:
        7b. Primary Server Netaddress:
        7c. Primary Server Hardware:
        7d. Primary Server Software:

  (8) The secondary server information.

        8a. Secondary Server Hostname:
        8b. Secondary Server Netaddress:
        8c. Secondary Server Hardware:
        8d. Secondary Server Software:

(9) Please briefly describe the organization for which this domain is being registered. If the domain is for an organization that already has a domain registered, please describe the purpose of this domain. For further information contact InterNIC Registration Services:

        Via electronic mail: HOSTMASTER@INTERNIC.NET
        Via telephone: (703) 742-4777
        Via facsimile: (703) 742-4811
        Via postal mail: Network Solutions
                         InterNIC Registration Services
                            505 Huntmar Park Drive
                            Herndon, VA 22070

The party requesting registration of this name certifies that, to her/ his knowledge, the use of this name does not violate trademark or other statues.

Registering a domain name does not confer any legal rights to that name and any disputes between parties over the rights to use a particular name are to be settled between the contending parties using normal legal methods.

(See RFC 1591)

```
1.    Top-level domain.....:
2.    Complete Domain Name.:
3a.   Organization name....:
3b.   Organization address.:
4.    Operational Date.....:
Administrative Contact:
5a.   NIC Handle (if known):
5b.   Name (Last, First)...:
5c.   Organization.........:
5d.   Postal Address.......:
5e.   Phone Number.........:
5f.   Net Mailbox..........:
Technical/Zone Contact:
6a.   NIC Handle (if known):
6b.   Name (Last, First)...:
6c.   Organization.........:
6d.   Postal Address.......:
6e.   Phone Number.........:
6f.   Net Mailbox..........:
7a.   Prime Server Hostname...:
7b.   Prime Server Netaddress.:
7c.   Prime Server Hardware...:
7d.   Prime Server Software...:
```

```
8a.   Second Server Hostname..:
8b.   Second Server Netaddress:
8c.   Second Server Hardware..:
8d.   Second Server Software..:
9.    Domain/Org Purpose/Desc.:
```
Notes: In Sections 3b, 5d, & 6d use multiple lines for addresses.
If contacts are registered, only 5a and 6a are needed. If servers are
registered, only 7a&b and 8a&b are needed.
If there is more than one secondary server, just copy Section 8.
The party requesting registration of this name certifies that, to her/
his knowledge, the use of this name does not violate trademark or other
statues.
Registering a domain name does not confer any legal rights to that name
and any disputes between parties over the rights to use a particular
name are to be settled between the contending parties using normal
legal methods.
(See RFC 1591)

IN-ADDR.ARPA Registration

[netinfo/in-addr-template.txt]   [04/93]
The Internet uses a special domain to support gateway location and
Internet address to host mapping. The intent of this domain is to
provide a guaranteed method to perform host address to host name
mapping, and to facilitate queries to locate all gateways on a particular network in the Internet.

IN-ADDR.ARPA Registration
The following information is needed for delegation of registered
networks in your domain for inclusion in the IN-ADDR.ARPA zone files:
       * the IN-ADDR.ARPA domain
       * the Network name
       * the Hostnames of the two hosts on networks that will be acting
         as IN-ADDR servers
IN-ADDR domains are represented using the network number in reverse.
For example, network 123.45.67.0's IN-ADDR domain is represented as
67.45.123.IN-ADDR.ARPA.

       For example:
       IN-ADDR domain   Network Name   IN-ADDR Servers
                                                 (Hostname)
                                                 (NetAddress)
                                                 (CPUType/OpSys)
```
```

```
41.192.IN-ADDR.ARPA    NET-TEST-ONE    BAR.FOO.EDU
                                        123.45.67.89
                                        VAX-II/VMS
                                        ONE.ABC.COM
                                        98.76.54.32
                                        SUN/UNIX
```

- -

NOTE: Unless specified, new hosts registered as IN-ADDR servers will be
registered in the root servers only and will not appear in the
HOSTS.TXT file.

Please have the Network Coordinator complete and return the following
information for those networks needing IN-ADDR registration.

- -

Completed templates and questions can be directed to Hostmaster at
HOSTMASTER@INTERNIC.NET, or mailed to:

Network Solutions
InterNIC Registration Service
505 Huntmar Park Drive
Herndon, VA 22070

APPENDIX

Further Reading

Albitz, P., and C. Liu. *"DNS and Bind" Help for UNIX System Administrators*, O'Reilly and Associates, Inc., 1992 October.

Braden, R. T., and J. B. Postel. *Requirements for Internet Gateways*. Marina del Rey, CA: University of Southern California, Information Sciences Inst.; 1987 June; RFC 1009. 55 pp. (DS.INTERNET.NET POLICY RFC1009.TXT).

Comer, Douglas E. *Internetworking with TCP/IP, Volume I.* 2nd ed. Englewood Cliffs, NJ: Prentice Hall, 1991.

Cooper, Postel. *The US Domain*. Marina del Rey, CA: University of Southern California, Information Sciences Inst.; 1992 December; RFC 1480. 31 pp. <rs.internic.net:policy/rfc1480.txt>.

Deering, S. "ICMP Router Discovery Messages," RFC 1256, 1991 September

Feinler, E. J., O. J. Jacobsen, M. K. Stahl, and C. A. Ward, eds. *DDN Protocol Handbook*. Menlo Park, CA: SRI International, DDN Network Information Center; 1985 December; NIC 50004 and NIC 50005 and NIC 50006. 2749 pp.

Garcia-Luna-Aceves, J. J., M. K. Stahl, and C. A. Ward, eds. *Internet Protocol Handbook: The Domain Name System (DNS) Handbook*. Menlo Park, CA: SRI International, Network Information Systems Center; 1989 August; 219 pp. AD A214 698.

Garfinkel, Simson, and Gene Spafford. *Practical UNIX Security.* Sebastopol, CA: O'Reilly & Associates, Inc., 1991.

Gerich, E. *Guidelines for Management of IP Address Space.* Ann Arbor, MI: Merit Network, Inc.; 1993 May; RFC 1466. 10 pp. (DS.INTERNIC.NET RFC1466.TXT).

Hafner, Kathryn, and John Markoff. *Cyberpunk: Outlaws and Hackers on the Computer Frontier.* New York: Touchstone, 1991.

Hare, Chris, and Emmett Dulaney, et al. *Inside UNIX.* Indianapolis, IN: New Riders Publishing, 1994.

Harrenstien, K., M. K. Stahl, and E. J. Feinler. *DoD Internet Host Table Specification.* Menlo Park, CA: SRI International, DDN Network Information Center; 1985 October; RFC 952. 6 pp. (NIC.DDN.MIL RFC:RFC952.TXT). Obsoletes: RFC 810.

_____. *Hostname Server.* Menlo Park, CA: SRI International, DDN Network Information Center; 1985 October; RFC 953. 5 pp. (NIC.DDN.MIL RFC:RFC953.TXT). Obsoletes: RFC 811.

Haskins, D. "Default Route Advertisement in BGP2 and BGP3 Versions of the Border Gateway Protocol," RFC 1397, 1993 January.

Hunt, Craig. *TCP/IP Network Administration.* Sebastol, CA: O'Reilly & Associates, Inc., 1992.

Internet Activities Board. *Internet Official Protocol Standards.* 1994 March; RFC 1600. 34 pp. (DS.INTERNIC.NET POLICY RFC1600.TXT). [Note: the current version is always available as "STD 1."]

Internet Engineering Task Force, and R. T. Braden. *Requirements for Internet Hosts—Application and Support.* Marina del Rey, CA: University of Southern California, Information Sciences Inst.; 1989 October; RFC 1123. 98 pp. (DS.INTERNIC.NET RFC1123.TXT).

_____. *Requirements for Internet Hosts—Communication Layers.* Marina del Rey, CA: University of Southern California, Information Sciences Inst.; 1989 October; RFC 1122. 116 pp. (DS.INTERNIC.NET RFC1122.TXT).

Lazear, W.D. *MILNET Name Domain Transition.* McLean, VA: MITRE Corp.; 1987 November; RFC 1031. 10 pp. (NIC.DDN.MIL RFC:RFC1031.TXT).

Lottor, M. *Domain Administrators Operations Guide.* Menlo Park, CA: SRI International, DDN Network Information Center; 1987 November; RFC 1033. 22 pp. (NIC.DDN.MIL RFC:RFC1033.TXT).

Malkin, G. "RIP Version 2 Carrying Additional Information," RFC 1388, 1993 January.

Mockapetris, P. *DNS Encoding of Network Names and Other Types.* Marina del Rey, CA: University of Southern California, Information Sciences Inst.; 1989 April; RFC 1101. 14 pp. <rs.internic.net:policy/rfc1101.txt>.

_____. *Domain Names—Concepts and Facilities.* Marina del Rey, CA: University of Southern California, Information Sciences Inst.; 1987 November; RFC 1034. 55 pp. <rs.internic.net:policy/rfc1034.txt>.

_____. *Domain Names—Implementation and Specification.* Marina del Rey, CA: University of Southern California, Information Sciences Inst.; 1987 November; RFC 1035. 55 pp. <rs.internic.net:policy/rfc1035.txt>.

Mogul, J., and J. B. Postel. *Internet Standard Subnetting Procedure.* Stanford, CA: Stanford University; 1985 August; RFC 950. 18 pp. (DS.INTERNIC.NET POLICY RFC950.TXT).

Nemeth, Evi, Garth Snyder, and Scott Seebass. *UNIX System Administration Handbook.* Englewood Cliffs, NJ: Prentice Hall, 1989.

Partridge, C. *Mail Routing and the Domain System.* Cambridge, MA: BBN Labs., Inc.; 1986 January; RFC 974. 7 pp. (NIC.DDN.MIL RFC:RFC974.TXT).

Postel, J. B. *Domain Name System Structure and Delegation.* Marina del Rey, CA: University of Southern California, Information Sciences Inst.; 1994 March; RFC 1591. 7 pp. <rs.internic.net:policy/rfc1034.txt>.

_____. *Address Mappings.* Marina del Rey, CA: University of Southern California, Information Sciences Inst.; 1981 September; RFC 796. 7 pp. (DS.INTERNIC.NET POLICY RFC796.TXT). Obsoletes: IEN 115 (NACC 0968-79).

_____. *Internet Control Message Protocol.* Marina del Rey, CA: University of Southern California, Information Sciences Inst.; 1981 September; RFC 792. 21 pp. (DS.INTERNIC.NET POLICY RFC792.TXT).

_____. *Internet Protocol.* Marina del Rey, CA: University of Southern California, Information Sciences Inst.; 1981 September; RFC 791. 45 pp. (DS.INTERNIC.NET POLICY RFC791.TXT).

_____. *Transmission Control Protocol.* Marina del Rey, CA: University of Southern California, Information Sciences Inst.; 1981 September; RFC 793. 85 pp. (DS.INTERNIC.NET POLICY RFC793.TXT).

_____. *User Datagram Protocol.* Marina del Rey, CA: University of Southern California, Information Sciences Inst.; 1980 August; RFC 768. 3 pp. (DS.INTERNIC.NET POLICY RFC768.TXT).

_____, and J. K. Reynolds. *Domain Requirements.* Marina del Rey, CA: University of Southern California, Information Sciences Inst.; 1984 October; RFC 920. 14 pp. (NIC.DDN.MIL RFC:RFC920.TXT).

Rekhter, Y., B. Moskowitz, D. Karrenberg, and G. de Groot. *Address Allocation for Private Internets*, IBM Corp., Chrysler Corp., RIPE NCC; 1994 March; RFC 1597. 8 pp. (DS.INTERNIC.NET RFC1597.TXT).

Reynolds, J. K., and J. B. Postel. *Assigned Numbers*. Marina del Rey, CA: University of Southern California, Information Sciences Inst.; 1992 July; RFC 1340. 139 pp. (DS.INTERNIC.NET POLICY RFC1340.TXT). [Note: the current version is always available as "STD 2."]

Stahl, M. K. *Domain Administrators Guide*. Menlo Park, CA: SRI International, DDN Network Information Center; 1987 November; RFC 1032. 14 pp. <.internic.net:policy/rfc1032.txt>.

Stevens, Richard W. *UNIX Network Programming*. Englewood Cliffs, NJ: Prentice Hall, 1990.

_____. *TCP/IP Illustrated, Volume I: The Protocols*, Addison-Wesley, 1994.

APPENDIX

Utilities at a Glance

The following list contains the most commonly used TCP/IP utilities and a description of their purpose:

arp

A diagnostic command for modifying the IP-to-Ethernet or Token Ring physical address translation tables. These tables are used by the *Address Resolution Protocol* (ARP).

finger

Used to ascertain additional information about an individual user. The output varies significantly from system to system.

ftp

The file transfer protocol that is used to transfer files to and from a remote computer running the ftp service.

hostname

An optional command that returns the name of the host. Invariably, on a Unix machine this is the same as the node name, and can also be found with uname -n.

ipconfig

A diagnostic utility that shows all network configuration values.

netstat

All protocol statistics and current connect information can be obtained via the netstat command. This command can tell foreign addresses, local addresses, protocols, and states.

ping

A diagnostic utility that verifies whether a connection is live or not. It can be used to loop through the internal card and verify it, or verify a connection to a remote host.

rcp

Enables files to be remotely copied to and from one host to another.

rlogin

Enables a user from one host to log into another host. Primarily used on Unix hosts, it is available with a few TCP/IP packages written for other operating systems.

route

Used to manipulate the routing table of gateway entries.

rsh

Also known as remsh on some systems, it enables commands to be run on one host from another.

ruptime

A Unix-based TCP/IP command that lists hosts currently visible to the host from which the command is run.

rwho

A Unix-based TCP/IP command that lists users currently visible to the network.

telnet

A protocol and utility that establishes connections with remote hosts.

tftp

Trivial File Transfer Protocol is similar to ftp but does not require user authentication.

GLOSSARY

ACK

acknowledgment. A response from a receiving computer to a sending computer to indicate successful reception of information. TCP requires that packets be acknowledged before it considers the transmission safe.

active open

An action taken by a client to initiate a TCP connection with a server.

address classes

Grouping of IP addresses with each class, defining the maximum number of networks and hosts available. The first octet of the address determines the class. Class A networks (first octet value between 1-126) can have 16,777,214 hosts per network. Class B networks (128-191) can have 65,534 hosts per network. Class C networks (192-223) can have up to 254 hosts per network.

address mask

A 32-bit binary number used to select bits from an IP address for subnet addressing.

address resolution

A translation of an IP address to a corresponding physical address. See *ARP*.

agent

The software routine in an SNMP-managed device that responds to get and set requests and sends trap messages.

ANSI

American National Standards Institute. The membership organization responsible for defining U.S. standards in the information technology industry. ANSI is a member of ISO and participates in defining network protocol standards.

API

Application Programming Interface. A language and message format that enables a programmer to use functions in another program or in the hardware.

ARP

Address Resolution Protocol. A protocol in the TCP/IP suite used to bind an IP address to a physical hardware address.

ARPANET

Advanced Research Projects Agency Network. A research network funded by ARPA (later DARPA), a government agency, and built by BBN, Inc. in 1969. It was the first packet-switching network and served as the central Internet backbone for many years.

AS

Autonomous System. A collection of routers and gateways that falls under the control of a single administrative entity. The collection cooperates closely to provide network routing information using a common Interior Gateway Protocol.

baseband

A network technology that requires all nodes attached to the network to participate in every transmission. Ethernet is a baseband technology.

best-effort delivery

Characteristic of a network technology that does not ensure link level reliability. IP and UDP protocols work together to provide best-effort delivery service to applications.

BGP

Border Gateway Protocol. A protocol that advertises the networks that can be reached within an Autonomous System.

big endian

A format for storage or transmission of data in which the most significant byte (or bit) comes first. See also *little endian.*

BOOTP

Bootstrap Protocol. A protocol used to configure systems across internetworks.

bps

bits per second. A measure of the rate of data transmission.

bridge

A computer device that connects two or more physical networks and forwards packets among them. Bridges usually operate at the physical level.

broadband

A network technology that multiplexes multiple network carriers onto a single cable. The technology uses less cable, but equipment is more expensive.

broadcast

A packet destined for all hosts on the network.

brouter

A computer device that works as both a bridge and a router. Some traffic may be bridged, while other traffic is routed.

buffer

A storage area used to hole input or output data.

checksum

A computed value used to verify the accuracy of data in TCP/IP packets and check for errors.

CMIP

Common Management Information Protocol. An OSI network management protocol.

connection

A logical path between two protocol modules that provides a reliable delivery service.

connectionless service

A delivery service that treats each packet as a separate entity. Often results in lost packets or packets out of sequence.

CRC

Cyclic Redundancy Check. A computation about a frame of which the result is a small integer. The value is appended to the end of the frame and recalculated when the frame is received. If the results differ from the appended value, the frame has presumably been corrupted and is therefore discarded. Used to detect errors in transmission.

CSMA

Carrier Sense Multiple Access. A simple media access control protocol that enables multiple stations to contend for access to the medium. If no traffic is detected on the medium, the station may send a transmission.

CSMA/CD

Carrier Sense Multiple Access with Collision Detection. A characteristic of network hardware that uses CSMA in conjunction with a process that detects when two stations transmit simultaneously. If that happens, both back off and retry the transmission after a random time period has elapsed.

datagram

A packet of data and delivery information.

DHCP

Dynamic Host Configuration Protocol. A protocol that provides dynamic address allocation and automatic TCP/IP configuration.

directed broadcast address

An IP address that specifies all hosts on a network.

DNS

Domain Name System. A distributed database system used to map IP addresses to their system names. DNS also provides the location of mail exchangers.

DNS name servers

The servers that contain information about a portion of the DNS database.

domain name space

The database structure used by DNS.

EBONE

European IP Backbone.

EGP

Exterior Gateway Protocol. A protocol that advertises the networks that can be reached within an Autonomous System.

fair queuing

A technique used to control traffic in gateways by restricting every host to an equal share of gateway bandwidth.

FCS

Frame Check Sequence. A computation about the bits in a frame of which the result is appended to the end of the frame and recalculated when the frame is received. If the results differ from the appended value, the frame has presumably been corrupted and is therefore discarded. Used to detect errors in transmission.

FDM

Frequency Division Multiplexing. A technique of passing multiple signals across a single medium by assigning each signal a unique carrier frequency.

flow control

A mechanism that controls the rate that hosts may transmit at any time. Used to avoid congestion on the network, which may exhaust memory buffers.

FQDN

Fully Qualified Domain Name. A combination of the host name and domain name.

fragment

A piece that results when a datagram is partitioned into smaller pieces. Used to facilitate datagrams that are too large for the network technology it must traverse.

frame

A packet as transmitted across a medium. Differing frame types have unique characteristics.

FTP

File Transfer Protocol. A high-level protocol that supports file copying between systems. Requires client and server components.

gateway

A computer that attaches multiple TCP/IP networks for the purpose of routing or delivering IP packets between them. Used interchangeably with IP router.

GOSIP

Government Open Systems Interconnection Profile. A U.S. Government document that defines a specification of a set of OSI protocols that agencies may use.

hardware address

The physical address of a host used by networks.

HDLC

High-Level Data Link Control. A standard data link level protocol.

header

Data inserted at the beginning of a packet that contains control information.

hop count

A measure of distance that measures the number of gateways that separate two hosts.

host

Any computer system or device attached to the internetwork.

host ID

The portion of an IP address that identifies the host in a particular network. Used in conjunction with network IDs to form a complete IP address.

HOSTS file

A text file that contains mappings of IP addresses to host names.

III

Appendixes and Glossary

IAB

Internet Architecture Board. An independent group responsible for policies and standards for TCP/IP and the Internet

ICMP

Internet Control Message Protocol. A maintenance protocol that handles error messages to be sent when datagrams are discarded or when systems experience congestion.

IGMP

Internet Group Management Protocol. A protocol used to carry group membership information in a multicast system.

IGP

Interior Gateway Protocol. A generic term that applies to any routing protocol used within an autonomous system.

internet

A collection of packet-switching networks connected by IP routers and appearing to users as a single network.

Internet

The worlds largest collection of networks that reaches universities, government research labs, business organizations, and military installations in many countries.

IP

Internet Protocol. Along with TCP, one of the most fundamental protocols in TCP/IP networking. IP is responsible for addressing and sending datagrams across an internet.

IP address

The 32-bit address assigned to hosts that identifies a node on the network and specifies routing information on an internetwork.

IS-IS

Intermediate System to Intermediate System protocol. A protocol that can be used to route both OSI and IP traffic.

ISO

International Standards Organization. An international body founded to draft standards for network protocols.

LAN

Local Area Network. A physical communications network that operates over short geographical areas.

little endian

A format for storage or transmission of data in which the least significant byte (or bit) comes first. See also *big endian*.

LLC

Logical Link Control. A protocol that provides a common interface point to the MAC layers.

MAC

Media Access Control. A protocol that governs the access method a station has to the network.

mail bridge

A gateway that screens mail between two networks to make sure it meets administrative constraints.

MAN

Metropolitan Area Network. A physical communications network that operates across a metropolitan area.

MIB

Management Information Base. A database made up of a set of objects that represent various types of information about a device. Used by SNMP to manage devices.

MSS

Maximum Segment Size. The largest amount of data that can be transmitted at one time. Negotiated by sender and receiver.

MTU

Maximum Transmission Unit. The largest datagram that can be sent across a given physical network.

multihomed host

A TCP/IP host that is attached to two or more networks, requiring multiple IP addresses.

name resolution

The process of mapping a computer name to an IP address. DNS and DHCP are two tools for resolving names.

network ID

The portion of an IP address that identifies the network. Used in conjunction with host IDs to form a complete IP address.

III

Appendixes and Glossary

NFS

Network File System. A distributed file system developed by Sun Microsystems that uses IP to enable clients to mount remote directories on their local file systems, regardless of machine or operating system. Users can access remote files as if they were local.

NIC

Network Information Center. A central administration facility responsible for providing users with information about TCP/IP and the Internet.

NIS

Network Information Service. A naming service from SunSoft used to provide a directory service for network information.

NSFNET

National Science Foundation Network. A network that serves as part of the current Internet backbone funded by the NSF.

NVT

Network Virtual Terminal. A set of rules that define a very simple virtual terminal interaction used at the start of a telnet session.

OSF

Open Software Foundation. A nonprofit organization formed of hardware manufacturers who attempt to produce standard technologies for open systems.

OSI

Open Systems Interconnection. A set of ISO standards that define the framework for implementing protocols in seven layers.

packet

The unit of protocol data sent across a packet-switching network.

ping

Packet internet groper. A program used in TCP/IP internetworks to test reachability of other hosts. A ping is simply an ICMP echo request that waits for a reply.

port ID

The method used by TCP and UDP to specify which application is sending or receiving data.

PPP

Point-to-Point Protocol. An industry standard protocol for data transfer across serial links. It allows for several protocols to be multiplexed across the link.

protocol

A set of rules used to govern the transmission and receiving of data.

RARP

Reverse Address Resolution Protocol. A protocol that enables a computer to find its IP address by broadcasting a request. Used by a diskless workstation at startup to find its logical IP address.

repeater

A device that amplifies or regenerates the data signal in order extend the transmission distance. Only two repeaters can appear between any two machines on an Ethernet network.

resolver

Client software that enables access to the DNS database.

RFC

Request for Comment. Official documents containing Internet protocols, surveys, measurements, ideas, and observations. These documents are available online from the Network Information Center.

RIP

Routing Information Protocol. A router-to-router protocol used to exchange information between routers. RIP supports dynamic routing.

RMON

Remote Network Monitor. A device that collects information about network communication.

route

The path that network traffic takes from its source to its destination.

router

A computer responsible for deciding the routes network traffic will follow, and then sending traffic from one network to another.

RPC

Remote Procedure Call. An interface that allows an application to call a routine that executes on another machine in a remote location.

segment

A protocol data unit consisting of part of a stream of bytes being sent between two machines. Also includes information about the current position in the stream and a checksum value.

SLIP

Serial Line Internet Protocol. A simple protocol used to transmit datagrams across a serial line.

III

Appendixes and Glossary

SMTP

Simple Mail Transfer Protocol. A protocol used to transfer electronic mail messages from one machine to another.

SNA

System Network Architecture. A protocol suite developed and used by IBM.

SNMP

Simple Network Management Protocol. A protocol used for network management data. NSNMP enables a management station to configure, monitor, and receive trap messages from gateways and the networks to which they are attached.

socket

A bidirectional pipe for incoming and outgoing data that allows an application program to access the TCP/IP protocols.

source route

A route identifying the path a datagram must follow, determined by the source device.

subnet

Any lower network, identified by the network ID, that is part of the logical network.

subnet mask

A 32-bit value that distinguishes the network ID from the host ID in an IP address.

TCP

Transmission Control Protocol. Along with IP, one of the most fundamental protocols in TCP/IP networking. TCP is a connection-based protocol that provides reliable, full duplex data transmission between a pair of applications.

Telnet

Remote terminal protocol that allows a terminal attached to one host to log into other hosts, as if directly connected to the remote machine.

TFTP

Trivial File Transfer Protocol. A basic, standard protocol used to upload or download files with minimal overhead. TFTP depends on UDP and is often used to initialize diskless workstations. It has no directory or password capability.

TLI

Transport Layer Interface. An AT&T-developed interface that enables applications to interface to both TCP/IP and OSI protocols.

transceiver

A device that connects a host interface to a network. Used to apply signals to the cable and sense collisions.

trap

A block of data that indicates some request failed to authenticate. An SNMP service sends a trap when it receives a request for information with an incorrect community name.

TTL

Time-To-Live. A measurement of time, usually defined by a number of hops, that a datagram can exist on a network before discarded. Used to prevent endlessly looping packets.

UDP

User Datagram Protocol. A simple protocol that enables an application program on one machine to send a datagram to an application program on another machine. Delivery is not guaranteed, nor is it guaranteed the datagrams will be delivered in the proper order.

universal time

An international standard time reference, formerly called Greenwich Mean Time.

UTC

Coordinated Universal Time. See also *universal time.*

UUCP

Unix-to-Unix Copy. An application that allows one Unix system to copy files to or from another Unix system over a single link. UUCP is the basis for electronic mail transfer in Unix.

WAN

Wide Area Network. A physical communications network that operates across large geographical distances. WANs usually operate at slower speeds than LANs or MANs.

X.25

A CCITT standard for connecting computers to a network that provides a reliable stream transmission service, which can support remote login.

X.400

A CCITT standard for message transfer and interpersonal messaging, like electronic mail.

XDR

External Data Representation. A data format standard developed by Sun that defines datatypes used as parameters, and encodes these parameters for transmission.

X Windows System

A software windowing system developed at MIT that enables a user to run applications on other computers and view the output on their own screen. Window placement and size are controlled by a window manager program.

III

Appendixes and Glossary

INDEX

INDEX

INDEX

INDEX

INDEX

INDEX

INDEX

INDEX

INDEX

INDEX

INDEX

INDEX

INDEX

INDEX

INDEX

INDEX

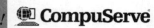

PLUG YOURSELF INTO...

THE MACMILLAN INFORMATION SUPERLIBRARY™

Free information and vast computer resources from the world's leading computer book publisher—online!

FIND THE BOOKS THAT ARE RIGHT FOR YOU!

A complete online catalog, plus sample chapters and tables of contents give you an in-depth look at *all* of our books, including hard-to-find titles. It's the best way to find the books you need!

- **STAY INFORMED** with the latest computer industry news through our online newsletter, press releases, and customized Information SuperLibrary Reports.

- **GET FAST ANSWERS** to your questions about MCP books and software.

- **VISIT** our online bookstore for the latest information and editions!

- **COMMUNICATE** with our expert authors through e-mail and conferences.

- **DOWNLOAD SOFTWARE** from the immense MCP library:
    - Source code and files from MCP books
    - The best shareware, freeware, and demos

- **DISCOVER HOT SPOTS** on other parts of the Internet.

- **WIN BOOKS** in ongoing contests and giveaways!

TO PLUG INTO MCP: ➜ WORLD WIDE WEB: **http://www.mcp.com**

GOPHER: gopher.mcp.com

FTP: ftp.mcp.com

WANT MORE INFORMATION?

CHECK OUT THESE RELATED TOPICS OR SEE YOUR LOCAL BOOKSTORE

CAD and 3D Studio

As the number one CAD publisher in the world, and as a Registered Publisher of Autodesk, New Riders Publishing provides unequaled content on this complex topic. Industry-leading products include AutoCAD and 3D Studio.

Networking

As the leading Novell NetWare publisher, New Riders Publishing delivers cutting-edge products for network professionals. We publish books for all levels of users, from those wanting to gain NetWare Certification, to those administering or installing a network. Leading books in this category include *Inside NetWare 3.12*, *CNE Training Guide: Managing NetWare Systems*, *Inside TCP/IP*, and *NetWare: The Professional Reference*.

Graphics

New Riders provides readers with the most comprehensive product tutorials and references available for the graphics market. Best-sellers include *Inside CorelDRAW! 5*, *Inside Photoshop 3*, and *Adobe Photoshop NOW!*

Internet and Communications

As one of the fastest growing publishers in the communications market, New Riders provides unparalleled information and detail on this ever-changing topic area. We publish international best-sellers such as *New Riders' Official Internet Yellow Pages, 2nd Edition*, a directory of over 10,000 listings of Internet sites and resources from around the world, and *Riding the Internet Highway, Deluxe Edition*.

Operating Systems

Expanding off our expertise in technical markets, and driven by the needs of the computing and business professional, New Riders offers comprehensive references for experienced and advanced users of today's most popular operating systems, including *Understanding Windows 95*, *Inside Unix*, *Inside Windows 3.11 Platinum Edition*, *Inside OS/2 Warp Version 3*, and *Inside MS-DOS 6.22*.

Other Markets

Professionals looking to increase productivity and maximize the potential of their software and hardware should spend time discovering our line of products for Word, Excel, and Lotus 1-2-3. These titles include *Inside Word 6 for Windows*, *Inside Excel 5 for Windows*, *Inside 1-2-3 Release 5*, and *Inside WordPerfect for Windows*.

Orders/Customer Service **1-800-653-6156** Source Code **NRP95**

New Riders Publishing 201 West 103rd Street ◆ Indianapolis, Indiana 46290 USA

Name _____ Title _____

Company _____ Type of business _____

Address _____

City/State/ZIP _____

Have you used these types of books before? ☐ yes ☐ no

If yes, which ones? _____

_____

How many computer books do you purchase each year? ☐ 1–5 ☐ 6 or more

How did you learn about this book? _____

Where did you purchase this book? _____

Which applications do you currently use? _____

_____

Which computer magazines do you subscribe to? _____

_____

What trade shows do you attend? _____

_____

Comments: _____

_____

_____

Would you like to be placed on our preferred mailing list? ☐ yes ☐ no

☐ **I would like to see my name in print!** You may use my name and quote me in future New Riders products and promotions. My daytime phone number is: _____

New Riders Publishing 201 West 103rd Street ◆ Indianapolis, Indiana 46290 USA

Fax to **317-581-4670** Orders/Customer Service **1-800-653-6156** Source Code **NRP95**

Fold Here

‖‖‖

BUSINESS REPLY MAIL
FIRST-CLASS MAIL PERMIT NO. 9918 INDIANAPOLIS IN
POSTAGE WILL BE PAID BY THE ADDRESSEE

NEW RIDERS PUBLISHING
201 W 103RD ST
INDIANAPOLIS IN 46290-9058